Multilateral Sanctions in International Law

C. Lloyd Brown-John

The Praeger Special Studies program—utilizing the most modern and efficient book production techniques and a selective worldwide distribution network—makes available to the academic, government, and business communities significant, timely research in U.S. and international economic, social, and political development.

Multilateral Sanctions in International Law
A Comparative Analysis

PRAEGER SPECIAL STUDIES IN INTERNATIONAL POLITICS AND GOVERNMENT

Praeger Publishers   New York   Washington   London

Library of Congress Cataloging in Publication Data

Brown–John, C   Lloyd.
    Multilateral sanctions in international law.

    (Praeger special studies in international politics
and government)
    Bibliography: p.
    1. Sanctions (International law)   I. Title.
JX1246. B76   341. 5'8   73–15181
ISBN 0–275–28775–0

341.5
B881m

PRAEGER PUBLISHERS
111 Fourth Avenue, New York, N.Y. 10003, U.S.A.
5, Cromwell Place, London SW7 2JL, England

Published in the United States of America in 1975
by Praeger Publishers, Inc.

75-4666

Printed in the United States of America

PREFACE AND ACKNOWLEDGMENTS

Multilateral Sanctions in International Law: A Comparative Analysis is a first and perhaps somewhat hesitant step toward grappling with one of the more critical issues and areas in international law, the concept and techniques of enforcement. Unlike many of the works cited in the text, this volume seeks to explore, in a tentative manner, a series of assumptions upon which rather extensive multilateral international agency decisions have been premised.

This is not a conventional comparative essay based upon models formulated in the literature and research of social science and law. Nor is the volume associated exclusively with a particular discipline. Rather, it utilizes political, historical, economic, legal, and some sociological materials to attempt an initial assessment of a fundamental concept. The concept--or premise, if you prefer--can be stated simply: Sanctions, and especially economic sanctions, can be used to enforce decisions of multilateral international agencies taken in pursuit of established principles of international law and its violators.

The discussion, therefore, is limited and does not purport to range the entire breadth from unilateral to multilateral sanctions. It reviews only three cases that all possess the common theme of international collective sanctions as response to a determined delict in law. The cases are the League of Nations and Italy (1935-36), the Organization of American States and the Dominican Republic (1960-62), and the United Nations and Rhodesia (1965-present). The discussion provides information sufficient for any reasonable person to be able to derive interpretations. Because of the immensity of the subject and the paucity of this type of research, this effort cannot aspire to be definitive. Thus, the discussion does not presume to be a detailed economic analysis of the consequences of sanctions, although it contains enough statistical material to facilitate a comprehensive economic evaluation. Further, the discussion cannot allege to be complete in every aspect of politics, either domestic or international, of the subject states, although generally there is enough information to permit fairly accurate sensing of political climates. Finally, the discussion is not so immersed in the "law of sanctions" (law of retaliation, retortion, embargo, navicerts) as to be authoritative in that respect, for the basic approach has been to interpret relevant law in a clear and simple (unencumbered) manner. In summary, therefore, what is done in the book is to suggest that the question of international law enforcement, under the circumstances specified, is a complete field requiring considerably more study, analysis, and effort than has been the case in the past. We very much require more clinical work and considerably less pontificating.

The volume describes the background situation in each case, explains the international organization's decision, and appraises the results in an implied cost-benefit context, although that type of specific analysis is not undertaken. The discussion concludes that sanctions are essential in international law but that they could be made considerably more effective in both major and minor circumstances if those charged with devising sanctions schemes approached the subject broadly and decisively rather than timidly and vaguely. Further, sanctions schemes in international law could rely much more extensively upon delegated authority while responsibility remained located at the delegating agency. This latter point is especially crucial in minor law violations, for there really is no alternative to sanctions in international law and politics.

Over the years that this subject has been fermenting in my studies, many persons have contributed, including librarians at the United Nations, the OAS, the National Library of Canada, the Canadian Parliamentary Library, the University of Michigan, the University of Toronto (law school), and the libraries of the University of Windsor. Friends and colleagues in the Canadian Foreign Service and in political science, economics, and law at the University of Windsor would probably prefer to remain anonymous. Others need not (although they might wish otherwise). Dean Ronald St. J. MacDonald, Faculty of Law, Dalhousie University, Halifax, Nova Scotia; Professor James Barros, Department of Political Economy, University of Toronto; Professor Leland Goodrich, School of International Studies, Columbia University; and Professor Charles Bourne, Faculty of Law, University of British Columbia, all warrant immense appreciation.

To my wife Marilyn and my daughters Lara and Michelle, I offer my most affectionate appreciation for allowing me to encroach upon our family time. To my parents, Clive and Doris, I dedicate this humble effort because, like many of us, they believe that law, human dignity, and peace are vital to our human relationship. I thank them deeply for inculcating those beliefs.

CONTENTS

LIST OF TABLES

x

LIST OF FIGURES

LIST OF ABBREVIATIONS

AJIL   American Journal of International Law

Annals   Annals: American Academy of Political and Social Science

APSR   American Political Science Review

ASIL   American Society of International Law

BYIL   British Yearbook of International Law

Cmnd   Command Papers (Great Britain)

OAU   Organization of African Unity

RGDIP   Revue générale de droit international public

RIAA   Reports of International Arbitral Awards

RIIA   Royal Institute of International Affairs

UDI   Unilateral declaration of independence

There has been a continuing and perplexing dilemma facing proponents of international law throughout this century. How can we talk of law unless we have some efficient means for enforcing that law? And, if we develop the means, how shall the enforcement provisions of international law be applied? This issue, perhaps more than any other in international law, has befuddled the international community and its organizations since at least the second Hague Conference in 1907. To solve the problem, international organizations have turned to the only apparent alternatives: sanctions and war. The latter has increasingly become an impractical alternative in functional terms, while the former, in consequence of experience, seems to be fruitless in practice.

With this ongoing conundrum in mind, and with the intent to explore the peaceful alternative somewhat more closely, the following study was undertaken. About the only preconceived notion implicit in this discussion is that there must be a better means than war and violence to enforce international law principles, at least the sort that emerge from the debates and harangues of international forums. Given that premise, this attempt to evaluate--more satisfactorily than has been done elsewhere--is offered. All three cases revolved about dramatic historical events: conquest, assassination, and rebellion. All three cases resulted in major confrontations between politics and law; and in only one case, broadly interpreted, did law manage to prevail more or less unscathed. As for sanctions, they appear to have been successful in all three cases--but this belief depends heavily upon your perspective. Sanctions have a place in international law, providing we do not burden their use with excessive overexpectation.

Multilateral
Sanctions in
International Law

SANCTIONS AND
NONDESTRUCTIVE
COERCION

> Because it is of the nature of Punishment, to
> have for end, the disposing of men to obey the
> Law: which end (if it be lesse than the bene-
> fit of the transgression) it attaineth not, but
> worketh a contrary effect.
>
> Thomas Hobbes, <u>Leviathan</u>

Underlying this discussion are some basic premises pertaining to sanctions and the concept of nondestructive coercion. First, the use of the term "nondestructive coercion" is simply a matter of descriptive convenience. Nondestructive coercion, as employed here, means the utilization of coercive techniques against a state with the intent
to alter that state's behavior while simultaneously maintaining the state as a viable political system. Systems
maintenance under stress is a key ingredient of applied
sanctions, from both the viewpoint of states sanctioned and
that of states sanctioning.

The second premise relates to sanctions. Conceptually,
sanctions are viewed as a broad spectrum ranging in degrees
of intensity from "soft" techniques, such as diplomatic and
political actions, through economic and financial manipulations, and ending with "hard" techniques, such as physical
threats and limited or precisely defined uses of force.
The employment of the concept of a spectrum in no manner
connotes that sanctions would be imposed in any progression,
from soft to hard, against an offending state. Quite obviously the decision to blockade a state suggests that a
range of other possible measures already would have been
taken.

Finally, implicit in this discussion is the assumption that the condition of world or regional peace is preferable to chaos or war. That being the case, sanctions of every, or any, variety are preferable to outright aggression. (In some respects this resembles the view that peace is the normal state of man; however, rather than enter a philosophical discussion, suffice it to say that peace seems to be the preferred state of man.)

As many contemporary situations suggest, sanctions may be the only valid choice, given the obvious conclusion that direct aggressive action would be an overreaction to some of the offenses committed in international society--for example, harboring aircraft hijackers. Unfortunately for the concept of sanctions in international law and relations, they have been victims of international overexpectation; and when the utility of sanctions has fallen below anticipated goals, the concept has suffered accordingly. This discussion suggests an intrinsic value in the employment of sanctions in international law, providing the available techniques are employed correctly and with a full and acute awareness of the limitations.

In a juristic sense a sanction is a hyphen between prescribed law and law enforcement, although certainly sanctions tend to be more closely related to enforcement than to prescribed law. Be the sanction implicit in existing societal norms or explicit within prescribed law, its primary roles are to function as a deterrent to unacceptable behavior and to exist as a means for enforcing prescribed behavior when the deterrent fails. Thus, in domestic or municipal law where there exists a prescribed law "A" there also will be a correlated sanction "B" that will be imposed should the law require enforcement. The law is subscribed to because the deterrent sanction "B" is known to exist and it is known, or at least generally believed, that sanction "B" will be imposed if the law is violated. The process has been simplified, of course, but the essential relationships nevertheless stand.

Attempts have been made to encompass the juristic process into the body of international relations. For example, Article 2(4) of the UN Charter provides that members shall refrain in their international relations from the threat or use of force against any other state. Article 39 sets out a procedure whereby a determination is to be made by the Security Council that an act of aggression has occurred. Finally, Articles 41 and 42 outline examples of the techniques that the Security Council may decide to employ if it

ascertains that a violation of law has occurred. Law, for
purposes of this brief outline, is any international state
activity or behavior not condemned by the UN Security Council, the UN Charter or other regional document, or the customary and prescribed rules of interstate relations as set
out, for example, in Article 38 of the Statute of the International Court of Justice. Such a loose definition
seems useful, given the ongoing fluidity of customary and
normative international law. It also accommodates those
areas of international state relations that are essentially
political and where law acquires an ancillary relationship,
the proverbial "rules of the game." Hence, any situation
that results in any multilateral international organization
or agency's deciding to impose any type of sanctions constitutes an enforcement of international law.

This type of definitional usage essentially lays waste
to parallels between international and domestic or municipal law. But that parallel has had dire consequences for
international law in any case. The apparent built-in pre-
dispositions that lawyers seem to have for rigidified or
codified juristic processes and law appears frequently to
be detrimental to the processes of international law. International law has an intricate relationship with politics
that is unusual in many domestic jurisdictions. If nothing
else, the following pages anticipate making it quite apparent that sanctions cannot even purport to succeed without
massive injections of political maneuvering. Consequently,
sanctions are as much a component of political weight-throw-
ing as they are of strict law enforcement. In suggesting
this there is a temptation to visualize the point in terms
of a cliché. Yet the frequency with which it has been assumed that sanctions <u>alone</u> could be used to enforce international decisions is disconcerting. Such sentiments were
expressed at Versailles in 1919 and found incarnation in
Article 16 of the League of Nations Covenant. Again, in
San Francisco in 1945, with more subtlety and some cynicism,
the same expectation became embodied in the UN Charter.
And, by 1947, with somewhat more skepticism, the expectation was embedded in Article 8 of the OAS Inter-American
Treaty of Reciprocal Assistance (the Rio Treaty).

Suppositions about the utility of sanctions in times
of relative peace appear to have been founded upon the use
of economic techniques during war. Thus blockades and embargoes during World War I provided proof positive of the
value of economic warfare. Yet the concept of economic
warfare is qualitatively distinct from sanctions employed
in pursuit of law enforcement. Economic warfare was de-

scribed by one observer as "economic measures which directly enhance a country's relative strength" vis-à-vis a target state. It was noted that the measures were to be taken primarily, though not exclusively, during a military conflict in order to supplement other forms of warfare.[1] Under these conditions sanctions are a related function of the primary state purpose, success in war.

The context within which sanctions are reviewed in this discussion is much less precise. First, we are concerned with a limited range of sanctions, that is, to the point where the target state's political, economic, and social systems are maintained. Second, the utilization of sanctions for enforcement is the dominant purpose of states involved in the imposition. Third, unlike war, the interests of many of the participating states may be marginal (if not contradictory) to the objectives of the sanctions. Fourth, we are concerned here with the effective use of sanctions on a multilateral basis and thus are faced with a constant need to achieve forms of interest accommodation and conflict resolution or compromise among participating states. Fifth, the enforced law is so imprecise and sanctions are often so vague that a method for determining degrees of offenses committed and sanctions to be employed is lacking; thus, states are not in a position to employ refinements that permit minute distinctions between harboring airline hijackers and committing outright armed aggression. Finally, the nature of the law itself is changing and activities that at one time in history would have prompted an outraged response no longer arouse the same passions.*

Perhaps the most significant defect in any concept of international law enforcement through sanctions, aside from misdirected expectations, is the inability of the enforcement process to be anticipatory or preemptive. That is, a vacuum exists in the legal and enforcement process, and this vacuum poses immense difficulties for the systematic utilization of various types of sanctions.

---

*The slaying of missionaries, for example, was the immediate excuse for more than one 19th-century invasion. In the latter part of the 20th century, nationals are more or less on their own and cannot expect the marines to bail them out. Of course, if the downfall of Salvador Allende in Chile in September 1973 is any example, corporate citizens may still obtain some protection even if it is surreptitious.

4

In 1938 the British Royal Institute of International Affairs (RIIA) defined international sanctions as "action taken by members of the international community against an infringement, actual or threatened, of the law."[2] Beyond the vagueness of its description of the international community (does it mean a formal community, such as the United Nations; or a formal subset, such as the OAS; or would it include informal subsets, such as all states hostile to Israel?), the definition contains an ingrained expectation of the sense of international law. The suggestion that action could be taken against "threatened" infringements of law is more like a prescriptive injunction to the international community than a depiction of actuality. Of course, reality is some distance from desirability. Article 16(1) of the League of Nations Covenant was close to political reality because it required a "resort to war in disregard" of the provisions of the Covenant before action could be taken by the Council under Article 16(1) and (2). Yet it was this resort-to-war provision, an apparent reflection of the inability of the 1907 Hague Conference system to prevent World War I, that has been judged historically to have been one of the more significant defects of the League sanctions system. In addition, the requirement of a resort to war invariably would have placed the members of the League at a great strategic disadvantage.

Wary of repeating the error, subsequent international collective security agencies attempted to accommodate anticipated situations. Article 39 of the UN Charter permits the Security Council to determine "the existence of any threat to peace."[3] Article 6 of the Inter-American Treaty of Reciprocal Assistance enpowers the Organ of Consultation to respond to any "fact or situation that might endanger the peace of America" (emphasis added). Yet there is not a universal consistency and, possibly in recognition of the limitations of such preemptive provisions, more recent international organizations appear to have returned to the League's constraints. Thus, the 1964 Organization of African Unity (OAU) Protocol of the Commission of Mediation, Conciliation and Arbitration provides that a dispute must exist before the commission can become involved.[4] Of course, the determination of when a dispute exists is much more permissive (or vague) than the very restrictive "resort to war" wording of the League Covenant.

Nevertheless, despite the breadth of the OAS and UN provisions and the more restrictive tones of the OAU document, the fact remains that the concept of "threat" (intent to commit an offense) is difficult to operationalize

5

in international law. Consequently, while Article 2(4) of
the UN Charter forbids states to threaten the use of force,
it is difficult to castigate a state that does threaten
another, and considerably more difficult--if, indeed, pos-
sible--to employ the provisions of Articles 41 and 42 (sanctions) to respond to an armed threat. As a result, one of
the major deficiencies in a multilateral resort to sanctions
appears to originate with lacunae in applied international
law. The absence of an adequate means for determining when
a state might be "loitering with intent to commit a felony"
or "is in possession of burglar tools" (armaments) is a
structural as well as a philosophical defect of international law. Clearly the gaps are more evident in those
areas where a precise definition of an offense is more complex. For example, external support for a national liberation movement against an existing government is not an offense subject to punishment by sanctions under existing international circumstances. Yet the external supporter may
be an accessory before, during, and after the fact. Such
relationships would make the party culpable in many domestic jurisdictions. Again, however, it is the domestic law
model that keeps encroaching; and the temptation to employ
the model can be appreciated when it is recalled that "ac-
cessories" to the fact were deeply responsible for that
major threat to world peace, the Vietnam conflict.

The inability of multilateral organizations effectively
to employ sanctions in a preemptive manner is a serious
enough defect in international law and relations, but the
problem is further compounded by the lack of precision in
determining what constitutes an act of aggression. For example, Italy physically invaded Ethiopia on October 3, 1935,
after several months of sustained and obvious military
buildup. However, on September 12 the British Foreign Secretary, Sir Samuel Hoare, had delivered a solid speech before the League Assembly in which he appeared to make explicit Britain's determination to resist Mussolini's intentions in Ethiopia.[5] Apparently unknown to Hoare, a large
section of the British home fleet had arrived at Gibraltar
the same day, in apparent support of the Mediterranean
fleet, which had taken up a position near Suez.[6] Hoare's
speech, in combination with the fleet movements, was widely
interpreted as a preemptive move against Mussolini. Yet
Mussolini naturally viewed the combined events as an aggressive series of actions and by some standards--for example,
those set forth in Article 2(4) of the UN Charter--such an
action (the fleet movements) without the approval of the
multilateral agency clearly might be identified as a threat

to peace and, therefore, aggressive. The inability to be precise about what actions constitute aggression and what actions are designed to thwart aggression, poses difficult challenges to the effective utilization of sanctions in international law and relations.

A final point worth noting concerns the concept of "defined benefit." Thus a major distinction that may, or should, exist between sanctions and economic warfare is that sanctions utilized as an enforcement action should provide no accrued benefit to the states imposing sanctions. That is, the imposing states would not usually derive long-term strategic, economic, or other advantages over the target state. Economic warfare, on the other hand, should be designed to devolve substantial advantage and benefit upon the state(s) employing the techniques. The reason for such a restrictive use of sanctions for enforcement purposes is quite simple. If it could be demonstrated that sanctions, under the guise of law enforcement, bestowed benefits upon the imposing states, then there would be an incentive to instigate sanctions more frequently and perhaps with greater enthusiasm. Moreover, given the necessity for a broad interpretation of the term "law" in this context, the abuse could be quite extensive.[7]

An attempt to grapple with this difficulty was made by Julius Stone, who suggested that the term "peace enforcement" would be preferable to the term "sanction."[8] Stone noted that the term "peace enforcement" encompasses a range of threats to peace or acts of aggression warranting a peaceful type of response, whereas sanctions are tied too closely to the necessity of a resort to war. It seems implicit in Stone's attempt to distinguish between the terms that motivation is the dominant factor. That is, Stone appears to have seen a sentiment of altruism tied to "peace enforcement" that in some manner would motivate states to "enforce" peace without reference to means; sanctions, on the other hand, imply a beneift, or material result, for the imposing states and Stone finds this unacceptable. As will become more evident later in the discussion, "disbenefits" are the more common consequence of sanctions. Thus Stone's conclusion stands to be contradicted.

For the purposes of this discussion, the term "sanctions" will connote the techniques of law, rather than peace, enforcement. This distinction is significant because the two terms need not be synonymous. Moreover, sanctions as a technique of law enforcement permit the discussion to range into areas where sanctions might be employed in response to a situation that is not a direct threat to international peace.* Skyjacking and hijacking, kidnappings, and assorted acts of terrorism might then be included within the focus of sanctions activity.

Within the spectrum of sanctions there appear to be four distinct, but broad, categories available to any multilateral agency that proposes to enforce law: moral and political, economic, financial, and physical. Boycott, embargo, retortion, quarantine, blockade, retaliation, and reprisal are specific types of action within the broad categories.

MORAL AND POLITICAL SANCTIONS

Moral Sanctions

Sir Henry Maine once observed:

> It is always easy to say that a man is guilty on manslaughter, larceny or bigamy, but it is often most difficult to pronounce what extent of moral guilt he has incurred, and consequently what measure of punishment he has deserved.[9]

The lumping together of moral and political sanctions has not been done strictly for convenience, although it does tend to downgrade tautological arguments about the moral content of politics. For purposes of the immediate discussion, the matter of a moral content in politics is incidental. In terms of sanctions the important point is that the two may be interchangeable in practice, although "moral" does tend to suggest modes of expression. For example, if a foreign minister chooses not to attend--or, more pointedly, chooses to ignore--a national day reception, this can constitute a form of political sanction. The motivation for not attending a reception may be varied, but if it expresses disapproval of an action or policy of the host state--for example, apartheid in South Africa--it becomes a moral judgment manifested in a political act. However, this is a narrow interpretation, and the nature of moral sanctions can be appraised more accurately by considering

---

*This observation denotes a view of the international system as essentially stable in terms of the prospects of major world conflict.

them as a general sanction of international law. Hsu Mo observed:

> The great body of rules that govern international
> relations have heretofore been mainly enforced,
> not objectively by force, but subjectively by a
> common sense of decency existing among the members
> of the civilized international community.[10]

A feature, then, of moral sanctions is that they are a consequence of subjective state determinations.

The natural-law proponent might argue, of course, that a moral sanction is subjective only insofar as the state does not fear the wrath of a deity. The positivist, by comparison, might retort that subjectivity is limited only to the extent that failure to be dissuaded by moral sanctions could lead to more severe forms of sanctions. A strong inclination exists to be pragmatic and lean toward the positivist because the apparent error of the naturalists is the tendency to translate prescribed individual moral behavior into collective moral behavior and then to deduce a conclusion about states on the basis of observations about collective behavior. Humans generally are expected to be capable of distinguishing between right and wrong and to be able to achieve the objects of self-interest by right means. States, while they may ordinarily seek self-interest by right means, cannot afford the luxury of rejecting wrong means for the sake of national self-interest.

Nevertheless, in international law and relations a political rebuke may serve as a sanction when its aims are generally conceded to be morally acceptable. States do distinguish between right and wrong at the foreign policy level; it is actual behavior that varies dramatically.[11] John Foster Dulles viewed the role of moral sanctions as follows:

> We recognize that moral pressure is an indispensa-
> ble element in any system of international law and
> order. Just as in the ordering of the life of a
> community it is impossible to accomplish anything
> effective in the long run unless it is responsive
> to the sentiment of the community and has back of
> it moral pressure, so also in the community of na-
> tions it is not going to be possible to accomplish
> anything unless it has moral pressure behind it.
> But, also as in that of the community, moral pres-
> sure alone does not suffice.[12]

9

Inherent in expressed moral sanctions are both positive and negative features. Positively, states may be impelled to seek consensus in their disputes, while negatively, they may annoy another state and its population to an extent necessary to force the state into an expanded conflict.

A fundamental subtype of the moral sanction, or perhaps the foundation, is public opinion. It is probably a truism to say that "opinions matter for policy,"[13] but it is a truism that becomes significant when foreign policy and the employment of sanctions are at issue. First, sanctioning states will find it essential to convey to the target state the impression that the action for which it is condemned by the international agency is universally disapproved by the imposing states' populations.[14] Second, the target state invariably will seek support for its action from its own population, since this is vital to success in any resistance to sanctions. Third, both contenders will doubtless consider it imperative that every effort be made to convince opposing populations that their policy is correct while that of their opponent is foolish.[15]

Generally, as a sanction of international law, public opinion is precarious. For example, the inability of persons to determine what is, and what is not, objective in the face of a barrage of conflicting claims can cause confusion, thereby spawning a decay in resolve. Similarly, no statesman can afford to trust to the chimeralike nature of public opinion, especially if sanctions implementation or the enforcement policy in general is projected for the long run. Taken together, these elements raise the obvious specter that public opinion, as an applied sanction, is of very limited utility. The problem is not so much that of generating opinion as it is of sustaining enthusiasm and cohesiveness. If all foreign policy could be concluded while newspapers and other media could still find headline copy, then perhaps public opinion would be more significant --or possibly "useful" is a better word. Of course, this does not mean that opinion would be better informed.

> Public opinion, particularly in democratic countries, is an important sanction against transgression. Ample evidence of this is to be found in the efforts made by all Governments which have been involved in war, particularly since 1914, to convince their own people and the world that their country has been the innocent victim of unjust aggression. Without popular support success in war is impossible.[16]

10

One corollary that can be extracted from this assessment is that popular support, appropriately employed, is essential to the success of diplomacy. Also, since 1914 it has been of value to control mass media for opinion-molding purposes. It matters not whether the opinion to be mustered is in support of or in opposition to the projected or ongoing policy.

A major limitation on the employment of public opinion as a sanction is the possibility that excessive damnation may arouse latent sympathies for the target state. The concurrent danger is that such condemnation may lead to a solidification of what otherwise might have been weak or indifferent opinion in the target state.*

Theoretically public opinion could be utilized, or manipulated as necessary, to promote support for a policy within the sanctioning state and dissension within the target state. In practice, the success of such an approach will depend heavily upon the nature of the political system and, invariably, the capacity of that system to direct or respond to opinion as reflected by available media. Conceivably, the more monolithic the political system, the greater the apparent unity of public opinion. Alternatively, if sanctions can be depicted within the target state as a threat to that state's survival, then it is possible that almost any population will tolerate extensive controls over the direction of opinion formation through media controls.[17] Within sanctioning states the necessity of unified public opinion is vital to the success of any such policy. Inevitably there is consolation to the target state if it has a reasonable expectation that opinion opposing the employment of sanctions has a substantial chance of success. The Rhodesian Information Office in Washington, D.C., has been particularly active in its efforts to appeal to potential American investors and to urge them to exert pressure upon the U.S. government to modify its attitude toward Rhodesia.[18] These efforts were capped with partial success in November 1971, when U.S. restrictions on imports of Rhodesian chrome were removed.

During the Italian-Ethiopian dispute, extensive use was made of overseas Italian-language newspapers and special press releases with attached glossy photographs of al-

---

*This was especially true in Rhodesia and, to a lesser extent, in Italy during 1935 and 1936. But the reverse appears to have occurred in the Dominican Republic in 1960. Naturally, as a defensive measure, target states promote the victim sentiment.

leged Ethiopian atrocities committed against Italian soldiers.[19] Doubtless the photographs were intended to be supportive of Italian pretensions about a civilizing mission in Abyssinia, and thereby to undermine public support for Ethiopia and especially League sanctions.

Various opinions have been offered on the limitations of public opinion as a sanction.

> The claims made in behalf of public disapproval
> as an international sanction appear greatly exaggerated. The organized means by which the community pressures make themselves felt within a state are largely lacking at an international level. And when popular opinion is manifest, short of positive action by states, it is in behalf of international morality and not the more or less technical rules of international law. In so far as international law and international morality coincide, there will be popular support for the law, but sanctions dispensed at the bar of world opinion are moral rather than legal sanctions.[20]

If the offending state is prepared to live with public opprobrium—and many appear willing—then it may violate the assumed morality of interstate relations with relative impunity. Sanctions, to be effective, must have a much more solid foundation than unguided popular opinion. Moreover, the limitations of public opinion as a sanction are further determined by factors that should be, but are not, extraneous to international law: isolationist, pacifist, and ideological sentiments, not infrequently couched in moralistic terms, that tend unreliably to distort public opinion.

Public opinion as a moral sanction of international law is a victim of its own vagaries and inevitably must lag behind the offense committed, thereby becoming little more than a nominal and often routine deterrent. In addition, a population may become so bewildered by the claims and counterclaims involved in a dispute that it loses perspective of the sequence of offense and punishment. Include with this the combined difficulties of generating and maintaining public opinion, and the usefulness becomes even more tenuous.[21]

While a discussion of public opinion as a sanction in international law may be employed to display the proximity of moral and political sanctions, the unity is more aptly illustrated by canvassing the formal modes of expressing

political disfavor. Specific political sanctions may be
motivated by altruistic moral and ethical impulses or by
purely pragmatic considerations. In either case the motivation ultimately may prove quite immaterial. As a general
observation it can be suggested that a multilateral agency's
response to an alleged violation of international law will
have a more valid claim to a moralistic motivation than a
single, unilateral, rebuke. This point is certainly more
evident in the Rhodesian case, where numerous subjective
state positions were amalgamated, in the long run, into a
rather weighty series of Security Council resolutions.
These tended to carry more authority because the UN resolutions made the event a worldwide concern, thus obstructing
any possible British attempts to conclude a surreptitious
deal with Rhodesian rebels.[22]

Political Sanctions

Under the heading of political sanctions are included
those techniques of international coercion that in some
manner involve the processes of regular diplomatic intercourse:* verbal communication, joint or unilateral diplomatic protest, and rupture of diplomatic relations.
The efficacy of a verbal communication depends to a
large extent upon the relative importance of the issuing
state, the relative frequency or infrequency of resort to
verbal reprimands, the nature of the language employed
(vitriolic or conventionally diplomatic), and the importance
of the issuing state in terms of its usual capacity to influence the target state. The verbal communication may express disapproval, serve as a reminder, or act as a warning.
Less frequently it may convey a direct threat.[23] The most
common means of conveying such communications are orally
or by the use of aide-mémoires.[24] "Joint protests" or
"identical notes"[25] may be less effective as a sanction

———————

*By limiting the discussion to diplomatic means, I have
purposely excluded the inadequately explored area of private
group activities and their direct and indirect relationships
to foreign policy outputs. It could be demonstrated, for
example, that the 1968 Commonwealth Prime Minister's meeting in London on Rhodesia was largely in response to a concerted campaign conducted by various Rhodesian interest
groups, journalists, certain African diplomats, and at
least one head of state.

than single-state communications because of deficiencies
and habitual defects inherent in any verbal sanction--that
is, inflammatory words cloaking passive intentions--because
multilateral objections tend toward a lower or more moderate common denominator. Also, joint protests require joint
consultation, thereby making time a crucial factor. The
inability to respond immediately also could be interpreted
as reticence on the part of the states involved, thereby
signaling the target state that there was disunity in the
ranks. This is a fairly common occurrence in a multipol-
arized world. Finally, there is the possibility that a delay will provide the offender with time to consolidate its
position.[26] However, all things considered, a more coordinated effort on the part of many states may proportionately enhance the impact of the objection on the offending
state.

The rupture of diplomatic relations is a serious sanction; and recent years have witnessed certain peculiar uses,
or abuses, of the technique.[27] Nevertheless, the technique
still vividly conveys disapproval of an alleged violation
of international law or other unfavorable act. The obvious
but frequently forgotten disadvantage is that severance of
diplomatic relations is usually reciprocal.

> The further step of breaking off formal diplomatic
> intercourse altogether by withdrawing embassy and
> staff, and refusing to receive an embassy from the
> offender . . . does put the offending government
> to some measure of inconvenience. . . . But the
> inconvenience is mutual, and may indeed be greater
> to the country which breaks off relations than to
> the other. . . . The method, however, constitutes
> an emphatic gesture, as a warning that effective
> ostracism may follow.[28]

The inconvenience is aggravated by severance of direct
lines of communication, thereby impeding possible courses
of negotiated settlement. In general, diplomatic sanctions

> are not efficacious in themselves. So far as the
> moral sanction is effective, diplomacy plays its
> part in mobilizing it, expressing it, and in bring-
> ing it into action. So far as more concrete mea-
> sures are possible and effective as sanctions,
> diplomacy may render their actual enforcement un-
> necessary by conveying a warning of their imminent
> use. But if the moral sanction is ineffective,

diplomacy cannot reinforce it; and unless concrete sanctions really are imminent, the warnings of diplomacy may well be useless.[29]

The actual termination of diplomatic relations may be counterproductive as a form of sanction unless it is part of a more comprehensive sanctions pattern. The real sanction, insofar as it can be effective, is probably the threat to break off relations. In this respect there is a certain parallel between the threat and the remaining type of political sanction, nonrecognition: Neither requires a physical effort by the sanctioning state(s) but each expresses its own peculiar brand of disapproval.* Nonrecognition is a form of sanction that may be classified according to the two usual varieties of recognition: "constitutive," or factual acknowledgment that a state exists regardless of its government, and "declaratory," or an expression of approval or disapproval of a particular government. During the past 50 years or so, the preponderance of declaratory recognition (or nonrecognition) has tended to create the anomoly that de facto recognition (or nonrecognition) is considerably more important in practice than de jure status.[30]

For purposes of this discussion, nonrecognition as a sanction is interpreted restrictively, that is, only to the extent that it relates directly to the application of international law. This more restricted approach avoids an incidental discussion of nonrecognition as an ideological weapon.[31]

The September 1931 Japanese invasion of Manchuria, and the creation of the puppet state of Manchukuo, prompted the United States and other nations into defining the general sorts of conditions under which recognition would, or would not, be accorded in response to overt violations of international law. The American "Stimson doctrine" of nonrecognition was defined as

---

*The extent to which South Africa's refusal to extend formal recognition to Rhodesia is in response to UN, British, and U.S. pressure is not clear. However, both South Africa and Portugal have been very cautious about discussing formal ties. The Rhodesians, aware of this delicacy, have refrained from pressing their friends. On one or two occasions, in fact (November 1971), Portugal had quietly encouraged Rhodesia to settle with Britain. Neither Portugal nor South Africa has appreciated world attention attracted to that part of Africa.

a prelude to concerted international action
against a wrongdoer whatever form it may take--a
complete economic boycott of its trade, expulsion
of its ships and its nationals from other countries, rupture of diplomatic relations, and so
forth--a policy of non-recognition may in certain
circumstances act as a deterrent.[32]

The doctrine contemplated nonrecognition in conjunction with
other types of sanctions, but nonrecognition was still to
be viewed as a form of opprobrium, that is, a distinct sanction. Critics of the Stimson doctrine leveled objections
at the absence of expressly defined supportive coercive
measures and suggested that the appeal of nonrecognition
was that it was "much less painful" than economic sanctions.[33]
     The appeal of moral and political sanctions stems from
the minimization of direct costs (internal as opposed to
external costs) to the sanctioning states. Yet there is
no necessary correlation between minimal costs and success.
The crucial variables, which would result in success or
failure of a sanctions program, are too dependent upon a
wide range of other elements to draw such a direct relationship. This is discussed more comprehensively later.
     In general, moral and political sanctions are of lim-
ited utility unless they are an acknowledged preface to
other, more direct and more "costly" types of sanction.
They are simply one phase of a comprehensive sanctions
scheme and must be evaluated in that context.

ECONOMIC SANCTIONS

     Roughly, economic sanctions may be grouped into three
types: embargoes, boycotts, and blockades or "quarantines."

     The employment of economics as an instrument of
     coercive policy may, in broad statement, be de-
     scribed as the management of access to a flow of
     goods, services and money, as well as to markets,
     with the end of denying the target-state such ac-
     cess while maintaining it for oneself. All the
     familiar methods of economic warfare developed in
     the last two world wars may be included, such as
     the blocking and freezing of the target's assets;
     the imposition of import and export embargoes,
     total or selective; blacklisting of foreign firms
     and individuals who deal with the target-state;

drying up of foreign supplies by preclusive buying; control of re-exportation from a non-participant's territory; and control of shipping through selective admission to credit, insurance, stores, fuel, port and repair facilities.[34]

The parallel drawn between the specific methods of economic sanctions in pursuit of unilateral or multilateral foreign policy objectives--the techniques of pressure--and economic warfare is not absolutely correct.[35]

The distinction between economic warfare and economic sanctions in international relations and law essentially originates with differences in goals sought. Warfare, unless defined with limited objectives, seeks to effect an absolute change in the status of the target state and perhaps, incidentally, to spark structural changes within that state's political and economic systems. Economic warfare is a tactical component of an overall military strategy. Economic sanctions may be designed to affect the entire social system, as in Rhodesia. Generally, however, a more usual goal is to impose a price for the offending state's continuation of an offensive policy or practice and, if necessary, to cause a change in that state's political system or political attitudes--that is, to force the offender to renounce or alter a policy or mode of behavior. The main purpose of economic sanctions, when utilized by a multilateral agency, is not to destroy a state, or for that matter, irreparably to impair its economic, political, or social systems. It seems to be acknowledged universally that economic sanctions of the types described here should present no threat to state continuance, an element not normally conterminous with a strategy of war.[36]

The embargo is a basic form of economic sanction. One study drew a distinction between what were termed active and passive embargoes:

An embargo may be (i) passive, or, (ii) active;
. . . (i) It may be applied by each state upon
its own territory, merely by abstaining from export.
Such a passive embargo will be completely
successful only if all producing and exporting
states in the world participate in it and if the
country against which it is applied is not entirely
self-sufficient . . . (ii) It may be enforced
actively by blockading the shores and
land frontiers of the recalcitrant state and preventing
goods and supplies from passing in over
them.[37]

17

The defect in these definitions is that they blend the embargo with the blockade and designate them collectively as
simply an embargo. A more accurate description of these
two types of activities would be to describe the passive
as an "economic boycott" while the active might best be
described as an "economic blockade." Their primary similar-
ities are that they are directed exclusively toward material goods and that they do not usually involve direct intervention in the internal affairs of the target state.

Another observer has classified embargoes and boycotts
as forms of reprisals; and although this classification
contributes little to the development of concepts of positive international law, it does serve as a means of viewing
these types of sanctions from another perspective. The embargo is

> a form of reprisals consisting of forcible deten-
> tion of the vessels of the State alleged to have
> committed a breach of international law. In the
> first instance, it was applied only to such ves-
> sels as were in the ports of the State laying the
> embargo, but in practice was extended to such ves-
> sels also as were apprehended at sea and even
> within the coastal waters of the offending State.
> This type of reprisal is more or less a relic of
> the past.
>
> An embargo upon the export of certain goods
> or materials, for example, of arms or special
> metals, has now become a fairly common measure,
> and has been adopted by the United States in par-
> ticular, not only to deny access to belligerents
> of implements or materials of war out of respect
> of neutral duties, but also to preclude an alleged
> aggressor State from increasing its war-making
> potential, or to prevent the aggravation of civil
> strife in a State where domestic violence pre-
> vails.[38]

It is this latter description of the economic embargo that
is implicit in any further references to embargoes.[39]

Julius Stone described a boycott as

> a modern form of reprisals whereby a State may in-
> stitute by itself and through its nationals an in-
> terruption of commercial and financial relation-
> ships with another State and that State's nationals.
> Opinion is divided as to whether independently of

any illegal acts committed by the State against
which the boycott is directed, it is a breach of
public international law. It is at least an un-
friendly act, but some writers go further and say
that in some circumstances it may amount to an
act of economic aggression which should be prohibited by law.[40]

The interesting aspect of Stone's descriptions of embargoes
and boycotts is that they tend to be couched in terms of
reprisals. This closely approximates the approach taken by
a number of commentators, for example, on the 1923 Italian-
Greek (Corfu) incident. Charles de Visscher suggested that
reprisals might be categorized according to the nature of
their intention. Thus, armed reprisals would include an
armed blockade and possibly even bombardment, while anything less than the use of armed force would be purely an
economic sanction.[41]
    That both Stone and de Visscher agree that embargoes
and blockades are little but reprisals poses a dilemma of
reconciling such a conclusion with the necessities of positive international law enforcement. However, two points
must be noted. First, both commentators focused upon the
act-of-state doctrine. This rules out informal and formal
restraints (such as consensus resolutions) that would be
inherent in a multilateral context; and it permits the suggestion that sanctions are an unhindered progression from
the aide-mémoire to armed intervention, or that all categories and types of sanctions are imposed simultaneously.
Second, both observers omitted reference, presumably because it was not considered essential for their purposes,
to whether the techniques described would be pursuant to
law enforcement or of more narrowly defined unilateral foreign policy goals, be they related to international law or
not. Regardless of whether boycotts and embargoes are forms
of reprisals in bilateral state relations, the concept of
reprisals is deficient for the purposes of international
organizations and their processes of law implementation.
This will become more evident later, when the position of
Venezuela (as the aggrieved party) in the Dominican Republic case is outlined.
    In the cases under review, international organizations
have by no means considered their imposition of sanctions
to be a reprisal. While Article 41 of the UN Charter and
Article 8 of the Rio Treaty may appear to imply that sanctions should be implemented in a sequential manner, and
that in some way they should be proportional to the offense,

practice has demonstrated that they may be imposed collectively and without regard to assessments of the extent of the offense.[42] Embargoes, boycotts, and blockades, while they may be employed for purposes of reprisal, should not be considered reprisals in terms of positive multilateral law enforcement. They have been applied quite independently, and in some instances not applied, as the organizations have considered necessary. In view of this, it might be suggested that the concept of reprisals should have no place in the lexicon of international organizations. For multilateral purposes each form of economic sanction must be treated quite independently of the others, thereby permitting the organization to select the most appropriate type, or combination of types, of sanction for the particular situation. Broad categorizations may be appropriate for bilateral, or even limited multilateral, purposes but not for international agency enforcement.

Economic embargoes and boycotts consist of a number of specific actions, the most obvious being import controls.* This is easiest to apply, with the exception of problems surrounding determination of the value-added content of goods, because it is controlled within domestic jurisdiction by a national customs administration. The reverse of import control is export control or an export embargo. This is considerably more difficult to enforce domestically, unless each state involved in imposing the embargo is prepared to permit the application of foreign law extraterritorially within its municipal jurisdictions.[43] Further, it has been the practice of some states to allow private agencies to supervise and control export licenses and export manifests, a situation that has proved liable to abuse. The consequence is a tendency to consider the stated place of destination as the actual destination, without regard to the possibility of transshipment or, more common, the production of false documents. Import embar-

---

*In this sense there is a tendency to view the embargo as being officially prescribed and thus enforced by municipal law, whereas the boycott is considered to be less formal and tends to lack the mandatory nature of the embargo. Of course, there are numerous occasions when a boycott is official state policy--for example, the UAR's boycott of products of American origin if the manufacturer has branches in Israel. This may change somewhat, however, since the United States and Egypt resumed diplomatic relations in February 1974.

goes tend to be favored over export embargoes simply because
they are administratively easier to apply (there is no need
to duplicate government services) and they cost less.[44]
    The cumulative impact of either embargoes or boycotts
is increased considerably when the ratio of applicants to
nonapplicants is high. Also, it is obvious that among those
applying sanctions there should be included dominant exporting and importing states. As well, third-party concurrence
--or at least acquiescence--is vital for the most efficient
application of economic sanctions. In the following cases
of applied mandatory sanctions, the position of third parties has been of considerable tactical importance.
    A variation of the economic embargo is the straight-
forward arms embargo.[45] An arms embargo is usually the
first economic sanction imposed, and the reasons are clear.
Generally, arms embargoes are proclaimed "to protect the
civilian population" or "to prevent the spread of hostilities." Both these reasons were advanced by League members
during the 1935 Bolivia-Paraguay (Chaco) dispute. The ade-
quacy of arms embargoes depends upon the resources of the
target state or states and upon the availability and costs
of alternative sources of supply from private dealers.

> The arms embargo can only be effectual against ag-
> gression if the aggressor is not able to supply
> its own needs; it can be rendered ineffective by
> the abstention of one important arms-producing
> state. It may even be rendered ineffective by the
> action of business interests which contrive to
> circumvent government control . . . since a coun-
> try which is running short of arms will offer very
> attractive inducements in order to provide such
> temptation.[46]

Ostensibly neutral states (for example Sweden) and ideological adversaries have often filled the arms gap, as Trujillo
discovered.
    A variation of the general economic embargo is one
directed specifically at raw materials. As a single form
of economic sanction this is of limited utility unless the
target state is significantly dependent upon raw materials
for its industry or trade. In 1932 the Committee of Economic Sanctions, made up of American citizens, reviewed
weapons of that day and observed:

> Going over the various supplies needed for actual
> front-line operations we find that only a few of

21

them need be expressed in large units per man per
year. Steel, for arms, ammunition, light railways,
and trench shelters may total three tons per capita; that amount would have involved the previous
production of some six tons of coal and six to
eight tons of iron ore. In the next line comes
petroleum, which at various front-line and transport uses may attain a military consumption of
one ton per capita or more. . . . All other supplies fall far below these rates: from 100 to
200 pounds each of nitrates, sulphur or pyrite,
cement, manganese, copper and lead; down to from
five to twenty pounds each of such things as cotton, wool, rubber and the minor munition metals
(tin, nickel, antimony, aluminum, zinc and quick-
silver).[47]

Allegedly, in 1932, a state lacking in any one or more of
these types of commodity would find its ability to conduct
an aggressive or offensive act impaired. Even its ability
to resist sanctions would be problematic. Alleviation of
some target state deficiencies might be accomplished by
converting goods from normal peacetime uses to military
purposes, but much would depend upon the rate of change-
over and the availability of approximate substitutes.
Stockpiling, either generally or for strategic purposes,
is another common and quite viable practice; and thus any
multilateral agency would be well advised to attempt estimates of stockpiled resources within any projected target
state.[48] In Rhodesia the reverse also occurred, that is,
a normal export (tobacco) was stockpiled and subsidized by
the government until surreptitious markets were developed.
It is also possible, as a result of conquest or by virtue
of control over peripheral states, to offset deficiencies
by utilizing resources of these appendages, for example,
Israel's exploitation of oil resources in the occupied
Sinai since the 1967 war. If necessary, poor-quality ore
bodies, normally considered unworkable, could be brought
into production, although at considerable additional expense. Finally, a state could salvage or requisition domestic supplies of goods for various purposes, such as India's
requisition of domestic gold supplies during the 1961 Sino-
Indian border dispute.[49]
   An economic boycott or embargo, while the most obvious
form of economic sanction, is not necessarily the most propitious. Numerous states, for example, have imposed boycotts, and often embargoes, on the Republic of South Africa

in accordance with either their own inclinations or pursuant
to decisions of the UN General Assembly. Yet these activities appear to have achieved little but a hardening of that
country's resolve to pursue its racial policies and, incidentally, to force upon the South Africans a greater degree
of economic self-sufficiency. A 1964 conference on economic
sanctions directed against South Africa suggested that "a
policy of total economic sanctions against South Africa is
feasible and practical and can be effective."[50] The conference arrived at this conclusion despite South African
government assertions that such onslaughts can be with-
stood.[51] Pronouncements such as those emanating from the
1964 conference become meaningless unless accompanied by
an acute awareness of the problems of applied economic sanctions. A brief digression will illustrate the point.

The matter of transshipment of goods has been one of
the more perplexing features of applied economic sanctions.
Transshipment is the procedure of delivering goods from
one place to another via a third, and often fourth, party
or state (for example, the movement of Rhodesian tobacco to
European markets via South African processors). It may
also involve the physical transfer of goods from one carrier to another en route, on land or at sea (the latter is
the more difficult both to undertake and to control).
Transshipment on land must involve a third party. For example, goods are transported from state "X" (the one imposing sanctions) to state "Y" (the state certified to receive
the goods); the latter may repackage, remanufacture, or
perhaps not even alter the product before passing it on to
state "A" (the target state). This situation raises the
additional question of neutrality as a perplexing test of
the efficacy of sanctions implementation,* and thus it becomes a political problem of highest magnitude.[52]

Transshipment at sea involves the primary difficulty
of control. This is further complicated by the existence
of free ports, such as Hamburg and Tangier, and the ease
with which ship registry may be altered.** More frequent,

---

*That is, notwithstanding the equally perplexing tech-
nical question of value-added content. It was tragically
amusing that senior statesmen on the League's Committee of
18 debated at length whether the wrappers placed, in Spain,
around Italian-grown oranges constituted sufficient value-
added content to warrant classification as non-Italian.

**Enforcement of economic sanctions against Rhodesia has
been plagued with cases involving the use of free ports to

but not impossible, is the transfer of goods between carriers in remote locations. A curtailment of some practices might result from more rigid issuance of certificates of cargo origin and destination and perhaps some form of verification with an international control board or agency. Certificates for neutral shipping, known as navicerts, permit free transit in the vicinity of the target state and constitute a form of immunity as long as no suspicious actions are observed nor contraband discovered.

A remaining economic sanction, and one not totally unrelated to other types, is the economic blockade. The blockade is a more complex and dangerous form of operation, and has not been considered particularly feasible by international organizations.[53] Possibly because the blockade appears to portend more direct aggression, its use has been confined, even recently, to little more than a form of bilateral and multilateral coercion.[54] The reason for apprehension appears to be fear that resistance on the part of the target state will lead to open hostilities.

Julius Stone, in a rather elaborate discussion of blockades, argued that noncollective blockades (under Article 42 of the UN Charter) are not admissible enforcement measures. He suggested that the term "pacific blockade" has a "tinge of absurdity because a blockade is undeniably a warlike act." The term "pacific" probably only means peacetime, as opposed to blockades established during outright war.*

---

unload cigarettes containing Rhodesian tobacco. The tobacco originates in Rhodesia, and is processed there and in South Africa. There are also cases of ships altering registry to avoid prosecution in domestic courts, the classic case being that of the Johanna V in April 1966. The ship, registered in Panama, was owned by a group in New York with a board of directors in Montreal. While the ship was in Beira harbor, the owners transferred ownership from one Panamanian company to another. Ultimately the ship became stateless and was allowed out of Beira only after it acquired Greek registry. The British have maintained an air base in Madagascar to observe ship movements into ports in Mozambique.

*Stone notes that blockades have not always been in the interests of peace--for example, the Spanish insurgent blockade of 1931 or Egypt's blockade of Suez in 1951. These he designates as quasiblockades.

Yet the absurdities notwithstanding, Stone discerned certain characteristics of pacific blockades since 1827.

> First, the majority of pacific blockades have been conducted by Great Powers acting in concert against a weaker or lesser Power. Second, in most instances the purpose aimed at was one of international concern, such as for example, the protection of a small State's independence, the prevention of the outbreak of war, and the proper execution of treaties (the role now occupied by the international organizations). Third, in practice the blockades were conducted so as to involve a minimum of interference with third States. These considerations, coupled with the fact that there has been no case of true pacific blockade since 1919 (with the possible exception of Japan's blockade of China in 1937) . . . suggests that apart from questions of its legality under the United Nations Charter, the procedure of pacific blockade has now become obsolete.[55]

Stone's dismissal of blockades to the category of historical relic is possibly as premature as it is cynical. The error is to impose upon a peacetime condition the rigors of wartime procedure. Thus, the role of third-party neutrals might have significance were it not that the concept of neutrality is better adapted to war and warlike conditions than to collective enforcement of decisions made by international agencies. In essence, Stone's comments about third-party rights amounts to a view that, in cases of neutrality and legitimate trading practices, third-party rights are only as good as the credibility of the state that claims them. Practice does not absolutely support this position, for, as demonstrated by Chile and Costa Rica during the League's Coordination Committee consideration of sanctions against Italy, even small powers can claim neutral rights in the face of popular opinion. Switzerland also demonstrated during the same event that it was possible to combine both neutrality and adherence, in principle, to a sanctions scheme.

A final point, and one partially related to financial sanctions, involves the depletion of foreign-exchange reserves brought about as a consequence of an embargo, boycott, or blockade. This is particularly crucial when the sanctions-imposing states hitherto have been valuable trad-

ing partners of the target state. The tendency of states
to trade in hard currencies or gold has exacerbated the
problem for potential target states. The target state must
acquire reserves, and they must be in a form that is readily convertible. Thus, efforts must be made to convert soft
currencies into hard currencies or gold--which conversions,
of necessity, must be done rather surreptitiously. No matter how available goods may be through third states or elsewhere, the absence of an appropriate exchange currency can
wreak havoc upon an economy under pressure.

One factor to be seriously considered in preparation
for a proposed sanctions program is the retaliatory capacity and position of the target state. During the League's
consideration of the sanctions to be imposed against Italy,
retaliation by Italy was the source of many quaverings by
representatives before the Committee of 18 and the Coordination Committee. (Romania feared loss of oil markets in
Italy and was threatened by Italian Foreign Minister Ciano
in early 1936; Poland feared loss of shipbuilding contracts;
and Albania feared loss of general trade.) The RIIA, commenting upon the role of possible retaliation for Britain's
attitude toward Bolivia during the Chaco dispute, observed:

> The imposition of an embargo may have indirectly
> an adverse repercussion in the country imposing
> it, if the country against which it is directed
> retaliates. For instance, the Government of
> Bolivia made the claim in 1934 that the British
> embargo contravened the Anglo-Bolivian Agreement
> of 1911; and threatened that if it were imposed,
> extra war taxation would be imposed on British
> companies in Bolivia, from which they had been
> hitherto exempt under the agreement.[56]

The broad conclusions that may be derived regarding
economic sanctions, be they considered as reprisals or as
retribution, are fairly uncomplicated. First, no state
can be totally detached from the imposition of economic
sanctions as an imposing state, target state, or third
party (neutral, if such can exist under multilateral circumstances); economic sanctions affect all trading patterns.
Second, the effectiveness of the enforcement program will
depend upon international unity (or unanimity) either actively or, at minimum, passively. This may result from
collaboration within an international organization or from
coordination between the organization's members and nonmembers. Third, the impact of economic sanctions will be

effective in a direct relationship to the nature of the
target state's economy. While there may not be direct proportional relationships between effectiveness, or nonef-
fectiveness, and single-crop economies versus highly industrialized economies, there is certainly reason to suggest
the potentially greater effectiveness of economic sanctions
in the single-crop over those in the industrialized category.
More will be said on this topic later. Fourth, it is obvious that a target state will have friends; and such friendly
states may find it possible to thwart, interfere with, or
otherwise detract from the full impact of the sanctions.
Such known and possible relationships must be taken into
account in any sanctions scheme. Finally, any form of sanction could be interpreted by the target state as an act of
aggression, more so when an armed blockade is included.
Such an interpretation automatically could raise the problem of retaliation and neutral rights; and hence the imposing state(s) must be prepared to assess its(their) respective position(s) and goals in terms of the probable increased strain in relations with the target state, themselves, and third parties and/or neutrals. Theoretically
this is of lesser consequence for a universal multilateral
agency such as the United Nations.

FINANCIAL SANCTIONS

Related to economic sanctions, although sufficiently
distinct to warrant individual consideration, are sanctions
that can best be described as financial sanctions. The
most obvious feature of imposed financial sanctions is the
correlation between "large" or creditor states and "small"
or debtor states. Almost without exception, wealthier
states are in much better positions to impose financial
sanctions on less wealthy states. Moreover, the short-term
loss of return is more readily absorbed by wealthier states.
Hence economically disadvantaged states, even when united
in action, are scarcely able to consider an effective reciprocal response to wealthy-state offenses in international
law. For this reason financial sanctions are little better than a corollary of big-power politics, perhaps illustrated to a certain extent by the African states' frustrations over an apparent inability to cope with large-power
protection of the Republic of South Africa and Portugal.
The requirements of economic development demand the
acquisition of foreign developmental capital in the form
of credits, exchange reserves, loans, increased trade, fa-

cilities for the sale of bonds, funding for insurance programs, and outright bilateral and multilateral financial assistance.[57] Financial sanctions function on the premise that if foreign capital sources are controlled and internal exchange resources are exhausted, then a target state may be forced into financial collapse and eventually into some form of submission.

A relatively recent variation on the conventional types of financial sanctions is use of development assistance as a means of exerting pressure upon recipient states.[58] From the perspective of the international organization, the suspension of developmental assistance and other forms of financial support is of restricted value because such support tends to have an impact on a limited number of states: those in need of aid. The imbalance between wealthier and poorer states is not conducive to equitable enforcement of international decisions. Of course, as was demonstrated in the Dominican situation in 1961, a U.S. offer of massive amounts of assistance could act as an inducement to a change in Dominican government policy. This offer of aid, as opposed to withholding aid, might be termed a positive sanction--an incentive to comply with the benefactor's wishes.

The variety of potential financial sanctions is almost unlimited. Forbidding the target state to take advantage of previously arranged credit agreements, the prevention of the raising of loans on international money markets, the prohibition of the sale of target-state bonds and securities, the restriction of acquisition and collection of insurance policies and premiums, and the freezing of bank assets are all viable techniques.[59]

Restrictions on the movement of goods can be imposed with relative ease by the revocation or suspension of most-favored-nation clauses in bilateral and multilateral treaties and agreements, and by raising tariffs on imports from the target state, including a required real percentage value-added tax. Under the conditions of a full trade embargo, these techniques would be employed only in circumstances where the matter of value-added content was a problem--that is, where the percentage of any given product that originated within the target state, without being the entire product, was such that the product might be classed as originating in the target state.

As a last resort the major enforcing states could consider a short-term revaluation of the target state's currency. In more drastic circumstances, the enforcing states and/or international agency might seek to have those states

28

with major supplies of hard currencies or gold reserves revalue their domestic currencies, that is, peg them at an artificially high level vis-à-vis the target-state's currency and major reserves. Either of these two procedures would involve one of two processes: devaluation, to prevent the imposing states' nationals from purchasing the target state's products, or supravaluation, to prevent the target state's purchase of goods from the imposing states, either directly or through third parties or states. These procedures could not be undertaken unilaterally because they would impose an incredible burden upon the trade of the state revaluing a currency. Supravaluation, in effect, could amount to an unofficial devaluation of the target state's currency. But the task of multilateral coordination would be immense. Manipulation of currency is dangerous for all parties involved and it is improbable, except in extreme circumstances, that many states would wish to become involved in such precarious and largely speculative ventures.

Naturally, as easily as financial sanctions are mechanically imposed, so are they circumvented. A target state might obtain foreign currencies by mobilizing the overseas holdings of its nationals, particularly if this can be facilitated through neutral states' banks. Such an undertaking may involve the seizure of titles to such holdings by the state or the requirement that ownership of foreign holdings be registered with, and placed at the disposal of, the state. If an enforcing state were recalcitrant about releasing funds, it would be possible for the target state to have titles transferred to holding companies resident within neutral and/or third-party convenience states. Hence, with a little extra cost it would be possible to have credits and dividends from privately held overseas investments and properties channeled back (probably indirectly) to the target state.

A further possibility is the clandestine acquisition of foreign currencies through barter arrangements, individual borrowings, and life insurance policies, all transacted through the financial institutions of neutral states. It is possible too that a target state could acquire adequate loans from within the enforcing states through, for example, Swiss banks. Government-supported, purportedly private individuals making loans abroad would be immensely difficult to detect.* When the financial rewards are suffi-

_____

*Numerous instances of all these practices can be documented in the Rhodesian case, while in the Dominican case,

29

ciently large, and neutral states are available, there is almost no limit to the means whereby investors could conclude transactions that would benefit the target state.

As a final note on the subject of financial sanctions, a mention must be made of contracts. Two preliminary questions arise on this subject. First, if there exists a contract between two private companies, is one state justified in seizing the goods or in refusing to permit the transfer of payments in fulfillment of the terms of the contract? Second, in cases of contracts between private companies, what action should, or could, the offended company take if a state intervenes? One attempt to answer these questions was made by the Legal Subcommittee of the League's Coordination Committee. It recommended that there should be a definite cutoff date for conclusion of contracts and that contracts in the process of being completed on the effective date of sanctions commencement (that is, in transit) be permitted to reach completion.[60] Essentially this meant fulfillment of commercial contracts within a specified time period. The matter of liability would depend upon whether the contract was terminated unilaterally or whether it was terminated in response to a decision of an international agency. The League's Legal Subcommittee did advise that termination should be without prejudice to future claims against the contract once sanctions had been suspended or lifted. As will be explained later, this advice would still appear to be appropriate.

So much of the success or failure of financial sanctions depends upon the long-term financial relationships between enforcing and target states and the general buoyancy, or lack of it, of participating states' economies. It became very evident during 1935 and 1936, for example, that states recovering from a depression are not anxious to become excessively altruistic, particularly when entire economies are under severe strain. It might also be recalled that the Dominican Republic was just beginning to recover from the 1959 recession when the OAS sanctions were leveled against the country in August 1960. Balance-of-payments and creditor-debtor relationships, in all probability, will determine the efficacy of financial sanctions and their variations. In fact, even this may be deceptive, for even if the target state has a debtor relationship with an enforcing state, it has recourse by withholding payments

---

Trujillo's private Swiss bank accounts were doubtless of immense value.

on matured bonds, interest, or dividends from capital in-
vested within its boundaries. In addition, there always
remains the possibility of additional taxes and other financial impositions against foreign-owned properties, as well
as outright nationalization. These response tactics can
be employed to generate opposition to the sanctions from
within the sanctioning states. There is also the possibility that a target state will threaten, if not undertake,
to withhold financial returns, and even services, from
shared activities--for example, Rhodesian threats against
Zambia over distribution of Kariba Dam power.

All of these points illustrate, of course, that the
use of financial and financially related sanctions can be
most hazardous. In addition, even a brief discussion
should have emphasized the highly complex and interrelated
nature of the international financial structure, a point
not to be taken too lightly or too readily oversimplified.

PHYSICAL SANCTIONS

The extreme aspect of the spectrum of types and categories of sanctions is the use of force short of war. It
will be recalled, of course, that within the context of
this discussion any use of force would be limited to the
point where it is not destructive of the target state's political system. The use of a flyby by the U.S. Navy over
Santo Domingo in November 1961 would certainly fall into
this category. In this instance the result was the total
elimination of the Trujillo family from the Dominican Republic. However, the Dominican political system continued
uninterrupted, but with relatively new actors. Such a military show of force had not been anticipated in any OAS
resolution and thus amounted to a unilateral U.S. action.
More will be said on this general subject later.

Force, as a sanction of international law and relations, overtly or covertly implies the employment of military equipment and personnel. Perhaps implicit in every
enforcement decision by an international agency is the potential use of force, although this parallel is based upon
a municipal law analogy and for that reason some caution
is advised. Whether force will be available in practice
depends upon a host of other related matters. For example,
the successful conclusion of the agreements necessary to
implement Article 43 of the UN Charter would significantly
define the extent to which the international agency was
prepared to tolerate the employment of direct force.

31

It cannot be denied that the effective enforcement
of all sanctions must, in the last resort, depend
on the will and the power to employ military force.
Even those most opposed to the use of force in any
circumstance may agree that its collective organization, actual use, or the knowledge that it will
be used, when need arises, to suppress its indis-
criminate and irresponsible use by individual
States, should diminish the frequency with which
its employment is required.[61]

This might be termed the theory of "imminent force," and a
parallel might be drawn between it and the "balance of terror" that apparently figures so significantly in East-West
relations.

In functional terms, the "imminent force" theory of
international legal enforcement has been as useless in preventing violations of international law as has been the balance of terror in preventing outbreaks of violence with
conventional weapons. The use of force, however, has been
as much a corollary of the unilateral imposition of sanctions as the nonuse of force, in current terms, has been of
multilateral sanctions. It should be remembered that the
French and British studiously avoided implying that they
were prepared to use force against Italy in 1935, that the
British announced very early in the Rhodesian situation
that they were not inclined to use force against the rebel
regime (after a secret study had been conducted on the possibilities and ramifications), and that even Venuzuela accepted the inappropriateness of the use of force under
Article 8 of the Rio Treaty and the OAS members emphasized
this point before the UN Security Council. The consequences
for sanctions of such preliminary commitments are immense.

A decision by a single state, a number of states, or
an international organization to adopt military sanctions
hinges upon a number of factors:

1.   The advisability of direct military action against
a target state's territory
2.   The probable extent of armed resistance and the
possibility that the conflict will spread
3.   The probability that the target state will occupy
contiguous territory, thereby compounding the seriousness
of the situation
4.   The geographical remoteness of the object situation from the primary interests of the states being called
upon to impose sanctions and commit military forces

5. The feasibility of assistance to the state or party against which the offense was committed
6. The possibility of a major, drawn-out conflict
7. The capacity of the target state to involve allies by virtue of subsidiary agreements or political sympathy.*

Regardless of the reluctance of international organizations to consider force as a sanction in international law,** it is still essential to review the potential of force and its role in the enforcement process. As many of the above points suggest, force is the most readily available sanction--on a unilateral basis--yet it is the one approached with greatest reluctance by international agencies and their members. Perhaps the question of force in international law most vividly portrays the individual components of collective complex decisions.

Clearly, because of the magnitude of the problems inherent in the use of force, states will be extremely cautious about committing their fates to decisions involving extensive military preparations. The tendency, therefore, has been for force to be employed as a unilateral sanction. Most studies on the subject tend to depict force, employed under the rubric of a sanction, as little but a variation of aggression. In theory, an international organization could authenticate the use of force by one or some of its members pursuant to a decision by that agency.*** This

---

*Many of these factors were evident in the U.S. attempts to expand participation by its allies in Vietnam.
**The UN operations in Korea and the Congo, and the various peacekeeping operations, are in a qualitatively different category, although the relationship could be suggested if the concept of force as an international sanction was broadened--that is, whether international policing is law enforcement or crime prevention. In a similar but opposite vein, the activities of the U.S. fleet off the Dominican coast in November 1961 might be termed a police act to ensure that the letter of the OAS decision was strictly followed. Of course, the United States had no organizational mandate for such a unilateral action.
***If the mood of the African states at the UN had prevailed in November 1965, Britain might have found itself authorized by the Security Council to employ force against Rhodesia. The United States successfully and quietly moved to obtain the compromise resolution of November 20, which edged Britain out of a tight spot. Britain did consider a

has been a fascinating sidelight of the relationship between the OAS and the United Nations and is discussed below.

Judge Hsu Mo once differentiated legitimate from il-
legitimate force by describing one as "horizontal" and the
other as "vertical."[62] Horizontal was the "application of
force without mandate by one individual state against another." This, he added, was no longer permissible except,
of course, "in case of self-defence." Legitimate, or vertical, force was described as force that

> emanates from sources whose validity rests on
> the common consent of the international community
> itself, it should be considered, not as horizon-
> tal and individual, but as vertical and collec-
> tive.[63]

He noted further that the processes involved were "not yet
perfect and efficacious," but that there was developing a
tendency in "the direction of establishing a clear sanction
of international law in the case of the breach of the
peace." His optimism has not yet been shared by those who
must generate and direct that tendency.

The imposition of military sanctions, in a strict
"vertical" sense, abounds with uncertainties. A major problem centers on the existence, or absence, of unanimity
among members of the multilateral or collective security
agency. Even from the purely practical perspective of
logistics, such as the availability of sufficient forces,
an international military endeavor can be problem-ridden.
Furthermore, there are difficulties of agreements, command,*
liability, supply of materials, and coordination of action.
None have been resolved adequately. Hence, military sanctions as a technique of international enforcement must be
described very loosely and usually in theoretical terms.
Minor enigmas include national public sentiment within each
participant state both for and against the target state;
public opinion for and against the international organiza-

---

military response to the unilateral declaration of independence (UDI) but, for various reasons, it was rejected.

*Hsu Mo, writing at the time of the UN action in Korea,
doubtless did not appreciate problems such as command. In
retrospect, there is little doubt that the UN involvement
in Korea was going to be under the command of U.S. General
Douglas MacArthur.

tion; the estimated strength of the target state (in order
to avoid, or at least minimize, the possibility of defeat
of the organization's forces); the political inclinations
and importance of the target state; the economic significance of the target state to other states' economies; and
the degree of force to be applied, both to achieve the desired results and in relation to the magnitude of the offense. All of these decisions pose crucial practical difficulties for any potential participant state in the collective action.

The frequency with which internationally sponsored
military enforcement could, or should, be employed would
depend in large measure upon the strength of the international organization relative to its constituency. There is
reason to suppose that the regional organization would be
more able to exert influence by military means, partly because of an apparent desire of members to keep disputes regional. Within the OAS pleas of hemispheric interest have
been potent, and there appears to be little doubt that the
OAU would prefer to be able to handle its internal disputes
as matters of African interest. If the organizations can
create and sustain impressions of stern resolve, a potential regional transgressor might be inclined to act more
hesitantly. The OAS, in the Dominican case, went to great
lengths at the United Nations to demonstrate not only that
the Dominican problem was hemispheric but that the OAS
alone was capable of handling the matter.

Theoretically, an effective international organization,
with the capacity to enforce its decisions militarily,
would act as a deterrent to law violation. However, because international politics is a real milieu, the theory
must remain just that. The suggestion, therefore, is that
force, as a sanction for international law enforcement,
will continue to be a function of unilateral state action
in response to unilaterally determined violations, real or
alleged. What might be more practical, as hinted above,
is the greater use of regional organizational adaptations
of multilateral provisions that permit the employment of
force as a sanction in response to an international offense.
Of course, the very existence of international organizations
acts as a type of restraint on the use of aggressive force,
and states that have resorted to force in contravention of
UN or other obligations go to great lengths to justify
their aggression.

Walter Raeburn, in a reply to Hsu Mo, summed up the
practical situation succinctly when he observed:

Sanctions sound very well in theory, but they are
useless unless they are backed by the ultimate resort to physical force. Whàt is therefore essential is to be able to count on public support in
justification of the cause, and at the same time
on overwhelming physical force capable, if need
be, of carrying it into effect.[64]

Essentially, the comment is valid; but the failure to appreciate that, and the unwillingness to consider it in
practice, have been the source of the major problems bedeviling the practical employment of a wide range of sanctions.

A brief observation on the generalizations of the preceding pages suggests that the successful employment of
sanctions depends, to a large degree, upon unanimity or
minimal acquiescence of the members of the international organization or agency. Sanctions, of whatever type, must
be adapted to the political and economic exigencies at the
time of application. The system of international states
is much more resistant to change than is the theory of
that system and, thus, it is the theory rather than the actions of states that must be altered to accommodate more
realistic state perceptions and actions. At the very least,
theory must endeavor to accommodate reality and to avoid
too many prescriptions directed at state behavior.

NOTES

1. Yuan-li Wu, Economic Warfare (New York: Prentice-
Hall, 1952), p. 6.
2. Royal Institute of International Affairs (RIIA),
International Sanctions: A Report (London: Oxford University Press, 1938), p. 16. For a more restrictive definition of sanctions, see J. Kunz, "Sanctions in International
Law," AJIL 54 (1960): 324.
3. The UN Security Council Resolution on Rhodesia of
November 20, 1965, employed the expression "continuation
in time" as a basis for designating Rhodesia's unilateral
declaration of independence as a threat to peace (thus not
a domestic British issue). This was certainly a preemptive
action. S/Res. 217(1965).
4. OAU, Documents (Addis Ababa: OAU, 1965): II, 18-
19.
5. See Viscount Templewood, Nine Troubled Years (London: Collins, 1954), pp. 169-71.

6. A brief summary of these events may be found in G. W. Baer, The Coming of the Italian-Ethiopian War (Cambridge, Mass.: Harvard University Press, 1967), pp. 334, 351-58.

7. On the broad interpretation of the word "law," see G. L. Williams, "International Law and the Controversy Concerning the Word 'Law,'" BYIL 22 (1945): 146-53.

8. J. Stone, Legal Controls of International Conflict (London: Stevens & Sons, 1959), p. 176, n. 55.

9. Sir Henry Maine, Ancient Law (Everyman's ed.; London: J. M. Dent, 1960), p. 223.

10. Hsu Mo, "The Sanctions of International Law," Transactions: Grotius Society 35 (1949): 4. Also see L. Cavaré, "L'idée de sanctions en droit international public," RGDIP 3rd ser., 11 (1937): 385-445. The relationship between moral and political sanctions is best typified by the diplomatic protest. J. C. McKenna, Diplomatic Protest in Foreign Policy (Chicago: Loyola University Press, 1962), p. 21. McKenna describes the protest, in part, as an appeal "to reason and principle. . . . There is also an implicit appeal to the nation's will, based upon its sense of honour and its desire to be regarded as fair and just." Also see F. Pfluger, Die einseitigen Rechtsgeschäfte im Volkerrecht (Zurich: Schulthess, 1936), pp. 215-16, where it is argued that a participant in a protest is expected to investigate and to reply in good faith.

11. Admittedly, what is right or wrong at the foreign policy level is relative to each individual state participant. However, as Easton has observed, interaction between participants in any system, "to enforce compliance with their allocations," presupposes forms of coercion to enforce "the prevailing norms the bulk of the membership may consider . . . to be legitimate." D. Easton, A Framework for Political Analysis (Englewood Cliffs, N.J.: Prentice-Hall, 1965), p. 51. The distinction between right and wrong is thereby defined and constrained by requirements of individual state interaction, the nexus of international relations.

12. J. F. Dulles, "Should Economic Sanctions Be Applied in International Disputes?" Annals: American Academy 162 (1932): 103-07, at 106-07. He does, however, raise the important question of whether this moral basis of international relations would permit the wholesale starvation of a civilian population.

13. R. C. Hennessy, Public Opinion (Belmont, Calif.: Wadsworth, 1965), p. 351. An interesting discussion of the role of objectivity in public opinion formation at the international level may be found in G. G. Grisez, "Moral Objectivity and the Cold War," Ethics 70 (1960): 291-305.

14. There is a fascinating converse of this situation: when a population seeks to impress a view upon government, particularly as it relates to projected foreign policy. One fine example was the British "Peace Ballot," as documented in Dame A. Livingstone, The Peace Ballot: The Official History (London: Victor Gollancz, 1935). The American debate on Vietnam was a more recent example.

15. An interesting, and perhaps intentional, comment on the role of public opinion in international relations is made by H. L. Childs in his book Public Opinion (Toronto: Van Nostrand, 1965), where he includes a chapter titled "International Propaganda," pp. 322-47.

16. RIIA, op. cit., p. 22. Also C. P. Anderson, "The Power of Public Opinion for Peace," AJIL 16 (1922): 241-43.

17. In the Dominican case the political system was far too monolithic for one to speak realistically about opinion formation. However, in the Rhodesian situation the white community has tolerated extensive press controls (for example, over half the front page of the Rhodesia Herald of March 5, 1968, is blank, the result of the censor's pen). However, while the white minority may be split over support for the Smith government, there appears to be much greater unity of opinion in respect to the future of the country. Moreover, divisions will become less noticeable as Rhodesia adjusts to its status. Essentially, therefore, the white community is monolithic despite internecine differences. J. L. Talmon, The Origins of Totalitarian Democracy (New York: Praeger, 1960), is instructive on this point, pp. 1-13. Also see A. Inkeles, "The Totalitarian Mystique: Some Impressions of the Dynamics of Totalitarian Society," in C. J. Friedrich, ed., Totalitarianism: Proceedings of a Conference (Cambridge, Mass.: Harvard University Press, 1954), pp. 87-107.

18. Since 1966 Rhodesian Commentary, and more recently Rhodesian Viewpoint, have been organs of this campaign. Limited and much less widely known was an opposition publication, Zimbabwe News, the organ of the Zimbabwe African National Union, Lusaka, Zambia.

19. See, for example, Giornale italiana (Montreal), various issues during the autumn of 1935. Glossy photographs of alleged Ethiopian atrocities were widely circulated to Canadian newspapers.

20. F. B. Sloane, "Comparative International and Municipal Law Sanctions," Nebraska Law Review 27 (1947): 9-10.

21. A classic case of the vagueness of public opinion involves the attitude of American commentators toward India. In the 1950s Americans were able to tolerate, if not en-

courage, Indian neutrality. For example, see an address by
President Eisenhower before the American Society of Newspaper Editors, Washington, D.C., April 21, 1956, in U.S.
Department of State, Bulletin (April 30, 1956): 700; and a
speech by Adlai Stevenson in Chicago, September 15, 1953,
New York Times, September 16, 1953. However, when these
conciliatory attitudes are compared with statements about
"pro-communist Nehru's India" (Bob Siegrist, "MBS News,"
September 27, 1960) and similar comments made during the
same period, some idea of the extent of opinion shift may
be obtained. Transcripts of Siegrist's, and others',
broadcasts during the period September-October 1960 may be
found in U.S. Senate, Freedom of Communications: Final Report, IV (Washington: U.S. Government Printing Office,
1961).
     22. At the 1959 annual meeting of the American Society
of International Law, O. J. Lissitzyn briefly reviewed the
moral factor in international law from the Soviet and Western perspectives. "Communist ideology . . . leaves no room
for the sense of moral observance of international law."
O. J. Lissitzyn, "Western and Soviet Perspectives in International Law," Proceedings: ASIL 53 (1959): 21-30.
     23. RIIA, op. cit., p. 23.
     24. "An aide-mémoire is an informal summary or record
of a diplomatic interview or conversation, serving as its
name indicates, merely as an aid to memory." U.S. Department of State, Correspondence Handbook (Washington: U.S.
Government Printing Office, 1961), p. 1.
     25. RIIA, loc. cit.
     26. For example, the rapid Soviet invasion of Czecho-
slovakia in 1968 or the 1961 Indian invasion of Goa. The
Allied response to the Soviet invasion of Finland and the
German invasion of Poland in 1939 illustrate some of the
defects in joint protests, especially when time is a factor.
See McKenna, op. cit.
     27. Yehezkel Dror would describe some aspects of this
as "crazy state behaviour." Crazy States (Lexington, Mass.:
Lexington Books, 1971).
     28. RIIA, op. cit., p. 24. While the United States
officially severed diplomatic relations with the Dominican
Republic in August 1960, it did retain personnel in Ciudad
Trujillo in order to maintain both communication and influence. The Canadian government, a good two years in advance of its official recognition of the People's Republic
of China, did conduct a survey into Canadian property (diplomatic) holdings retained in Peking after 1949.

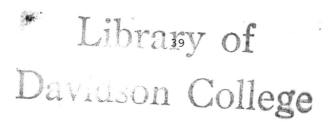

29. Ibid., p. 25. Britain, despite extreme provocations during the 1967 Chinese Cultural Revolution, seriously
considered breaking diplomatic relations. This did not
occur largely, it would appear, because of the arguments
advanced by Britain's beleaguered chargé d'affairs D. C.
Hopson, who, even while his embassy was burning, still retained immense calm.

30. For more on this see H. Lauterpacht, ed., Oppenheim's International Law: Peace, 1 (8th ed.; London: Long-
man's, 1955): § 75, pp. 148-51.

31. Clearly there could be a coincidence of ideological and legal reasons for nonrecognition--for example, the
United States and North Korea prior to, and after, the invasion of South Korea. But this discussion has been confined to the purely legal or formalistic aspects of nonrecognition as a sanction, preferably at the behest of an
international agency.

"Ces buts 'politiques', que l'on ne saurait distinguer
d'une manière satisfaisante d'avec les buts 'juridiques'
ne sont pas deféndus par le droit des gens et ne constituent
pas, par conséquent, un detournement des sanctions de leur
but legitime." L. Reitzer, La Réparation comme conséquence
de l'acte illicite en droit international (Liège: G.
Thone, 1938), pp. 74-75.

32. A. McNair, "The Stimson Doctrine of Non-recognition," BYIL 14 (1933): 65-74, at 74.

33. R. L. Buell, "Are Sanctions Necessary for International Organizations?" Annals: American Academy 162
(1932): 95.

34. M. S. McDougal and F. P. Feliciano, Law and Minimum World Order (New Haven, Conn.: Yale University Press,
1961), pp. 30, 31-32. Wu, op. cit., reviews in detail each
of these techniques and numerous others: blacklisting,
pp. 51 ff.; export licensing, pp. 60 ff.; export-import
price fixing, p. 67; preemptive buying, pp. 83 ff.; freezing of assets, pp. 92 ff.; substitutions, p. 175; and a
more recent form of sanction, foreign aid, pp. 185-243.
On this latter subject, see especially G. Liska, The New
Statecraft: Foreign Aid in American Foreign Policy (Chicago: University of Chicago Press, 1960), pp. 58-64; J. D.
Montgomery, The Politics of Foreign Aid (New York: Praeger,
1962); and C. J. Olmstead, "Foreign Aid as an Effective
Means of Persuasion," Proceedings: ASIL 58 (1964): 205-11,
at 207.

35. A review of some of the literature on economic
warfare precludes this type of parallel as a logical conclusion. However, the parallel appears to have been made

first by analogy and second on the basis of experience, especially in World War I. Medlicott's studies of the blockade during World War II did little to dampen interest. A short list of references is contained in the bibliography. Other notable works would include W. N. Medlicott, Economic Blockade, 2 vols. (London: His Majesty's Stationery Office, 1946-47); B. Emery, The Strategy of Raw Materials (New York: Macmillan, 1934); E. C. Eckel, Coal, Iron and War (New York: Henry Holt, 1930); G. O. Smith, The Strategy of Minerals (New York: Appleton & Co., 1919); F. M. Surface, The Grain Trade During the World War (New York: Macmillan, 1928); Sir A. Slater, Allied Shipping Control (New York: Oxford Press, 1921); and J. C. Lawrence, The World's Struggle with Rubber, 1905-1931 (New York: Harper & Bros., 1931).

36. On economic sanctions as a direct form of political pressure, see R. O. Freedman, Economic Warfare in the Communist Bloc (New York: Praeger Special Studies, 1970).

37. RIIA, op. cit., pp. 28-29.

38. Stone, op. cit., p. 291.

39. The "relic of the past" definition of embargoes (that embargoes are a form of reprisal) is the premise upon which McNair was able to construct a distinction between war as a reprisal and war as an aggression. A. D. McNair, "The Legal Meaning of War and the Relation of War to Reprisals," Transactions: Grotius Society 11 (1926): 29-51. Nicolos Politis, Greek Foreign Minister at the time of the Italo-Ethiopian war, dwelt upon the more common description in an article, "Les représailles entre États membres de la Société des Nations," RGDIP 31 (1924): 3-24.

40. Stone, loc. cit.

41. C. de Visscher, "L'interpretation du Pacte au lendemain du différend Italo-Grec," Revue de droit internationale 51 (1924): 328 ff. On the Corfu (Janina) incident, see James Barros, The Corfu Incident of 1923: Mussolini and the League of Nations (Princeton, N.J.: Princeton University Press, 1965); A. J. Toynbee, Survey of International Affairs, 1920-23 (London: RIIA, 1925), p. 349; League of Nations, Official Journal (1923), 1413; K. Strupp, "L'incident de Janina entre la Grèce et l'Italie," RGDIP 31 (1924): 255; and D. J. Hill, "The Janina Corfu Affair," AJIL 18 (1924): 98-104.

42. This is covered, in part, in the Portuguese-German arbitral decision (the Naulilaa Incident of 1928), in RIIA 2 (1928), 1011. The tribunal noted:

Reprisals are an act of self-help . . . of the injured state, in retaliation for an unredressed

act of the offending state contrary to international law. . . . They will be illegal unless a
previous act in violation of international law
has furnished the justification. They tend to
impose on the offending state reparation for the
offence or the return to legality and avoidance
of new offences. This definition does not require
that the reprisal be proportioned to the offence.
On this point authors, unanimous for some years,
are now divided in opinion. The majority consider
a certain proportion between offence and reprisal
a necessary condition of the legitimacy of the
latter.

This closely parallels de Vattel's observation in Les
droits des gens (1758) that a reprisal is the forcible taking by one nation of a thing belonging to another in response or satisfaction for an injury committed (bk. 2, ch.
18, sec. 342).

43. The possibility of extraterritorial application
of law was certainly explicit in UN Security Council Resolution S/232 (1966), of December 16, 1966. Paragraph
2(b)(d)(e) and (f) employs the wording "any activities by
their nationals" as distinct from activities within state
territory.

44. Wu, op. cit., p. 18, suggests that the fundamental
purpose of any embargo is to stop exports to the enemy, not
imports of the enemy's products. This is probably a more
accurate depiction of the Cold War context within which Wu
wrote (1952) than it would be for the regular processes of
international law enforcement that are set forth in this
discussion.

45. It is classed as a form of economic sanction rather
than as a moral sanction because, on balance, the reverse
situation must be considered--that is, why arms are exported. The reasons appear to be strictly pragmatic: export sale and support of friends and allies. Hence, for
pragmatic reasons, it is included in this section. On
arms embargoes in the classic sense, see RIIA, op. cit.,
p. 35; and H. Lauterpacht, "Boycotts in International Relations," BYIL 14 (1933): 124-40.

46. RIIA, loc. cit. As will be outlined later, Trujillo's European arms purchases were made at a considerable
expense to his government.

47. E. Clark, ed., Boycotts and Peace: A Report of
the Committee on Economic Sanctions (New York: Harper &
Bros., 1932), p. 174. On the same subject, see H. Feis,

Seen from E.A.: Three International Episodes (New York: Knopf, 1947; repr. Norton & Co., 1966).

48. On stockpiling in the United States, see G. H. Snyder, Stockpiling Strategic Materials: Politics and National Defense (San Francisco: Chandler, 1966).

49. These possibilities and others may be found in D. T. Jack, Studies in Economic Warfare (London: P. S. King & Son, 1940).

50. R. Segal, ed., Sanctions Against South Africa (Harmondsworth: Penguin Books, 1964), p. 270.

51. An address by H. L. T. Taswell, former South African Ambassador to the United States, warrants note. Speaking to the Executive Club of Chicago, March 4, 1966, he cited his country's ability to resist sanctions. Reprinted in Progress Through Separate Development (New York: South African Information Service, 1966), p. 105.

52. On this subject, see R. Pélloux, "Mésures d'embargo et neutralité," RGDIP, 3rd ser., 8 (1934): 58-75, is interesting. A good deal of material on neutrality may be found in studies by P. S. Wild and G. G. Wilson in International Law Situations and International Law Materials (United States Naval War College), for 1931, 1934, 1936, and 1969. Also see P. Q. Wright, ed., Neutrality and Collective Security (Chicago: University of Chicago Press, 1936).

53. The literature on blockades is immense, and a more comprehensive list is provided in the bibliography. In addition, since 1962 a modest list has appeared on the subject of "quarantines." Historically, one significant document is in the League of Nations Official Journal (1927), app. II; M. Giraud, "Memorandum on Pacific Blockade up to the Time of the Foundation of the League of Nations."

54. E. S. Colbert, Retaliation in International Law (New York: King's Crown Press, Columbia University, 1948), p. 62, n. 4, provides a list of blockades and acts of force short of war.

55. Stone, op. cit., pp. 292-93.

56. RIIA, op. cit., p. 33; and R. Pélloux, "L'embargo sur les exportations d'armes," RGDIP 3rd ser., 9 (1935): 146-55.

57. McDougal and Feliciano, op. cit., p. 31, offer other possibilities.

> Dumping large quantities of currency to compel the target-state to pay in gold; by psychological methods calculated to cast doubt on the target-state's ability or willingness to pay; and by simple counterfeiting of its currency. Other techniques in-

clude the creation of artificial scarcity and high
prices and the retarding of technological development through cartelization and control of patents.

Counterfeiting was a technique employed by the Italians
against Ethiopia when they acquired the plates for the Marie
Theresa thaler from the printer in Austria. The currency
was printed in Italy and distributed primarily within northern Ethiopia for payoffs and generally to undermine the
economy.

    58. In addition to the materials cited in note 4, the
following warrant mention: J. S. Berliner, Soviet Economic
Aid (New York: Praeger, 1958); W. G. Brown, "The Use of
Foreign Aid as an Instrument to Secure Compliance with International Obligations," Proceedings: ASIL 58 (1964):
210-17; and B. W. Jackson, "Foreign Aid: Strategy or Stopgap?" Foreign Affairs 41 (1962): 9, 100.
    59. The New York Times, May 13, 1964, records an in-
stance where France suspended aid to Tunisia following
Tunisian nationalization of French-owned agricultural lands.
The British did not follow this approach in 1967 after
Tanzania nationalized British-owned banks. However, Britain
did forbid Rhodesian trading on the London money markets
after November 11, 1965.
    60. League of Nations, Official Journal, special supp.
no. 146 (1936), pp. 48, 69-73, 73-75.
    61. RIIA, op. cit., pp. 43-45.
    62. Hsu Mo, "The Sanctions of International Law,"
Transactions: Grotius Society 36 (1950): 8.
    63. Ibid., p. 9.
    64. Walter Raeburn in response to Hsu Mo, in Mo, op.
cit., p. 18.

CHAPTER

2

INTERNATIONAL
ORGANIZATIONS
AND SANCTIONS

In situations where more than one state institutes sanctions, of whatever types, there is a multilateral imposition of enforcement measures. Such multilateral action may result from the coordinated decisions of a number of states--for example, the 1901 great-power blockade of Venezuela--or the action may be a consequence of a collective response to a decision by some formal or informal decision agency--for example, the UN Security Council resolutions on Rhodesia. This discussion is predominantly concerned with the latter processes. However, even here there are degrees of multilateral "authenticity" or legitimacy as perceived by the respective parties.

The primary consideration in terms of multilateral action is that which results from decisions made by openended international agencies--international agencies for which there is no significant restriction on membership (other than geography). In order for the definition to be broad enough, it is important to add that the international agency should be concerned fundamentally with matters pertaining to peace or matters that are functionally conducive to international peace. Finally, the international agencies should not exist exclusively for the particular interests of a restricted membership. Thus, the Arab League's boycott and blockade of Israel does not fall clearly into the definition of an international agency action in pursuit of peace.[1] Neither do the activities of the European Economic Community, which exists to serve the material ends of its European (and associated) members. Nor does the activity of NATO fit into the definitions of multilateral agency suggested above, because it exists for the primary purpose of defense and has a restricted membership and geographical area.

Essentially, then, what all this leads to is an uncomplicated statement that for purposes of this discussion, only a limited number of international organizations qualify as nonexclusive multilateral international law-enforcement agencies: the OAS, the OAU, the United Nations, and, historically, the League of Nations. A subgroup probably would include UN specialized and related agencies--ICAO, UNESCO, FAO, WHO, IBRO, IMF, ITU, ILO--providing they are functionally oriented toward international peace through regularized legal or constitutional processes that are universally acknowledged as authoritative.

Consequently, the parameters within which this review and evaluation of the use of multilateral sanctions occur are defined as follows. The decision-making body must be universally or regionally international. Its membership should normally encompass all states within the international or regional system, regardless of incidental criteria beyond a desire to belong. The organization must have a formally constituted body with inscribed powers to make mandatory decisions.* The organization must have a procedure for formally reaching a decision and for requiring that members subscribe to the decision in an obligatory manner. Finally, the organization must be regarded as definitive or authoritative in its sphere of international activity.

Establishment of organizational parameters leaves only the requirement that such organizations will utilize their decision procedures to impose the enforcement provisions of their constitutional documents against a state deemed to have violated premises of international law. There are three major historical instances where this has occurred. First, there was the League of Nations decision under Article 16 of the League Covenant to impose sanctions against Italy (October 3, 1935-July 15, 1936). Second, there was a decision by the OAS to impose military and limited economic sanctions against the Dominican Republic (August 21, 1960-January 4, 1962). Third, there is the decision by the United Nations to impose sanctions against Rhodesia (November 15, 1965 and continuing).** In this latter case manda-

---

*Subject, as always, to the inevitabilities of individual state sovereign prerogatives.

**Two other apparently obvious cases not considered here are the UN sanctions against the Republic of South Africa and the U.S. quarantine of Cuba. The former case is a consequence of General Assembly decisions; hence the sanctions

tory Chapter VII sanctions really were not imposed until
December 30, 1966, although the first Security Council Resolution was in November 1965.

Broadly speaking, the three decisions sought to achieve
similar ends, the decision processes were roughly equivalent,
and the available enforcement techniques were approximately
similar. The variations among these three cases stem from
differing expectations and divergent consequences. The expectations were most crucial. In two cases, states directly
aggrieved were most intent upon sanctions achieving desired
results: Venezuela and, more pointedly, Ethiopia had something to gain from a successful recourse to sanctions. In
the Rhodesia situation, expectations are not so directly
evident. Thus Britain, the specifically aggrieved party
(Rhodesia's offense is to have unilaterally declared independence), had less to gain from successfully implemented
sanctions than a host of states that find the absence of
majority rule a greater offense than the unilateral declaration of independence (UDI). This immense distinction became lost after the September 1966 Commonwealth Prime Minister's meeting and the early December 1966 H.M.S. Tiger
talk, for Britain's commitment to NIBMAR (No Independence
Before Majority Rule) tended to obscure the constitutional
issue.

Various other comparisons and/or parallels in these
three cases will be discussed later.

Quite obviously the utility of multilateral sanctions
will depend upon varying confluences of multitudes of pressures. Moreover, there appears to be a greater degree of
acceptability among states if the sanctions are authorized
by a multilateral agency.

> It is the essence of law that its sanctions are
> collective . . . that they are accepted by the
> community as a necessary element of law to ensure
> its enforcement and are applied with and by the
> general authority and not by the individual. It
> is these conditions that render possible the
> reign of law in the national sphere.[2]

---

are not mandatory. In the latter case the OAS involvement
was pro forma and after the fact; that is, after the essential actions had been taken and had succeeded on a unilateral basis.

If sanctions can be "legitimized" by an international agency, surely the next question is whether sanctions need to be imposed impartially. That is, is justice the necessary corollary of law application? M. A. Kaplan and N. de B. Katzenbach suggest that impartiality need not be a factor in the decisions of an individual foreign office.[3] Clearly, each state must consider its actions to be correct, regardless of the circumstances of a particular situation; hence its single viewpoint, although alleging impartiality, need not--and perhaps cannot--preclude partiality. Transposing the matter of impartiality to the context of the international organization, it would seem, at least superficially, that because the output of such an organization is a composite of many individual inputs and conflict resolutions, the very process of consensus construction would therefore assure impartiality as a general rule. But even that can be illusory. For example, in the past few years the United Nations has witnessed an outpouring of anticolonial sentiments and resolutions, a display that might lead to the supposition that impartiality has been sacrificed to the emotion of nationalism. This is possibly a premature assessment, because it may be that the governing premises of the United Nations are being updated, in which case this cannot be seriously construed as a parody of impartiality. On the point of impartiality, and for the purposes of this discussion, it is assumed that an international agency's decision to impose sanctions will tend to more closely approximate an objective consensus than would a similar unilateral decision and action. This observation is made with the full knowledge that in collective decision-making models (and despite Max Weber) "rational" decisions need not be "rational" and "objective" decisions thus probably need not imply "objectivity."

Two final points to be noted concern latent force and flexibility of employment. By the municipal law standard, force, as a type of sanction, is latent in every decision to enforce a law. It is the latent, or always prevalent, nature of force that makes its actual use relatively infrequent, despite an overall societal acceptance of the law as a legitimate expression of social norms. The municipal enforcement of law is thus facilitated by the public's awareness of the reality and omnipresence of coercion. The same feature cannot be observed so readily in respect to international law enforcement. Admittedly force, whether legitimized by the international organization or unilaterally undertaken, is a fact of international relations. It is not, however, a fact of the pursuit of international law by international agencies. Without latent multilateral force the psychological impact of sanctions is noticeably decreased, providing all other factors are held constant.

Finally, the employment of sanctions in international law lacks the flexibility generally inherent in municipal law, at least in the British common law jurisdictions. Municipal law, because it is a product of a relatively coherent political system, tends to retain flexibility in terms of law creation and application. What Sir Henry Maine referred to as "legal fictions" facilitate a society's ready acceptance of changes in law, provided the changes do not radically diverge from accepted historical, social, and ethical norms.

> If the decision-maker's operating assumptions are strongly out of line with the latent forces of history, decisions may be made but they will not produce the intended results.[4]

Unless it can be concluded that the concept of natural law fulfills the "legal fiction" role, it must be assumed that international law lacks such guiding principles. As a result, the very existence of an unstable international political system causes apprehension when proposals are advanced for changes in the delicate regime of law that functions between states.

For the proponent of the rule of law in international relations, it is essential to remember that not only should law be enforceable but, additionally, it should be sufficiently flexible as to be able to accommodate varying degrees of offense and response. This form of peaceful adaptation might be termed an "organic development" of law application. In the past, too much effort has been exerted in setting forth the standards and types of international enforcement without simultaneous attempts to corroborate international practice. A crucial defect of the enforcement provisions of both the League Covenant and the UN Charter were, and are, their prescriptive natures. While they proclaim that sanctions of all varieties should be applied and describe the types of sanctions available, in practice neither organization fully appreciated the difficulties inherent in practical application before the organizations were actually committed to implementation.

The RIIA said of sanctions that they

> operate in two ways; negatively, in that the
> knowledge of the will and power to apply them may

deter a would-be wrongdoer from transgressing the
law; positively, in that their application checks
a wrongdoer in the act of transgression or com-
pels him, after a transgression has been committed,
to submit to the law and deprives him of the fruit
of his transgression.[5]

In operation, international sanctions appear never to
have functioned fully negatively or positively. In the
first instance, they have never completely deterred states
from violating international law, although they may have
induced a degree of reticence. When necessary, states have
sought the interstices of the law and its sanctions, and
have justified their actions accordingly. Positively,
sanctions have failed to the extent that they seldom have
been effective against a state that viewed its actions as
being of vital national interest.[6]
Despite this rather gloomy conclusion, provisions to
employ sanctions in international law must continue to
exist. Additionally, efforts must be made to incorporate
enforcement provisions within the framework of international
organizations. Finally, attempts should continue to be
made to utilize the law enforcement and disciplinary provisions available in international law, if for no other reason than to prevent a withering of the entire concept.
Before turning to the three major cases under consideration
in this discussion, a brief review of some of the relevant
enforcement provisions of selected international agencies
will be set forth in order to emphasize that the need for
sanctions provisions is deemed to be continuing.

INTERNATIONAL CIVIL AVIATION
ORGANIZATION

The International Civil Aviation Organization (ICAO)
serves as both an arbitrator and a regulator of civil aviation disputes and problems. The ICAO Council has the capacity to resolve disputes either by advisory reports or by
binding decisions, providing the parties to a dispute agree
in advance on the Council's role. The ICAO Convention
relies, where individuals are involved, upon the domestic
law of member states. Thus, Article 12 obligates states
to prosecute persons violating regulations. Article 62 em-
powers the organization to suspend voting rights in the organization for failure to discharge financial obligations,
and at various times this power has been employed (for ex-

ample, in 1947 Bolivia, Nicaragua, Paraguay, and Poland were suspended from voting).

Under certain circumstances, most notably the arbitration procedures of Articles 85-87, the ICAO Council may decide to prohibit an airline from operating within other members' airspace. These provisions, however, require undertakings by members not to allow prohibited aircraft operational facilities. ICAO sanctioning provisions, as outlined here, rest upon the willingness of member states to employ their domestic resources and law to enforce Council decisions.

The only organizationally imposed sanction, and here the term is used in a sense not hitherto discussed, is expulsion from membership under Article 93 of the ICAO (Chicago) Convention.[7] ICAO began its relationship with the United Nations by barring Spain from membership in the organization. In 1947 the General Assembly required ICAO to amend its constitution to prohibit membership to any state barred from membership in the United Nations.[8] In 1965 an attempt was made by 31 African states to further amend Article 93 to exclude from ICAO membership any state that practiced apartheid. The proposal was successful at the Executive Committee stage but failed to obtain the necessary two-thirds vote of the membership at the plenary Assembly stage.[9]

In August 1973, the ICAO Assembly, in response to an Israeli diversion of a Lebanese civilian aircraft, condemned Israel and called upon it to desist from further acts of this nature. The resolution (approved 87-4-1) warned that the Assembly was prepared to "take further measures against Israel to protect international civil aviation."[10] It is not clear what other measures might be taken, unless Article 93 were to be amended to exclude Israel from membership. Clearly, however, a more practical sanction would be to prohibit Israeli aircraft from overflights and landing rights in member states, along the lines of Article 87.

INTERNATIONAL LABOR ORGANIZATION

The original International Labor Organization (ILO) Convention was part of the Treaty of Versailles (April 11, 1919). However, it is presently governed under an Instrument of Amendment of the Constitution of September 26, 1946.[11] The ILO Constitution contains a number of provisions that might be considered appropriate as sanctions; for example, Article 13(4) provides for the loss of voting

51

privileges if a member falls into arrears in its financial contributions.

Like other specialized agencies, the organization's ability to enforce its decisions is related to its specific area of competence, the ILO Convention. Articles 24-34 provide for a series of procedures that permit the ILO to review and inquire into complaints that a member "has failed to secure in any respect the effective observance within its jurisdiction of any Convention" (Art. 24). A commission of inquiry may be appointed, and members undertake (Art. 27) to place at the disposal of such a commission all information in their possession pertaining to the complaint. Such commissions of inquiry report, ultimately, to the Governing Body (Art. 29); and if satisfactory resolution of the problem is not achieved, it may be referred to the International Court of Justice (ICJ). The ICJ is empowered (Arts. 31 and 32) to render final decisions that may affirm, alter, or reverse the findings and/or recommendations of a commission of inquiry.

Thus far, of course, only the procedure has been set forth. Insofar as this discussion is concerned, the core issue is the ILO's capacity to enforce final decisions of the ICJ upon its members. Detailed sanctions are not specified, although Article 33 states that in the event a decision of the ICJ or a commission of inquiry is not fulfilled, the Governing Body may recommend to the International Labor Conference "such action as it may deem wise and expedient to secure compliance." The provisions under Article 33 have not been employed; and on occasions when recourse might have been remotely considered, the ILO has relied upon the moral sanction of public exposure and opinion.[12]

African states began their efforts to remove South Africa from membership in the ILO in 1961. By 1963 this pressure resulted in a declaration that the credentials of South African workers' representatives were invalid. Finally, in July 1964, two amendments were made to the ILO Constitution, one of which permitted the International Labor Conference to suspend or exclude from membership any state suspended or excluded from the United Nations. The second amendment permitted the General Conference to exclude any member that had been declared by the United Nations to be guilty of practicing apartheid (approved 253-24-35). In the meantime, however, South Africa voluntarily left the ILO and the provisions therefore have not been employed.[13]

UNESCO

The United Nations Educational, Scientific and Cultural Organization has a relationship with the United Nations that provides, like the Intergovernmental Maritime Consultative Organization (IMCO), for suspension or expulsion from membership if a state is suspended or expelled from the United Nations. Beyond this provision, the UNESCO Constitution (in force November 4, 1946) has nothing else that might be deemed a sanctioning capacity.

Portugal has been the object of attacks within UNESCO since 1965 (South Africa is not a member). In May 1965 the Executive Council decided that Portugal would not be invited to attend UNESCO meetings pending the outcome of a study into the educational situation in African territories under Portuguese administration.[14] Portugal demanded that this decision be submitted to the ICJ for an advisory opinion.[15] This proposal was rejected at the 14th session of the UNESCO General Conference in November 1966. The decision led one observer to remark, "The attitude of the UNESCO organs seems to imply a lack of assurance about the juridical basis of the decision taken in respect of Portugal."[16] Incidentally, the General Conference, by the same resolution, decided that it was competent to rule on its own constitutional act.[17]

In a letter dated June 18, 1971, Portugal informed the Director General of UNESCO that it would withdraw from the organization, and did so on December 31, 1972.[18]

WORLD HEALTH ORGANIZATION

The World Health Organization (WHO), like other international organizations, may refer disputes to the ICJ. Under provisions of Article 75 of the Constitution (July 22, 1966) the World Health Assembly shall make reference to the ICJ "unless the parties [to a dispute] agree on another mode of settlement." Once again, the primary issue has surrounded efforts by African states to expel South Africa. Beginning in 1963 and culminating in 1965 with a substantial resolution, the pressure was maintained.[19] However, as had happened before, South Africa withdrew from the organization (in March 1964) before it was formally expelled. (South Africa withdrew from the Food and Agricultural Organization in December 1963 and was expelled from the International Telecommunications Union in 1965.)[20]

53

UNIVERSAL POSTAL UNION

Perhaps the most successful international organization is the Universal Postal Union (UPU). Essentially, it is a highly independent and functional agency with the capacity to control the activities of its members because it provides a service. Article 30 of the 1874 Bern Convention governs disputes. The procedures for resolving disputes between members or groups is fairly straightforward, involving informal inquiries from the International Bureau, followed by arbitration and final adjudication. M. A. K. Kenon noted:

> To the credit of the UPU during its first seventy-five years, there was never a refusal to accept a verdict despite the fact that no means to enforce adjudication are on the statutes.[21]

And J. J. LeMouël, long associated with UPU, stated:

> It is hard to imagine any sanction or repressive action in the UPU, since any country attempting to rebel against the common rule would thereby exclude itself from the Postal Union and preclude any possibility of communication with the rest of the members of the Union, which is quite inconceivable.[22]

WORLD BANK AND INTERNATIONAL
MONETARY FUND

The International Bank for Reconstruction and Development (IBRD), or World Bank, and the International Monetary Fund (IMF) are interlocking agencies possessing three basic forms of sanction. Article VI(2)(3) of the Bretton Woods Agreement provides for suspension of membership in the bank and in the IMF. Article V(5) of the IMF agreement permits the IMF to restrict a member's access to the fund's resources and, in fact, to deny access should this prove necessary. Article XV(2)(a-c) covers these points procedurally under the title "compulsory withdrawal." Finally, IMF has the capacity to reprimand members, as, for example, in 1945, when France, in contravention of Article IV(6), altered par value of its currency on January 26. IMF refused to assign France an official par value, thereby denying France access to the fund's resources.

54

It is interesting, of course, that IMF does become directly involved in domestic matters—for example, the December 1947 review of Australian and Canadian subsidies to gold producers. However, the bank and the fund do serve very specific needs and for that reason their role, like that of the UPU, is essentially perceived to be functional.

There are a number of other international (UN-related) agencies—the Intergovernmental Maritime Consultative Organization, the World Meteorological Organization, International Finance Corporation, International Development Association—that appear to follow a general pattern. First, where they appear to provide a specific service or fulfill a need to all members in their mutual relations, such sanctions as exist appear effective (this may simply reflect perceived need). Second, where the functional ability of the organization is not apparent to all members, disciplinary sanctions have frequently involved expulsion (or withdrawal) of the offending state. Such expulsions do not appear to have served any significant purpose, for the expelled states had little to gain from membership and presumably the expulsion was not considered a serious blow. Expulsion from membership is not a terribly effective sanction in international law and should be resorted to with exceptional caution. For the organizations noted in the preceding paragraphs, expulsion has usually been blunted by resignation; thus the impact is so insignificant as to be of questionable worth.

It will become apparent in the next three chapters that when the organization's functional utility is perceived to be low, from the individual state's viewpoint, its ability to require and/or enforce behavior is seriously limited. Thus, the specific services of the United Nations are not so readily apparent as are those, for example, of the UPU or IMF. Hence, to paraphrase Herbert Simon, unless directly affected, states tend to seek "satisficing" rather than "maximizing" decisions and obligations relative to the international agency.[23] In the following three cases it will be demonstrated that the degree of perceived interest was a primary determinant of state behavior in all instances.[24]

NOTES

1. The Arab League's boycotts and blockades were not broadened into an international agency action either by the activities of sympathetic states—for example, the Soviet Union—or by the USSR's 1953 embargo on oil shipments

to Israel. See M. Domke, "The Israeli-Soviet Oil Arbitration," AJIL 53 (1959): 787-806.

2. Royal Institute of International Affairs, Sanctions: The Character of International Sanctions and Their Application (London: Chatham House, 1938), p. 6. Also see A. E. Hindmarsh, "Self-help in Time of Peace," AJIL 26 (1932): 315-26, at 324; and A. Berenstein, "Le Mécanisme des sanctions dans l'Organisation international du travail," RGDIP 3rd ser., 11 (1937): 446-64. The concept of "reign of law" closely parallels A. V. Dicey's view of "rule of law" within common law jurisdictions. Law of the Constitution (10th ed.; Toronto: Macmillan, 1964), pp. 183-205.

3. M. A. Kaplan and N. de B. Katzenbach, The Political Foundations of International Law (New York: Wiley, 1961), pp. 231-64.

4. K. Boulding, "Toward a Theory of Peace," in R. Fisher, ed., International Conflict and the Behavioral Sciences (New York: Basic Books, 1964), p. 71.

5. RIIA, op. cit., p. 5.

6. "Law serves as a focal point, as the tool for 'internationalizing' a national interest." Stanley Hoffman, "Introduction," in L. Scheinman and D. Wilkinson, International Law and Political Crisis (Boston: Little Brown, 1968), p. xiv.

7. Expulsion from membership, of course, is a form of sanction. One author, in fact, has referred to the suspension of the rights of membership as a "disciplinary sanction." D. Ruzie, Organisations internationales et sanctions internationales (Paris: Armand Colin, 1971), p. 27. While more will be said on the matter of suspension later, it will be noted here that suspension from membership places the target state outside the bonds of any organizational control. Thus the target state acquires the status of outlaw (in a figurative sense), thereby undermining the overall capacity of the organization to function. Incidentally, Ruzié classes suspension from membership and most of the other sanctions available to UN agencies as "internal discipline," as opposed to the types of sanctions considered in Chapter 1, which he would refer to as "exterior constraints."

8. Ibid., p. 46; and L. H. Phillips, "Constitutional Revision in the Specialized Agencies," AJIL 62 (1968): 654-78, at 660.

9. ICAO, Doc. 8522, A.15-Ex/43; and Doc. 8516, A.15-P/5.

10. ICAO, resolution of August 30, 1973, 20th extraordinary session of the Assembly (Rome).

11. Another document, the "Philadelphia Declaration" of 1944, in addition to the Preamble to the Constitution, set forth the basic ILO objections.

12. J. M. Dehousse, Les organisations internationales, essai de théorie générale (Liège: Gothier, 1968), p. 362.

13. United Nations, Yearbook (1964) (New York: United Nations, 1964), p. 493.

14. United Nations, Yearbook (1965), p. 775.

15. International Legal Materials 6 (1967): 190.

16. Ruzié, op. cit., p. 48.

17. International Legal Materials 6 (1967): 188.

18. In accordance with UN Resolutions G. A./2758 (XXVI) of October 25, 1971, and 396 (V) of December 4, 1950, a number of UN specialized agencies decided to recognize the government of the People's Republic of China as the only legitimate representatives of China in the organizations. This action perhaps constituted as much a matter of credentials recognition as expulsion of Taiwan. Some of the effective dates were International Labor Organization (ILO), November 16, 1971; Food and Agriculture Organization (FAO), November 25, 1971; United Nations Educational Scientific, and Cultural Organization (UNESCO), October 29, 1971; World Health Organization (WHO), May 10, 1972; International Civil Aviation Organization (ICAO), November 19, 1971; Universal Postal Union (UPU), February 28, 1972; International Telecommunication Union (ITU), session 27, 1972; World Meteorological Organization (WMO), February 25, 1972; Intergovernmental Maritime Consultative Organization (IMCO), May 23, 1972; International Atomic Energy Agency (IAEA), December 9, 1971; International Finance Corporation (IFC), International Bank for Reconstruction and Development (IBRD), International Development Association (IDA), and International Monetary Fund (IMF), no action.

19. United Nations, Yearbook (1965), p. 725.

20. Ibid., p. 775.

21. M. A. K. Menon, "Universal Postal Union," International Conciliation 552 (March 1965): 47.

22. J. J. Le Mouël, "The Universal Postal Union," Union postale 75 (1950): 117, as quoted in Menon, ibid. Also see L. Chaubert, L'Union postale universelle (Bern: Ed. H. Lang, 1970).

23. Simon, of course, is discussing humans within the control of organizational behavior. H. Simon, Administrative Behavior (2nd ed.; New York: The Free Press, 1965).

24. In some other types of organizations--for example, the European Economic Community--rather more complex and elaborate forms of enforcement sanctions exist. It has

not been discussed here partly because of its limited utility in terms of types of broadly based international organizations, and partly because the law is fairly well established and the sanction is clearly the loss (among other things) of special economic (and presumably advantageous) considerations. On the law of the EEC perhaps the best volume is Xavier de Roux and Dominique Voillemot, <u>Le droit de la concurrence des communautés européennes</u> (Paris: Dictionnaires André Joly, 1972).

3

In the last few years, perhaps in consequence of the availability of diplomatic papers, a wealth of material has been produced on the Italian-Ethiopian affair of 1935-36.[1] Hence there is no attempt to reproduce this material. The main discussion, therefore, is prefaced by a brief historical account of events leading to the imposition of sanctions under Article 16 of the League of Nations Covenant, followed by a discussion of Article 16. The chapter concludes with a more detailed discussion of the work of the League's Coordination Committee and a review of the Italian economy during the period in question.

BACKGROUND

Italy was late to acquire colonies; and by the time it entered Africa, virtually every scrap of territory was taken. Perhaps because of this Italy, rather than the colonial powers of Britain and France, was less suspect in Ethiopian eyes. Thus, when the Ethiopian King Menelik of Shoa wrote to Italian King Victor Emmanuel II in 1872, his intent seems to have been both to seek outside support for his efforts to unify Ethiopia and to create an offsetting influence to the French and British threats on his borders. Between 1878, the year of the first Italian trade expedition to Menelik's Kingdom of Shoa, and 1889, when, through Italian involvement, Menelik became uncontested Emperor of Ethiopia, relations progressed. However, by 1891 Menelik had wearied of Italians' absorbing segments of Ethiopian territory. An attempt to resist Italian encroachments in Tigré province resulted in Italian occupation of Ethiopian

villages. After a series of diplomatic blunders, and in
the face of growing Italian antagonism along the Eritrean
border region, an Ethiopian revolt broke out in Eritrea in
December 1894. By March 1895 the Italians replied by in-
vading Ethiopia; and in a classic battle at Aduwa on March
1, 1896, the Italians were crushed. It was not until October 6, 1935, that the Italians were able to avenge the dead
of Aduwa.[2]

Revenge of Aduwa became a consuming ambition for Italian militarists, and consequently Italian attention tended
to focus directly upon matters relating to Ethiopia. The
growing influence of Germany in the country had led to a
secret European tripartite treaty in 1906.* Italy's territorial ambitions, while conceded in the 1906 treaty, were
a problem in terms of implementation; Italy was forced to
wait nine years before another opportunity arose.

In "an excessively badly drafted document"[3] known as
the Treaty of London of April 26, 1915, Italy was given
concessions for entering the war against Germany. Fortunately for Ethiopia, the European states were occupied with
their war; and by the time Italy sought to obtain some results from the 1915 treaty, neither Britain nor France was
prepared to lend support. Furthermore, when the colonial
loot was divided up after the war, Italy received nothing.
The combination of desire for revenge and pique at having
been cheated tended to focus Italian attention on the one
area in Africa where it still retained some influence,
Ethiopia.

In 1923 Ethiopia applied for, and obtained, membership
in the League of Nations; Italy took the initiative in lobbying for Ethiopian membership in the face of British opposition.[4] Unfortunately for the Italians, Ras Tafari, as
heir to Menelik, undertook a European tour in 1924 that
included Italy. His trip apparently was not exceptionally
successful, and he returned to Ethiopia rather disillusioned.
To counter this setback and yet to maintain pressure, Mussolini initiated what ultimately became the Italian-British
agreement of 1925, whereby Britain acknowledged exclusive

---

*Under provisions of this treaty, Ethiopia was arbi-
trarily divided into three spheres of influence: Britain
received the Nile basin; France, the railway from Djibouti
to Diredawa (and eventually Addis Ababa); and Italy was
promised a "territorial connexion between Eritrea and Italian Somaliland." It was this "connexion" that later led to
Italy's claim to a lion's share of Ethiopia.

Italian economic influence in western Ethiopia while the
Italians reciprocated by agreeing to support the British
efforts to obtain a concession for dam construction at the
outlet of Lake Tana, the source of the Blue Nile.[5]
    Ethiopian resistance to this absorptive pressure appar-
ently paid off in 1928, with the conclusion of an Italian-
Ethiopian 20-year treaty of friendship.[6] From 1928 until
the failure of the European Disarmament Conference in 1934,
official Italian interest in Ethiopia cooled.[7] It was not
until March 18, 1934, that Mussolini announced that Italy
was prepared "to introduce Africa more fully into the cir-
cle of the civilized world."[8] By December 20, 1934, Mussolini had "personally compiled the Directions and Plan of
Action for the solution of the Italo-Abyssinian question."[9]
    There are probably various reasons why Mussolini chose
1934. Referring to "the basic sterility of Fascism" in
the face of the world economic crisis of the 1930s, George
Baer commented:

> Without a broad and viable program for the peace-
> ful development of Italy, Mussolini came to lean
> more and more on the pursuit of militant nation-
> alism to give the appearance of direction and
> energy to his regime. The Ethiopian adventure was
> almost certainly contrived, at least in part, as
> an alternative to social reform.[10]

Further, Baer noted:

> The demands of an Ethiopian campaign would absorb
> the idle energies of the population. Prepara-
> tions for war would revive the economy, increase
> profits, provide employment, and raise wages.
> Army service would drain off more of the unem-
> ployed. . . . Victorious battles overseas, par-
> ticularly the avenging of Aduwa, would renew the
> glory of the Duce and enable his regime to share
> in the mythic grandeur of imperial Rome.[11]

In summary, an Ethiopian campaign capped with success
suited every aspect of Mussolini's needs. And, as became
apparent only in later years, this was traditional imperialism in the twilight of the age of imperialism. Nevertheless, Italy needed a provocation.[12] The Ethiopians, meanwhile, had begun to become nervous; and on September 29,
1934, at their insistence, a joint Italian-Ethiopian communiqué was issued affirming mutual friendly relations in
accordance with the 1928 treaty.[13]

The necessary "provocation" came on December 5, 1934, at an obscure waterhole roughly 50 miles inside Ethiopia on the poorly demarcated Ethiopia-Somaliland boundary. Walwal consisted of 359 wells located in the semiarid portion of Harar province known as the Ogaden plateau. The area had been annexed to Ethiopia in 1895, and the boundary between Italian Somaliland and Ethiopia was vaguely mapped in 1897. After a disastrous expedition into the region (from which only 7 of 7,000 Ethiopians returned), the Ethiopians did little more than collect taxes (when possible) from nomadic tribesmen every five years.

Between 1926 and 1930 Italians moved into and effectively occupied the Walwal oasis and an attempt by Haile Selassie to regain control of the location was withdrawn in 1931. Sporadic Ethiopian efforts followed in 1932 and 1933, until finally in 1934 Selassie commissioned both diplomatic and military moves that were designed, apparently, to reassert Ethiopian claims over the lost territory. Italy's sought-for provocation was emerging rapidly.[14] Italy had struck an uncompromising stance vis-à-vis Ethiopia throughout the summer of 1934, and this became even more adamant after Walwal.

The actual incident was essentially nothing more than a violent culmination of a 10-day standoff between Italians at Walwal and Ethiopians seeking to recover the lost oasis. On December 5, 1935, fighting broke out; and when it was over the next morning, 107 Ethiopians and 30 Italians were dead. Thereafter Ethiopia proposed the application of Article 5 of the 1928 treaty, the provisions of which bound both parties to conciliation and arbitration without resort to armed force.

A refusal by the Italian government to submit the dispute to arbitration led the Ethiopian government to bring the problem before the League of Nations under Article XI(a).[15] Mussolini responded to the Ethiopian initiative in two ways. Between December 20 and 30, 1934, he proposed a secret "Directive and Plan of Action for the Resolution of the Italian-Abyssinian Question."[16] This directive essentially laid the groundwork for Italian action in the ensuing year, including the invasion of Ethiopia with at least 100,000 metropolitan soldiers. Second, the Italians responded to the Ethiopian request before the League by indicating a desire to apply Article 5 of the 1928 treaty. This second response, however, came only after immense pressure was placed upon the Italians by the British, in the interest of their mutual desire to avoid an open discussion before the League Council. Thus, after numerous demands for compensation, Italy agreed to arbitrate on January 19, 1935, and Ethiopia agreed.[17] From then on, events moved with astonishing singularity of direction and rapidity.

Italy's approach was to stall for time while preparations for the Ethiopian war continued unabated. The approach, perhaps in retrospect, was evidenced by both delays in Italian responses to Ethiopian communications and the nature of the responses.[18] Ethiopian patience finally expired on March 16 and 17, 1935, when the government formally requested consideration of the dispute by the League Council. In a letter to Joseph Avenol, the League's Secretary-General,[19] the Ethiopians sought League consideration under Article 15 of the Covenant.

> The Ethiopian Government hereby calls attention
> to the imminent danger of a rupture; for nothing
> is more to be apprehended than that some local
> incident may serve as a pretext for military ac-
> tion. The independence of Ethiopia . . . is in
> peril.[20]

The Italians were obviously caught off guard with this request, because their stalling tactics had culminated in an agreement fixing a neutral zone on March 13. Hence, in a series of letters the Italians reiterated their intent to negotiate, as "ordinary diplomatic methods cannot be said to be exhausted."[21] Of course the troop movements were defended as defensive while diplomatic quibbling continued over the meaning of Article 5 of the 1928 Treaty.

Eventually Italy did agree to direct negotiations with Ethiopia.[22] But when activity proved slow in emerging, Haile Selassie appealed to the League with a request that Article 15 of the Covenant be implemented if Italy failed to agree to the essential points in the arbitration.[23] The Arbitration Commission (consisting of two Italians, a Frenchman, and an American) was formally appointed after much negotiation on May 25, and it was agreed that it would report on August 25. By July 25 the Commission had not agreed on a fifth member, and on July 31, 1935, the League Council met to review the issue.[24]

Meanwhile, Britain and France effectively conspired with Italy to circumvent the League. Thus, on July 31, 1935, a plan was submitted to the Italians by the French whereby Italy would agree to the appointment of a fifth member (Nicoli Politis, Greece) for the Arbitration Commission, in return for which there would be tripartite talks (without Ethiopia) designed to placate Italian demands.

The Italians realized that if tripartite negotiations so early sought by the British, could be
held outside the League's jurisdiction, not only
would this be a slap in the face for the League
and a diplomatic disaster of the first magnitude
for Ethiopia--both contrived and delivered by
Britain and France, no less--but it would afford
Italy a new mechanism for delay by forestalling
League action at this time. No one would want to
endanger the private negotiations of the leading
powers of Europe by threatening Italy with League
sanctions if it appeared that a settlement was in
the offing.[25]

For all intents and purposes Ethiopia had been aban-
doned; and while the charade of negotiations would continue
for the next two months Italy would press, Ethiopia would
falter, and the world would wait. Furthermore, it would
become increasingly obvious that the League and Article 16
would be challenged. "The word Sanctions was on no one's
lips; but it was in everyone's mind."[26] The Arbitration
Commission finally reported on September 3, 1935, that it
was "of opinion that in respect of these minor incidents
no international responsibility need be involved."[27] Pitman Potter (one of Ethiopia's arbitrators), in a rather
optimistic vein, observed that the report of the Commission
was "an illuminating clinical study in the organization
and practice of arbitration and an integral item in the
first effective League action to halt an aggressor."[28] The
League Council met on September 4 and was immediately faced
with an aggressive Italy indicating that Walwal was no
longer of significance. Instead, the Italian delegate,
Baron Aloisi, stated:

Italy can no longer adopt a passive and forgiving
attitude towards an uncivilized State incapable
of controlling itself or its own people. . . .
The Ethiopian Government does nothing to fit itself for membership of the community of civilized
nations.
    Italy's dignity as a civilized nation would
be deeply wounded were she to continue a discussion in the League on a footing of equality with
Ethiopia.[29]

And while the Ethiopian representative, Gaston Jèze, could
correctly argue that Walwal was now res judicate, and there-

64

fore there no longer existed a reason for the continuation of Italian military preparations,[30] his reasoning fell upon ossified and intimidated minds. In addition, the Italians came well prepared with an extensive memorandum that set forth every possible real and imagined grievance and example of uncivilized state behavior.

> Every delegation, including that of Italy, knew very well that, even if all that was said in the Memorandum were true, it could not justify the assertion that Italy could now make war on Ethiopia without violating the Covenant.[31]

The Italians' refusal to negotiate with an allegedly uncivilized state led to their walkout from the League Council on September 5. This dramatic, but erroneous, tactic opened the way for the Council to appoint a committee of five to review the situation.[32] The committee, under the chairmanship of Salvador de Madariaga (Spain), reported on September 24, outlining several reforms that would raise Ethiopia to the level of its obligations under the Covenant.[33]

The Italian response to the committee's report concluded that the situation could not be settled by the Covenant "because the Covenant does not contemplate the case of countries which, though unworthy and incapable of participation in the League of Nations, continue to claim the right and to demand the observance of the obligations that such participation involves."[34] On September 25 the Ethiopian Emperor notified the League that his troops had withdrawn 30 kilometers from the frontier in order to avoid incidents that might serve as a pretext for the Italian invasion. The League Council met the next day under Article 15, which, in review, appeared to have exhausted this recourse. Article 15 set the stage for further League action should the dispute in question not be resolved by conciliation, arbitration, and the issuance of reports. Consequently, when the Council met on September 26 there was not much left for it to do and it therefore formed itself into a committee of 13 (excluding Italy) to draft a final statement of facts and recommendations to the League Assembly. F. P. Walters commented regarding the Council:

> It now had no alternative but to declare that its work of conciliation had failed and its work of judgement must begin. This, as all knew, was the first constitutional step towards the application of sanctions . . . if Ethiopia accepted the Coun-

cil's judgement and Italy then attacked her, the
violation of the Covenant would be self-evident
and the application of sanctions would be the
plain duty of every Member.[35]

Haile Selassie ordered general Ethiopian mobilization
on September 28, 1935. In a telegram to the League Council
on October 3, the Italians informed the Council that in
view of the Ethiopian mobilization and the strategic 30-
kilometer withdrawal, Italy was obliged to take defensive
measures. Then, in the light of an Ethiopian appeal under
Article 16, the Council appointed another committee, which
found Italy guilty of resort to war in contravention of its
obligations under the Covenant.[36]

Initially League reaction to the Italian aggression
was swift and direct, and will be discussed in greater detail below. The concept of collective security retained
some credence until the secret Hoare-Laval plan was divulged
in December.[37] Haile Selassie fled his country on May 2,
1936, and appeared before the League Assembly on June 30.
By May 9, 1936, Ethiopia was declared part of the Italian
empire, and on July 15 League sanctions were removed. In
the face of concerted aggression both the League and Ethiopia were doomed to failure. In the remaining sections of
this chapter, Article 16 of the League Covenant is discussed, followed by a review of its only application, on
the occasion of the Italian-Ethiopian war. The chapter
concludes with an assessment of the impact of the sanctions
on Italy.

ARTICLE 16, LEAGUE OF
NATIONS COVENANT

The enforcement provision of the League of Nations
Covenant was Article 16, supplemented by a 1921 League Assembly resolution. Article 16 was a restricted statement
of fact, for resort to war in violation of Covenant obligations was essential to the operation of the League's response procedures. Threats to peace were only vaguely ac-
commodated in Article 15. There are some parallels between
the UN Charter and the League Covenant, but all tend to
highlight the restrictive nature of the latter.[38]

A careful scrutiny of the League Covenant in general,
and Article 16 in particular, reveals one essential fact.
Nowhere in the document is there an irrevocable obligation
on members to act deferentially toward League Council or

Assembly decisions.[39] The textual provisions were statements of general principles established for the guidance of
members, apparently on the assumption that principles could
be effective by being considered morally binding. To a
limited extent there was merit in this approach, for in the
early stages of the League's development, when states did
violate the Covenant, justification was sought within the
framework of that document.

In a functional sense the defects of Article 16 permitted individual state determination that a resort to war
had occurred in disregard of League covenants. Thus, if a
state determined that a condition of war did not exist, it
was not pledged to adopt and apply the sanctions set forth
in Article 16. Conversely, if a determination were made
that a state of war existed, a state was pledged to commence
a response. Therefore, the pledge to adopt enforcement
procedures within the League Covenant depended upon each
state's satisfactorily concluding that the Covenant provisions had been violated. States were expected to undertake
reasonable measures according to a reasonable interpretation of the relevant Covenant provisions. The only apparent beneficial consequence resulting from a practical interpretation of Article 16 was that it obviated the necessity
of unanimity among members.

> The legal interpretation of Article XVI was . . .
> that no authority could decide whether or not a
> State had resorted to war in violation of the
> Covenant except each individual Member State it-
> self. . . . It avoided the difficulty . . . of
> seeking to obtain a binding decision of the As-
> sembly or even of the Council including the de-
> faulting Member, in accordance with the unanimity
> rule.[40]

This was the context, then, within which League enforcement
procedures were to function.

The inherent weakness of the League procedure was obvious: would members necessarily be unanimous (assuming
unanimity was absolutely essential) in their decision as to
what constituted "a resort" to war? If honorable decisions
could have been assured, in preference to politically value-
laden responses, the answer would probably have been "yes."
A refusal to honor the Covenant pledge and obligations, or
a decision on any other basis, would, and in fact did, neu-
tralize the system. The unanimity rule, an essential basis
for the successful application of Article 16, did not, how-

ever, ruin the system, although it did provide a convenient
escape from moral commitments.

> The League Council's position in relation to peace
> enforcement was, therefore, converted, from a posi-
> tion of loose, anarchic co-operation, undermined
> by the unanimity rule, into a machine of interna-
> tional co-ordination which, up to a certain point
> at any rate, was a streamlined and effective in-
> strument.[41]

The "certain point" to which J. Stone refers above was essentially a low and illusory one. Article 16 represented
an anomaly in world order. In one respect it was general
enough to permit functioning of the "streamlined" League,
while in another respect the same generality led to its
impotence.

The defects of Article 16 and the enforcement system
it sought to create were numerous--for example, it sketched
the general methods but not the details. It was not designed to prevent war in its nascent stages but to prohibit
the successful achievement of the goals of war once it had
been undertaken. In this sense Article 16 did not permit
preemptive actions, although in conjunction with other provisions for the settlement of disputes (Articles 10, 11,
and 15), it might have been possible to interpret Article
16 as a logical progression along the lines of the spectrum
concept outlined in Chapter 1.

Specifically, Article 16 lacked that degree of precision common to constitutional documents, and, unfortunately,
the appropriate court lacked sufficient judicial capacity
to interpret. This led F. Bradley to state:

> Certain lacunae in the original wording of Art.
> XVI may be briefly noted. What is the relation
> between the various paragraphs of the article so
> far as action by organs of the League as well as
> the individual States is concerned? How is the
> 'mutual support' stipulated in paragraph 3 to be
> provided and of what is it to consist? What is
> the nature of the 'intercourse' and of the 'trade
> and financial relations' envisaged in paragraph
> 1? To what extent and in what manner is co-or-
> dination of the action of individual States Mem-
> bers of the League to be achieved? How 'immediate'
> must the action by the individual Members be?[42]

For example, "immediacy of action" presented insoluable problems for interpreters of the League Covenant. Did "immediately" mean "immediately in response to a warlike outbreak," or did it mean "immediately upon each state's satisfying itself that an outbreak had occurred"? One attempt was made by the 1920 Blockade Committee in its 1921 resolution, when it concluded that "immediate" meant when the Council agreed on a date at which unanimous action might be secured. In practice, as simple a point as this was never solved and "immediate" stretched from 1921 to 1939.

There were other more substantial problems involved with the application of Article 16; and while the Coordination Committee and the Committee of 18 made valiant efforts in the autumn of 1935, failure ensued. In summary, some of the unresolved questions included:

What is left of the neutrality of League Members in case of application of economic and particularly military sanctions? What is the relation of Members and non-Members of the League during the application of sanctions? Could, for instance, a blockade, pacific or otherwise, be applied to the vessels or property of non-Member states? While the geographical situation of the Suez in relation to the scene of the [Italo-Ethiopian] aggression made its closing a matter of discussion, what is the effect of other treaty obligations between Members and non-Members of the League upon the obligation of the former in the application of the Covenant?[43]

Finally, the economic sanction provisions of Article 16 encountered a problem that in many respects is an obstacle to systematic attempts to impose sanctions: self-interest. A state that offends international law and sensibilities does not, for various reasons, offend all states equally. Implicit, therefore, in the practical imposition of sanctions is the self-interest of the participating states. A single state, directly offended, will readily consider self-interest to be harsh punishment of the transgressor. But attempts to expand that indignation to include the world community is a formidable task.

What is thus true of the considerations leading one country to employ economic measures against another apparently applied equally, as a practical

matter, to a country which is a member of the
League when called as such to apply economic sanctions against an aggressor state. Strong considerations of self-interest would seem to be necessary before wholehearted action under Article XVI
would be undertaken.[44]

Thus, self-interest becomes a particular consideration not
apt to be arrogated for another state's unilateral satisfaction.

The League Covenant, and specifically Article 16, had
three loopholes in the enforcement procedure. These gaps
represented "outs" whereby states could circumvent the
prohibition on war while retaining the aura of legality.
First, if neither disputant complied with a unanimous Council or Assembly report, the Covenant was silent about League
recourse. Second, as they deemed appropriate, all members
were free to act against the party (or parties) that failed
to accept the unanimous report. Third, when the Council or
Assembly failed to reach a unanimous report, members were
permitted "to take such action as they shall consider necessary for the maintenance of right and justice" (Art. 15[7]).

The very cacaphony of names of the thirty-four
working committees, which practice brought to fill
the silences of the Covenant indicate the wide ramifications of the task of applying economic sanctions.[45]

Article 16 represented good intentions but lacked the pressure toward unity that was axiomatic to results; it was
non efficit affectus nisi sequatur effectus.

An attempt was made in 1920 to remedy the defects of
Article 16 through an International Blockade Committee,
which was to strive to coordinate action that might be contemplated under Article 16. The committee drafted four
sets of questions:

(1) Under what conditions should sanctions be ap-
    plied?;
(2) Whose duty is it to decide that the necessity
    for sanctions has arisen?;
(3) At what moment and by whom should these mea-
    sures be applied?; and,
(4) How should they be applied?[46]

To these questions the Blockade Committee responded:

70

(1) The economic sanctions in the first instance
should be applied not as a measure of war but
as a form of peaceful pressure.

(2) While each Member, as a sovereign State, must
decide for itself whether a resort to war in
breach of the Covenant has in fact taken place,
there are obvious difficulties involved in
isolated or individual action. Centralisa-
tion is necessary. The Council is the obvious centralising authority. All branches of
the Covenant should be referred to the Council as a matter of urgency, and the Council
should draw up a common plan of action.

(3) The Council should fix a date at which measures should be taken, and these measures
should be measures of increasing stringency
[an obvious attempt to mitigate the earlier-
mentioned problem of the word "immediate"].
A simultaneous severance of diplomatic relations might have a great effect. But it might
be desirable to qualify this by allowing diplomatic representatives of exalted rank to
remain. Consular representatives need not in
the first instance be withdrawn. Commercial
prohibition should vary and develop with the
circumstances of the case. Personal relations
need only be severed in so far as they have
any economic bearing. The cutting off of food
supplies should be regarded as a very drastic
and extreme measure. Humanitarian relations
should continue. With regard to non-Members,
the whole action of the League must be affected
by the fact that great exporting countries remain outside the League, but efforts should
be made to secure at least their passive co-
operation.

(4) While all States must be under an obligation
to apply the concerted measures, it may be
necessary to grant special exemptions in
cases where the full application to some
States of the measures laid down would create
such hardships and dangers as to be almost
intolerable--or, in other words, to small
States in dangerous situations. [In regard
to this point an amendment was suggested to
the effect that

71

The Council may, however, at the request
of a Member which can show that the facilities demanded are essential to its
political or economic security, grant
such exemptions as in its opinion will
not conflict with the aim of Art. XVI.]

Special duties might be assigned to particular States. "It might be advisable that some
Members of the League should exercise the
belligerent right of visit and search at sea"
--but only "after the economic measures have
been imposed and have been found in practice
to require such support."[47]

The report of the International Blockade Committee was
considered by the League Assembly and was referred to its
First and Third Committees for general consideration and
possible amendments to the Covenant. The intent of economic sanctions as a form of "peaceful pressure" was agreed
upon, yet it was broadly accepted from the outset that
League members would be granted a certain flexibility in
applying the sanctions of Article 16 and that a resort to
war would come about only if a defaulting state continued
to violate its Covenants.

It was the first piece of constructive work on
the text of the Covenant which the Assembly had
attempted, and its members worked at the task
with enthusiasm. At the same time there was a
certain indisposition to sharpen and define
things in advance. There was a general eagerness
to explain away the word "immediately." The Assembly, like the Blockade Committee, disclaimed
the idea of giving any guidance to individual
States in the way of legislation, and even re-
nounced the investigation of the attractive and
very critical question of the "pacific blockade."[48]

The end result of the report was the adoption by the
Assembly of 18 resolutions and 4 amendments to the Covenant.
This result stemmed from a compromise whereby it was finally agreed that the amendments and resolutions adopted
by the Assembly were to constitute only rules for guidance
that the Assembly recommended to the Council and to the
members of the League.

In summary, the amendments were as follows:

The first of these Amendments substituted resi-
dence for nationality as the basis for severance
of relations.

The second declared that it was for the Council to give an opinion whether or not a breach of
the Covenant had taken place, and that in deliberations on the subject in the Council the votes of
the States concerned would not be counted.

The third authorised the Council to notify
the date it recommends for the application of
economic pressure under the Article.

The fourth provided for very carefully
guarded exemptions of particular States from the
obligation to apply the sanctions.[49]

The last amendment prevailed throughout the history of the
League. The 1921 resolution did expand the scope of Article 16, but effectiveness was eventually limited by insuf-
ficient ratifications. And since neither the amendments
nor the resolutions were ratified, they served only the
purpose of directives to the member states.

By 1935, therefore, there was simply Article 16 as
the League's enforcement provision. It is troublesome to
pluck Article 16 from context and consider it as a separate
entity, but the mechanics were fairly simple. All breaches
of the Covenant were to be referred to the Council as a
matter of urgency, and the Council was to meet and summon
representatives of the conflicting parties. The Council
would examine the circumstances and consider whether a
breach of the Covenant had occurred. In the event of a
finding that a breach occurred, recommendations on necessary responses were forwarded to each League member. Decisions on whether recommendations would be implemented
were the prerogatives of member states (sovereign prerogative).

There were other weaknesses besides sovereignty, although most were less fundamental. For example, there was
no provision for an explicit determination of the existence
of a state of war. An obligation upon states to act was
implied, but Article 16 did not extend beyond the mere implication. Clearly, it would appear that the drafters of
the Covenant had foreseen that measures "short of war"
would provide a recourse in lieu of war; but should these
measures fail, then presumably war remained legal even among
League members.[50]

When a situation developed to the point of applying
enforcement measures, further defects emerged. For example,

a proposed technical committee to determine the date of application of sanctions never came into existence. Similarly, provisions for considering the preliminary measures to be taken and action to be permitted in lieu of immediate sanctions application--for instance, postponement for special reasons--were never developed. A system of compensation for losses incurred while imposing sanctions met an identical fate.

By 1935, world opinion and the development of the League machinery seemed to reveal a greater willingness by states to take enforcement action. In the period 1932-35, the League had developed a number of understandings that apparently made states more receptive to the application of sanctions:

1. That the Council was to recommend the imposition of economic sanctions before states undertook domestic action;
2. That the Council would define the scope and nature of sanctions and when they were to take effect;
3. That there would be universal application;
4. That the legal, political, and economic capacities of members to perform sanctions were to be considered;
5. That the relationship of members to third-state nonmembers was to be considered.

The basis of the understandings may be found in the 1921 resolutions. But even with the constitutional development in the period 1932-35, and the recognition by states that the Japanese rape of Manchuria was a complete violation of the Covenant, sanctions against Italy failed. Nevertheless, League action in 1935 dissipated partly because of a lack of organization for collective security by the international and municipal enforcement agencies. An integrated system of sanctions, internationally organized, municipally implemented, and designed for rapid application, might have led to greater success. The effectiveness of sanctions, in all cases, is impaired by the absence of operative and rapid enforcement machinery. Unanimity of sanctions is essential, as is rapidity. All requirements depend upon a well-developed (and perhaps specifically functional) international organization, as defined and supported by the individual state's willingess to participate. The League, to a disastrous extent, lacked these essential requirements. The lessons derived from the brief League experience are not many, but they are significant. The technique of applied sanctions had to be worked out from the beginning, for the concept of universal application was new to the world community. The League took time to develop its techniques, and even more time in an attempt to put them into effect.

One consolation was the League's achievement in directing some 50 states to adopt a common policy toward a transgressor of law. The League provided a practical lesson in possible enforcement techniques and functioned for the unification of public condemnation.

> The moral weight and prestige of the League, in spite of any temporary impairment, is strengthened in the long run if the world looks to it as a vehicle for the expression of the moral judgements of the community of nations without any element of physical coercion. Coercive measures in the Covenant that are not likely in practice to be employed, are a source of weakness rather than strength.[51]

Many of the techniques and modes of publicity that the League evolved were later incorporated into the UN Charter. The organization's failure to achieve anything beyond moderate success in any dispute, particularly its limited application of economic sanctions in the Italo-Ethiopian dispute, leaves no solid ground for placing the attempt in disrepute. The techniques of applying economic sanctions are still not beyond the nascent stages, so we are not even permitted the wisdom of mature hindsight. In summary, therefore, the League effort was, and still is, the only instance when international law enforcement resembled the objectives of the written instrument. Second, the preliminary steps of reaching consensus, planning coordination, supervision, and implementation at both the international and municipal level were undertaken. Third, the situations facing the League revealed the now-obvious fact that the political and economic conflicts of states lie at the bases of effective peace enforcement. And finally, the problems of coordinating the actions of many states are only peripheral to the real source of disputes in international intercourse. The difficulties from which the League of Nations suffered stemmed from attempts to mold political reality to the word of the Covenant. (Non jus ex regula, sed regula ex jure.)

THE LEAGUE'S SANCTIONS

If it can be acknowledged in advance that the League's experiment with sanctions against Italy failed, it really cannot be suggested that this was due to a lack of formal organization; at a minimum 12 committees and subcommittees may be identified. The largest was the Coordination Committee, consisting of all League members (except Italy and Ethiopia). The most important functional group was the "Little Coordination Committee," more commonly known as the Committee of 18.[52] It was supported by five subcommittees: Economic Measures (13 members); Financial Measures (7 members); Mutual Support (9 members); Military Experts (4 members) and Legal (6 members). In November 1935, the Committee of Experts (12 members) was appointed to assist the Chairman of the Coordination Committee and created four subcommittees: Petroleum (12 members); Transport (3 members); Substitutes (membership unknown); and Supply and Consumption (11 members). The structure looked something like Figure 3.1.

During the period October 11, 1935–July 6, 1936, these committees and subcommittees formally convened about 93 times.* The work of the committees was divided into sessions, as follows:

Coordination Committee
First session, October 11–19, 1935
Second session, October 31–November 6, 1935
Third session, July 6, 1936

Committee of 18
First session, October 11–19, 1935
Second session, October 31–November 6, 1935
Third session, December 12–19, 1935
Fourth session, January 12, 1936
Fifth session, March 2–4, 1936
Sixth session, July 5–6, 1936

Committee of Experts
First session, November 27–December 12, 1935
Second session, January 29–February 1, 1936
Third session, March 4–9, 1936
Fourth session, April 21, 1936

---

*It is difficult to be accurate on this point for the official record often simply records that a subcommittee submitted a report without indicating when it met.

FIGURE 3.1

Committee Structure of

the League of Nations

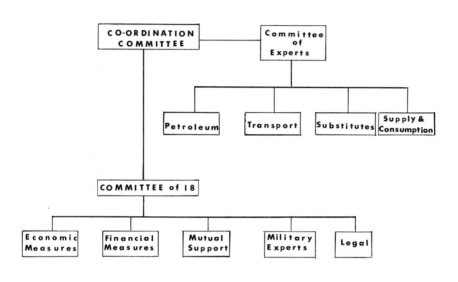

As is frequently the practice at international meetings
and during the regular proceedings of international organizations, staff, advisory, and delegation committees tend
to meet in the intervals between primary committee sessions
(it might also be worth including informal gatherings,
such as those held in New York at the offices of delegations among friends or caucuses, delegates' lounge sessions,
and even corridor meetings). In the period until December
1935, activity emanated from and surrounded the various
subcommittees of the Committee of 18, while after January
1936, impetus shifted to the various subcommittees of the
Committee of Experts. Two possible reasons may be advanced
for this alteration in emphasis. First, during 1935 empha-

sis was placed upon the mechanics of economic sanctions, with fine details to be worked out later. Second, the mechanics were worked out in late 1935 and, proving fruitless, forced the League members to place emphasis in early 1936 upon retention of the fiction of operation by generating noises about tightened sanctions.

In retrospect, the latter interpretation is more plausible, because available materials do not suggest that League members had sufficient vision to see where sanctions would lead. Thus, it is more probable that the detailed work of early 1936 was designed to placate segments of world opinion that were still optimistic. In sum, the charade of early 1936 was a means of softening the final blow of July 6, 1936.[53]

Briefly, as outlined earlier, the League Council met under the provisions of Article 16 on September 26. After assessing the situation, the Council resolved itself into the Committee of 13 and on October 5 issued its report.

> This report was a document of the highest historical importance. It represented the judgement of thirteen states . . . they reached conclusions completely unfavourable to the Italian case. No great international dispute has ever been the subject of a clearer verdict.[54]

Meanwhile, events had overtaken the League, and the Italian invasion of Ethiopia had been launched on October 3. Anthony Eden records that he met that evening with his French counterpart Pierre Laval at the Quai d'Orsay and Laval urged upon him the possibility of further negotiations with Mussolini. Eden agreed to relay the suggestion to London, but he doubted that either government would be in a position to offer concessions "which went further than those previously offered."[55]

Subsequently, at the Council meeting on October 5 Eden proposed that a committee be appointed to consider the facts of the situation and "report within twenty-four hours whether either of the parties was in breach of the Covenant."[56] This six-member committee met early the next day and by evening had issued its report. In it the committee concluded that Italy had resorted to war in violation of its obligations under Article 12 of the Covenant. "Condemnation in these terms involved Article XVI."[57]

On the afternoon of October 7 the Council met for a private session "as notable for its sense of urgency as the deliberations of the Committee of Six had been."[58] At

this meeting the nature of the sanctions were discussed
but decisions were not taken, in view of an impending Assembly meeting.

At the League Assembly meetings on October 9 and 10,
the members (except Austria and Hungary) accepted the Committee of Six recommendation that sanctions be imposed
against Italy. To initiate the process a committee (virtually of the whole Assembly) was established to coordinate.

> The Assembly . . . taking into consideration the
> obligations which rest upon the Members of the
> League in virtue of Article XVI of the Covenant
> and the desirability of co-ordination of the mea-
> sures which they may severally contemplate,
> Invites the Members of the League (other
> than the parties) to set up a committee, composed
> of one delegate, assisted by experts, for each
> Member, to consider and facilitate the co-ordina-
> tion of such measures.[59]

The first meeting of the Coordination Committee was
on October 11, 1935, eight days after the Italian invasion
of Ethiopia began. Its precise legal status was not clearly
defined, for it was created by recommendation of members
of the Assembly to the members of the League. The Council was advised of its creation but Council approval was
neither sought nor, apparently, deemed essential.

On the invitation of the Portuguese representative,
Agustode Vasconcellos, a subcommittee of the Coordination
Committee (eventually known as the Committee of 18) was
created to guide the former in its deliberations.* In order to provide every member of the Coordination Committee
the opportunity to serve on the Committee of 18, the latter was empowered to add members whenever advisable. The
Committee of 18 met that same afternoon (October 11). Vasconcellos, the chairman, indicated that its purpose was to
make recommendations on specific sanctions to be employed
and to report that afternoon to the Coordination Committee.
At the same time he raised a query about the status of the
1921 resolution.[60]

As noted earlier, the 1921 resolution was an attempt
to make workable the simple rigidity of Article 16; this
was especially important after the U.S. failure to join the

---

*These sorts of procedural anomalies are not unusual
in international organizations.

League. France's subsequent fear of weakening the security it derived from the Covenant proved to be the main stumbling block to a more satisfactory appraisal of Article 16.[61] Nevertheless, the League Assembly had taken the modest precaution of requiring that the Council be guided by the intent of the 1921 resolution. Eventually, when the Ethiopian situation emerged, the resolution did offer some practical guidance in respect to the League's position vis-à-vis nonmembers. However, paragraph 4 of the 1921 resolution ultimately proved a big enough loophole for all serious sanctions evaders to skip through. It allowed each League member to decide for itself whether a state of war existed. This respect for sovereignty is the essential bedeviling feature of international law. In any case, after some discussion it was generally agreed that the 1921 resolution did not prohibit the Committee of 18 from making some concrete suggestions. At this point there was still considerable resistance to states being "guided" in their actions by "unfettered sovereignty."[62] However, over time that resistance wavered and collapsed.

It was Anthony Eden who proposed that the Committee of 18 turn immediately to the matter of an arms embargo. Now that Italy had been judged an aggressor, and in view of the need for an obvious and immediate League response, suspension of the arms embargo to Ethiopia was appropriate. Eden initially suggested that the list of states embargoing arms to Italy should be expanded to include all manufacturing countries, whether League members or not. In one respect this was not as problematic as it might have been.

On August 31 the United States had implemented the first Neutrality Act; and while its terms would not assist Ethiopia in acquiring arms, it did prohibit arms shipments to Italy. Thus, insofar as a League arms embargo was concerned, the position of the United States was literally neutralized.[63] Germany was committed to a policy of neutrality in the dispute. It had assured Italy that it would not export arms to Ethiopia while refraining from a pro-Italian campaign, "for this might endanger the lives of German citizens living in Ethiopia."[64]

The delicacy with which the proposed arms embargo was approached was exemplified by suggestions that the Committee of 17 (18) draft a list of embargoed arms.* Eden (Britain) suggested that for practical purposes "the Committee

---

*In 1935, the Committee of 17 coopted Mexico to its membership and was known thereafter as the Committee of 18.

might adopt the list issued by President Roosevelt."[65]
Interestingly, he proposed the American list ostensibly for
practical, as opposed to political, reasons. The approach
was justified by observing that the U.S. list was sufficiently broad to be adaptable to League purposes. More important, however, it was necessary to emphasize that the
League was capable of operating independently while simultaneously demonstrating that it would avoid a direct confrontation with the United States. For practical purposes
the committee was constrained to accept the U.S. list or a
lesser version (in fact it added powder and explosives).
Only with difficulty could it have pressed significantly
beyond the U.S. Neutrality Act, and thus it was this list
of embargoed arms that became Committee of Coordination
Proposal I.[66] Eventually the American list of embargoed
arms, after some modification, became an annex to Proposal
I. In addition, the Committee of 18 added a provision relating to contracts in the process of execution. This was
to take into account substantial rumors concerning a variety of sales of war and "nonwar" materials to Italy.[67]
The proposal was finally prepared and was submitted to the
Coordination Committee at its second meeting, early in the
evening of October 11.

    Before terminating its first meeting, the Committee
of 18 established two subcommittees: Financial Measures
and Military Experts. The latter was empowered only to
consider and complete, if necessary, the list of arms, am-
munitions, and implements of war.

    The Coordination Committee's receipt of the recommen-
dations of the Committee of 18 confirmed the latter as an
advisory body to the former. In approving Proposal I, the
Coordination Committee also adopted the conclusion that
members were requested (not required) to inform the Secretary-General, in the shortest possible time, of measures
taken in conformity with Proposal I. The following day
the instruction was observed by the League's Secretary-
General with the request that "chaque gouvernement communique le texte des lois, décrets, proclamations ou autre instruments formulant ces mesures ou les mettant eu vigueur."[68]
For the next two months replies drifted in.

    Of the many dilemmas faced by League members respond-
ing to the Secretary-General's call, perhaps nothing was
as complicated as the situation of Switzerland. The Swiss
imposed an arms embargo on both Ethiopia and Italy in accordance with the requirements of Swiss neutrality.[69] Of
course, as Swiss Foreign Minister Guiseppe Motto pointed
out, the practical consequences of the arms embargo were

not significant because Ethiopia lacked money to purchase arms and because Switzerland produced no arms. In addition, Switzerland was faced with geographical and ethnic proximity to Italy, a fact that posed immense problems for the country.[70]

The problems that neutrality poses for international organizations are complex. The Legal Subcommittee of the Committee of 18 had decided that the obligations of the Covenant took precedence over specific treaty obligations. Swiss neutrality was dependent upon treaty, and thus it could be assumed that the obligation of the Covenant took precedence. Yet the 1920 Declaration of London was neither a treaty nor an amendment of the Covenant; apparently it was a statement of understanding, and hence the question of its relationship to the Covenant was open. A broad interpretation of the "act of state" doctrine presumably permitted upholding the Swiss interpretation of neutrality. But the doctrine assumes that a state will act only within the recognized principles of international law and that "a state cannot abolish or create International Law."[71] Doubtless, under the circumstances, a rather idyllic view.

In retrospect the Swiss interpretation of their neutral status, vis-à-vis the League Covenant, was manifestly defective. International law that assured neutrality was law defined by states acting in concert in 1815, 1907, and 1919. The League Covenant was international law similarly created, and certainly was beyond the capacity of Switzerland or the parties to the London Declaration to modify. Neutrality had been altered by the League Covenant, and appeals to pre-Covenant neutrality certainly amounted to little more than a veiled defense of an expedient act of state.* The appreciation of this dilemma clearly influenced Switzerland's decision against membership in the United Nations.

Moving with some rapidity, the newly appointed Subcommittee on Financial Measures convened for its first meeting on October 12, 1935, and eventually produced a document known as Proposal II (dealt with below).[72] Meanwhile, other committees were proceeding apace.

It must be recalled, of course, that this was the first attempt by an international organization to impose sanc-

---

*The appreciation of this dilemma clearly influenced Siwtzerland's decision against membership in the United Nations. However, as evidenced in the Rhodesian case (see Ch. 5), neutrality is still a perplexing issue.

tions; thus it is understandable that considerable time
was devoted to overviews and subsequent details. For example, one difficulty facing the Committee of 18 centered
upon nonparticipating League members and the status of nonmembers. At one point, in the Subcommittee on Economic
Measures, Robert Coulondre (France) explained that "it was
hoped that certain non-participating countries would assist and that they would take similar measures of embargo."[73]
The reason was that the League could effectively sanction
only commodities over which participating member states had
substantial control. In this vein Walter Riddell (Canada)
observed that while tin and tin ores were restricted, tin
cans were not, because no League members exclusively controlled can production and tin cans were a product Italy
required.[74]

Consequently, while the Committee of 18 first grappled
with the vexation of nonmembers, it was not prepared to
pursue the implications of the conundrum. C. T. teWater
(South Africa) summarized the issue: "In order to obtain
a plan of sanctions that would be viewed by the world as
something courageous, something that had been drawn up in
earnest and would work, the problem [of nonmembers and nonparticipating member states] must be viewed as a whole."[75]
At an early stage, therefore, the dominant concerns of the
League's sanctions machinery were to establish the credibility and validity of any measures proposed, and to achieve
mutual assurances that proposed measures would be enforced
by all members.

The requirement of credibility was essential if nonmembers were to be expected to accede to any system of sanctions. This explains why the members devoted so much effort to the technical issues and why each of the major proposals was reviewed in detail by a technical subcommittee.
The two concerns were interrelated, of course, because it
was widely believed that the attitude of nonmember states
would depend largely upon what they considered to be the
effectiveness of the proposed measure: "A coherent and
effective system should be established and then application should be made to nonmember states whose accession
might exercise an influence on the measures decided upon."[76]
For nonparticipating member states (Austria, Hungary, and
Albania) the Committee of 18 initially suggested stern
measures.[77] However, in conceding the problems posed by
nonmembers and nonparticipants, the Committee was not dis-
posed to tackle the issue directly. It turned instead to a
more immediate and perplexing problem, the disproportionate
impact projected sanctions would have on participating member states.

Clearly a state that depended heavily upon exports to
Italy would be at a considerable disadvantage in contrast
with a state with more diverse export interests. Article
16(3) of the Covenant provided for mutual support among
members "in order to minimise the loss and inconvenience"
resulting from imposed sanctions. The issue was raised on
the assumption that the obligations of Article 16(3) were
binding upon all members. Eventually, after some disagreement, the question was resolved (not solved) by the increasingly common expedient of appointing another subcommittee, this one on Mutual Support. Hence, despite the protestations of some respresentatives, the League's sanctions
machinery began the process of "miring-in" for the duration.[78]

Meanwhile, the Subcommittee on Financial Measures had
concluded its initial work in the form of Proposal II (control over private and public borrowing by Italy and its
citizens), and by October 14 it superficially appeared that
the League was functioning. Members were requested to impose restrictive measures on credit and banking facilities
as quickly as possible and to the extent permitted by existing domestic legislation. In practical terms the proposal
clearly affected branches of foreign banks in Italy and
Italian banks abroad. Essentially it involved restrictions
(to the extent permitted by domestic law) on foreign banks
providing credits to the Italian government and prohibitions
on Italians utilizing deposits abroad as credits for Italian imports. These restrictions also applied to insurance
policies contracted with non-Italian firms. Finally, Proposal II had raised some questions about its direct appli-
cability to individuals--that is, to prevent private citizens
from negotiating loans surreptitiously for the Italian government. The issue was never satisfactorily resolved;
and ultimately the Committee of 18 was forced to include a
rather innocuous provision calling upon states to apply,
without recourse to new legislation, practical measures to
control financial transactions of their nationals with
Italy by October 31, 1935.[79]

Throughout this early period it was becoming increasingly evident that British and French interests were beginning to diverge over the obligations of Article 16, especially the mutual support provisions of paragraph 3.
French representatives on the committees invariably referred
to France's willingness to adhere to all Covenant obligations; yet, when pressed on detailed sanctions provisions,
the French equivocated. The British clearly were leading
the deliberations, and League sanctions therefore were be-

ginning to resemble the British lowest denominator. The
reasons for the French shying away included a long-standing
distrust of the British, improving French relations with
Italy, and France's ongoing concern about European security.[80] Eventually, and despite French protestations, the
Subcommittee on Mutual Support was created.[81]

In addition to the increasingly uncertain political
situation, progress toward sanctions was beginning to en-
counter detailed and very thorny issues. Thus, questions
about restricting the export of strategic materials to
Italy, nonmembers, and transshipment remained vexatiously
unanswered. It was one thing for states to refuse to import Italian products, but exports were more problematic.
Many members of the League had favorable trade balances
with Italy, particularly during 1935 (Italy's major war
preparation year), and thus it was an attractive market.
Moreover, one of the largest exporters to Italy was the
United States; and there was apprehension that if League
members ceased exporting, the United States would take up
the slack. Clearly, therefore, the collaboration of nonmembers was essential for members attempting to fulfill obligations, yet it was becoming clear that somebody would
have to consult with nonmembers. However, the League was
neither programmed nor structured to undertake negotiations
as an entity in itself. This meant, of course, that the
role of the Secretary-General became very significant. Unfortunately for the League, Secretary-General Joseph Avenol
apparently foresaw no significant political role for his
position.

> Avenol inherited and followed the lead set by
> Drummond, and he inclined even more toward the
> primarily administrative content of his office,
> rarely taking any initiative to strengthen the
> political bases of the League. This lack of
> leadership was a serious source of weakness for
> the international body, although such passivity
> was what self-serving member states often
> wanted. . . . He did not believe in the enforce-
> ment machinery of the League. . . . He consid-
> ered this unworkable and thought that Article 16
> should be abandoned by amendment. . . . Avenol
> wanted the League revamped, made non political.[82]

On relations between the League and nonmembers, Avenol
had not been excessively informative: "Such co-operation
is constantly increasing and we have derived benefits from

that which we can set off against the loss which we have suffered by their non-membership."[83] If neither the organization nor its Secretary-General was able or inclined to represent the members in negotiations with nonmembers, what of the members themselves?

Only Britain and France were in a position to undertake any initiative, for they were the only major powers, besides Italy, directly involved. However, it was apparent that neither of the former was prepared to lead the League in pursuit of its objectives. France, as noted earlier, was cast as a reluctant follower of Britain. And Britain, despite Samuel Hoare's well-received speech of September 11, was beginning to vacillate as the magnitude of the situation emerged. Very succinctly stated, "Britain, and France behind it, deserted the Covenant and this is the major significance of the Italian-Ethiopian War."[84] Thus the League, in its relations with nonmembers, was effectively thwarted. Negotiations, if they could have been conducted with nonmembers, would have taken place in a vacuum because neither the League nor its major powers were prepared to take any initiative. From this point on, the sanctions exercise became something like shadowboxing. The inclination of the major powers to hold the minor states to their mutual Covenant obligations waned; and as this occurred, new ways were found to circumvent the elaborate procedures devised.

Sanctions for the League were probably dead before they started; and if they were alive, the fourth meeting of the Committee of 18 on October 14, 1935, constituted an unheralded coup de grace. That the pretense of sanctions lingered on for nine more months is explicable. There appeared to be the faint hope that somehow, despite the League's failure on this situation, something could be salvaged. In any event, the charade continued and the Committee of 18 established the Subcommittee on Economic Measures "to undertake an immediate study of the application of measures concerning the embargo on raw materials and products essential to Italy for the continuance of hostilities, and concerning the cessation of Italian exports to countries, Members of the League."[85] Finally, because of a number of legal problems that had arisen, the Committee created the Legal Subcommittee. It was charged to render an opinion on the status of private contracts, commercial treaties (including most-favored-nation clauses), and treaties of friendship and nonaggression that existed between various members and Italy.

During the afternoon of October 14 the Coordination
Committee held a meeting at which it considered a declaration on mutual support.[86]

> Les Membres de la Société conviennent, en outre,
> de se prêter l'un à l'autre un mutuel appui dans
> l'application des mesures économiques et finan-
> cières à prendre en vertu du présent article pour
> réduire au minimum les pertes et les inconvénients
> qui peuvent en résulter. Ils se prêtent également
> un mutuel appui pour résister à toute mesure spé-
> ciale derigée contre l'un d'eux par l'Etat en
> rupture de Pacte.[87]

The declaration simply represented an immediate policy
statement the details of which were to be considered by
the Subcommittee on Mutual Support. The interesting point
is that the declaration was designed to create an obligation to render mutual assistance in the event Italy took
reprisals against member states. Theoretically, the statement represented a comprehensive interpretation of Article
16(3) of the Covenant; in practice, however, the system
broke down.

The Coordination Committee next reviewed Proposal II
(Financial Measure). The most closely scrutinized aspect
of Proposal II was the provisions relating to extension of
credit. Alfred De Nickl (Hungary) pointed out that the
proposals "applied only to creditor countries and not to
debtor countries like Hungary."[88] Richard Schüller (Austria) agreed, and drew attention to the fact that Italy
"had guaranteed 20% of the League of Nations loan and 100%
of the obligations entailed for Austria by the Südbohn
agreements.[89] Italy had also granted Austria large commercial credits." M. Tytus Komarnicki (Poland) explained
that "the proposed arrangements did not in any way affect
the service of debts" and that "Proposal II should be interpreted as meaning that everything not expressly prohibited in it was permitted." The committee agreed, and Proposal II was approved.

One unfortunate feature of Proposal II was that it
permitted the servicing of outstanding debts to Italy.
The loophole was created for the benefit of countries such
as Austria and Hungary, in order to avoid excessive claims
by Italy after sanctions were removed. Strangely, the commitment was made with the full realization that outstanding Italian debts would not be serviced. In most respects,
therefore, the sanction actually amounted to a favorable

exchange for Italy and, in the long run, would prove to be a major weakness in the entire sanctions program because it provided Italy with another lever to extract concessions from League members. It should be recalled that sanctions are a form of warfare, and thus the object state must employ every means at its disposal to weaken their application:

> To cut the enemy off from outside supplies means, usually, to deny oneself the benefit of the enemy's production. It is possible that the enemy may be hurt more. Indeed it is this belief that underlies most action in economic warfare. But it would be irrational to regard the sacrifice as completely one-sided.[90]

The Italians took advantage of loopholes in the sanctions program and exploited doubts and fears of League members.

Before continuing with the broad perspective, it is worth digressing to review the activities of two major subcommittees, Mutual Support and Economic Measures.[91]

Mutual Support

Mutual support, as envisaged by League diplomats, was a process whereby sanctioning states mutually interacted to support each other when losses were incurred in trade or production as a consequence of imposing sanctions. Perhaps the concept might be described best as a process of temporarily taking up the slack in trade and production. Clearly there are a number of complex features in such a system--for example, single-crop or single-product economies are precariously situated. Second, it was certainly apparent at the League that members did not foresee permanent alterations in trading patterns.[92] Third, a comprehensive mutual support system doubtless could be developed; but it would require the acquisition and digestion of vast quantities of statistical materials relating to trade, trade patterns, and national economies--a process the League was not prepared to undertake. Nor, in retrospect, does it appear that League members were very deeply committed to an advanced form of worldwide trade liberalization that marginally would have facilitated the requirements of mutual support. On one occasion, for example, it was suggested that members establish a mutual support fund consisting of a 1 percent duty on all imported goods. The fund, to be administered by a technical subcommittee of the League, would be used to grant foreign exchange advances to states unable to absorb goods normally exported to Italy and to assist procurement elsewhere of goods usually imported from Italy.[93]

By far the most perplexing phase of a projected mutual support program revolved about the status and requirements of existing commercial treaties, especially those containing most-favored-nation (m.f.n.) clauses. Theoretically, restrictions on imports and exports would violate m.f.n. clauses, thereby violating treaties, which would permit Italy to denounce treaties--possibly in perpetuity. Clearly, long-term trading patterns stood to suffer considerably. Conversely, some states were perturbed by the prospect of granting m.f.n. status to states not normally accorded the privilege, such as the Soviet Union.

Advice on the status of m.f.n. clauses was sought from the Committee of 18's Legal Subcommittee.[94] The subcommittee was asked whether a state that benefited from concessions made to Italy under commercial treaties with sanctioning states could continue to derive benefits even though the sanctions had resulted in suspension of the concessions made to Italy. The Legal Subcommittee replied that it was within the spirit of Article 16(3) that advantages should continue to be accorded independently of m.f.n. clauses because it was inconceivable that mutual support should render economic relations more difficult than before sanctions. To a considerable extent the Legal Subcommittee was being as realistic as it was legalistic in its interpretation. Nevertheless, it did recommend a paragraph for inclusion in Proposal V (the proposal being drafted by the Subcommittee on Mutual Support) that would have granted states participating in League sanctions the same advantages that would have accrued normally to Italy "on the new ground of mutual support." At this point the League clearly was creating law, for in effect it was saying that for the duration of the emergency, League members would grant each other concessions equivalent to standard m.f.n. clauses.

Ultimately this rather equitable provision was discarded in favor of a diluted version that appeared as paragraph I(d) of Proposal V, which called upon sanctioning states that had suffered no loss in respect of any given commodity to refrain from demanding the application of any m.f.n. clause. This restrictive provision permitted only sanctioning states that had suffered losses to request the privileges usually accorded to Italy.

A second question that had been directed to the Legal Subcommittee was whether countries entitled to m.f.n.

89

clauses would be justified in claiming temporary preferential treatment for the goods of another participating state whose exports had been specifically restricted as the result of sanctions. The Legal Subcommittee concluded that m.f.n. clauses did not justify the extension of the advantages to third states. The reasons were the following, as cited in Special Supplement no. 150:

> First, that such advantages would have an exceptional as well as a temporary character and would be the consequence of a special obligation existing between the states concerned in virtue of Article 16, paragraph 3, and secondly, that the m.f.n. clause is a provision peculiar to commercial treaties, which are treaties in which it is found, and, accordingly, is one which must be interpreted as not contemplating economic relations of so exceptional a nature as those which are here under consideration. [PP. 11-12.]

The opinion effectively quashed attempts to equate m.f.n. status with preferential treatment. Trade liberalization was to be interpreted to the extent permitted by existing treaties and was not to be expanded so as to encroach upon domestic trade policy.

As the work of the Mutual Support Subcommittee continued, it became evident that certain states, such as Romania and Yugoslavia, would suffer more than other states from imposing sanctions. Various solutions were proposed, and ultimately responsibility for accommodating special cases was turned over to the Technical Committee (eventually the Committee of 18) under provisions of Proposal V (1)(d).

By October 19, Proposal V was before the Committee of 18 and was being promoted as a technique for employing m.f.n. clauses as a basis for mutual support.[95] However, it was not pointed out that the temporary concession of m.f.n. privilege was not mandatory but simply a moral obligation. Second, the requirement of mutual support was not conceived to be in any manner restrictive of sovereign prerogative; thus, while mutual support was acknowledged in principle, the League was not prepared to encroach upon a state's prerogative to determine what concessions might be granted. Third, the mutual support scheme did not provide recourse should states fail to grant any concessions whatsoever.

Proposal V was basically adopted as presented, with the exception that the League did attempt, in paragraphs

II(1)(2), to assert "the League's authority in relation to all countries in the globe."[96] This was done by calling upon League members to increase imports from countries that had suffered hardship through the loss of their Italian market while simultaneously reducing, to an equitable degree, imports from nonparticipating countries.[97] In sum, therefore, mutual support amounted to a moral directive to temporarily alter trading patterns to benefit League members that had suffered from trade restrictions with Italy.

Economic Measures

The Subcommittee on Economic Measures was created for two purposes: to consider an embargo on raw materials to Italy and to consider means of halting Italian exports.[98] The results of its work were Proposals III and IV (prohibition of imports of Italian goods and embargo on certain exports), adopted by the Coordination Committee on October 19, 1935.[99]

The primary objective of the subcommittee was to create procedures "to prevent the belligerent country as far as possible from continuing to receive products which were essential to it in the pursuit of hostilities."[100] Initially the subcommittee viewed its task as a whole because questions relating to exports and imports pose essentially the same types of difficulty: goods en route, partly completed contracts, goods in transit (especially through third countries), and transshipment via third-party facilities. Italian exports posed the additional difficulty of value-added content, particularly insofar as Italian value-added might constitute a proportion of a third state's exports. The significance of this latter issue is underscored by the fact that Germany and the United States were major Italian trading partners by 1934-35 and also of numerous League members.

Quite obviously, a prohibition on imports from Italy was a primary element in the emerging sanctions scheme, and it was also a necessary corollary to Proposal II (financial measures). Clearly, the reduction of belligerent trade would reduce Italy's ability to purchase abroad materials essential to the Ethiopian war. Anthony Eden (Britain) proposed the framework for the import embargo when he suggested (1) that goods be regarded as Italian unless a minimum of 25 percent of the value was added after the goods left Italian territory; (2) that goods en route (in transit), on the dates on which individual states imposed

the sanctions be excluded; (3) that goods subject to existing contracts not be excluded; and (4) that gold or silver
bullion and coins be excluded.

With the exception of the rather generous value-added
proposal, the framework for an import embargo was fairly
realistic. The rather weak value-added restraint doubtless
reflected the general concern over the importance of Italian trade to a world trade just emerging from a stunning
depression. In practice the 25 percent value-added proposal meant that up to 75 percent of the value of a good
could be of Italian origin without the product being considered Italian for purposes of import embargo. Such a
provision functions to the disadvantage of states that have
unfavorable trade balances with a target state.* The intent of such provisions, among other basic objectives,
clearly is to force the target state to purchase necessary
goods with hard currencies or, in the case of Italy, gold.
The League sought to force Italy into a rapid depletion of
gold reserves, thereby reducing its ability to conduct a
prolonged war.[101]

In the end, Eden's proposals were put together and
presented to the Committee of 18 on October 19, 1935 as
Proposal III (prohibition of importation of Italian goods).
The only difficulty was the matter of fixing the date for
implementation. The Committee of 18 finally compromised
and agreed to meet on October 31 to consider, "in the light
of the replies received, the date of the coming into force
of the said measures."[102]

The next stage was a meeting of the full Coordination
Committee, also on October 19, and it was here that real
hard-core opposition to the import embargo emerged.[103]
The increasing frustration--indeed, the desperation--of
Austria and Hungary emerged in the form of challenges to
the legal status of the League Covenant vis-à-vis the peace
treaties. For example, Austria invoked Article 284 of the
Treaty of Saint Germain (Articles 1-26 contained the League
Covenant), guaranteeing freedom of transit through Austria
for all countries. "The Italian market was the only market of Austria's which showed any expansion. Italy was
the only country except Switzerland with which Austria had
a considerably active trade balance."[104] Similarly, Hungary equivocated in the light of a 1925 Italian-Hungarian

---

*There was also the problem faced by Switzerland. It
had barter arrangements with Italy under which Italy accepted Swiss goods in place of gold or currency.

bilateral trade agreement that was "called the spinal column of Hungary's commercial policy. Since it had come into force, the whole economic life of Hungary had turned on it as on a pivot."[105]

The question of the status of such treaties in the light of Covenant provisions is not really complex. Clearly, the League Covenant prevailed:

> Application of sanctions by a State having a commercial treaty with Italy may, to a greater or lesser degree, prevent the execution of the treaty. Italy would, however, have no legal right to complain, since the situation so created would be the result of the provisions of the Covenant, which is legally binding on both Italy and the other State and prevails over the treaty in question.[106]

On that note, and with Austrian and Hungarian abstentions, Proposal III was approved without amendment.

In most respects Proposal IV (embargo on certain exports to Italy) was the reverse of Proposal III, with the added feature that Proposal IV was sort of an extension of Proposal I (export of arms): paragraph 2 of Proposal I was extended to include transport of animals, rubber, and a wide range of metals and ores. Crucial to Proposal IV were the opinions of the Legal Subcommittee on the matter of private contracts. In summary, the questions and opinions were as follows:

Preliminary
What would happen between a Government and one of its residents or citizens if a contract, in the process of implementation, was adversely affected by the sanctions?

Opinion
This question will be settled by the internal public law of the State concerned.[107]

Q1. What if an Italian has a contract with a national of a State participating in the sanctions and the Italian suffers loss owing to the sanctions preventing the contract from being performed?

(a) Opinion
If the Italian sues in the courts of that
State, the action will fail because prevention of the execution of the contract is the
result of a prohibition lawfully imposed.*

(b) Opinion
If the Italian sued in an Italian court and
the judgement is for him as the plaintiff,
the judgement cannot be executed in the defendant's country because the requisite authority for its execution will not be obtainable,
even if claimed in virtue of treaties, for
the treaties could not override the effect of
Article 16 of the Covenant. . . . If it were
to be possible for execution of the judgement
to be sought and obtained in the plaintiff's
country, this would have to be considered to
be a breach of the international obligations
created by the Covenant.

(c) Opinion

If the claim for execution were brought before the courts of a third participating
state, the same reason should lead to their
rejection.

(d) Opinion

If the claim were submitted to arbitration,
the same result would follow.

(e) Opinion

If the claim were brought before an International Tribunal, the same result would follow.

Q2. If the application of sanctions by a State
having a commercial treaty with Italy, to a

---

*Presumably the Legal Subcommittee meant by "prohibition
lawfully imposed" a prohibition imposed by municipal law
pursuant to obligations under the Covenant. They could not
constitutionally have said this, however, because they were
not in a position to direct municipal jurisdictions.

greater or lesser degree, prevented the execution of the treaty, what recourse had Italy?

(a) Opinion

Italy would have no right to complain, since the situation so created would be the result of the provisions of the Covenant, which is legally binding on both Italy and the other state and prevails over the treaty in question.

Q3. Would the principle of reciprocity permit Italy to withhold the execution of her obligations under the treaty or to annul or suspend the performance of contracts in the process of execution?

Opinion
Because the Covenant is binding on all parties, Italy would incur international liability by refusing to carry out the commercial treaty or by annulling or suspending the performance of contracts in the process of execution.

Q4. What is the obligation under a treaty of friendship and non-aggression in which the parties undertake "not to participate in any international entente preventing purchase or sale of goods or provision of credits from or to the other party"?

Opinion
Since the parties are members of the League, it is clear that the treaty must be interpreted subject to Article 16 and 20 of the Covenant.* It follows that application of sanctions by one of the contracting parties against the other is legitimate, even if the treaty contains no reservation regarding the provisions of the Covenant or if one of the contracting parties was not a mem-

---

*Article 20 of the Covenant referred to obligations inconsistent with the Covenant; membership included abrogation of all inconsistent treaties.

ber of the League of Nations at the moment when
it concluded the treaty.*

The Legal Subcommittee's opinions established a series
of workable international legal precepts that would justify
the unilateral suspension of treaties during a period of
multilateral international law enforcement.** The constraints of municipal law were avoided by implying that an
obligation flowed from the Covenant. Action was to occur
within the limits of municipal law and in precedence to
any bilateral treaty relations.

Other subjects considered by the Economic Measures
Subcommittee included transshipment.[108] Unfortunately for
the subcommittee, it never agreed, and two proposals were
finally recommended to the Coordination Committee. Meanwhile, other difficulties surrounded the timing for imposing embargoes and, again, the attitude toward nonparticipating states. On this latter point it appears to have
been largely Britain's (Eden's) initiative. The subcommittee, over French objections, agreed to meet on October 31
to consider replies received to the proposals and to fix
a date for the coming into force of the measures.

Resolution of the difficult question of nonparticipating states was attempted both through suggested moral declarations and through quotas based upon annual average of
imports of a given product over a period of years.[109] No
solution proved acceptable; and eventually the subcommittee
fell back upon the expedient of having the Secretary-General formally convey the contents of Proposal IV to nonparticipants, in hopes it would appeal to their senses of de-
cency.

Proposal IV was finally accepted by the Coordination
Committee after some dispute at the Committee of 18 stage
over the matter of reexport of goods (paragraph 2). The
original text was reduced from a "requirement" to "taking
steps to secure against re-exportation." As Gajardo (Chile)
observed:

---

*Literally this is nothing more than a broad interpre-
tation of Article 20.
**There was no question of the abrogation of commercial
treaties. The suspensions were considered to be temporary,
ipso facto while sanctions were in effect. Italy was to
be deprived of its public and private international law
rights (and obligations) only temporarily.

The fact that a proposal prohibited such and such
a transaction, did not necessarily involve _ipso
facto_, the prohibition of that transaction in law.
The Co-ordination Committee had only been set up
to assist, by framing and preparing texts, the
Governments of countries applying sanctions in
the performance of their task.[110]

Hungary, Albania, and Spain were even more forthright, expressing direct reservations.[111]
    By October 19, 1935, the Coordination Committee had
completed the first stage of its work.[112] By then 22 countries had agreed to impose an arms embargo, and a modest
mood of optimism prevailed. The states were improvising
with a fledgling form of international cooperation, one
for which neither precedent nor adequate model existed,
while they faced the formidable reluctance of states to
jeopardize burgeoning recovery from economic depression.
Arnold Toynbee remarked:

The architects of these sanctions had to overcome
first a general disinclination to impose any fresh
economic strain upon a social fabric which had
barely begun to recover from a devastating economic depression, and then the particular disinclination of each sanction-taking state to make
national sacrifices--a disinclination which was
a formidable force in an age when national self-
ishness was being cultivated as the quintessence
of public virtue under the name of _sacro egoismo_.
Moreover, the difficulty of demanding such sacri-
fices was accentuated by the inevitable inequality of the incidence of the sacrifice as between
this country and that.[113]

The euphoria of the Coordination Committee's early work
had resulted, therefore, in the five ingredients of the
League's sanctions scheme directed against Italy:[114]

Proposal I: Export of arms, ammunition and implements of
            war (October 11, 1935)
        I(a): Amended list of articles considered as arms,
            ammunition, and implements of war (October
            16, 1935)
Proposal II: Financial measures (October 14, 1935)
        II(a): Clearing agreements (November 6, 1935)

Proposal III: Prohibition of importation of Italian goods
(October 19, 1935, with report of the Legal
Subcommittee)
Proposal IV: Embargo on certain exports to Italy (October
19, 1935, with report of the Legal Subcommit-
tee)
IV(a): Extension of the embargo (November 6, 1935)
IV(b): Indirect supply (November 6, 1935)
Proposal V: Organization of mutual support (October 19,
1935, with report of the Legal Subcommittee).

The groundwork having been completed, the Committee of 18
then began work, at its second session, on a series of
complicated details. Very briefly these included the following:

1. Consideration of contracts
   a. Fully paid
   b. Partially paid but in the course of execution
2. Outstanding claims (credits) against Italy and
   the related matter of clearing agreements
3. Extension of the embargo (Proposal IV)
4. Indirect supply
5. Exceptions to the prohibition on importation of
   Italian goods
6. Consideration of special cases arising from the
   application of the proposals
7. The date of entry into force of Proposals III and
   IV.

The matter of fully paid contracts was handled rather
expeditiously after Anthony Eden (Britain) and Robert Coulondre (France) sorted out their interests and agreed that
the contracts should be completed, providing payment had
been made in full by October 19, 1935.[115] Contracts partially paid and parties to barter arrangements posed more
difficult problems. The latter was peculiar, because barter arrangements involve no currency transactions; hence
the case was made by Poland and Turkey that there really
was no accrued benefit to Italy.[116] Eden, apparently exas-
perated at the thought that a deluge was beginning, expressed doubts about special cases "which were not special
at all and which had simply been thought of by Governments
since they applied."[117] Yet there certainly seemed to be
a "me too" or, at best, a "maybe me too" approach to the
bailing-out process of the requirements of Proposal III
(3). Of course the issue of contracts partially completed

was not anticipated to be a major breach of the sanctions because it should have been interpreted as a short-term issue.

Eventually the subject was passed on to a series of subcommittees of the Economic Measures Subcommittee of the Committee of 18. Initially an attempt was made to define terms of reference within which contracts in the process of execution might be considered.[118] Unfortunately, the definition included a reference to "an institution belonging to the state" as well as contracts conducted by states. This raised a vast range of questions about the relationship between states, private enterprise, and state enterprise, all of which provided pegs upon which to hang exceptions to constraints on terminating partially fulfilled contracts.

In an attempt to answer the array of questions, a number of draft resolutions were proposed, each of which sought to meet specific objections.[119] Eventually agreement was reached and a resolution was approved by the Committee of 18 on November 6, 1935.[120] In brief, contracts in the course of execution were considered subject to completion if they were of "essential importance to the importing State," were concluded before October 19, and were not less than 20 percent paid by that date. Barter agreements that would have made goods banned by Proposal IV available to Italy were not excepted. Finally, the League was to have available details of contracts for which exception was sought.

The end result of the deliberations on the matter of unfulfilled contracts was basically a solid resolution. Recognized was an easily overlooked aspect of sanctions that relates to the difficulty of terminating or suspending extended contracts. The solution's weakness was the broad definition of state involvement, which might permit ready circumvention of the sanctions if a private enterprise were in a position to exert pressure on a government to have its imports from Italy considered as "of essential importance." The delegates were aware of the possibility of deception, but apparently were prepared to place confidence in each state's commitment to the obligations of Article 16. This, as will become more evident later, is the essence of any successful sanctions scheme, and failure can be measured against the lack of same among participating states.

Even more complicated than unfulfilled contracts were outstanding claims (credits) and clearing agreements. The two matters are related because a creditor relationship may result from the operation of a clearing agreement as well as from normal trade relations. Sanctions interfere with clearing and debt-settlement arrangements to the extent that they prevent a country from accepting the target state's goods as payment for debts that have fallen due. Therefore sanctions can recoil against sanctioning states. Moreover, if a target state were to offer to pay off a debt and the sanctioning-creditor state refused payment because of the application of the sanctions, then the target state might ipso facto consider itself relieved of the debt.

> If the sanctions scheme was to work at all, it would have to be on the basis that once that particular measure came into force no more Italian goods would be received; otherwise . . . if commerce continued, it would be virtually impossible to say whether it was being continued in fulfillment of the final stage of a clearing agreement or whether it was due to some further arrangement made subsequently.[121]

Debate on the related subjects was extensive in the Economic Measures Subcommittee, with members being pressed vigorously to accept the authenticity of the sanctions over limited national interest.[122] As one delegate observed, "Some nations wished to play their part at little or no cost to themselves. . . . The thing could not be done without cost."[123]

> It was obvious that, where private interests were at stake, the most ingenious means would be employed to get around any Government measures taken.
> It was a case of force majeure. The obligations entered into, in virtue of the Covenant released them (members), under Article 20, from other undertakings in regard to clearing or commercial agreements. When the sanctions came to an end, they would be in possession of the same rights as before.[124]

The Swiss delegate even went so far as to challenge the status of the Coordination Committee and its affiliates.

> It was obvious that the Co-ordination Committee and its organs could not take any decision. They could not authorize or prohibit this or that to everybody or anybody, since any such action would

raise the question whether unanimity or a majority vote was required. The Committee could, however, study the problem and exercise an influence on the Governments. . . . It would be imprudent to attempt, by any kind of multilateral agreement, to codify all the questions which might arise in various forms in the relations of fifty countries with Italy. Guiding principles must be laid down and discussed and their application might also be studied; but a codification in the absolute sense was impossible.[125]

The bubble of collective response to armed aggression was surely beginning to strain. The Swiss, for the first time, clearly had attacked the status of the League's sanctions effort. In addition, the boldness of the Swiss assault gave impetus to other states to find excuses to wiggle from beneath inconvenient League commitments. Finally, the Swiss equivocation highlighted the immense difficulties involved in arriving at basic multilateral agreement on a sanctions scheme. This latter point is fundamental to sanctions, and its importance will be highlighted on numerous occasions hereafter.

The Economic Measures Subcommittee, perhaps taking a cue from the Swiss objections, vacillated. First it agreed to a Mexican proposal that states be polled on the extent of clearing agreements. Then it acknowledged the complexity of the issue and deferred back to the Committee of 18.[126] On November 2 the draft resolution was adopted, as proposed, by the Coordination Committee.[127] In summary, the concept of mutual support was elongated in two directions. First, members were expected to support each other when sanctions were discontinued, to ensure that Italy discharged its credit obligations. Second, and with some futility, states were requested to expand the principle of Article 16(3), of their own volition, to assist states incurring severe losses because of the restrictions on credit arrangements.

Clearing agreements were finally resolved separately in Proposal II (a), approved by the Coordination Committee on November 6, 1935.[128] Clearing agreements permitted payments between importers and exporters in local currency through a domestic bank. Thus, transactions remained within one currency while goods moved between two countries. Usually on an annual basis, outstanding balances were cleared in favor of creditor countries by transfers of hard currency or gold. Coordination Committee discussion of the subject arose in recognition of an Anglo-Italian exchange of notes of April 27, 1935. The British had argued in a reply to Proposal II that the method of Italian payment for British exports set out in the April 1935 agreement did not contravene Proposal II (and enabling British Orders-in-Council), providing payment was made by deposit of lire in an Italian bank on or before the delivery of the goods.[129]

Discussion of the subject revealed substantial variations in opinions between the British and some other delegates (Sweden, Yugoslavia). The latter believed that a proper interpretation of Proposal II left no doubt that governments would "have to suspend their clearing or other similar agreements."[130] The issue was resolved by submission to another subcommittee (on clearing agreements), which drafted a resolution including a provision to abrogate all clearing or payments agreements.[131] The general lack of enthusiasm that greeted this proposal probably reflected the fear of making permanent decisions in a fluid sanctions situation. Needless to say, the proposal was so in excess of expectations that it was returned to the subcommittee for reconsideration. Subsequently it went through the process again and was approved by the Committee of 18 on November 6.[132]

With the increased emphasis upon the Committee of 18, it was becoming apparent that the locus of League sanctions was altering. Committee of 18 meetings were private, while Coordination Committee meetings were public forums. The British, having been mildly stung on clearing agreements, were wary of any more exposure than necessary, particularly in view of the greater ease with which they and the French could maneuver the Committee of 18 as opposed to the Coordination Committee. Proposal II was becoming a practical hoax, a sop to public opinion, that was so circumscribed by caveats as to be ignored with impunity.

Support for this conclusion may be found in the activities of the Italian representative in Geneva, Baron Pompes Aloisi.[133] He met with Samuel Hoare and Pierre Laval on November 1 and 2, the major subject for discussion being the proposed "gentleman's agreement" for military détente in the Mediterranean. Aloisi realized that with an approaching election in Britain, that government was faced with the task of maintaining momentum against Italy.[134] In return for not pressing Britain on sanctions, Aloisi sought some relief from the pressure of the British fleet in the Mediterranean and made it clear that he expected the situation with Britain to improve after the election.[135] Consequently, by November 6, 1935, the British, French, and Italians had achieved recognition of each other's mutual

interests--they agreed to disagree. Other members quietly
conceded their positions.

The final two sentences of Proposal IV delegated to
the Committee of 18 authority to extend the document to
certain other articles. On November 2 the Committee of 18
introduced a draft proposal to extend the list contained
in Proposal IV to petroleum and derivatives, coal, and iron,
cast iron, and steel.[136] Two interesting features of the
draft stood out: first, it proposed that implementation
occur after the Committee of 18 assessed replies to the
proposal, and second, it was apparent that the products
listed essentially were beyond direct control of League
members.[137]

The draft proposal was submitted to the Economic Measures Subcommittee on November 4. Ultimately, after reference to a drafting subcommittee, and over the objections
of Yugoslavia, the extension of the embargo became Proposal
IV(A), approved by the Committee of 18 on November 6,
1935.[138]

Proposal IV(A), perhaps more than anything else, af-
firms the sort of shadowboxing role being played by smaller
states on the matter of sanctions. The extended sanctions
were not attractive to the major powers, although they
would tend to placate public opinion; consequently, the apparent tightening of sanctions was illusory because the
major powers were making deals elsewhere.

One of the more explosive issues to face the Committee
of 18 was "indirect supply," the provisioning of a target
state by transshipment, false bills of lading, barter arrangements in third states, and a host of other deceptive
means to maintain trade despite sanctions. The League
committees, in accord with the diplomacy of the day, shied
from accusations that states would do anything untoward in
their mutual dealing. As a result, the solution to the
question of indirect supply found form in Proposal IV(B),
approved November 6, 1935, as a rather bland general injunction to states to "immediately take such steps as may
be necessary to prevent supplies reaching Italy or Italian
possessions by indirect routes" in the event of abnormal
increases in exports of embargoes goods.[139] Beyond improving customs procedures and creating more elaborate
forms (navicerts), there really was not much else available.*

---

*Since at least the 1973 Arab-Israeli war, Saudi Arabia
has very rigidly controlled oil shipments. Ship captains

Indirectly, Proposal IV(B) raised an often overlooked area of sanctions utilization, an element that might be referred to as the "contiguous factor." That is, states bordering on the target state have increased difficulties employing sanctions against their neighbor both because of the likelihood of traditional trading patterns and, as a consequence, because loyalties may be stronger to the contiguous (target) state than to the international organization. The Committee of 18 chose to avoid the issue despite its being raised.[140] However, the seriousness of intent of Proposal IV(B) must be questioned simply because it confined its prescription to platitudes rather than providing realistic and more specific guidance for standardized means of verifying destinations and "abnormal" exports.

The remaining major area reviewed at the second session of the sanctions committee were exceptions to the prohibition on imports of Italian goods (Proposal III). This issue boiled to the surface as approval for certain Italian published materials (books, maps, music, newspapers) to be excepted and circulated freely was sought. This exception became Proposal III(A), approved by the Committee of 18 on November 6, 1935.[141]

The remaining two issues, special cases and date of entry into force, were handled with some expeditiousness. The Coordination Committee finally fixed November 18, 1935, as the date for commencement of the five proposals. Meanwhile, special cases (arising from responses to the proposals) were referred to the Committee of 18. Thus, by November 6 League sanctions committees had completed their second session. By then a gelatinlike set of sanctions had been developed covering a broad range of specific and intricate subjects. Yet the superficiality of the entire affair was beginning to emerge; and it was only a matter of time before the final collapse occurred, if for no other reason than the "gentleman's agreement" that was fermenting between Britain, France, and Italy.

The Committee of 18, as the steering committee of the League's Coordination Committee, did not meet again until December 12, 1935. It began its third session that day and completed its work on December 19. In the interval between November 6 and December 12, the Committee of Ex-

---

must produce loading and unloading certificates for all cargoes. This double check has been used, among other things, to control crude oil supplies to refineries in Italy and Greece supplying the U.S. 6th Fleet in the Mediterranean.

perts met, beginning November 27, to review state replies
to Proposals I-IV and to seek clarification and explanation
where necessary, should replies not appear to fulfill the
requirements contained in the four proposals.[142]

In this same period events external to the League and
sanctions occurred that effectually neutered the sanctions
and subsequently undermined, if not destroyed, the League.
Most significant, of course, was the Hoare-Laval agreement
of December 8, 1935. However, before commenting upon this
coup de grace to the League's sanctions, a brief note is
in order on the dying gasps of the League's sanctions
scheme.

The Committee of Experts reviewed the various replies
through a series of specialized subcommittees and their
reports.[143] In a series of meetings held up to December
10, the Committee of Experts delayed preparing its final
report until states cited for failure to comply with the
proposals were given time to fill in the explanatory gaps.[144]
The final report was submitted to the Committee of 18 on
December 13,[145] and contained a summary of the status of
replies received to each of the proposals. The committee
reported again on January 30, 1936; the summary is reprinted
in Table 3.1. There was no significant change between the
status summaries contained in the two reports with the exception of Peru. The first report had contained a series
of detailed questions[146] that might have warranted more
investigation and answers had not Samuel Hoare and Pierre
Laval pulled the rug out from beneath the sanctions.

There really is not much merit considering the Hoare-
Laval agreement, the reasons for it, and the maneuverings
that preceded that nefarious but understandable act.[147]
Nor is there great merit exploring the apparent betrayal
of the mandate given to British Prime Minister Baldwin by
the British electorate at the general election of November
14, 1935. The impression that "the electorate was resolved
to ensure League victory over Italy"[148] was shattered by
the revelation on December 9 that Hoare and Laval had concluded a secret agreement in Paris the preceding day.
That the agreement was divulged in Paris before it was
known to the Italians, the Ethiopians, or even the British
cabinet was doubly galling. The fact that the Hoare-Laval
agreement resembled the 1921 tripartite agreement on
spheres of economic influence in Ethiopia (with the exception that Britain and France basically withdrew their
claims) makes suspicious the entire intent of British-French
activity at the League from late 1934 on.

TABLE 3.1

Summary of Government Replies to League Proposals
(as of January 30, 1936)

Country	Proposal I	Proposal II	Proposal III	Proposal IV	Proposal V
Afghanistan	In force	In force	In force	In force	Accepted
Albania	--	--	--	--	--
Argentina	In force*	In force*	Bill drafted for Parliament	In force*	[a]
Australia	In force*	In force*	In force*	In force*	Accepted
Austria	--	--	--	--	--
Belgium	In force*	In force*	In force*	In force*	Accepted
Bolivia	In force*	In force*	In force*	In force*	Accepted
Bulgaria	In force*	In force*	In force*	In force*	Accepted
Canada	In force*	In force*	In force*	In force*	Accepted
Chile	In force*	In force	In force[b]	In force	Accepted
China	In force	In force	In force	In force	Accepted
Colombia	In force*	In force*	In force*	In force*	Accepted
Cuba	In force*	In force*	In force*	In force*	Under consideration
Czechoslovakia	In force*	In force*	In force*	In force*	Accepted
Denmark	In force*	In force*	In force*	In force*	Accepted
Dominican Republic	In force*	In force*	In force*	In force*	Accepted
Ecuador	In force	In force	In force	In force	Under consideration
Estonia	In force*	In force*	In force*	In force*	Accepted
Finland	In force*	In force[c]	In force*	In force*	Accepted
France	In force*	In force*	In force*	In force*	Accepted
Greece	In force*	In force*	In force*	In force*	Accepted
Guatemala	Accepted in principle	Accepted in principle	Accepted in principle	Accepted in principle	Accepted
Haiti	In force	In force	In force	In force	Accepted
Honduras	In force	In force*	In force	In force	Accepted
Hungary	--	--	--	--	--
India	In force*	In force*	In force*	In force*	Accepted
Iran	In force*	In force*	In force*	In force*	Accepted
Iraq	In force*	In force*	In force*	In force*	Accepted
Irish Free State	In force*	In force*	In force*	In force*	Accepted
Latvia	In force*	In force*	In force*	In force*	Accepted
Liberia	In force*	In force*	In force*	In force*	Accepted

Lithuania	In force*	In force*	In force*	In force*	Accepted
Luxembourg	In force*	In force*	In force*	In force*	Accepted
Mexico	In force*	In force*	In force*	In force*	Accepted
Netherlands	In force*	In force*	In force*	In force*	Accepted
New Zealand	In force*	In force*	In force*	In force*	Accepted
Nicaragua	In force*	Before Parliament	Before Parliament	Before Parliament	a
Norway	In force*	In force*	In force*	In force*	Accepted
Panama	In force	Will take necessary measures	Will take necessary measures	Will take necessary measures	Accepted
Paraguay	--	--	--	--	--
Peru	In force*	In force*	Will be enforced*[d]	In force*	Under consideration
Poland	In force*	In force*	In force*	In force*	Accepted
Portugal	In force*	In force*	In force*	In force*	Accepted
Romania	In force*	In force*	In force*	In force*	Accepted
Salvador	Accepted in principle but considered unnecessary to apply	Accepted in principle but considered unnecessary to apply	In force*	Accepted in principle but considered unnecessary to apply	Accepted
Siam	In force*	In force*	In force*	In force*	Accepted
Spain	In force*	In force*	In force*	In force*	Accepted
Sweden	In force*	In force[c]	In force*	In force*	Accepted
Switzerland	In force*	In force*	--	In force*	a
Turkey	In force*	In force*	In force*	In force*	Accepted
Union of South Africa	In force*	In force*	In force*	In force*	Accepted
Union of Soviet Socialist Republics					
United Kingdom	In force*	In force*	In force*	In force*	Accepted
Uruguay	In force*	Before Parliament	Before Parliament	In force*	Accepted
Venezuela	In force*	Under consideration	Under consideration	Under consideration	Accepted
Yugoslavia	In force*	In force*	In force*	In force*	Accepted

*Texts have reached Geneva.
[a]Reply not quite explicit.
[b]With exception of imports arising from clearing operations.
[c]The governments of Finland and Sweden have put Proposal II into force by administrative measures and in consequence no legislative texts have been received.
[d]For goods having left Italy after February 20, 1936.

Source: Second Report of the Committee of Experts, February 1, 1936, League of Nations, Official Journal: Coordination Committee: Minutes of Committee of Experts, Special Supplement no. 148, 33.

The Hoare-Laval pact demoralized the League.

> With the publication of the French-British plan,
> all the ground thus gained, and much more, was
> lost in a few hours. The relief in Germany, the
> dismay in America, were unmistakable. The effect
> on the members of the League and on their capacity
> for collective resistance to aggression was still
> more crushing.[149]

But, when Eden replaced Samuel Hoare as Foreign Secretary
on December 22, a glimmer of hope flickered and there was
some belief that the sanctions were beginning to achieve
results.[150]

In February a special Coordination Committee subcommittee of petroleum experts unanimously concluded that
Italy's petroleum resources would be exhausted in three to
four months and that even with imports from the United
States, the effectiveness of the embargo would not be
diminished significantly. Unfortunately the impetus had
been lost, and members shuffled the report into limbo.
Meetings and more meetings were held during March 1936,
and in April there was even some talk of additional sanctions. But events in Ethiopia had reached their conclusion.

On May 5, Marshal Pietro Badoglio's mechanized columns
entered Addis Ababa. Mussolini proclaimed the founding of
the Fascist Empire on May 9, and two days later the League
Council met. The Council resolved to maintain its resistance for a period (a sense of mourning prevailed for a
respectable month); and on June 30, 1936, the League Assembly met in a "mood of ill humour and discouragement"[151] to
put _fini_ to the sanctions experiment. On July 4 the Coordination Committee met for the last time and voted to remove the sanctions, effective July 15, 1936. With a whim-
per the League began its descent into oblivion.

SANCTIONS: AN ASSESSMENT

Fundamentally, the only thing remaining is to attempt
to assess whether the elaborate sanctions scheme constructed
by the League of Nations had any impact upon Italy. Herbert Feis, in a brief note on the sanctions, remarked:

> The sanctions that were put into force did not
> seriously interfere with the Italian conquest
> of Ethiopia nor deeply disturb its economic life.

They were neither universal, extensive, nor prolonged enough to do so.[152]

To this observation must be added the proverbial grain of
salt because, as will become clear, there was evidence of
two trends in Italy during 1935-36. First, there was some
evidence of an inflationary trend in the economy (Tables
3.5, 3.10, 3.11, 3.14).* Second, there was evidence of a
broad economic slowdown during 1936, that is, the rate of
change in various indexes was either downward or, at best,
marginally upward (Tables 3.4, 3.7, 3.8, 3.9). There are
two possible explanations for this apparent slowdown in
the economy: the sanctions were having an impact or Italy
was entering a minor postwar depression. While this latter
factor might be one element in explaining the apparent
sluggishness in the Italian economy in 1936, it is difficult to sustain because Italy maintained a state of full
war preparedness at least until the capture of Addis Ababa
in May, and probably for a period thereafter to combat guerrillas. (There was also the Spanish expedition.)
    Figures 3.2 and 3.3 clearly display major declines for
the period 1934-36. Exports reached their lowest level in
1934, climbed marginally in 1935 and climbed further in
1936. Imports reached their lowest level in 1936, doubtless reflecting the impact of the League sanctions on Italy.
The index from which the import-export graphs were derived
provides an even more striking illustration of the impact
of League sanctions on Italian imports. Between 1935 (51.3)
and 1936 (54.3), exports increased by three points on the
index while imports decreased from 66.3 (1935) to 51.7
(1936), a 14.3-point decline after only six months of somewhat indifferently applied economic sanctions. The pre-
cariousness of the Italian import-export trade may also be
noted in the rather insignificant alterations in inports
and exports of gold and specie for 1936 (Tables 3.2 and
3.3). There is no doubt, therefore, that Italian trade
was affected by the League's sanctions, but two essential
questions remain: What repercussion, if any, did this
have upon the Italian domestic economy? If there had been

------

*Unfortunately, some significant information is not
available. Thus, real disposable per capita income, components of real disposable income, and output per person
employed (generally and by sectors) are not available. This
information would have provided a basis for determining the
possible rate of inflation during the period in question.

FIGURE 3.2

Italy: Exports, 1931-38

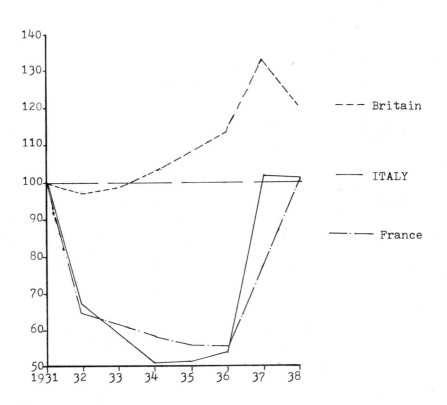

Source: League of Nations.

a repercussion, could it have affected Mussolini sufficiently to deter his continued aggression in Ethiopia?

Obviously a number of factors are at issue on these
points. First, how stable was the Italian economy? Second, was it in any manner vulnerable to particular sanc-
tions--that is, was the economy weak in any major respect?
Third, to what extent was Mussolini committed to his actions in Ethiopia? Fourth, would it be possible for eco-

nomic sanctions to achieve a sufficient result within a
relatively short time? Fifth, what other factors, political or economic, might intervene to dilute or thwart the
intent of sanctions? These and numerous ancillary questions can be answered more adequately in retrospect than
was possible in 1935 and 1936. But, to answer some of them,
consider a comment from one apparently jaundiced but nevertheless accurate observer. The Italian government,

> like many others during the early 1930s, had in-
> stituted import restrictions as depression mea-
> sures. Once, therefore, the League declared sanc-
> tions against Italy, already existing machinery

FIGURE 3.3

Italy: Imports, 1931-38

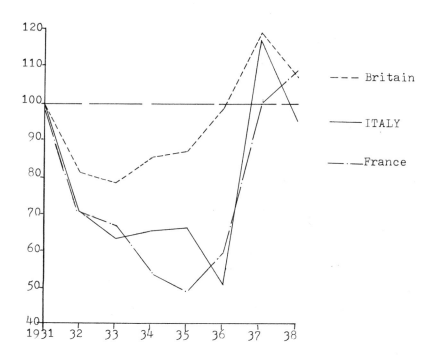

Source: League of Nations.

111

TABLE 3.2

Exports: Bullion and Specie, 1931-38
(change over preceding year; 1931 = 100)

Year	France	Britain	Italy
1931	100	100	100
1932	75.3	100.4	85.1
1933	346.0	47.0	429.1
1934	390.0	101.1	1,068.5
1935	763.5	163.8	22.8
1936	798.0	74.9	12.5
1937	917.2	161.3	64.0
1938	373.0	237.3	27.4

Source: League of Nations, Statistical Yearbook, 1939-1940.

TABLE 3.3

Imports: Bullion and Specie, 1931-38
(change over preceding year; 1931 = 100)

Year	France	Britain	Italy
1931	100	100	100
1932	108.1	149.9	50.7
1933	80.5	245.5	370.6
1934	30.5	266.8	18.9
1935	58.1	266.8	9.9
1936	31.7	310.5	10.2
1937	24.2	295.5	0.1
1938	40.0	241.5	0.4

Source: League of Nations, Statistical Yearbook, 1939-1940.

could operate to apply even more stringent restrictions. The government then paralleled this device with a rigidly enforced system of price controls upon articles of general consumption. Four other circumstances aided Mussolini even more importantly in weathering the crisis: the period of sanctions did not last long enough to harm Italy's economy irreparably; the vital supply of oil had never ceased to flow; 27 nations kept trading with Italy; and finally, the war against Ethiopia moved rapidly.[153]

The Italian economy was functionally quite stable, although its economic base was about 50 percent dependent upon agriculture in the 1930s. However, between 1931 and 1941 agriculture was diminishing in favor of manufacturing and service industries.[154] Moreover, as suggested in Tables 3.6 and 3.14, the manufacturing and metallurgical sectors were comprehensive and diverse. Consequently, with the exception of petroleum, Italy was not an excessively vulnerable country in 1935-36; and with the collapse of the League's petroleum sanction, even this weakness posed few problems.

On the matter of Mussolini's commitment to aggression, few descriptions can adequately depict either the intensity or the apparent historical significance of his dream of empire. The entire fascist regime was dependent upon the Ethiopian conquest; and presumably, if the sanctions had succeeded, Mussolini and fascism might have collapsed.

Obviously the Hoare-Laval agreement provides a major clue to the intensity of opposition by major League members to Mussolini. The desire by France to protect its rear flank in order more directly to face Germany explains not only the Hoare-Laval agreement but also the rapidity and ease with which the major powers allowed themselves to be bailed out of League obligations. To this must be added the inability of the smaller states to effectively maintain an initiative against Italy,[155] as well as the lack of incentive on the part of countries just emerging from devastating economic calamity.

Finally there was the question of time. It has been noted earlier, and will be repeated below, especially in the Rhodesian case, that time is a crucial factor. Sanctions require time to be effective. And any achievement in the time allotted to the Italian situation would have had to be gained either by supplying Ethiopia with large quantities of arms or by restricting transport of Italian arms to the battle zone—for example, by restricting passage through the Suez Canal. Neither of the major League powers was prepared to follow these courses.

The following pages contain a series of statistical tables that provide some insight into the impact of the sanctions on the Italian economy in 1936, the crucial year.

Generally the materials suggest that 1936 was a year of declining economic activity relative to 1935 and 1937. A slight increase in the index of employment in industry (Table 3.4) coupled, for example, with a substantial rise in the wholesale price index (Table 3.10), suggest that the focus of productivity was being directed into more labor-intensive industries while some inflation was occurring. This is further supported by the relatively large increase in the index of wages (Table 3.5) while the general index of industrial production declined (Table 3.6).

TABLE 3.4

Index of Employment in Industry, 1929-39
(percent change from preceding year; 1929 = 100)

Year	Italy		Selected States Combined, Average	Difference, Italy Versus Average
	Index	Percent Change		
1929	100.0	--	--	--
1930	97.3	-2.7	-9.7	+7.0
1931	88.8	-8.5	-9.6	+1.1
1932	78.5	-10.3	-9.2	-1.1
1933	79.2	+0.7	+3.1	-2.4
1934	82.9	+3.7	+7.5	-3.8
1935	94.0	+11.1	+3.7	+7.4
1936	94.9	+0.9	+6.1	-5.2
1937	104.5	+9.6	+8.0	+1.6
1938	110.7	+6.2	-0.3	+5.9
1939	113.3	+2.6	+6.0	-3.4

Note: The five states selected for creation of a comparative index were Hungary, France, Germany, United States, and Great Britain.

Source: League of Nations, Statistical Yearbook, 1939/40 (Geneva: League of Nations, 1940), p. 73.

TABLE 3.5

Index Numbers of Wages, 1929-38
(index change from preceding year)

Year	Italy		Selected States Combined, Average	Difference, Italy Versus Average (above/below)
	Index	Percent Change		
1929	100	--	--	--
1930	99	-1	-.4	-.6
1931	93	-6	-5.2	-.8
1932	91	-2	-6.0	+4.0
1933	89	-2	-4.2	+2.2
1934	86	-3	-1.2	-1.8
1935	85	-1	-1.0	--
1936	90	+5	+.8	-.3
1937	101	+11	+3.8	+7.2
1938	108	+7	+5.2	+1.8

Note: The states were Netherlands, Norway, Poland, Great Britain, and Romania.

Source: League of Nations, Statistical Yearbook, 1939/40 (Geneva: The League, 1940), p. 77.

Two capital-investment-related industries (cement, Table 3.7, and steel, Table 3.8) show significant declines in Italy in 1936 with recoveries in 1937. This is in contrast with the situation in comparable countries (Germany, France, Britain), where increases in production were recorded for almost all years after 1932. Translating this economic slowdown into other terms, it seems apparent from

TABLE 3.6

Index Numbers of Industrial Production: Italy, 1929-38
(1928 = 100)

	General Index	Chemicals	Mines	Engineering	Textiles	Paper	Construction	Metallurgy
1929	109	na	na	104	102	107	140	111
1930	100	na	na	95	91	106	131	93
1931	85	na	na	83	82	99	88	79
1932	73	na	na	71	67	103	79	73
1933	81	na	na	72	76	111	93	88
1934	87	na	na	75	74	121	136	92
1935	102	100	99	102	77	140	162	112
1936	96	107	110	120	70	123	92	106
1937	109	133	128	132	84	150	96	114
1938	108	130	135	134	83	143	91	121

na = not available

Source: League of Nations, Statistical Yearbook, 1939/40 (Geneva: The League, 1940), p. 173. Statistics were supplied by the Italian Ministero delle Corporazioni.

TABLE 3.7

Cement Production, Selected Countries, 1930-38
(1,000 metric tons)

	Italy	Germany and Saar	France	Britain
1930	3,482	5,672	4,989	5,111
1931	3,018-	3,837-	5,547+	4,969-
1932	3,125+	2,888-	5,714+	4,320-
1933	3,554+	3,931+	5,221-	4,470+
1934	4,092+	6,625+	4,872-	5,674+
1935	4,196+	8,807+	4,371-	6,054+
1936	3,859-	11,689+	4,638+	6,700+
1937	4,258+	12,605+	4,285-	7,300+
1938	4,587+	15,600+	--	7,900+

Source: League of Nations, Statistical Yearbook, 1939/40 (Geneva: The League, 1940), p. 127.

TABLE 3.8

Steel Production, Selected Countries, 1930-38
(ingots and castings, 1,000 metric tons)

	Italy	Germany, Saar (s), Austria (a)	France	Britain
1930	1,743	11,371	9,444	7,443
1931	1,409-	8,176-	7,816-	5,286-
1932	1,396-	5,624-	5,638-	5,346+
1933	1,771+	7,453+	6,577+	7,137+
1934	1,832+	11,696+	6,155-	8,992+
1935	2,212+	16,144+(s)	6,255+	10,017+
1936	2,026-	18,756+(s)	6,686+	11,974+
1937	2,099+	19,356+(s)	7,920+	13,192+
1938	2,307+	23,208+(s,a)	6,174+	10,565-

Source: League of Nations, Statistical Yearbook, 1939/40 (Geneva: The League, 1940), p. 145.

TABLE 3.9

Index of Automobile Production, 1929-38
(percent change over previous year; 1929 = 100)

Year	Italy Index	Italy Percent Change	Index, Average	Italy, Above/Below
1929	100.0	--	--	--
1930	80.0	-20.0	-22.2	+2.2
1931	43.3	-36.7	-17.0	-19.3
1932	48.6	+5.3	-9.8	+15.1
1933	69.6	+21.0	+14.3	+6.7
1934	74.7	+5.1	+19.5	-14.4
1935	82.0	+7.3	+21.3	-14.0
1936	85.1	+3.1	+14.7	-11.6
1937	125.2	+40.1	+12.0	+28.1
1938	115.2	-10.0	-13.0	-3.0

Note: Index based upon average production in Germany, Canada, United States, France, and Britain.

Source: League of Nations, Statistical Yearbook, 1939/40 (Geneva: The League, 1940), p. 165.

TABLE 3.10

Wholesale Price Indexes: Italy and Selected Countries, 1929-38
(1929 = 100)

Year	Italy Index	Italy Index Change from Previous Year	Selected States, Index Change from Previous Year	Italy, Percent Change from Previous Year	Selected States, Percent Change from Previous Year
1929	100.0	--	--	--	--
1930	89.5	-10.5	-12.0	-10.5	-12.0
1931	78.1	-11.4	-9.5	-12.8	-10.7
1932	73.0	-5.1	-7.4	-6.6	-9.5
1933	66.5	-6.5	-4.0	-9.0	-5.7
1934	65.0	-1.5	-0.2	-2.3	-0.7
1935	71.5	+6.5	+0.5	+9.1	+1.1
1936	80.1	+8.6	+4.2	+10.8	+6.0
1937	93.1	+13.0	+11.6	+14.0	+14.1
1938	100.3	+7.2	-.3	+7.2	-0.6

Note: Selected States Index based upon aggregated indexes of Germany, France, Hungary, Netherlands, and the United Kingdom.

Source: League of Nations, Statistical Yearbook, 1931/40 (Geneva: The League, 1940), pp. 206, 207.

TABLE 3.11

Cost-of-Living Indexes: Italy and Selected Countries, 1929-38
(1929 = 100)

Year	Month	Italy	Hungary	Germany	France	Britain	Switzer-land
1929		100.0	100.0	100.0	100.0	100.0	100.0
1930		96.6	90.5	96.2	104.5	96.3	98.1
1931		87.3	85.7	88.4	102.3	89.9	93.2
1932		83.1	83.3	78.3	94.6	87.8	85.7
1933		79.6	77.3	76.6	93.5	85.4	81.4
1934	March	78.6	75.3	77.9	94.6	84.8	80.8
1934	June	73.5	77.0	78.3	93.9	86.0	80.1
1934	September	73.4	76.1	79.0	91.9	87.2	80.1
1934	December	74.5	75.1	79.4	90.7	87.2	80.1
1935	March	74.5	76.2	79.4	88.9	84.8	78.9
1935	June	76.4	76.8	79.9	88.1	87.2	78.9
1935	September	76.8	79.4	80.2	84.4	88.4	80.1
1935	December	80.6	79.5	80.2	86.0	89.6	80.7
1936	March	81.0	81.6	80.6	87.4	87.8	80.7
1936	June	82.9	81.3	80.8	89.4	89.0	80.7
1936	September	82.6	82.6	80.7	90.6	90.2	80.7
1936	December	85.0	83.2	80.7	91.2	92.1	82.0
1937		90.7	87.3	81.2	111.3	93.9	84.9
1938		98.0	87.8	81.6	125.5	95.1	85.1

Source: League of Nations, Statistical Yearbook, 1939/40 (Geneva: The League, 1940), pp. 209, 210.

the index of automobile production (Table 3.9) that Italy
was lagging well behind all other producing countries in
this item.

Table 3.11, which presents cost-of-living indexes,
is significant because it suggests long-term inflationary
trends in Italy, as the following table on the rates of
change in the cost-of-living index shows.

	Italy	Hun-gary	Ger-many	France	Brit-ain	Swit-zerland
October 1935						
to June 1936	+2.3	+1.8	+.6	+3.4	−.6	0
1935 and 1936	+10.5	+7.0	+1.3	+2.3	+7.3	+3.1
1934 to 1938	+19.4	+12.5	+3.7	+30.9	+10.3	+4.3

Source: Table 3.11.

Only France exceeded Italy in rate of inflation for the period 1934-38, but in the crucial period 1935-36 Italy was
highest. Once again this suggests movement into labor-
intensive industries with fixed, if not diminished, wages.

Table 3.12, in relation to Tables 3.2 and 3.3, provides further evidence of the precarious state of the
Italian balance of payments in 1934-36. Clearly the large
depletion of gold between 1933 and 1935 is attributable to
war preparation. One example of this may be viewed in
Italian and "Italian African" trade statistics with the
United States (Table 3.13).[156] Herbert Feis concludes:
"The rise in exports to Italian Africa was concentrated in
the second half of 1935 and plainly was for the Italian military operations."[157] Substantial commodity purchases from
the United States seem to explain, in large measure, the
rapid decline in gold and exchange reserves. The remaining information (Tables 3.14, 3.15, and 3.16) is included
to provide broad-based views of the Italian economy.
Table 3.14, with a series of increases in productivity in
various raw materials, suggests that the Italian economy
was moving toward a more credible industrial base.[158]

It can be fairly readily ascertained that at least
for the early part of 1936--that is, during the period of
League sanctions--the Italian economy suffered. However,
it was not even a near-fatal blow, partly because the economy was diverse (hence somewhat flexible) and because the
sanctions were undermined by states fundamentally unwilling to lose potential Italian support on the European
scene. The League sanctions scheme was by far the most
complex ever developed by an international organization;

TABLE 3.12

Gold and Foreign Assets Reserves*: Italy, 1931-39
(million lira)

Year	Gold	Exchange
1931	5,626	2,170
1932	5,839	1,305
1933	7,092	305
1934	5,811	72
1935	3,027	367
1936	3,959	63
1937	3,996	32
1938	3,674	152
1939	2,738	393

*This table is based on the League of Nations source cited below. The note on parity was in the original and is thus included here. Presumably the Italian government altered the ratio of gold to lira to combat a deflationary trend in the economy. This has statistical advantages as well because such an alteration would tend to obscure significant statistical index changes.

Note: In 1936 Italy altered its legal gold parity.

Source: League of Nations, Statistical Yearbook, 1939/40 (Geneva: The League, 1940), p. 214.

TABLE 3.13

American Trade with Italy and Italian Africa, 1934-36

Total American Trade with Italy
(million current dollars)

	Exports to Italy	Imports from Italy
1934	64.6	35.7
1935	73.4	38.7
1936	59.0	40.3

Total American Trade with Italian Africa
(1,000 current dollars)

	Exports to Africa	Imports from Africa
1934	276	213
1935	4,558	214
1936	771	224

American Exports to Italy and Italian Africa
(1,000 current dollars)

	Italy	Italian Africa
October 1934	6,226	45
November 1934	8,445	18
December 1934	4,821	4
January 1935	6,257	20
August 1935	na	1,704
September 1935	na	508
October 1935	6,529	363
November 1935	9,125	590
December 1925	7,944	374
January 1936	5,420	22

na = not available

Source: H. Feis, Seen from E.A.: Three International Episodes (New York: Norton, 1966), pp. 307,350.

122

TABLE 3.14

Italy: Production, 1930–38

Year	Natural Gas Consumed (million cubic meters)	Coal (all types)	Py-rites	Sul-fur	Sul-furic Acid	Man-ganese Ore	Iron Ore	Pig Iron
1930	8.7	808	717	370	831	3.7	359	588
1931	12.1	600	646	374	633	2.3	285[b]	554
1932	12.9	631	517	375	562	0.1	214	495
1933	13.8	717	733	402	678	1.6	264	567
1934	15.0	783	812	366	818	2.5	252	582
1935	12.0	998	833	331	858	3.3	286	704
1936	13.0	1,575	865	349	1,021	8.9	449	828
1937	15.7	2,023	915	364	1,094	12.0	530[b]	874
1938	17.0	2,282	930	397	1,150[b]	15.0	520	929

(continued)

123

TABLE 3.14 (continued)

Year	Steel	Cop-per	Lead Ore	Lead	Zinc Ore	Zinc	Bauxite Crude Ore	Aluminum
1930	1,743	0.3	29.9	24.3	79.6	19.3	161.2	8.0
1931	1,409	0.7	24.1	24.9	47.1	16.9	67.4	11.1
1932	1,396	0.4	21.6	31.5	32.2	18.0	86.6	13.4
1933	1,771	0.1	17.9	26.4[c]	29.1	23.3	94.8	12.1
1934	1,832	0.5	19.1	53.7[c]	46.1	24.9	131.3	12.8
1935	2,212	0.1	24.8	50.7[c]	62.2	28.4[c]	170.1	13.8
1936	2,026	0.5	40.4	48.1[c]	69.7	28.4[c]	262.2	15.9
1937	2,099	1.5	35.0[b]	46.7[c]	80.0[b]	38.0	386.5	22.9
1938	2,307	3.0	40.0[b]	50.7[c]	88.0[b]	33.7[c]	360.8	25.8

Year	Tung-sten	Cad-mium	Anti-mony Ore	Quick-silver	Molyb-denum Ore	Silver	Gold (Italy) (kilos)	Gold (Eritrea)[b] (kilos)
1930	--	--	413	1,933	--	15.7	92	--
1931	--	8	336	1,298	--	13.6	77	6
1932	--	6	378	1,016	--	12.2	58	59
1933	--	7	364	607	--	10.7	85	123
1934	--	8	361	441	--	12.2[b]	106	250
1935	1	16	461	972	--	15.6	121	134
1936	4	55	493	1,473	9	19.6[b]	237	78
1937	2	91	610	2,308	--	22.2[b]	208[b]	na
1938	3	59	925	2,301	--	25.5[b]	385[b]	na

na = not available.

[a]Excluding output of state powder works.
[b]Estimated.
[c]Includes small amounts of secondary recovery.

Note: Amounts are 1,000 metric tons unless otherwise indicated.

Source: League of Nations, Statistical Yearbook, 1939/40 (Geneva: The League, 1940), pp. 136-61.

125

TABLE 3.15

Italy: Commercial Bank Deposits, 1931-37
(million lira)

	1931	1932	1933	1934	1935	1936	1937
Deposit accounts	19,789	19,808	20,351	20,311	20,614	22,613	24,053
Current accounts	4,611	4,434	5,093	4,949	4,996	4,733	5,742
Savings	8,917	8,967	8,641	8,612	8,586	11,269	11,268
Fixed deposits	5,614	5,739	5,986	6,009	6,208	6,135	6,499
Deposits in securities	647	668	631	741	824	476	544
Correspondent creditors	21,717	19,782	18,847	18,029	15,165	18,426	18,664
Total	61,295	59,398	59,549	58,651	56,393	63,652	66,770

Source: League of Nations, Statistical Yearbook, 1939/40 (Geneva: The League, 1940), p. 232.

TABLE 3.16

Italy: Savings Bank Deposits and Savings Certificates, 1931-38
(million lira)

	1931	1932	1933	1934	1935	1936	1937	1938
Savings accounts	29,755	32,627	36,004	37,282	36,121	39,242	43,023	44,982
Post office savings bank	14,547	16,883	19,263	20,295	19,826	22,188	25,398	27,907
Savings banks	15,208	15,744	16,741	16,987	16,295	17,054	17,625	17,075
Other deposits*	3,102	3,132	2,923	2,717	2,434	1,814	1,504	1,326
Post office savings bank	129	133	139	132	131	121	125	117
Savings banks	2,973	2,999	2,784	2,585	2,303	1,693	1,379	1,209
Total	32,857	35,759	38,927	39,999	38,555	41,056	44,527	46,308

*Judicial deposits, ordinary savings banks.

Source: League of Nations, Statistical Yearbook, 1939/40 (Geneva: The League, 1940), p. 237.

that it crumbled was not the fault of the scheme so much as it was a collapse of spirit. More will be said when a final overview is set forth in Chapter 6.

APPENDIX 3.A: TEXT OF THE PROPOSALS, DECISIONS AND RESOLUTIONS ADOPTED BY THE CO-ORDINATION COMMITTEE AND THE COMMITTEE OF EIGHTEEN

Mutual Support

Declaration Adopted by the Co-ordination Committee on October 14th, 1935[159]

With a view to facilitating for the Governments of the Members of the League of Nations the execution of their obligations under Article 16 of the Covenant, it is recognised that any proposals for action under Article 16 are made on the basis of the following provisions of that article:

> "The Members of the League agree, further, that they will mutually support one another in the financial and economic measures which are taken under this article, in order to minimise the loss and inconvenience resulting from the above measures, and that they will mutually support one another in resisting any special measures aimed at one of their number by the Covenant breaking state."

EXECUTION OF OBLIGATIONS WHICH FLOW FROM ARTICLE 16 OF THE COVENANT

Resolution Adopted by the Co-ordination Committee on October 16th, 1935[160]

The Committee of Co-ordination,
Considering that it is important to ensure rapid and effective application of the measures which have been and may subsequently be proposed by the Committee;
Considering that it rests with each country to apply these measures in accordance with its public law and, in

128

particular, the powers of its Government in regard to execution of treaties:

Calls attention to the fact that the Members of the League, being bound by the obligations which flow from Article 16 of the Covenant, are under a duty to take the necessary steps to enable them to carry out these obligations with all requisite rapidity.

APPENDIX 3.B: PROPOSAL NO. 1

Adopted by the Co-ordination Committee
on October 11th, 1935[161]

Export of Arms, Ammunition and Implements of War

With a view to facilitating for the Governments of the Members of the League of Nations the execution of their obligations under Article 16 of the Covenant, the following measures should be taken forthwith:

(1) The Governments of the Members of the League of Nations which are enforcing at the moment measures to prohibit or restrict the exportation, re-exportation or transit of arms, munitions and implements of war to Ethiopia will annul these measures immediately;

(2) The Governments of the Members of the League of Nations will prohibit immediately the exportation, re-exportation or transit to Italy or Italian possessions of arms, munitions and implements of war enumerated in the attached list;

(3) The Governments of the Members of the League of Nations will take such steps as may be necessary to secure that arms, munitions and implements of war, enumerated in the attached list, exported to countries other than Italy will not be re-exported directly or indirectly to Italy or to Italian possessions;

(4) The measures provided for in paragraphs 2 and 3 are to apply to contracts in process of execution.

Each Government is requested to inform the Committee, through the Secretary-General of the League, within the shortest possible time of the measures which it has taken in conformity with the above provisions.

Annex

List of Articles, Considered as Arms, Ammunition and
Implements of War, Adopted by the Co-ordination
Committee on October 11th, 1935[161]

Category I
    1. Rifles and carbines using ammunition in excess of
calibre 26.5 and their barrels.
    2. Machine-guns; automatic rifles and machine-pistols
of all calibres and their barrels.
    3. Guns, howitzers and mortars of all calibres, their
mountings and barrels.
    4. Ammunition for the arms under 1 and 2 above--i.e.,
high power steel jacketed ammunition in excess of calibre
26.5; filled and unfilled projectiles, and propellants with
a web thickness of 0.015 inch or greater for the projectiles
of the arms enumerated under 3 above.
    5. Grenades, bombs, torpedoes and mines, filled or
unfilled, and apparatus for their use or discharge.
    6. Tanks, military armoured vehicles and armoured
trains.

Category II
    Vessels of war of all kinds, including aircraft-car-
riers and submarines.

Category III
    1. Aircraft, assembled or dismantled, both heavier
and lighter than air, which are designed, adapted and intended for aerial combat by the use of machine-guns or of
artillery, or for the carrying and dropping of bombs, or
which are equipped with, or which by reason of design or
construction are prepared for, any of the appliances referred to in paragraph 2 below.
    2. Aerial-gun mounts and frames, bomb-racks, torpedo-
carriers, and bomb or torpedo release mechanisms.

Category IV
    Revolvers and automatic pistols of a weight in excess
of 1 lb. 6 oz. (630 grammes) using ammunition in excess of
calibre 26.5 and ammunition therefor.

Category V
    1. Aircraft assembled or dismantled, both heavier
and lighter than air, other than those included in Category
III.

2. Propellers or air-screws, fuselages, hulls, tail units and under-carriage units.
3. Aircraft-engines.

Category VI
1. Livens projectors and flame-throwers.
2. Mustard gas, Lewisite, ethyldichlorarsine and methyldichlorarsine.
3. Powder and explosives.

PROPOSAL NO. IA

Adopted by the Co-ordination Committee on October 16th, 1935
The Text of the Proposal is the same as that of
Proposal No. I (see page 129)[162]

Annex

Amended List of Articles Considered as Arms, Ammunition
and Implements of War, Adopted by the Co-ordination
Committee on October 16th, 1935,[163] in Substitution
for the First List Attached to Proposal No. I

Category I
1. Rifles and carbines and their barrels.
2. Machine-guns, automatic rifles and machine-pistols of all calibres and their barrels.
3. Guns, howitzers and mortars of all calibres, their mountings, barrels and recoil mechanisms.
4. Ammunition for the arms enumerated under 1 and 2 above; filled and unfilled projectiles for the arms enumerated under 3 above, and prepared propellant charges for these arms.
5. Grenades, bombs, torpedoes and mines, filled or unfilled, and apparatus for their use or discharge.
6. Tanks, armoured vehicles and armoured trains. Armour-plate of all kinds.

Category II
Vessels of war of all kinds, including aircraft-carriers and submarines..

Category III
    1. Aircraft, assembled or dismantled, both heavier
and lighter than air, and their propellers or air-screws,
fuselages, aerial gun-mounts and frames, hulls, tail units
and under-carriage units.
    2. Aircraft-engines.

Category IV
    Revolvers and automatic pistols of a weight in excess
of 1 lb. 6 oz. (630 grammes) and ammunition therefor.

Category V
    1. Flame-throwers and all other projectors used for
chemical or incendiary warfare.[164]
    2. Mustard gas, Lewisite, ethyldichlorarsine, methyl-
dichlorarsine, and all other products destined for chemical
or incendiary warfare.[164]
    3. Powder for war purposes, and explosives.

PROPOSAL NO. II

Adopted by the Co-ordination Committee on
October 14th, 1935[165]

Financial Measures

    With a view to facilitating for the Governments of
the Members of the League of Nations the execution of their
obligations under Article 16 of the Covenant, the following
measures should be taken forthwith:
    The Governments of the Members of the League of
Nations will forthwith take all measures necessary to
render impossible the following operations:

        (1) All loans to or for the Italian Gov-
    ernment and all subscriptions to loans issued
    in Italy or elsewhere by or for the Italian
    Government;
        (2) All banking or other credits to or
    for the Italian Government and any further ex-
    ecution by advance, overdraft or otherwise of
    existing contracts to lend directly or indi-
    rectly to the Italian Government;

132

(3) All loans to or for any public authority, person or corporation in Italian territory and all subscriptions to such loans issued in Italy or elsewhere;

(4) All banking or other credits to or for any public authority, person or corporation in Italian territory and any further execution by advance, overdraft or otherwise of existing contracts to lend directly or indirectly to such authority, person or corporation;

(5) All issues of shares or other capital flotations for any public authority, person or corporation in Italian territory and all subscriptions to such issues of shares or capital flotations in Italy or elsewhere;

(6) The Governments will take all measures necessary to render impossible the transactions mentioned in paragraphs (1) to (5), whether effected directly or through intermediaries of whatsoever nationality.

The Governments are invited to put in operation at once such of the measures recommended as can be enforced without fresh legislation, and to take all practicable steps to secure that the measures recommended are completely put into operation by October 31st, 1935. Any Governments which find it impossible to secure the requisite legislation by that date are requested to inform the Committee, through the Secretary-General, of the date by which they expect to be able to do so.

Each Government is requested to inform the Committee, through the Secretary-General of the League, within the shortest possible time of the measures which it has taken in conformity with the above provisions.

Resolution Adopted by the Co-ordination Committee on
November 2nd, 1935[166]

The Co-ordination Committee notes that thirty-nine Governments of Members of the League of Nations have taken or are taking measures with a view to rendering impossible those financial operations with Italy and Italian possessions defined in Proposal No. II adopted by the Committee on October 14th, and that ten other Governments have expressed their willingness to take such measures.

It requests all Governments to take steps in order that the measures contemplated in Proposal No. II may take full legal effect by or before November 18th.

Each Government which has not already sent a communication to this effect is requested to inform the Committee, through the Secretary-General of the League, within the shortest possible time, of the measures which it has taken in conformity with this resolution.

Outstanding Claims

Resolution Adopted by the Co-ordination Committee on
November 2nd, 1935[167]

The Members of the League of Nations participating in the measures taken in regard to Italy under Article 16 of the Covenant,

Having regard, in particular, to Proposal No. III, under which they have agreed to prohibit as from November 18th all imports consigned from Italy or her possessions:

I. Consider that the debts now payable by Italy to them, under clearing agreements or any other arrangements, the payment of which becomes impossible by reason of the aforesaid prohibition, will remain valid at their present value notwithstanding any offers of payment in kind that may be made by Italy or any action that might be taken by her against the creditor States;

II. Recognise:

(a) That, on the discontinuance of the measures taken in regard to Italy under Article 16 of the Covenant, they should support one another in order to ensure that Italy discharges her obligations to the creditor States as she should have done if she had not incurred the application of Article 16 of the Covenant;

(b) Furthermore, that, if in the meantime particularly serious losses are sustained by certain States owing to the suspension by Italy of the payment of the aforesaid debts, the mutual support provided for by paragraph 3 of Article 16 will be specially given in order to make good such losses by all appropriate measures.

The Committee on Mutual Support will draw up a list of the debts referred to in paragraph I above and will examine the measures contemplated in paragraph II (b) above.

PROPOSAL NO. II A

Adopted by the Committee of Eighteen on November 6th,
1935[168]

Clearing Agreements

The Committee of Eighteen,
Entrusted by the Co-ordination Committee with the task
of following the execution of the proposals submitted to
Governments and empowered to make such new proposals as it
may think desirable, proposes that the following measures
should be taken:
In order to render effective the application of
Proposal No. II (4) and Proposal No. III, approved by
the Committee of Co-ordination, Governments represented
on the Co-ordination Committee will:
I. (a) Prohibit, as from November 18th, the
acceptance of any new deposit of lire into the
Italian clearing account in payment for exports
to Italy, and, in consequence,
(b) Suspend to the extent necessary the operation of any clearing or payments agreement that
they may have with Italy by or before November
18th;
II. Take, if need be, the necessary steps
to ensure that the purchase price of Italian
products already imported, or to be imported, in
respect of which payment has not yet been made,
shall be lodged in a national account, the resources of which will, if necessary, be employed
for the settlement of claims arising from their
exports.
Each Government is requested to inform the Co-ordination Committee through the Secretary-General of the League,
within the shortest possible time, of the measures which
it has taken in conformity with the above provisions.

135

PROPOSAL NO. III

Adopted by the Co-ordination Committee on October
19th, 1935[169]

Prohibition of Importation of Italian Goods

With a view to facilitating for the Governments of the
Members of the League of Nations the execution of their obligations under Article 16 of the Covenant, the following
measures should be taken:

(1) The Governments of the Members of the League
of Nations will prohibit the importation into their
territories of all goods (other than gold or silver
bullion and coin) consigned from or grown, produced
or manufactured in Italy or Italian possessions, from
whatever place arriving;

(2) Goods grown or produced in Italy or Italian
possessions which have been subjected to some process
in another country, and goods manufactured partly in
Italy or Italian possessions and partly in another
country will be considered as falling within the scope
of the prohibition unless 25% or more of the value of
the goods at the time when they left the place from
which they were last consigned is attributable to processes undergone since the goods last left Italy or
Italian possessions;

(3) Goods the subject of existing contracts will
not be excepted from the prohibition;

(4) Goods en route at the time of imposition of
the prohibition will be excepted from its operation.
In giving effect to this provision, Governments may,
for convenience of administration, fix an appropriate
date, having regard to the normal time necessary for
transport from Italy, after which goods will become
subject to the prohibition;

(5) Personal belongings of travellers from Italy
or Italian possessions may also be excepted from its
operation.

Having regard to the importance of collective and, so
far as possible, simultaneous action in regard to the measures recommended, each Government is requested to inform
the Co-ordination Committee, through the Secretary-General,
as soon as possible, and not later than October 28th, of

136

the date on which it could be ready to bring these measures
into operation. The Co-ordination Committee will meet on
October 31st for the purpose of fixing, in the light of the
replies received, the date of the coming into force of the
said measures.

Annex

Report Submitted by the Legal Sub-Committee on the
Application of Sanctions and Private Contracts, Commercial
Treaties and Treaties of Friendship and Non-Aggression

The Legal Sub-Committee has been asked to advise as to
the legal consequences of paragraph (4) of the Proposal No.
I dealing with the embargo on arms and of paragraph (3) of
the draft proposal for a prohibition on the importation of
Italian goods.[170] These paragraphs relate to contracts in
progress of execution and prevent their being performed.

A first question which need only be mentioned is that
of the difficulties which may be produced between the Government of a Member of the League and a national or a person resident in its territory by the prohibition of the
performance of contracts in progress of execution. This
question will be settled by the internal public law of the
State concerned.

There are other questions which arise which have an
international character.

1. One such question is that of the position of an
Italian who has a contract with a national of a State which
participates in the sanctions, or with a person resident
in its territory, and who suffers loss owing to the sanctions preventing the contract from being performed.

If the Italian sues in the courts of that State, the
action will fail because prevention of the execution of
the contract is the result of a prohibition lawfully imposed.

If the suit is brought in the courts of the plaintiff
(whether in virtue of general rules of jurisdiction or a
special provision in the contract) and if the judgment is
for the plaintiff, the judgment cannot be executed in the
defendant's country because the requisite authority for
its execution will not be obtainable, even if claimed in
virtue of treaties, for the treaties could not override the
effect of Article 16 of the Covenant, which constitutes
the law by which the two States concerned are bound. If

it were to be possible for execution of the judgment to be
sought and obtained in the plaintiff's country, this would
have to be considered to be a breach of the international
obligations created by the Covenant.

Should the original claim, or the claim for execution
of a judgment, be brought before the courts of another State
which was participating in the sanctions, the same reason
should lead to their rejection.

The result would be the same if the claim was submitted
to arbitration.

Finally, the same result should follow if a State
should find a possibility of bringing the issue before an
international tribunal.

2. A second question of an international character
arises out of the existence of commercial treaties between
Italy and the States which participate in the sanctions.
Application of sanctions by a State having a commercial
treaty with Italy may, to a greater or lesser degree, prevent the execution of the treaty. Italy would, however,
have no legal right to complain, since the situation so
created would be the result of the provisions of the Covenant, which is legally binding on both Italy and the other
State and prevails over the treaty in question.

It may be asked whether, on the principle of reciprocity, Italy would, in the same way, have the right to withhold the execution of her obligations under the treaty or
to annul or suspend the performance of contracts in progress
of execution. Having regard to the essential fact in the
case--namely, that the Covenant, in virtue of which the
sanctions are taken, is binding both on Italy and on the
other Members of the League of Nations--the reply must be
that Italy would incur international liability by refusing
to carry out the commercial treaty or by annulling or suspending the performance of contracts in progress of execution.

3. Finally, there is the question of application of
treaties of friendship and non-aggression, which may have
been concluded between Italy and some of the Members of the
League of Nations, under which each contracting party un-
dertakes not to participate in any international _entente_
preventing purchase or sale of goods or provision of credits
from or to the other party.

. It may be asked whether application of economic and
financial sanctions against Italy by a Member of the League
which has such a treaty with Italy is compatible with the
obligations of the treaty. Since the contracting parties
are Members of the League, it is clear that the treaty must

be interpreted subject to Article 16 and 20 of the Covenant. It follows that application of sanctions by one of the contracting parties against the other is entirely legitimate, even if the treaty contains no reservation regarding the provisions of the Covenant or if one of the contracting parties was not a Member of the League of Nations at the moment when it concluded the treaty.

Contracts Fully Paid

Decision Taken by the Co-ordination Committee on November 2nd, 1935[171]

The Co-ordination Committee agreed to the proposal of the Committee of Eighteen that, as an exception to Proposal No. III, contracts for which payment had been made in full by October 19th, 1935, might be executed.

Contracts in Course of Execution

Resolution Adopted by the Committee of Eighteen on November 6th, 1935[172]

The Committee of Eighteen instructs a Sub-Committee consisting of representatives of the United Kingdom, France, Mexico, Poland, Roumania and the Union of Soviet Socialist Republics to make proposals to the interested Governments on its behalf in regard to those contracts--other than those in respect of which payment had been made in full by October 19th, 1935--which might be executed by way of exception to paragraph 3 of Proposal No. III.

In making its proposals, the Sub-Committee will be guided by the following principles:

(a) Exception to be made only in the case of contracts concluded by a State or institution belonging to a State or entirely subject to its administrative control, or for their account, prior to October 19th, 1935, which relate to goods of essential importance to the importing State;

(b) Not less than 20% of the total sums due under the contract to have been paid by October 19th, 1935;

(c) Contracts stipulating for payment in goods, the export of which to Italy is prohibited under Pro-

139

posal No. IV, not to have the benefit of the exception
in question;
   (d) Governments to furnish the Sub-Committee, not
later than November 10th, with the full details of
each contract (nature of goods, total sums due, amount
paid prior to October 19th, 1935, and amount outstanding on November 10th, 1935).

The Sub-Committee will draw up, not later than November
12th, the final list of contracts in the case of which an
exception appears to it to be justified, and will communi-
cate the list forthwith for information to the Governments
represented on the Co-ordination Committee.

PROPOSAL NO. III A

Adopted by the Committee of Eighteen on November
6th, 1935[173]

Books, Newspapers, Etc.

   The Committee of Eighteen,
   Having been instructed by the Co-ordination Committee
to follow the execution of the proposals submitted to Governments, and being empowered to make such further proposals
as it may think expedient,
   Proposes that, as an exception to Proposal No. III,
the prohibition to import goods consigned from Italy or
Italian possessions should not be extended to books, newspapers and periodicals, maps and cartographical productions
or printed or engraved music.

PROPOSAL NO. IV

Adopted by the Co-ordination Committee
on October 19th, 1935[174]

Embargo on Certain Exports to Italy

   With a view to facilitating for the Governments of
the Members of the League of Nations the execution of their

obligations under Article 16 of the Covenant, the following
measures should be taken:

(1) The Governments of the Members of the League
of Nations will extend the application of paragraph
(2) of Proposal No. I of the Co-ordination Committee
to the following articles as regards their exportation
and re-exportation to Italy and Italian possessions,
which will accordingly be prohibited:

(a) Horses, mules, donkeys, camels and all
other transport animals;

(b) Rubber;

(c) Bauxite, aluminium and alumina (alumi-
nium-oxide), iron ore and scrap iron;

Chromium, manganese, nickel, titanium,
tungsten, vanadium, their ores and ferro-alloys
(and also ferro-molybdenum, ferro-silicon, ferro-
silico-manganese and ferro-silico-manganese-alumi-
nium);

Tin and tin-ore.

List (c) above includes all crude forms of the
minerals and metals mentioned and their ores, scrap
and alloys;

(2) The Governments of the Members of the League
of Nations will take such steps as may be necessary to
secure that the articles mentioned in paragraph (1)
above exported to countries other than Italy or Italian
possessions will not be re-exported directly or indirectly to Italy or to Italian possessions;

(3) The measures provided for in paragraphs (1)
and (2) above are to apply to contracts in course of
execution;

(4) Goods en route at the time of imposition of
the prohibition will be excepted from its operation.
In giving effect to this provision, Governments may,
for convenience of administration, fix an appropriate
date, having regard to the normal time necessary for
transport to Italy or Italian possessions, after
which goods will become subject to the prohibition.

Having regard to the importance of collective and, so
far as possible, simultaneous action in regard to the measures recommended, each Government is requested to inform
the Co-ordination Committee, through the Secretary-General,
as soon as possible, and not later than October 28th, of
the date on which it could be ready to bring these measures
into operation. The Committee of Co-ordination will meet
on October 31st for the purpose of fixing, in the light of

the replies received, the date of the coming into force of the said measures.

The attention of the Co-ordination Committee has been drawn to the possible extension of the above proposal to a certain number of other articles. It entrusts the Committee of Eighteen with the task of making any suitable proposals to Governments on this subject.

Annex

Report Submitted by the Legal Sub-Committee on the Application of Sanctions and Private Contracts, Commercial Treaties and Treaties of Friendship and Non-Aggression

Proposals Nos. III (Prohibition of Importation of Italian Goods) and IV (Embargo on Certain Exports to Italy)

Resolution Adopted by the Co-ordination Committee on November 2nd, 1935[175]

The Co-ordination Committee,
Taking note of the facts:
(1) That forty-three Governments of States Members of the League have already expressed their willingness to accept Proposal No. III and forty-four Proposal No. IV adopted by the Committee on October 19th, and that six others which, owing to their distance from the seat of the League, did not immediately receive the full text of these proposals have expressed their readiness to consider them favourably;

(2) That nearly all these Governments have declared themselves ready to put the proposed measures into force by the middle of November or by such date as may be fixed by the Co-ordination Committee:

Decides to fix November 18th as the date for the entry into force of these measures;

Invites all Governments of Members of the League to take the necessary steps so that these measures may be effectively applied throughout their territories by November 18th;

Requests each Government to inform the Committee through the Secretary-General of the League, within the shortest possible time, of the measures which it has taken in conformity with the above provisions.

PROPOSAL NO. IV A

Adopted by the Committee of Eighteen on November 6th, 1935[176]

Extension of the Embargo on Certain Exports to Italy

In the execution of the mission entrusted to it under the last paragraph of Proposal No. IV, the Committee of Eighteen submits to Governments the following proposal:
It is expedient that the measures of embargo provided for in Proposal No. IV should be extended to the following articles as soon as the conditions necessary to render this extension effective have been realised:

Petroleum and its derivatives, by-products and residues;
Pig-iron; iron and steel (including alloy steels), cast, forged, rolled, drawn, stamped or pressed;
Coal (including anthracite and lignite), coke and their agglomerates, as well as fuels derived therefrom.

If the replies received by the Committee to the present proposal and the information at its disposal warrant it, the Committee of Eighteen will propose to Governments a date for bringing into force the measures mentioned above.

PROPOSAL NO. IV B

Adopted by the Committee of Eighteen on November 6th, 1935[177]

Indirect Supply

The Committee of Eighteen,

143

Entrusted by the Co-ordination Committee with the task
of following the execution of the proposals submitted to
Governments and empowered to make such new proposals as it
may think desirable, is of opinion that the following measures should be taken:

In order to render effective the provisions of
point 2 of Proposal No. IV, Governments represented on
the Co-ordination Committee will take, as regards the
export of prohibited products, such measures as are
necessary to verify, by all means in their power, the
destination of such products.

Those Governments which do not immediately restrict their exports of these articles will keep under
constant review the volume and direction of such export. In the event of an abnormal increase in this
export, they will immediately take such steps as may
be necessary to prevent supplies reaching Italy or
Italian possessions by indirect routes.

Each Government is requested to inform the Co-ordination Committee, through the Secretary-General of the League,
within the shortest possible time, of the measures which
it has taken in conformity with the above provisions.

PROPOSAL NO. V

Adopted by the Co-ordination Committee on October
19th, 1935[178]

Organisation of Mutual Support

The Co-ordination Committee draws the special attention of all Governments to their obligations under paragraph 3 of Article 16 of the Covenant, according to which
the Members of the League undertake mutually to support
one another in the application of the economic and financial measures taken under this article.

I. With a view to carrying these obligations into
effect, the Governments of the Members of the League of
Nations will:

(a) Adopt immediately measures to assure that
no action taken as a result of Article 16 will de-
prive any country applying sanctions of such advan-

tages as the commercial agreements concluded by the participating States with Italy afforded it through the operation of the most-favoured-nation clause;

(b) Take appropriate steps with a view to replacing, within the limits of the requirements of their respective countries, imports from Italy by the import of similar products from the participating States;

(c) Be willing, after the application of economic sanctions, to enter into negotiations with any participating country which has sustained a loss, with a view to increasing the sale of goods so as to offset any loss of Italian markets which the application of sanctions may have involved;

(d) In cases in which they have suffered no loss in respect of any given commodity, abstain from demanding the application of any most-favoured-nation clause in the case of any privileges granted under paragraphs (b) and (c) in respect of that commodity.

II. With the above objects, the Governments will, if necessary with the assistance of the Committee of Eighteen, study, in particular, the possibility of adopting, within the limits of their existing obligations, and taking into consideration the annexed opinion of the Legal Sub-Committee of the Co-ordination Committee, the following measures:

(1) The increase by all appropriate measures of their imports in favour of such countries as may have suffered loss of Italian markets on account of the application of sanctions;

(2) In order to facilitate this increase, the taking into consideration of the obligations of mutual support and of the advantages which the trade of certain States Members of the League of Nations, not participating in the sanctions, would obtain from the application of these sanctions, in order to reduce, by every appropriate means and to an equitable degree, imports coming from these countries;

(3) The promotion, by all means in their power, of business relations between firms interested in the sale of goods in Italian markets which have been lost owing to the application of sanctions and firms normally importing such goods;

(4) Assistance generally in the organisation
of the international marketing of goods with a view
to offsetting any loss of Italian markets which the
application of sanctions may have involved.

They will also examine, under the same conditions, the
possibility of financial or other measures to supplement
the commercial measures, in so far as these latter may not
ensure sufficient international mutual support.

III. The Co-ordination Committee requests the Committee of Eighteen to afford, if necessary, to the Governments
concerned the assistance contemplated at the beginning of
Part II of the present proposal.

Annex

Report Submitted by the Legal Sub-Committee on the
Application of the Most-Favoured-Nation Clause

1. The Legal Sub-Committee has been asked to advise
whether a country participating in the sanctions which at
present, under the most-favoured-nation clause, benefits
by concessions made to Italy under commercial treaties with
other States which are participating in the sanctions can
continue to do so when the sanctions have resulted in suspension of the concessions made to Italy.

The Sub-Committee is of the following opinion:

The most-favoured-nation clause cannot give a right
to continued enjoyment of the advantages in question, since
application of most-favoured-nation treatment depends upon
the existence of a particular state of things. It is,
nevertheless, in conformity with the spirit of Article 16,
paragraph 3, of the Covenant, that the advantages should
continue to be accorded independently of the most-favoured-
nation clause, for one could hardly conceive that the
States participating in the sanctions, which are under an
obligation to support one another mutually, should proceed
to render their economic relations with one another more
difficult than before.

The Sub-Committee considers that this view might ad-
vantageously be expressed in the proposal dealing with
economic sanctions by the insertion therein of a provision
to the following effect:

146

"States participating in the sanctions which,
in virtue of most-favoured-nation treatment, have
up to the present been obtaining from other participating States advantages or benefits accorded by
the latter to Italy, of which Italy will be temporarily deprived through the application of sanctions, will continue to enjoy such advantages and
concessions on the new ground of the mutual support which the Members of the League of Nations are
bound to afford one another under Article 16, paragraph 3, of the Covenant."

2. The Legal Sub-Committee has been asked to advise
whether it is legally maintainable that countries entitled
to the benefit of the most-favoured-nation clause would
nevertheless not be justified in claiming for themselves
the advantages of preferential treatment accorded, temporarily and for the duration of the sanctions only, by one of
the participating States to the goods of another participating State whose exports had been specially restricted
as the result of the sanctions.
The Sub-Committee is of the following opinion:
The most-favoured-nation clause would not justify the
extension of the advantages in question to third States.
The reasons are, first, that such advantages would have an
exceptional as well as a temporary character and would be
the consequence of a special obligation existing between
the States concerned in virtue of Article 16, paragraph 3,
of the Covenant of the League of Nations, and, secondly,
that the most-favoured-nation clause is a provision peculiar to commercial treaties, which are the treaties in which
it is found, and, accordingly, is one which must be interpreted as not contemplating economic relations of so exceptional a nature as those which are here under consideration.

Report by the Legal Sub-Committee on the Application
of Sanctions and International Conventions
Concerning Freedom of Communications

The Legal Sub-Committee has been asked to advise upon
the following question:
"Do Conventions concluded with States not Members
of the League of Nations, which contain provisions
for freedom of communications, prevent the Members of
the League from taking such measures of interruption

or control of transit as may be necessary for the application of Article 16 of the Covenant?"

The Sub-Committee is of opinion that, in the contemplated case, the Members of the League may, at least if the Conventions are anterior to the Covenant, find themselves faced with two conflicting obligations, one towards the League of Nations and flowing from Article 16 of the Covenant and the other towards a non-member State which is a party to the Conventions in question.

The force and effect of the latter obligation is not a matter which the League of Nations has to appreciate. But so far as it is concerned, the League is entitled to hold that no individual Member can release itself from the obligations which result from Article 16 of the Covenant by invoking obligations assumed towards a country not belonging to the League.

NOTES

1. Among some of the better works are F. D. Laurens, France and the Italo-Ethiopian Crisis, 1935-1936 (The Hague: Mouton, 1967); G. W. Baer, The Coming of the Italian-Ethiopian War (Cambridge, Mass.: Harvard University Press, 1967); A. J. Barker, The Civilizing Mission (London: Cassell, 1968); and B. Harris, The United States and the Italo-Ethiopian Crisis (Stanford: Stanford University Press, 1964).

2. A respectable account of this early period may be found in C. Jesman, The Russians in Ethiopia (London: Chatto and Windus, 1958), ch. 7, pp. 61-79. Italian documentation for the period may be found in Documenti diplomatici presentati al Parlamento italiano--Avvenimenti d'Africa (Gennaio 1895-Marzo 1896) (Rome: Tipografia della Camera dei Deputati, 1896).

3. David Walder, The Chanak Affair (London: Hutchinson, 1969), p. 60.

4. "It turned out to be the most shrewd move that Rastafari could have made, for no doubt what happened in 1935 would have been little more than a passing squall on the political scene if it had not been for the fact that Ethiopia was a member of the League." Barker, op. cit., p. 26.

5. Baer, op. cit., pp. 16-18. The agreement was concluded in December 1925 but was not communicated to the Ethiopian government until June 9, 1926. Ras Tafari pro-

tested the agreement on June 15, and on June 19 he took it to the League of Nations. League of Nations, Official Journal, 1926, pp. 1517 ff.

6. G. Vedovoto, Gli accordi italo-etiopici dell'agosto, 1928 (Florence: Rivista di Studi Politici Internazionali, 1956).

7. On this period see Baer, op. cit., pp. 21-27.

8. Quoted in ibid., p. 29.

9. Emilio de Bono, Anno XIII: The Conquest of an Empire (London: Cresset Press, 1937), pp. 116-17. De Bono, in fact, said that Mussolini first spoke to him of the "coming operations" in East Africa in the autumn of 1933: "From this moment the Duce was definitely of the opinion that the matter would have to be settled no later than 1936." Ibid., p. 13.

10. Baer, op. cit., p. 31.

11. Ibid., p. 35.

12. Apparently at a meeting on May 31, 1934, Mussolini directed that a study be made of means whereby Ethiopia could be provoked indirectly into taking action of any type against Eritrea. See R. L. Hess, Italian Colonialism in Somalia (Chicago: University of Chicago Press, 1966), pp. 172-73.

13. New York Times, September 30, 1934. Copies of both the 1906 and 1928 treaties may be found in RGDIP 3rd ser., 9 (1935): 748-50.

14. More material on this incident may be found in the record of Chief Arbitrator Pitman B. Potter, The Wal-Wal Arbitration (Washington, D.C.: Carnegie Endowment, 1938); Baer, op. cit., pp. 45-61; and League of Nations, Official Journal, 1935. Also see P. B. Potter, "The Wal-Wal Arbitration," AJIL 30 (1936): 27-44; and his article in RGDIP 3rd ser., 9 (1935): 751-58.

15. League of Nations, Official Journal, 1935, pp. 270-74. For background see L. Kopelmanas, "L'article XI de Pacte de la S.D.N.," RGDIP 3rd ser., 9 (1935): 559-639.

16. A summary of the directive is contained in Baer, op. cit., pp. 58-61.

17. Ibid., pp. 96-106. Also see League of Nations, Official Journal, 1935, pp. 252-74; and the Italian offer to arbitrate, pp. 162-63.

18. For example, an Ethiopian note of February 1, 1935, was not replied to until February 6. Moreover, the Italian reply not only rejected an Ethiopian offer to withdraw troops from border regions but also levied additional allegations against Ethiopia. League of Nations, Official Journal, 1935, pp. 730, 731-32.

19. Avenol, a career diplomat, circulated all Ethiopian communications to the Italians in advance of publication in order to permit time for an appropriate reply. Baer, op. cit., p. 102; and James Barros, Betrayal from Within: Joseph Avenol, Secretary General of the League of Nations, 1933-1940 (New Haven, Conn.: Yale University Press, 1969).

20. League of Nations, Official Journal, 1935, pp. 571, 572.

21. Ibid., p. 742. The March 13 agreement is at p. 743, and other correspondence may be found at pp. 740-41.

22. Ibid., pp. 577-78.

23. Ibid., p. 721; and the Ethiopian memorandum to the Secretary-General on the situation, dated May 22, 1935, ibid., pp. 721-59.

24. Ibid., "Minutes of the 87th (Extraordinary) Session of the Council, 31 July and 3 August, 1935," pp. 963-70.

25. Baer, op. cit., p. 240.

26. F. P. Walters, A History of the League of Nations (London: Oxford University Press, 1960), p. 639.

27. The report of the commission may be found in AJIL 29 (1935): 690-98, at 697.

28. Potter, "The Wal-Wal Arbitration," p. 44. Also see his comments on the commission in RGDIP 3rd ser., 9 (1935): 751-58.

29. League of Nations, Official Journal, 1935, II, "Minutes of the 88th Session of the Council," pp. 1133-39, at 1135-37.

30. Ibid., pp. 1137-39.

31. Walters, op. cit., p. 644. The Italian memorandum is Council Document C.340.M.171, 1935 VII (September 11, 1935) and C.340(a).M.171(a), 1935 VII (September 28, 1935).

32. League of Nations, Official Journal, 1935, II, p. 1145.

33. League Document C.379.M-191, September 24, 1935, "Report of the Committee of Five to the Council." Also see Baer, op. cit., p. 344.

34. Baer, op. cit., p. 5. Italy regarded the project as its "mission in Africa" (p. 6).

35. Walters, op. cit., pp. 651-52.

36. Material on the Italo-Ethiopian dispute, at this stage, is quite extensive. One of the better studies was that undertaken by C. Rousseau, "Le conflit italo-ethiopien," in RGDIP 3rd ser., 10 (1936): 231-56, which has a useful series of documents on the conflict. Also see Nordisk tidskrift för international ret 6 (1935): 46-50, 155-57, 234-43, and 7 (1936): 56-58, 162-64.

37. "He [Laval] would not throw away his insurance on a minor affray. He was also bent on mitigating the Germans and looked on Mussolini as a link." Lord R. Vansittart, The Mist Procession (London: Hutchinson, 1958), p. 539.

38. For example, Article 16(2) conceptually might resemble Article 43 of the Charter; 16(3) approximates Article 50, while 16(4) tends to equate with Articles 5 and 6 of the Charter.

39. F. Bradley, "Some Legislative and Administrative Aspects of the Application of Article XVI of the Covenant," Transactions of the Grotius Society 22 (1937): 14.

40. J. Stone, "The Rule of Unanimity: The Practice of the Council and Assembly of the League of Nations," BYIL 14 (1933): 18-42.

41. J. Stone, Legal Controls of International Conflict (London: Stevens & Sons, 1959), p. 179.

42. Bradley, op. cit., p. 15.

43. Ibid., pp. 15-16. Also see P. Guggenheim, "Die Schweizer Neutralität und Artikel 16 der Volkerbandsatzung," Zeitschrift für offentliches Recht 8 (1927-28): 3 ff.; R. L. Buell, "The Suez Canal and League Sanctions," Geneva Special Studies 6 (1935); and "Report by the League Secretary General," May 17, 1927, Doc. A-14.1927.P.83, pp. 88 ff.

44. J. D. Greene, "Economic Sanctions as Instruments of National Policy," Annals: American Academy 162 (1932): 102.

45. Stone, Legal Controls, p. 181.

46. R.I.I.A., International Sanctions: A Report (London: Oxford University Press, 1938), p. 190.

47. Sir A. Bertram, "The Economic Weapon as a Form of Peaceful Pressure," Transactions of the Grotius Society 17 (1931): 139-174.

48. Ibid., p. 151.

49. Ibid., p. 152.

50. On this general point see J. L. Kunz, "Sanctions in International Law," AJIL 54 (1960): 324-48, at 329.

51. Greene, op. cit., p. 102.

52. As originally proposed by Dr. Agusto de Vasconcellos (Portugal), it was to be a Committee of 16. Laval (France) suggested that it be called the Committee of Initiative; wisdom appears to have led the members of the Co-ordination Committee to accept the less grandiose Committee of 16 (17, and finally 18) proposal. See League of Nations, Official Journal: Co-Ordination Committee: Minutes, Special Supplement no. 145, First Session, October 11, 1935, pp. 12-13.

53. Material for this section is drawn from the record of the minutes and proceedings of these various committees. League of Nations, Official Journal, Special Supplements nos. 145, 146, 147, 148, and 149 (hereafter cited as Official Journal, Special Supplement no. 145, etc.).

54. Walters, op. cit., pp. 652-53.

55. A. Eden, The Eden Memoirs: Facing the Dictators (London: Cassell, 1962), pp. 273-75. Presumably he meant the proposals of the Committee of Five.

56. Ibid., p. 276. In retrospect this seems like a fairly superfluous exercise.

57. Ibid.

58. Ibid., p. 278.

59. League of Nations, Official Journal, Special Supplement no. 145, October 11, 1935.

60. There is little doubt that the Coordination Committee members expected their work to be completed over the weekend of October 12-13 and the measures to be taken announced on the Monday. See League of Nations, Official Journal, Special Supplement no. 145, pp. 13-28.

61. Minutes are in Special Supplement no. 145, pp. 29-35. A summary is available in A. J. Toynbee, Survey of International Affairs, 1935, 2 (London: Oxford University Press, 1936), 223-28.

62. Walters, op. cit., p. 143.

63. See Harris, op. cit., pp. 25-29, 53-55. The text of the first Neutrality Act is in United States, Department of State, Peace and War, United States Foreign Policy, 1931-1941 (Washington, D.C.: U.S. Government Printing Office, 1943), pp. 266-71.

64. Baer, op. cit., p. 277. Baer draws upon M. Lambert et al., eds., Documents on German Foreign Policy, 1918-1945 serc. C, 4 (Washington, D.C.: U.S. Government Printing Office, 1962), 564-65, for this information. Also see W. E. Dodd, and M. Dodd, Ambassador Dodd's Diary, 1933-38 (New York: Harcourt Brace, 1941), p. 259.

65. The list was appended to the Neutrality Act. The minutes of this meeting of the Committee of 18, Special Supplement no. 145, contains as an annex a letter from Cordell Hull to the League's Secretary-General, dated September 25, 1935, in which Hull brought to the League's attention the existence of the Neutrality Act (a joint resolution of Congress) and the appended list of embargoed arms.

66. Two versions of the list and the proposal may be found in Special Supplement no. 150, 1936, pp. 2-3; and in P. Q. Wright, ed., Neutrality and Collective Security (Chicago: University of Chicago Press, 1936), pp. 208-11.

67. The list of military and "nonmilitary" contracts was long. See, for example, the Manchester _Guardian_, October 10, 1935, for a report of Turkish coal and cattle sales to Italy; the _Times_ (London), August 26, describes the sale by a Glasgow company of a water distillation plant to "ensure an adequate supply of pure water for troops" operating in East Africa; the _Times_, August 29, noted that an Italian order for 100,000 pairs of boots had been received by a British firm; the _Times_, September 6, reported that Italians were arranging for the purchase, from Poland, of coal and army blankets; the New York _Times_, September 22, reported large shipments of petroleum products, food supplies, and vehicle equipment from Kenya to Mogadishu; the New York _Times_, September 26, noted the activity of Swedish manufacturers in supplying Italian war needs. Throughout August, September, and until mid-October 1935, such reports are found daily in most major newspapers. Toynbee, op. cit., p. 221, referred to this as the "ghoulish traffic."

68. _Special Supplement_ no. 150, p. 13.

69. _Special Supplement_ no. 146, p. 41. The reference was to Article 4 of the 1907 Hague Convention on Swiss neutrality. Also referred to were Article 435 of the Treaty of Versailles and the Treaty of London of February 13, 1920.

70. See the Swiss reply to the Secretary-General in _Special Supplement_ no. 150, pp. 272-73.

71. L. Oppenheim, _International Law: A Treatise_, 1 (8th ed., H. Lauterpacht, ed.; London: Longmans, 1955), §148, p. 337.

72. Minutes of early meetings are in _Special Supplement_ no. 145, pp. 118-23. The historical significance of these meetings--collective enforcement of international law--seems generally to have escaped the participants.

73. Ibid., pp. 85-94.

74. Ibid., p. 81.

75. Ibid.

76. Ibid. (Coulondre), p. 37.

77. Ibid. (Vladimir Potemkine, U.S.S.R.), p. 39.

78. See the remarks of Sandler (Sweden), Komarnicki (Poland), and De Madariaga (Spain), ibid.

79. Ibid., pp. 53-59.

80. There was also Eden's unbridled dislike of Laval, a fact he recorded. See Eden, op. cit., p. 277. Also see Laurens, op. cit.

81. Proceedings in _Special Supplement_ no. 145, pp. 124-39.

82. Baer, op. cit., p. 101. Baer also questions Avenol's loyalty to the League, ibid., p. 102. "Avenol

showed all communications from Ethiopia to the assistant
Secretary General, the Italian jurist Pilotti, in advance
of circulation, so that the Italian government would have
ample time to formulate an appropriate response when the
matter arose formally." Baer cites A Berio, "L'affare
etiopico," Rivista di studi politici internazionali 25
(April-June 1958): 182, as the source. Also see Barros,
op. cit.
      83. J. Avenol, "The Future of the League of Nations,"
translation of an address given at Chatham House, London,
December 12, 1933, International Affairs 13 (1934): 142-58,
at 150.
      84. Baer, op. cit., p. 326.
      85. Special Supplement no. 145, p. 56. Minutes, ibid.,
pp. 85-117; Special Supplement no. 146, pp. 52-77.
      86. Special Supplement no. 145, pp. 15-16.
      87. Special Supplement no. 150, p. 1.
      88. Special Supplement no. 145, p. 17.
      89. A reference to the 1928 agreement between various
Austrian creditors that permitted Austria to float an in-
ternational loan. A major commercial treaty was signed by
Austria and Italy on April 28, 1924. See M. Currey, Italian Foreign Policy, 1918-1932 (London: Nicholson and Wat-
son, 1932), pp. 97-98, 135, 247. Italy's relations with
Austria always had been tense over the long-standing Alto
Adige question and competing aspirations in the Adriatic.
See L. Villari, Italy (New York: Scribners, 1929), pp.
311-32.
      90. Yuan-li Wu, Economic Warfare (New York: Prentice-
Hall, 1952), p. 13. H. Feis, Seen from E.A.: Three International Episodes (New York: Norton, 1966), p. 211, notes
that Italy had "prohibited the importation into Italy of
one hundred and twenty-eight commodities except under li-
cense. The calculation behind this measure was that some
members might be deterred from voting further sanctions by
fear of losing trade, while other members might be attracted
to the support of Italy by hope of gaining trade."
      91. Minutes in Special Supplement no. 145, pp. 85-117,
124-39.
      92. Ibid., p. 131.
      93. Ibid., p. 130. The fund never achieved fruition.
      94. A summary of the subcommittee's activities may be
found in Wright, op. cit., pp. 217-21. For the complete
report of the committee, see Special Supplement no. 150,
pp. 11-12.
      95. Committee of 18, Document no. 16; see Special
Supplement no. 145, p. 71.

96. Nicolae Titulescu, ibid., p. 73.

97. Proposal V, II(1)(2).

98. Special Supplement, no. 145, p. 56.

99. Full texts may be found in Wright, op. cit., pp. 212-15.

100. Coulondre (France), Special Supplement no. 145, p. 56.

101. See Feis, op. cit., p. 212.

102. This was the final sentence of Proposal III.

103. Special Supplement no. 145, pp. 22-27.

104. Special Supplement no. 145, pp. 22-23. In 1934 Austria purchased 2.4 percent of Italy's exports, while Italy purchased 11.1 percent of Austria's exports.

105. Ibid., p. 23. The treaty (signed in Rome, September 5, 1925), besides containing m.f.n. clauses, permitted export of Hungarian goods through the port of Fiume.

106. Report submitted by the Legal Subcommittee on the application of sanctions, appended to Proposal III, Special Supplement no. 150, p. 7.

107. Without wishing to become too immersed in the problem of the nonperformance of contracts in private international law, there is reason to suppose that the subcommittee's opinion on this point was far too simplified. That is, if the dictum set forth by Lord Bowen in Jacobs vs. Credit Lyonnais (1884), 12 Q.B.D. 589 (Court of Appeal), was still valid in 1935. This decision supported the view that applicable law in the case of a commercial trade contract was the proper law of the contract itself. Thus, the law of the place of performance was inconsequential unless otherwise provided. In practice a contract signed in Italy, for performance in Italy, but including a national of a sanctioning state, caveats notwithstanding, would be subject to Italian law. Litvinoff, in appreciation of the point, had suggested that the problem of contracts be submitted to the Permanent Court, with a view to establishing the doctrine that nonexecution of contracts as a result of the enforcement of sanctions was to be regarded as due to force majeure. His suggestion failed.

108. Canada's virtual world monopoly on nickel was an example of the problems faced. Large quantities of Canadian nickel were exported to the United States for processing and further export. This difficulty was appreciated by Riddell (Canada); Special Supplement no. 145, p. 103. Poland was faced with the dilemma of trading its coal for a new transatlantic liner and feared that Italy would "acquire a first-class ocean liner at Poland's expense." Switzerland (Gothard Tunnel Convention, 1869) and the

Netherlands (International Convention on Rhine Navigation) both pleaded special transportation consideration.

109. Special Supplement no. 145, p. 111.

110. Special Supplement no. 147, p. 22.

111. Special Supplement no. 145, pp. 20-28.

112. With the exception of an expanded and more specific arms embargo, Proposal I(A), a product of the Military Experts Subcommittee. Special Supplement no. 145, pp. 140-41. Proposal I(A) removed caliber references from weapons and ammunition, expanded the restrictions on aircraft and parts to all types, and the inclusion of all products related to chemical or incendiary warfare. Proposal I(A) was one of the few steps made toward strengthening the sanctions scheme. Also see Special Supplement no. 145, pp. 20-21.

113. Toynbee, op. cit., p. 228.

114. Special Supplement no. 150 contains the five proposals (pp. 2-12) and the official correspondence and communications relating thereto from League members (pp. 13-359).

115. Special Supplement no. 146, p. 19.

116. To Poland and Turkey were added Siam, Norway, U.S.S.R., Iran, and perhaps Ecuador. See Coordination Committee Documents 13(A), 51(B), 37(C), 19(A), 33(B), and 70(B).

117. Special Supplement no. 146, p. 20.

118. Ibid., pp. 69-73.

119. Ibid., p. 70; and Coordination Committee Document SCME-9. Also see Special Supplement no. 146, pp. 73-75; and Coordination Committee Document SCME-10.

120. Special Supplement no. 146, pp. 46-51, at p. 48. The text may be found in Special Supplement no. 150, p. 7.

121. Special Supplement no. 146, p. 24.

122. Ibid., pp. 52-59.

123. Riddell (Canada), ibid., p. 56.

124. Coulondre (France), ibid., p. 52.

125. Stucki (Switzerland), ibid., p. 53.

126. Ibid., p. 34.

127. Text in Special Supplement no. 150, p. 5.

128. Ibid. The use of clearing agreements has dwindled considerably since World War II, although such agreements are still employed between developing and developed countries. See C. P. Kindleberger, International Economics (Homewood, Ill.: Irwin, 1968), p. 144.

129. Paragraph 4, Coordination Committee Document no. 1, 10(d); Special Supplement no. 150, p. 65. Eden referred to the exchange of notes as a "payments agreement"; Special Supplement no. 146, p. 44.

130. *Special Supplement* no. 146, p. 61. Westman (Sweden) feared that "the proceedings were deteriorating into [a] sort of game of tennis"; p. 60.

131. Coordination Committee Document SCME 8.

132. There is some question here about both the legality of the Committee of 18 acting formally on behalf of the Coordination Committee and the technical propriety of converting a resolution into a proposal. However, these were unresolved (and apparently almost unnoticed) legal niceties. See *Special Supplement* no. 146, p. 54.

133. Baron Pompeo Aloisi, *Journal, 25 juillet 1932-14 juin 1936* (Paris: Librairie Plon, 1957).

134. Ibid., p. 320. He described Hoare's September 11 speech as an electoral speech (p. 303). The peace ballot campaign had just concluded in Britain.

135. Ibid. On a number of occasions Aloisi records that he met with delegates from other Committee of 18 members to woo them into wavering on sanctions (p. 303): "I sent a secret communication to Beck to incite Poland eventually to vote against the sanctions" (p. 304); "I went to see the Chilean delegate [leader] to ask that his country vote against sanctions" (p. 316); Switzerland (p. 317); Holland.

136. *Special Supplement* no. 146, pp. 33-42. Also see W. A. Riddell, ed., *Documents on Canadian Foreign Policy, 1917-1939* (Toronto: Oxford University Press, 1962), pp. 540-41.

137. In addition there is reason to suspect that the French had already made known their lack of enthusiasm for a petroleum embargo. Certainly later (November 26) Laval made his opposition known at a Cabinet meeting. Edouard Herriot, *Jadis II: D'une guerre à l'autre, 1914-1936* (Paris: Flammarion, 1952), p. 613.

138. *Special Supplement* no. 146, pp. 59-65; and *Special Supplement* no. 150, p. 10.

139. *Special Supplement* no. 150, p. 10.

140. *Special Supplement* no. 146, p. 38.

141. *Special Supplement* no. 150, p. 10.

142. The Committee of Experts was appointed on November 6, 1935, by the Committee of 18 "to study in Geneva the information furnished by Governments concerning the application of the measures proposed by the Committee of Co-ordination." *Special Supplement* no. 146, p. 50.

143. Minutes of the committee are in *Special Supplement* no. 147, pp. 20-45, with eight annexes following at pp. 46-62. Norway, Chile, and the Union of South Africa delayed implementation of the proposals beyond November 18

because of goods in transit over long distances. Ibid., p. 21, 31. Finland and Bolivia pleaded constitutional limitations (pp. 24, 27); Australia excluded its territories; and Panama begged off more or less completely (p. 24).

144. This was especially true of Switzerland, which, because of heavy trading with Italy, had concluded a clearing agreement with Italy that sought to effectively maintain a 1934 trade level. Special Supplement no. 147, pp. 39-42.

145. Ibid., pp. 9-10.

146. Ibid., p. 16.

147. Among the most useful material on the period is G. Warner, Pierre Laval and the Eclipse of France (London: Eyre & Spottiswoode, 1968); Viscount Templewood, Nine Troubled Years (London: Collins, 1946), pp. 176-92; W. C. Askew, "The Secret Agreement Between France and Italy on Ethiopia, January 1935," Journal of Modern History 25 (1953), 47-48; Aloisi, op. cit., pp. 308 ff.; P.-E. Flandin, Politique française, 1919-1940 (Paris: Nouvelles, 1947); R. Guariglia, Ricordi, 1922-1946 (Naples: Edizioni Scientifiche Italiane, 1950), pp. 781-82; and Walters, op. cit., pp. 668-76.

148. Walters, op. cit., p. 666.

149. Ibid., p. 672.

150. Note ibid., p. 675, where reference is made to diminishing Italian trade with Britain and France.

151. Ibid., p. 684.

152. Feis, op. cit., p. 297.

153. M. F. Neufeld, Italy: School for Awakening Countries: The Italian Labour Movement (Ithaca, N.Y.: Cornell University Press, 1961), p. 400.

154. Ibid., p. 527.

155. Ciano, in his 1937 Diary, cites numerous examples of his direct pressure on weaker states to remove the sanctions.

156. Feis, op. cit., p. 304, 305.

157. Ibid., p. 350. Feis points out that the average value of American petroleum products to Italy and Italian Africa during 1932-34 had been $480,000. In October 1935, the United States exported $1,084,000 worth of petroleum to these points (November 1935, $1,684,000; December, $2,674,000). Ibid., p. 307.

158. In the long run, of course, this trend was sustained and Italy now ranks fourth in European manufacturing production, although it still has one of the lower European per capita incomes (which emphasizes the continued significance of farm incomes). Economic Almanac, 1970-71 (London: Collier-Macmillan, 1970).

159. <u>Special Supplement</u> no. 145, pp. 15, 55.
160. Ibid., pp. 19, 52, 53, 60.
161. Ibid., pp. 14, 32.
162. Ibid., pp. 19, 63.
163. As Proposal No. I A was substituted for Proposal No. I, both proposals are indicated throughout the volume as Proposal No. I, unless the contrary is clearly stated.
164. It should be observed that the utilization of these articles has been, and still is, prohibited under the Convention of June 17th, 1925. These articles are only mentioned above because their manufacture being free (the more so, as in many instances they serve various purposes), the committee desires to emphasize that the export of such products could in no circumstances be tolerated.
165. <u>Special Supplement</u> no. 145, pp. 16, 45, 122.
166. Ibid. no. 146, pp. 8, 43, 81.
167. Ibid., pp. 12, 34, 52.
168. Ibid., pp. 48, 65, 76.
169. Ibid. no. 145, pp. 20, 65, 105, 115.
170. This paragraph was adopted without alteration as paragraph (3) of Proposal No. III.
171. <u>Special Supplement</u> no. 146, pp. 13, 19.
172. Ibid., pp. 48, 64, 69, 73.
173. Ibid, pp. 50, 73.
174. Ibid. no. 145, pp. 25, 78, 87, 100, 112.
175. Ibid. no. 146, pp. 8, 45.
176. Ibid., pp. 46, 61, 68.
177. Ibid., pp. 47, 64, 75.
178. Ibid. no. 145, pp. 25, 70, 132.

4

THE CASE OF THE
DOMINICAN REPUBLIC

BACKGROUND

There are two instructive themes in the history of
the Dominican people: their ability to survive assorted
natural and human catastrophes, and their capacity to live
in a form of racial harmony. These features have created
what may be described as a form of societal stoicism. It
was this quality that permitted Dominicans to accept, in
Rafael Trujillo's form of stability, one of Latin America's
worst tyrants while simultaneously seeming resigned to the
inevitable next round of chaos. The brief, almost euphoric
moments during which the country "suffered" peace, stability, and freedom appear, in retrospect, to have been only
rest stops between periods of continuing tragedy.

> Trujillo was the product of all the historical
> forces that have opposed the development of the
> Dominican people since Columbus discovered the
> island.[1]

Dominicans have a history of minor and major dictators interspersed with passing generals, conquerors, and owners.
Germán Arciniegos noted, in a preface to Sumner Welles's
Naboth's Vineyard, that the Trujillo era "was an era of
peace through terror similar to the Haitian occupation"
of 1822-44.[2] The country has resisted, often unsuccess-
fully, occupation by the "wrong people"--Haitians and Amer-
icans--and has openly sought absorption by the "right people"--the Americans and Spanish. This is only one of
numerous Dominican historical paradoxes.

But all the worst in Dominican politics--invasion, in-
trigue, terror, repression, and bankruptcy--culminated in
the "decomposición caudillista" of 1929 and the emergence
of Trujillo in 1930.[3] And if there was some inevitability
in Trujillo's rise to power, his consolidation of that position greatly depended upon the acquiescence of the mass of
the population to the traditional techniques of repression.
Thus while Trujillo sought self-aggrandizement, he varied
from habitual patterns by identifying his success with im-
provements in Dominican society. As a result he was able
to employ latent Dominican nationalism to successfully
equate himself with the state, and he solidified his power
by convincing Dominicans that attacks upon his person
and/or the state were synonymous.

"La Era de Trujillo" began officially on August 16,
1930, a date commemorated on numerous occasions.[4] Trujillo
was assassinated on the night of May 30, 1961, two and one-
half months short of his 31st year as leader of the country. During that 31-year period he succeeded in construct-
ing a regime that was superficially distinct from those of
the past. His appeal was to Dominican patriotism, and upon
this foundation he constructed an image allegedly the anti-
thesis of the past. "Trujillo's personality is all the
greater when viewed against the darkness of the past."[5]
Yet the techniques of rule were patterned upon the tyranny
employed by the Haitians during their occupation (1822-44)
and by many later Dominicans. Thus, Trujillo's most important personal accomplishment was the ruthless elimination
of competitors for his position.

But if Trujillo was a caudillo, then this reliance
upon a special relationship between the dictator and the
people was unusual. For he offered the masses peace, prosperity, discipline, and involvement; they reciprocated
with adulation that bordered upon deification. "It took
every form known to the long history of sycophancy, and it
increased year by year."[6] Trujillo's titles and medals
were legendary for their quantity: "Benefactor of the
Fatherland," "Restorer of Financial Independence"--and the
list droned on through 76 identifiable titles.[7]

And, if Trujillo had a philosophy of politics, it
scarcely could be classified among the great political
theories of the state. Such philosophy as existed lacked
any ideological pretensions beyond strict pragmatism; thus,
while various constitutions blandly proclaimed democracy
and liberty, there is little reason to suppose that they
were anything more than a technical facade.[8] For Trujillo,

democracy was action "directed towards the improvement of the community."[9] Order, peace, progress, and work were the guidelines for his political system.[10] Politics without the military would, of course, have been impossible.

Order, for Trujillo, was based upon submission and control of the population. His experience as a member of the Dominican National Guard during the American occupation (1916-24) demonstrated the dual advantages of a population disarmed and made submissive by terror.[11] The American occupiers had been able to control the population by disarming everyone, and Trujillo did not overlook the wisdom of continuing this practice. Once terror became politically inconvenient, and Dominicans were dissuaded from the practice of plotting conspiracies, the function of maintaining order devolved upon the military. In addition, the demise of internal opposition was compensated for by the growth of external opposition, notably among exile groups. External threats to the state permitted Trujillo to justify his burgeoning military establishment despite the very obvious fact that it most frequently functioned along the classical lines of the military in Latin American politics.[12] That is, it provided Trujillo with a large and dedicated body of custodians of the national interest.

Order was not based exclusively, however, upon a military monolith. R. D. Crassweller described the system for maintaining the structure as a "honeycomb of power" and outlined it as follows:

> The military power, the political power, the Church, were all represented in the multiple-cell walls of the comb, but--and in this lay the unique quality of the design--so was every important business interest, every financial power, every permit and licence and trade regulation, every tax, every exemption, every law; all joined together in their thousands and harmonized, each unit supporting every other, until the separate strengths of the components were as nothing in comparison with the strength and tenacity of the whole.[13]

The ingredients of the honeycomb, besides a subservient military and a detached and normally permissive Church, included extensive Trujillo personal and family involvement in virtually every sector of the country's economy, absolute control over all forms of mass media, total control over every level of the educational system, and complete

direction of every aspect of the formal processes of government: legislature, bureaucracy, and judiciary.

While estimates varied as to the extent of Trujillo
family wealth, there is general agreement that the sums
were large ($500 million to $1 billion) and the range of
activities diverse. Trujillo enterprises included everything from the salt monopoly to 12 of the country's 16
sugar mills, cement, shoes, dairy products, shipyards, construction companies, automobile sales, bottling works,
radio and television stations, insurance companies, lotter-
ies, gambling establishments, and brothels.[14] Control over
every aspect of the mass media served not only to propagate
the myth of Trujillo but also to insulate the regime from
foreign ideas and opinions.[15]

Controlled newspapers (i.e., La Nación and El Caribe)
served as authentic outlets for propaganda and praise of
the country and its leader, as means of perpetuating the
myth of Trujillo's divinity by constantly seeking out new
hagiographic adjectives, and as a device to control individuals within his empire by means of public exposure and
vilification.

The high illiteracy rate in the Dominican Republic in
1930 might have served, for another dictator, as a means
for maintaining the population in servitude. Trujillo's
technique was more astute. His much-lauded campaign to
increase literacy served the practical purpose of indoctri-
nation. Trujillo's 1933 Civic Primer and his wife's Moral
Meditations, both required reading, served as a basis for
the grade-school curriculum. Writers, musicians, and poets
praised el benefactor and were lavishly rewarded for doing
so.[16] Education became the process of inculcating submis-
siveness and mass adulation, in a generation and a half of
Dominicans.

Government was an effective mode of maintaining control and, in turn, was effectively controlled by Trujillo.*

_____

*The informal aspect is extremely important when it is
recalled that during the 31 years of the "era of Trujillo,"
he was president for only 18 years. Dominican presidents
were as follows: August 16, 1930 to August 15, 1938--Tru-
jillo; August 16, 1938 to his death, March 7, 1940--Jacinto
B. Peynado; March 8, 1940 to May 15, 1942--Manuel de Jesús
Troncoso de la Concha (vice-president under Peynado); May
16, 1942 to August 15, 1952 (two five-year terms by 1942
constitutional amendment)--Trujillo; August 16, 1952 to
August 15, 1960--Hector ("Negro") Bienvenido Trujillo;

Elections were as farcical as was the democratic regime
that proclaimed their results (see Tables 4.1 and 4.2).
And if elections were shoddy, so were the functions of
constitutional organs of government that purported to exist
at the behest of the population.

Legislative careers were ephemeral because they depended upon the whim of the dictator. The same pattern of
rapid turnover also may be ascertained in the careers of
judges, bureaucrats, local government officials, and other
high state employees. Some idea of the fluidity of government careers may be seen in a remark by Nanita that during
1950 the "Administrative Department of the Executive Power"
was responsible for 9,090 official appointments.[17] The
formal structure of government was important only to the
extent that it provided a facade of legitimacy for internal
consumption, and dulled adverse foreign criticism.[18] The
final component of the honeycomb, and one directly related
to the formal process of government, was the Partido Dominicano (P.D.), created in 1931. Although Trujillo found it
convenient periodically to create opposition parties--the
Trujillo Party (1942), the Partido Socialista Popular, the
National Democratic Party, and the Labor Party (1947), the
fact remains that only the P.D. was consistently Trujillo-
sponsored.*

Fundamentally the P.D. was a social organization that
performed many functions normally associated with the state:
distribution of milk, construction of parks, creation and
operation of clinics, hospitals, and ancillary institutions. It also provided libraries, newspapers, schoolbooks,
and other educational facilities.[19] Its greatest activity
was in the rural regions, thereby serving a population that
eventually came to identify hitherto unknown luxuries and
services with Trujillo. It also functioned as a two-way
communications system. By providing peasants with a modi-
cum of services, it identified progress and well-being with
Trujillo rather than with the government, thereby assuring
the regime of rural support or, at least, acquiescence.
It also served as an upward channel of communication for

August 16, 1960 through Trujillo's death and until late
1961--Joaquín Balaguer (vice-president under Hector Trujillo).

*Parties other than the P.D. were allowed to exist es-
sentially only during, and immediately after, World War II,
the period of temporary democratization in the face of U.S.
and world pressure.

TABLE 4.1

Dominican Republic: Representation in Senate and Lower
House, 1930-52

| | Senators | | Deputies | |
| | Number of Seats | Vacancies and Resignations | Number of Seats | Vacancies and Resignations |
Years				
1930-34	12	2	33	19
1934-38	13*	12	35	46
1938-42	16	30	50	83
1942-47	19	32	42	139
1947-52	21	41	49	122

*Only three Senators completed a full term of office.

Note: El Caribe, August 3, 1960, p. 13, contains an attendance list for members of the Lower House for the preceding month under the headings Absentees, Legitimate Excuses, Absences Without Excuse, and Absent with Permission. Probably a useful idea in theory, but an absurdity in the Dominican Republic under Trujillo.

Sources: Jesús de Galíndez, La era de Trujillo (Santiago de Chile: Editorial del Pacífico, 1956), pp. 210-18; and H. J. Wiarda, Dictatorship and Development (Gainesville: University of Florida Press, 1968), pp. 63-64.

rural complaints and pleas. In the absence of special farmers' interest groups or adequate legislative representation, it fulfilled the functions of such organizations. Equally important, in both the rural and urban contexts, was the party's role as a watchdog over local and national bureaucrats.

The P.D. served two other important roles: as a disseminator of Trujillo propaganda and as part of the national network of spies and informers.[20] It operated local "educational" programs for discussion of Trujillo's work. It was responsible for the promotion of patriotic slogans ("God and Trujillo"), organization of patriotic acts (renaming of Santo Domingo Ciudad Trujillo), and the production of patriotic studies (Balaguer's "God and Trujillo" paper read before the 1956 formal session of the Dominican Academy of History). The party was thus an all-encompas-

TABLE 4.2

Dominican Republic: Presidential Election Summaries, 1930-57

1930	Estrella Urena (Trujillo's candidate)(99 percent)	223,731
	Velásquez-Morales (Alinanza Nacional Progresista) (1 percent)	1,883
	Total registered voters	414,711
	Votes cast (55 percent of electorate)	225,614
1934	Partido Dominicano (Trujillo)	256,423
	Registered voters	286,937
	Gaceta oficial 4684 (May 29, 1934).	
1938	Total votes cast	319,680
	"The total votes cast were the same number of votes obtained by the candidates comprising those proposed and presented by the Partido Dominicano and the Trujilloists."	
	Gaceta oficial 5180 (June 6, 1938).	
1942	Total votes cast	581,937
	Partido Dominicano	391,708
	Partido Trujillista	190,229
	Trujillo was the candidate for both parties.	
	Gaceta oficial 5744 (May 17, 1942). The official results were published only two days after the elections, May 15, 1942.	
1947	Total votes cast	840,340
	Partido Dominicano	781,389
	Partido Nacional	29,765
	Partido Laborista	29,186
	Gaceta oficial 6632 (May 27, 1947).	
1952	Total votes cast	1,038,816
	"The number of votes cast equalled the number of votes obtained for each candidate of the Partido Dominicano."	
	Gaceta oficial 7428 (May 31, 1952). "Unanimity was perfect."	
1957	"His brother, Hector, won both [1952 and 1957] unanimously."	
	Wiarda, Dictatorship and Development, p. 66.	

Note: Quotations in the table are from Galíndez.

Sources: Jesus de Galíndez, La era de Trujillo (Santiago de Chile: Editorial del Pacífico, 1956), pp. 201-07; and H. J. Wiarda, Dictatorship and Development (Gainesville: University of Florida Press, 1968), pp. 65-66.

sing cement for the Trujillo structure of power. It was possible for a child to be born in a party clinic, to be fed and clothed by party largess, to be educated on Trujillo-oriented texts, and to work in a Trujillo-controlled operation, be it government, industry, service, or agriculture.

But, despite the honeycomb of power, the regime was beginning to show signs of weakness. While these will be enlarged upon in the following section, a brief jump ahead will permit a few factual paragraphs about the regime's collapse. It is important to remember that this was the consequence of events up to the date of Trujillo's assassination. The sanctions, as one of the causes, will be evaluated in greater detail below.

On April 1, 1960, Trujillo formally withdrew from Dominican politics in favor of his valued lieutenant Joaquín Balaguer.[21] On May 30, 1961, Trujillo was assassinated; on November 19 the U.S. fleet appeared off Santo Domingo in support of Balaguer's efforts to rid the country of the late dictator's brothers; and by January 16, 1962, Balaguer was heading into exile in the United States. In that 21-month period, therefore, dramatic events occurred, aided by the OAS and its sanctions but very clearly directed by the United States.[22]

It will probably never be established precisely who was responsible for Trujillo's assassination (providing the conspiracy theory is believed), but there is no doubt as to who the actual assassins were.[23] For that reason there is little cause to believe that the assassination in any manner represented a culmination of pent-up pressures against the regime. Moreover, it must be noted that the sanctions were not lifted after Trujillo's death; hence they must be viewed as being directed at every aspect of the regime rather than just at Trujillo, as was widely supposed in June 1961.

The implication of this observation is that a distinction could be drawn between factors that contributed to Trujillo's death and factors that contributed to critical political change within the country. Hence, it can be suggested that while sanctions may have been of limited utility as a weapon against Trujillo personally, they acquired substantial symbolic significance as a weapon against the Trujilloists. From the broader perspective of applied sanctions, this poses the possible hypothesis that as long as a sanctioned state possesses a powerful and resourceful leader, it may be capable of resisting sanctions indefinitely.

The assassination plot had been under way since at least late 1960 and was well developed by early 1961. Initially it involved about 20 people; but as it expanded, it became more complicated. The conspirators were organized into two groups, an action group to commit the deed and a political group charged with responsibility for setting up the provisional government.[24] Unfortunately for the conspirators, they did not contemplate the collapse of their scheme and thus failed to provide an escape plan. This error was fatal, for all but two of them subsequently lost their lives. Whether the U.S. government knew of the existence of the conspiracy is open to question. Teodoro Tejeda's "official" investigation linked the CIA to the plot, and his conclusions are supported by Arturo Espaillat.[25] American commentators usually acknowledge that the U.S. government knew of the plot but apparently did little to prevent it, although a futile effort was made to slow it down after the failure of the Bay of Pigs invasion. By that time, the plot was too far advanced and the channels of communication too unreliable to prevent culmination of the plan.[26] There is certainly not enough substantial evidence to support Espaillat's allegation of direct CIA involvement in the plot. But there is unquestionably circumstantial evidence, particularly that relating to the activities of certain American citizens in Ciudad Trujillo and the types of weapons used, to lend support to various assertions that the United States knew--or at least was informed--of the plot. Whether knowledge of a conspiracy necessarily implies approval or even active involvement is an entirely different matter.

As for the possibility of a relationship between the assassination and sanctions, very little concrete evidence is available. Tejeda stated:

> The punishment of the Dominican Republic by enforced economic isolation, besides the diplomatic sanctions . . . [was], at last, the determining cause in the death of the dictator. . . . The country began to suffer the errors of his governments.[27]

It would be stretching imaginations to accept Tejeda's opinion without reservations. His "official" report, prepared in June 1960, had to draw attention away from the Trujilloists still in power. Consequently, factors other than the defects and decay of the regime had to be accorded primary responsibility, although sanctions may have added momentum to the impetus of the conspirators. However, sanctions certainly did not directly trigger the assassination.

In the weeks immediately after the assassination, during the period of the ruthless pursuit of the conspirators, the incumbent President Balaguer was overshadowed by Trujillo's sons, Ramfis and Rhadames, and Trujillo's brother José Arismendi (Pétan). These three conducted an unrestrained campaign of search and destruction of persons associated with the conspiracy. In many cases this included relatives and associates of the conspirators who were in no manner involved.[28] Hence, for incumbent President Balaguer the situation was confusing. Now in command without the encumbrance of Trujillo, he was faced with uncontrollable outbursts by members of the Trujillo family. Thus, while he faced the responsibility of office, a factor that became more important as the OAS pressure continued, he was virtually powerless to exercise the functions of office. For Balaguer the task was to maintain stability and, if possible, appease the OAS. Conversely, Ramfis Trujillo sought to soothe discontent while retaining family control. He may have realized that Pétan also was a willing heir to Trujillo's mantle.

Throughout the period June-November 1961, sanctions began to resemble an internal Dominican political gambit. Initially they symbolized the presence of the OAS or other outside observers in the Dominican political process of establishing normalcy after Trujillo's death. Consequently, by July--after the initial butchery--the sanctions became a lever in the alleged democratization process. It must be observed, however, that this democratization process was clearly considered by those then in power to be taking place within the existing political framework.[29] It was a rejection of this premise by opposition groups (usually under the mantle and symbolic protection of OAS investigatory teams) that ultimately forced a decisive change in the politics of the country.

In September 1961, John Bartlow Martin arrived in Ciudad Trujillo at President Kennedy's behest. Martin saw his role, eventually, as that of providing direction to a people accustomed to obedience but who lacked a clearly defined leader.[30] U.S. involvement in the Dominican Republic, however, predated Martin's arrival and had been partially foreshadowed by Douglas Dillon before the U.S. House of Representatives Committee on Agriculture, August 24, 1960.

The Chairman. Do you then entertain hopes
that Trujillo will purge himself and will reform
and comply strictly with the terms of the OAS
Charter?

Mr. Dillon. Based on his record and his
situation to date, I have considerable doubts that
anything of that nature would be possible.

The Chairman. So then the only alternative
is to bring about the downfall of the Government?

Mr. Dillon. That would be something that
would be left to the Dominican people to determine themselves. There is no intention of inter-
fering in their internal affairs.[31]

Substantial, but detached, American pressure had occurred during the first half of 1961. On January 17, 1961,
President Eisenhower, in one of his last official acts, requested a nine-month extension of authority not to purchase
from the Dominican Republic a proportion of the sugar needed
to replace the former Cuban quota.[32] When Congress did act,
it extended the suspension of the Cuban sugar quota until
December 31, 1962, but specified only that the President
was not obliged to purchase sugar from any country "with
which the United States is not in diplomatic relations."[33]
While the result was not quite what the President had requested, it nevertheless proved to be useful in the Dominican situation.

In conjunction with this abrupt change of attitude toward the Dominican Republic there was a significant overall change in the U.S. approach to Latin America. This
change cannot be attributed exclusively to the Kennedy administration, because much of the groundwork for the attack
on Trujillo had been laid during Eisenhower's last year in
office.[34] Yet the impetus for a major reevaluation of
Latin American policy appears to have been a Kennedy initiative; and the objectives of the Alliance for Progress,
while drafted in economic terms, were undoubtedly related
to political developments as well. Trujillo and the Trujilloists were unquestionably anathema to the program. Had
the Cuban Bay of Pigs invasion of April 15, 1961 been successful, it is possible that the United States might either
have eased the pressure on Trujillo or have opted for a
similar exile-CIA invasion of the Dominican Republic. But
that embarrassing adventure eliminated the possibility of
an identical performance in the Dominican Republic. Hence,
the only available choices were economic pressure, and
political and economic persuasion.

The obsessive U.S. fear of another Castro-type turn of
events in the Dominican Republic clearly dominated the U.S.
approach to the country.[35] The OAS mantle therefore permitted a very direct involvement in the country while the
sanctions became a useful tool. By the end of September
1961, it had become apparent, however, that the immediate
threat to renewed stability was remnants of the Trujillo
family.[36] Thus the immediate task became that of removing
the family from contention while, it was hoped, maintaining
Balaguer in office. Martin presented his report to President Kennedy on October 5, and on the same day Kennedy dis-
patched George McGhee, Undersecretary of State, to the
Dominican Republic as a negotiator. By October 23, with
the exception of Ramfis, remnants of the Trujillo family
were on their way into exile.

However, the removal of the Trujillo family did not
mean the end of the Trujilloists, and this became the next
contentious issue over which the United States exercised
direct control. The first event was the move into exile
on November 17-18, 1961 of Ramfis Trujillo[37] under the
wing--or guidance--of the United States and its Chargé
d'Affaires in the country, John Hill. Ramfis' departure
was materially assisted by the brief return of his uncles
(Hector and Pétan) on November 15, followed by their almost
forcible ejection four days later. The appearance of a
U.S. fleet off Ciudad Trujillo while U.S. navy jets buzzed
the capital and surrounding area, plus the prospect of the
U.S. Marines landing (as in 1965) in support of Balaguer,
did much to persuade Trujilloists to behave.[38]

Once the Trujilloists were gone, full responsibility
for democratization fell squarely upon Balaguer. Unfortunately, the crowds in the streets were beginning to focus
their wrath upon Balaguer, who still reeked of Trujilloism.
On November 29 opposition parties successfully conducted a
general strike, and on December 9 Balaguer and the opposition parties reached agreement in principle on a provisional
government. The agreement was short-lived, for the following day Balaguer declared his intention to remain in office
until the expiration of his term in August 1962. Balaguer's
position was strengthened when General Rodríguez Echavarría
declared the armed forces in support of his position. However, after more street rioting, on December 17 Balaguer
announced a seven-member Council of State with himself as
President. He also announced his intention to resign whenever the OAS lifted sanctions.[39]

At this point U.S. President Kennedy expressed the
opinion that the OAS was considering lifting sanctions and

that a high-level U.S. economic assistance mission was being sent to the Dominican Republic to inquire into economic and social development projects.[40] Such financial assistance would represent a normal stage, that is, recovery assistance for the target state. In theory the San José meeting, which imposed the sanctions, would have considered this prospect. However, there is no evidence of such considerations.

More probable in this case is that the suspension of sanctions, the restoration of quota and nonquota sugar purchases, and the influx of various assistance missions were held out as the rewards--or employed as levers--to force Balaguer to resign and Echavarría to agree. There was also the equal probability that the U.S. fleet, while visibly out of Dominican waters, was not too far beyond the horizon. Possibly this latter persuader did more than anything else to convince Echavarría to withdraw his support of Balaguer within one week.

There seems to be little doubt that the United States alone was responsible for exerting this direct pressure. First, John B. Martin had outlined the entire scenario in his report to Kennedy on October 5. Second, the United States had demonstrated its capacity to direct the OAS Special Committee to consider lifting sanctions (November 14) or, when matters went askew, to defer a decision (November 16). Third, the United States had exclusive control over the fate of an important persuader, the Dominican portion of U.S. sugar quotas. Fourth, of all the OAS members, only the United States was in a position to supply the substantial sums required for the improvement and recovery of the Dominican economy.* Finally, only the United States controlled its fleet. In combination, these factors constitute a solid, and somewhat obvious, base from which to exert pressure or influence. As in other situations in Latin America, the OAS was used to legitimize the process by invoking, and later revoking, formal sanctions (the 1962 Cuban "quarantine"). But the ingredients for a solution that would meet U.S. primary goals were largely of American origin.

On December 29 the Dominican Congress approved a constitutional amendment that permitted the Council of State

------

*On January 22, 1962, the United States extended an emergency $25 million credit to the Dominican Republic, from Alliance for Progress funds, to ease the critical balance-of-payments problem.

to function as a provisional government until February 1963;
the Council of State was sworn into office on January 1,
1962. The OAS sanctions were removed on January 4, and two
days later the United States resumed diplomatic relations
and restored the Dominican sugar quota. A final effort by
Balaguer to retain office again was thwarted by the crowds,
and on January 16, 1962, he resigned. A coup on the same
day by General Echavarría was thwarted two days later by
an air force countercoup. On January 22 the United States
announced a $25 million credit, and by the end of the month
it had restored military hardware support.

It has been suggested on a number of occasions that
sanctions were influential in the events surrounding the
collapse of Trujillo and the Trujilloist regime. Whether
these dramatic consequences were intended by the OAS is
really difficult to determine, although there is no doubt
that the collapse of the regime was a much preferred goal
of some OAS members. However, while it can be broadly conceded that sanctions had a well defined role in political
events, it can be illustrated that Trujillo's regime was
under immense pressure. Some of these pressures are outlined in the following two sections.

TRUJILLO'S PRECARIOUS POSITION:
EXTERNAL THREATS

This section is divided into three parts: (1) comment
on the vanishing regimes of Latin America; (2) exile activity, including 1959 invasions; and (3) a note on the
Galíndez case. The latter is mentioned because it brought
the terror of the Trujillo regime into the continental
United States, thereby arousing anti-Trujillo opinion.
Galíndez's mysterious disappearance in March 1956, and
bungled attempts to cover up details, is frequently conceded to have been a major first crack in the regime's
public relations facade.

No attempt will be made here to explain, beyond a
cursory overview, political trends throughout Latin America
in the few years immediately preceding Trujillo's assassination.[41] While many of the factors involved in political
unrest in Latin America during 1959-60 can be attributed
to the very origins of the Latin American states, others
can be related more specifically to the post-World War II
period. As the following figure and table indicate, there
is little that can be interpreted as a pattern in Latin
American political upheaval in the period 1935-64.

FIGURE 4.1

Successful Coups d'Etat in Latin America , 1935-64
(number per year)

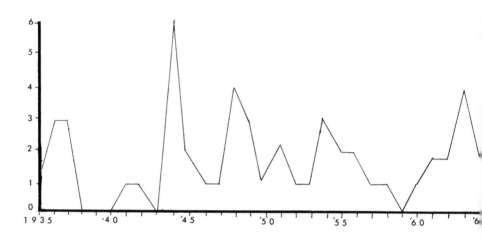

Source: W. C. Soderlund, "The Functional Roles of
Intervention in International Politics" (unpublished Ph.D.
dissertation, University of Michigan, 1970), p. 57.

Figure 4.1 is a visual summary of "successful"* coups
and, if anything, it seems to indicate that the years
1959-61 were almost the least propitious for such upheavals.
Even the longer-range perspective, shown in Table 4.3,
leads to virtually the same conclusion. The average num-

---

*"Successful" coups are defined as those that, through
political violence, deposed the previous chief executive
and in which the new government remained in office for at
least three months. Assassinations of chief executives in
office--Remon, Somoza, Armas, Trujillo, and Kennedy--are
not included because in no instance did the senior government officials change in the short run. Also, for uniform-
ity, regimes overthrown by paramilitary coups, such as Ba-
tista in 1959, are not included.

174

TABLE 4.3

Successful Coups d'Etat in Latin America, 1935-64:
Totals and Averages

Period	Total Number of Coups	Average per Year
1935-39	7	1.4
1940-44	9	1.8
1945-49	11	2.2
1950-54	8	1.6
1955-59	6	1.2
1960-64	10	2.0
Total	51	1.7
1955-61*	10	1.4

*Shown separately, as the period when Trujillo declined from his "pinnacle of power."

Source: Compiled from Figure 4.1.

ber of coups per year, prior to the Dominican upheaval, was the second lowest in the 30-year period 1935-65. This being the case, it is a moot point whether a "momentum" of coups necessarily threatened Trujillo.* The threat to Trujillo's regime appears to have been of a qualitative nature explained by postcoup events. Figure 4.2 partially illustrates this point. The net decline in unequivocally "dictatorial"[42] regimes throughout Latin America is evidence that some form of evolutionary process was under way by 1961.

Therefore, it may be suggested that coups contributed to the decline of dictatorships in Latin America. However, if some of the raw data in Figures 4.1 and 4.2 are combined, the result set forth in Table 4.4 is obtained.[43]

---

*The "momentum" concept supposes that the interaction of various exile groups and/or military officers tends to create a transmission line along which the "waves" from any single coup may travel. And where internal conditions in another state are propitious, another coup may follow. This in turn strengthens the appeal of the first coup, and so on, until there is a reaction and the process is reversed.

FIGURE 4.2

Incidence of Dictatorships in Latin America, 1935-64

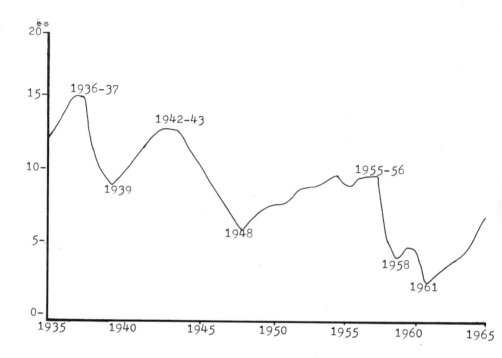

*Numbers refer to dictatorial governments in office for at least six months of the year.

Source: M. C. Needler, Political Development in Latin America: Instability, Violence, and Evolutionary Change (New York: Random House, 1968), p. 41.

Clearly, of course, a change toward constitutionality need not imply a change toward social and economic betterment, for constitutionality may be as reactionary as it is liberal. What is significant, however, is the rebirth of respect for some form of constitutional norms. Between 1950 and January 1961, the military intervened, established provisional governments, and restored adherence to the primacy of a constitution in seven Latin American states.

TABLE 4.4

Flow Chart: Latin American Countries in Which Coups Occurred,
1950-61

Coun-try	1950	1951	1952	1953	1954	1955	1956	1957	1958	1959	1960	January 1961

```
1    M-----------------------*M---P---------C*--------------C

2    Q----*M-Pml-C*-----------------------------------------C

3    C-------------------M--*Q(M)---C*-----------------------C

4    D--------------M-------------------*M-P---C*-------------C

5    C-----------M-----------------------------------Pml-D--------D

6    P-M---------------------------M----P--------------------P

7    C---------------M--P--M-------------------Q---------------Q

8    D-M--------------------------M----P----D---------------D

9    Q----------------------------D---*--P--C*-------------C

10   Q----P---*M-P--C*---------------------------------------C

11   D-----------------M-------------------------------------M

12   M-------------------------------------*M-P--C*---------C
```

M   = Military dictatorship, six months or more.
D   = Civilian dictatorship, six months or more.
P   = Provisional government, six months or more.
C   = Constitutional government, six months or more.
Q   = "Qualified" constitutional government, six months or
      more (a constitutional government that permitted lim-
      ited application of the prevailing constitution).
Pml = Change caused by paramilitary group.
* * = Period of military intervention to restore constitu-
      tionality. (Asterisks bracket period.)

1 = Argentina	7 = Guatemala
2 = Bolivia	8 = Haiti
3 = Brazil	9 = Honduras
4 = Colombia	10 = Panama
5 = Cuba	11 = Paraguay
6 = El Salvador	12 = Venezuela

Source: W. C. Soderlund, "The Functional Roles of Intervention in International Politics" (unpublished Ph.D. dissertation,
University of Michigan, 1970).

Table 4.4 may be summarized as follows:*

1950		January 1961
2 of 12	Military dictatorships	1 of 12
3 of 12	Civilian dictatorships	2 of 12
1 of 12	Provisional governments	1 of 12
3 of 12	Constitutional governments	7 of 12
3 of 12	"Qualified" constitutional governments	1 of 12

Without delving into the probable causes of such changes, it can be established reasonably well that by January 1961 the vanguard of political change in Latin America was running against Trujillo.

Exiles probably have had a more active role in political events in Latin America than in any other region of the world. Diversities of government, variations in levels of political maturity and economic development, and a fundamental homogeneity of language appear to have facilitated activities and ease of movement of exiles. There is also a peculiar Latin American custom of permitting political opponents an opportunity to obtain exile. Perhaps the recognition that almost any presidency may be short-lived, combined with a variation of "Do unto others what you hope they would do to you," allows this process to be perpetuated.

Trujillo's contests with exiles appear to have begun soon after he took office, in an event known as the Cibao-Santiago Plot of 1934. In the late 1930s an opposition vice-presidential candidate in the 1930 Dominican election operated from within the United States, under the unofficial patronage of Undersecretary of State Sumner Welles, against Trujillo.[44] But it was not until after World War II that intensive exile activity began with the 1947 Cayo Confites debacle, which involved, among others, the person who became president in 1962, Juan Bosch. From this failure emerged the somewhat shadowy "Caribbean Legion" based in Guatemala.[45] In June 1949 another disastrous exile invasion was attempted at Luperón. Thereafter, Trujillo re-

---

*The remaining eight Latin American countries on which material was gathered remained unchanged, with the exception of Peru's electoral ouster of the Odría regime. Chile, Costa Rica, Ecuador, Mexico, Peru (after 1956), and Uruguay were constitutional; the Dominican Republic and Nicaragua were military dictatorships as of January 1961.

mained relatively secure for about 10 years, and during that period his network of terror began to systematically eliminate exiles abroad.[46]

However, by 1958 Trujillo's archenemy Rómulo Betancourt was in office in Venezuela, and the following year Castro succeeded in Cuba. The latter proclaimed his intention to see Trujillo overthrown and, in keeping with this desire, he opened Cuba's doors to Dominican exiles in order for them to prepare to combat Trujillo. Possibly Trujillo's position would have been more secure if he had not had to contend with Betancourt, for the latter's presence severely constrained the United States from intervening on behalf of Trujillo against Castro, as had been done with Cuban President Grau to protect Trujillo during the 1947 Cayo Confites affair. Because of Betancourt's attractiveness as an ideological alternative to Castro, Trujillo was considerably less immune by 1959 to exile activities and the exiles, in turn, were much better organized, financed, and sponsored.

Nonetheless, Trujillo had resources of men and arms; and he supplemented these with a $50 million national defense fund and the hiring of former Spanish, German, and Yugoslav mercenaries. Consequently, when the 1959 invasions were launched, his superior armament of napalm, mortars, rockets, and bazookas, was able to crush the invaders.[47] Meanwhile, Trujillo made a pathetic attempt to overthrow Castro in July 1959 by supplying alleged remnants of the Escambray veterans with weapons. The entire project turned out to be a Castro-sponsored hoax, and Trujillo was publicly humiliated.

The most significant contribution the exiles made to Trujillo's downfall was unquestionably provocation and harassment. Of secondary importance was their focusing of adverse publicity upon Trujillo and, in some respects, embarrassment of American legislators who were in close association with his regime. Incidentally, one crucial consequence of their activity was that they did force Trujillo into some large expenditures on defense in anticipation of further exile invasions. At a third level of importance, the exiles slowly became acceptable and viable political alternatives to the Trujillo regime, which was crucial so far as the United States was concerned.

In one respect it can be suggested that it was the exiles, in collaboration with the sympathetic governments, who brought about Trujillo's confrontation with the OAS. Trujillo was unpopular in many Latin American countries; and when he responded against exile provocations, he was declared to be guilty of aggression. Latent and active

sympathy for exiles permitted them to carry on their activities virtually unhindered and, in some instances, to do so
with support from los simpáticos in official positions.
This obvious double standard also was related to the inability, or lack of desire, of states to place responsibility
upon the exiles for their activities, although they proved
most willing to attribute Trujillo's crimes directly and
personally. As fast as one group of exiles was broken up
by arrests or deportations in various Latin American locations, a new group emerged elsewhere. If he had confined
his activities to combating just the exiles, instead of
innovating and attacking los simpáticos, perhaps Trujillo
could have survived.

   As a final comment on the external sources of pressure
on Trujillo, it would be impossible to overlook the adverse
impact of the murder of Jesús de Galíndez, a 42-year-old
Basque nationalist who vanished without a trace from a New
York City subway station on the night of March 12, 1956.
Galíndez had fled Spain in 1939 and settled in the Dominican Republic, where he taught at a diplomatic school. In
1946 he went into exile and became active in and with Dominican and Latin American exile groups in New York. At
the time of his disappearance he had just completed his
Ph.D. dissertation at Columbia.[48] Galíndez's disappearance
was not discovered for a week, and efforts to trace him
failed.

   It was not until December 1956, for an entirely different reason, that details began to emerge. An American,
Gerald Murphy, died under peculiar circumstances in the
Dominican Republic. After his fiancée's parents pressured
their congressional representatives, it was discovered
that Murphy had been the pilot of an aircraft that had
picked up Galíndez's drugged body at an airport at Linden,
New Jersey.[49] The details of the plot are of no concern
here, nor, for that matter, are those of the FBI's inves-
tigations. Suffice it to say that Galíndez was transported
to the Dominican Republic, where, it is widely believed,
Trujillo personally murdered him.[50] Numerous others associated with the plot, including some who were remotely
aware of the strange movements that night (for example,
the watchman at the New Jersey airport), died mysteriously
in the weeks after Galíndez's disappearance. In a futile
attempt to clear himself, Trujillo hired a public relations
firm and a New York lawyer, Morris Ernst, to conduct an
investigation.

   The repercussions of the Galíndez case were far-
reaching. Many of Trujillo's American friends began to

abandon him--largely, it appears, out of fear of being implicated as recipients of financial favors. Exiles had
new fuel added to their claim that Trujillo was dangerous;
and for them, and many others, the disappearance of the
"frail professor" at Trujillo's apparent behest became a
cause célèbre. Galíndez unknowingly became a martyr to
the anti-Trujilloist movement; and Trujillo, never fond of
adverse publicity, found it in abundance after Galíndez.
The affair's contribution to Trujillo's unsteady position
was that it not only focused attention on him but also concentrated the publicity almost exclusively upon the sinis-
ter nature of his regime.

TRUJILLO'S PRECARIOUS POSITION:
INTERNAL STRESS

This section highlights the extent to which pressures
within the Dominican Republic were threatening the stability of the regime. They constituted a complex, and perhaps
formidable, confrontation for Trujillo and may be classified under five basic headings: financial problems, the
position of the military, the attitude of the Church, general corruption and malfeasance, and underground political
opposition.[51]
    Among Trujillo's numerous titles was "Restorer of Our
Financial Independence," to which he was especially attached, for at least until 1930, a major theme in Dominican
history had been abysmal indebtedness that frequently bordered upon national bankruptcy. Indebtedness led to the
brutal American occupation of the country from 1916 to 1922,
and this occupation regime pushed the country into even
deeper indebtedness through a series of public loans at
very favorable rates of interest for American creditors.[52]
Therefore, by 1930, the year Trujillo came to power, government revenues totaled only about $7.3 million, from
which $1.08 million (interest) and $1.80 million (amortization) were deducted, leaving a balance of $4.4 million for
public expenditures.
    From 1924 until 1940, as a result of a bilateral cus-
toms convention, the United States basically controlled
Dominican customs revenues as a means of securing debt
servicing. The Hall-Trujillo Treaty of September 7, 1940,
eased the burden somewhat by permitting amortization and
interest payments to be made through an exclusive American
banking facility. It was not until July 18, 1947, when a
representative of American debtholders received a cere-

monial check for $9,271,855.55, that the country was de-
clared free of all foreign debts. For a number of years
thereafter its financial position improved dramatically,
reaching a peak about 1958.[53] But by 1959 the decline had
begun, and Trujillo's financial independence was being
strained.

Three main factors seem to have been responsible for
the financial problems. First, the 1955 International Fair
of Peace and Brotherhood of the Free World amounted to a
classic financial blunder. Second, the general 1959 recession severely struck Latin America. Third, there was a
growth of revolutionary fervor in the Caribbean region,
and the anticipated threat forced Trujillo into inordinately
large military expenditures.

The International Fair, in which 42 states agreed to
participate, was designed primarily to draw world attention
to Trujillo and his achievements. Serious planning did
not begin until early in 1955, and yet it opened on December 20, 1955. In that period a major highway was constructed between Ciudad Trujillo and San Cristóbal, a major
hotel (the Embajador) was constructed, pavilions and a
stadium were erected, and an estimated $30-40 million was
spent.[54] This rough figure represented approximately one-
third of the total Dominican budget for 1955-56.

If the fair was something over which Trujillo could
have exercised control, the 1959 recession was not. E.
Leiuwen has summarized the problem:

> Contributing to the general Latin American pres-
> sures for a Cuban-type violent social revolution
> were the area's deepening economic woes. The
> trend which began in 1955, toward declining pro-
> duction and income quickened. During 1959 the
> per capita supply of goods and services dropped
> 1.9 per cent while the gross per capita growth
> was the lowest for any year in a decade (except
> 1959). During both years market conditions for
> Latin America's exports remained unfavorable,
> foreign investment declined, and population
> growth outpaced agricultural output to such an
> extent that 8 per cent more food had to be im-
> ported during 1960 than in 1956. In addition
> most governments were saddled with serious finan-
> cial problems.[55]

Adding to Dominican problems in 1959 were a poor sugar crop
and a major reduction in the world sugar price. The coun-

try's earnings from sugar dropped by 15 percent while its earnings from the two other major exports, coffee and cacao, dropped by 25 percent.[56]

The cost of living, while notoriously high in Ciudad Trujillo, climbed by an estimated 20 percent between July and October 1959.[57] V. Alvarez Sánchez, governor of the Dominican Central Bank, agreed that "the country was suffering the effects of a drop in raw materials prices on the world market."[58] Other reports indicated that by December 1959 unemployment had increased; the tourist trade was declining; and business was generally very slow.[59] Exports were down during 1959, as compared with 1958, by 5.1 percent while imports dropped in the same period by 26.3 percent.

By mid-1960, however, the governor of the Central Bank was able to report 1,409 new businesses in the first quarter, as opposed to 167 in the same quarter of 1959. In addition, he reported that, as of June 1, 1960, the total holdings of foreign exchange reserves were $51,287,000 and Central Bank reserves were $47,603,000.[60] It is possible to conclude that the Dominican economy might have recovered, under normal circumstances, by the end of 1960.

The third factor was extensive arms purchases after mid-1959. Trujillo's military was spendidly provided with sophisticated and modern weaponry, as well as rather substantial salaries and, at times, exhorbitant privileges.[61] The air force especially was favored; and when the United States refrained from selling jets, Trujillo turned to British and Swedish (American) jets at premium prices. This was in spite of American pressure upon European allies to refrain from selling arms.[62]

In part, the purchase of elaborate weapons was designed to placate the military and to affirm their special domestic status as an elite social group. In part also, purchases served to strengthen the position of the regime by adding to the domestic control arsenal. Finally, of course, Trujillo actually feared the 1959 invasions and the portent offered for future threats.* Thus, from 1959 on, Trujillo's Dominican Republic acquired the trappings of an armed fortress. It was reported in July 1959:

> The Dominican Republic has assigned $36,680,000
> of its total 1959 budget of $151,365,000 (24.23%)
> to defense. The Government also has available in

---

*Presumably it was his fears that led to the attack on Betancourt.

the budget $25,000,000 for "economic and social improvement and other objectives of national interest". Such an appropriation can likewise be used for a military program.[63]

And in October the same source reported:

Heavy purchases of weapons have forced the Dominican Government to obtain loans ranging up to $40,000,000 abroad, mostly from Canadian banks to help cover the growing deficit in the balance of payments.
   The operation was conducted secretly, as the Government appeared to fear the psychological impact at home of the news that it was borrowing money again.[64]

In addition, the quality of weapons was improving dramatically as Trujillo's era came to a close.[65]
   The most relevant aspect for purposes of this discussion of financial pressures is the extent of Dominican allocation of financial resources to armaments as opposed to other sectors of the economy. Quite clearly, a disproportionate redirection of resources to the military would place a significant burden upon an already strained economy. The 1956-57 Dominican budget was $122,728,500, of which the armed forces were allocated $28,685,110.87, or almost 25 percent.[66] An analysis of Dominican imports during 1960 is even less helpful. A reasonable scrutiny of all the remotely related entries in the Dominican Boletín de comercio exterior (1960)[67] fails to provide anything resembling an accurate basis for estimating probable military expenditures on imported hardware. The following list, compiled from the Boletín de comercio exterior illustrates the statistical futility.

	$R.D.
Arms and parts	94,458
Explosives	180,182
Aircraft and parts	567,348
Trucks and parts	1,236,827
Autos and parts	651,453
Bicycles and parts	136,195
	2,866,463

To this would be added wages and salaries, subventions and ancillary benefits, supplies (uniforms and food), and a total for arms and munitions produced domestically.[68]

A reasonably accurate figure is difficult to obtain. In 1959 President Hector Trujillo had reported a figure of $50 million as "extraordinary measures for national defense."[69] In addition, it can be assumed that a portion of the $40 million obtained from Canadian banks was used, bringing the total to $65-70 million. To this may be added the regular $38 million budgetary appropriation for the year 1959, bringing the grand total close to $100 million, or roughly two-thirds of the national budget.

Of the 1960 budget of $157.6 million, an appropriation of $42.6 million was designated for defense and $25 million for "economic and social improvement." Of this latter figure, the following can be accounted for:[70]

	$R.D.
Military aviation	3,419,890
Navy	3,778,096
"5 de Junio" Movement	3,668,970
National police	2,394,676
Rural police	1,175,504
Other, such as "Foreign Legion"	99,500
	14,336,636

Of the remaining approximately $10.7 million, no accurate account can be provided. In addition, although U.S. military assistance terminated on June 30, 1960, the sum of $445,000 can be included to that date for 1960.[71] There is also something of the Canadian bank loans left to include. Thus, the total 1960 expenditures on defense and the military can be estimated to have been as shown below:

	$R.D.	
Budgetary appropriation	42,000,000	
Social Improvement Fund	25,000,000	(est.)
U.S. assistance	445,000	
Bank loans for 1960	18,000,000	(est.)
	85,445,000	(est.)

Two points must be noted about this estimate of $85,445,000 (or 54.6 percent of the budget) for defense expenditures in 1960. First, it is only a rough calcula-

tion based upon what little information exists; it is
doubtful whether a totally accurate figure could be given,
and it probably is of no great consequence. For even if
the error were 10 percent, the estimate could be simply revised to range from $78 to $93 million for military expenditures in 1960. In either case the same general conclusion
stands: During 1959 and 1960 the Dominican Republic was
devoting an incredibly large sum to defense, and such a
disproportionate amount had a major adverse impact upon the
economy.

A further point in this context relates to Trujillo
family pilferage of the National Defense Fund. While an
overall estimate of defense expenditures may be provided,
there is no means available for estimating how much of this
may have been diverted to Trujillo family pockets. That the
habit was deeply ingrained is not doubted. What may seem
surprising is that even when the regime was seriously
threatened, Trujillo and the family proved unable to divorce
themselves from the temptation to misappropriate funds.

A final note on Trujillo's financial plight may be obtained by citing some features of the Dominican taxation
system during 1959 and 1960.[72] On October 10, 1959, a new,
more sweeping taxation scheme was canceled, a move widely
interpreted "as an admission that the nation could not afford any further economic strain to help finance General
Trujillo's military effort."[73] By early 1960 conditions
were becoming so desperate that taxes were increased or
imposed wherever possible.[74] These ad hoc responses to
the country's financial problems suggest something of the
regime's predicament.

In summary, Trujillo's position as "Restorer of Our
Financial Independence" was seriously in doubt by mid-1960.
The 1955 fair, the 1959 recession, and the 1959-60 military
expenditures were jointly responsible for creating unusual
financial pressures.[75] Hence, the country was economically
weakened by the time sanctions were imposed.

In the preceding pages a number of remarks have been
made about the privileged and well-provided military in
Trujillo's Dominican Republic. Yet if this were so, why
could the military be considered a threat to the regime?[76]
Basically Trujillo was a cautious person who sought to take
every safeguard against military overthrow. He constantly
rotated and purged senior personnel, paid officers high
salaries, created special clubs with corresponding social
status for senior personnel, provided subsidized housing
and quality military equipment, granted rapid promotions
and numerous awards and medals, and created a well-defined

internal domestic role for military personnel.[77] In addition, there was usually some form of external threat to which reference could be made if the military became idle or restless: Haiti's real or imagined territorial ambitions, the onslaught of international communism, the activities of exile groups, and, later, Cuban- and Venezuelan-supported invasion threats. The traditional functions of both the military and the government within the Latin American context thus were mutually acknowledged and respected. Yet there was substantial disaffection, and a brief attempt will be made to explain this contradiction. Two basic factors are foremost in this appraisal: the social status of the military and fear, both Trujillo's and the military's.

Trujillo was the offspring of humble parents and could not normally have expected to become a professional or to have been admitted to the ranks of high Dominican society. However, when the traditional elite reacted with disdain toward U.S. occupiers after 1916, Trujillo did not; and his success was capped with a maneuver for the presidency in 1930. Once in power, and as an expression of contempt for traditional elites, he destroyed the symbols of their status and replaced them with his own creations. Simultaneously, he replaced traditional elites with his own cronies and henchmen in positions of responsibility, and he consolidated his regime through the effective use of private armies of thugs. Consequently, over time he constructed a parallel elite hierarchy that overlapped with traditional society in later years and drew younger members of traditional families into its orbit.

The difference between the two elite structures was that wealth and background were solid footings for traditional society, while the new elite depended entirely upon the whims of El Benefactor. Hence Trujillo's upper and middle classes were motivated by fear of disgrace, obscurity, and even death. Unfortunately, social status usually meant wealth, and in Trujillo's Dominican Republic the means of acquisition were not always commendable. As a result Trujillo retained useful means for coercing members of his elite society. Fear fed upon the realization that wealth and position, once enjoyed, should never be lost. As Espaillat observed, "The Dominican Army, far from being a Praetorian Guard, was kept in a state of frightened subjugation."[78]

Yet it would be wrong to suppose that the senior military was staffed entirely by sycophants. Many younger officers were professionals who had been trained in the United States and France, and had opportunities to view their country from other perspectives. In addition, Trujillo's emphasis upon Dominican nationalism had been drummed into younger officers from their earliest years, thereby nurturing dual loyalties. Over time, therefore, many younger military officers began to view their role in terms of "custodians" of national interest. Trujillo inadvertently nourished this belief by synthesizing every attack upon him as an attack upon the Dominican people and the Dominican state.[79]

As long as the military could perceive the best interests of the Dominican state as being conterminous with the best interests of Trujillo, the latter remained secure. But when Trujillo's persistence in office began to threaten the Dominican state, attitudes began to polarize. And finally, when Trujillo's obdurate hatred of Betancourt led to an irrational attack upon the Venezuelan's life, and this triggered the ensuing isolation and denunciation of Trujillo, the interests of segments of the new and the traditional military elites coalesced for the first time in 30 years. As elements of Trujillo's military middle class assumed the mantle of social respectability, they nurtured the traditional military ethic, protection of the state. In doing so they assumed the habitual role of the Latin American military caste. There was extensive military opposition and discontent that Trujillo adroitly kept under control. Thus, he could prevent overt revolution but, as he probably knew, he was not able to thwart the obsessed few.

Arturo Espaillat, in reviewing Trujillo's relations with the Church, commented: "The Old Man never did really figure out how to cope with his church problem."[80] All Dominican constitutions from 1844 acknowledged the primacy of the Church, and this was formalized in a 1954 Concordat. The function of the Church was multifaceted and included fostering nationalism through education, as well as ministering to the well-being and souls of individuals. "Churchmen tended to interpret any attempt to alter the status quo as inimical to the religion itself."[81]

Generally Church-state relations within the Dominican Republic can be divided into six fairly arbitrary periods: 1502-1795 (the Spanish establishment period); 1796-1844 (the independence activity period); 1844-1929 (the political participation period); 1930-59 (the first quiescent period); 1959-65 (the political involvement period); and 1965 to the present (the second quiescent period). Details are of no concern to this discussion, although the latter two periods normally would be most characteristic.

During Trujillo's first 29 years, the Church tended
to confine its activities to traditional roles. Italian
Archbishop Ricardo Pittini, appointed in 1935, "totally submitted himself to the dictatorship, and on more than one
occasion pronounced eulogies to the dictator."[82] Support
was so extensive that the Archbishop Primate of America was
led to sign a letter to the New York _Times_ objecting to
references to Trujillo as a dictator.[83] The 1954 Concordat
marked the apex of Trujillo's relations with the Church,
although, as his later activities suggest, personal ambitions were not satiated. By 1960, and later in 1961, there
was a concocted public clamor to have Trujillo designated
"Benefactor of the Church," a title previously bestowed
only upon the Holy Roman Emperor Frederick Barbarosa in
1167.[84]

But changes were occurring in the Church, and no
longer would it blissfully support dictators while ignoring
the living conditions of people.[85] Encyclicals from _Rerum
novarum_ (1888), through _Quadragesimo anno domini_ (1931),
and culminating in _Mater et magistra_ (1961) and _Pacem in
terris_ (1965) map the direction of cumulative change in
Church attitudes. This, combined with a replacement for
89-year-old Archbishop Pittini by a younger Dominican,
Archbishop Octavio Beras, portended new pressures upon Trujillo. Beras, "unenthusiastic about the regime," expressed
sympathy for relatives of opponents of the regime (suffering in retaliation for the June 1959 invasion) rather than
affirm traditional support for Trujillo.[86] In October 1959
a new Papal Nuncio arrived, Archbishop Lino Zanini, a
known opponent of dictators.[87]

The definitive break came on Sunday, January 31, 1960,
when a pastoral letter was read to most congregations in
the country.[88] The letter called upon the government to
respect fundamental human rights, including regard for individual freedom, the right of privacy of the home, the
right to emigrate, the right to retain privacy of conscience,
and greater freedom of the press and assembly. Trujillo's
response to the letter was slow in coming; and when it did
appear, it was meek and somewhat conciliatory.[89] He promised the release of all female prisoners and absolute respect for legal rights of all others still in custody. He
warned, however, that he would not permit order, peace, and
stability to be upset by the forces of international communism; and he cautioned the Church to avoid contributing to
anarchy. He urged it to continue its task in the spirit
of harmony that had prevailed since the signing of the
Concordat.

In February, Archbishop Beras, at a mass in the national cathedral,

> spoke of the nation's history but failed to mention Trujillo's name. To omit speaking of the Generalisimo in any speech had long been considered a grave offense, and many believed that its omission by Beras was deliberate. Then clerics began to criticize the regime from their pulpits.[90]

Harassment of clergy and intimidation of laymen ensued. Canadian and American priests were expelled, and Dominican priests and their families were threatened.[91] The Church was accused of being ungrateful for Trujillo's long-standing financial support and of being spiteful for the government's toleration of Protestantism. Trujillo even sent an unsuccessful special mission to Rome in an effort to have the January pastoral letter rescinded. The Church replied with a second pastoral letter on March 6, 1960, calling for the release of all political prisoners before Easter.[92]

Another facet of the overall Church dispute, and one that became ludicrous, was the massive campaign that began early in 1960 to have Trujillo designated as Benefactor of the Catholic Church. From early February until mid-May, the project became a national crusade. Daily, El Caribe carried articles eulogizing aspects of Dominican-Church relations and the efforts by Trujillo to make them harmonious. Entire pages were devoted to letters from citizens lauding the idea of Trujillo's being designated with the highest lay title the Church could offer.[93] In a mid-February reply, the Church noted that it was unable to grant the title; but it assured Trujillo that "God would not let merit go unrewarded."[94] However, by June, Trujillo's patience with the Church had expired and the counter-campaign took on more bizarre, dangerous, and often fatal overtones.

While Trujillo could presume that his harassment campaign had brought the Church under control by December 1960 and in fact had received a letter explaining the January pastoral letter, this was simply an illusion before the final act. For while official "just harmony" prevailed, priests returned once more, as during the 1822-44 Haitian occupation, to revolution in the confessional. In a final, ironic move, President Balaguer again attempted, in early 1961, to revive the title of Benefactor of the Church for Trujillo as a demonstration of good faith by the Church.[95] But, in spite of official harmony, the Church's enthusiasm for the regime was entirely dissipated by early 1961. Consequently, a powerful element in Dominican society was alienated and added its weight to an already disenchanted upper class. The extent to which local clergy actively opposed Trujillo is unknown. However, there is no doubt that, like Perón in Argentina, Rojas Pinilla in Colombia, and Pérez Jiménez in Venezuela, the dictator's days were shortened once the Church turned.[96]

In one respect corruption and malfeasance may not be wholly reprehensible; and it might even be suggested that where private capital is scarce, peasants incapable of being taxed, and outside investment hesitant, corruption may serve as a short-term source of capital formation.[97] Germán Ornes remarked, "If it loses money, it is government owned, if it makes money, it's El Jefe's."[98] Trujillo's techniques were fairly simple and, in some respects, beneficial to the country. If an industry made money, he would endeavor to take it over. This could be achieved in one of two ways: (1) if it was privately owned by a Dominican, intimidation, oppressive taxation, coercion, or outright assassination might be employed to sway the owner; (2) if it was privately owned by a foreigner, coercion or taxation might be employed, followed by an offer to purchase. In other areas--for example, imported goods--Trujillo would either establish or take over an existing import business. If this was not possible, he would establish a domestic producer and then drastically increase tariffs on the competitive imported product. In any situation the important objective was the establishment of a Trujillo enterprise in a monopoly or dominant-share position. Frequently he dabbled in the creation of enterprises on the advice of close associates or itinerent schemers. In some cases public money was employed to establish an operation that, if profitable, was later transferred to Trujillo. In other instances Trujillo's money was utilized to create an enterprise, usually managed by a close friend or relative; and if it proved profitable, it was retained. Failing that, the government acquired another enterprise.

Supporting the entire entreprenurial structure in the Dominican Republic was a system of variable taxation, price controls, exorbitant interest rates on loans, and a semi-official system of kickbacks, bribes, and payoffs. For the system to succeed, of course, it could not be confined exclusively to Trujillo or even to his family. Consequently corruption and malfeasance were deemed to be the right of almost every petty civil or military bureaucrat. This had the triple advantage of keeping Trujillo supporters content, of creating a vested interest in his perpetuation, and of providing reasons for the removal from office of any official on charges of corruption should the official prove dangerous to Trujillo or too overtly obnoxious to the people.[99]

Unfortunately, commentators who focused exclusively upon Trujillo's personal corruption overlooked the most essential aspect of the relationship between corruption and the collapse of the regime. Trujillo, the promoter of the ethic of corruption, was held neither liable for the practice nor culpable for the result by the bulk of the Dominican population. Some observers, such as Juan Bosche, Germán Ornes, and Jesús de Galíndez, saw a relationship; but the mass of the population did not. Hence the paradox of people praising Trujillo for his attacks upon corruption while he simultaneously directed his massive piracy. Trujillo's corruption, however, served the identifiable purpose of materially improving the country, whereas that of his officials served only for their personal aggrandizement.

In view of the above discussion, an estimate of Trujillo's wealth and the extent of his holdings becomes incidental to an explanation of the relationship between corruption and the decline of the regime.

Estimates vary widely on the gross worth of the Trujillo family, but Howard J. Wiarda summarized a number of pre- and postassassination estimates. The latter are generally considered to be more accurate because of the large-scale seizure of properties within the country during 1961 and 1962.[100]

> The estimates of the amount of the fortune vary. Kraslow [Miami Herald, June 8, 1972, p. 1-B] put it at $500 million; both Ornes, Trujillo: Little Caesar, p. 234, and Jimenes-Grullón ["Trujillo: More Croesus than Caesar," The Nation 189 (December 29, 1959): 485-86], p. 485, stated that it was "more than $500 million"; Ziegler [Jean Ziegler, "Santo Domingo: Feudo de Trujillo," Cuadernos (Paris) no. 46 (January-February 1961): 98-102], p. 101, placed it in the neighbourhood of $800 million; and Hispanic American Report, XIV (July 1961), p. 412, estimated it at $1 billion. The figure of $800 million was chosen because (1) it is roughly the average of the several estimates, and (2) this is the figure at which the highly respected "National Zeitung" of Basel,

Switzerland (Trujillo's principal bankers) arrived.
See Geoffrey Bocca, "A Dictorator's Legacy" [This
Week (September 19, 1965): 3 ff.], p. 5.[101]

The figure of $800 million is plausible. Likewise, the na-
ture of the Trujillo holdings cannot be determined accurately. Various lists have been prepared, but they all faltered over the problem that very little of the property was
held in Trujillo's name.[102]

Generally, therefore, it can be estimated that Trujillo and Trujillo-related enterprises were principal pil-
lars in the Dominican economic system. Unfortunately,
large quantities of the profits were diverted out of the
country, thereby imposing a massive drain upon resources.
Moreover, the Trujillo example encouraged hosts of petty
thieves to prosper, much to the annoyance and disadvantage
of the population at large. As a consequence the population looked upon Trujillo with devotion and respect but
upon the regime with envy, frustration, and deep skepticism.

Doubtless there were other internal pressures upon
the regime, and clandestine groups began to consolidate
sentiments of opposition (Movimiento 14 de Junio, Unión
Cívica Nacional--largely businessmen and professionals).[103]
That much of this pressure welled forth during the regime's
final two years suggests an immense cumulative result.
The regime was under a veritable onslaught of interlocking
internal pressures, and thus it was in serious trouble by
the time OAS multilateral sanctions were imposed. The
ramifications will become clearer in the remainder of this
chapter.

THE OAS AND THE UNITED STATES

Generally this section reviews one major subject, although a number of ancillary matters are noted in passing.
Primarily the discussions review the background to the
OAS sanctions imposed, initially in August 1960, against
Trujillo's Dominican Republic. The reason for sanctions,
the procedure for imposition, and some of the international
legal aspects are considered. In addition, background
comments are offered on U.S. relations with the hemisphere
and the Dominican Republic.

The OAS and Venezuela's Complaint

Probably little needs to be said about the Organization of American States (OAS), for most observations of

consequence are much more adequately stated elsewhere.[104]
At the time of the Dominican sanctions it seems to have
been assumed, or believed widely, that the OAS represented
a fairly well defined, if not sophisticated, system of collective security lubricated and supported by a network of
inter-American social and economic institutions. Much of
what poses as collective security, however, has been an
elaborate defensive response by Latin Americans to the immense presence of the United States in the hemisphere.[105]

By 1960 the OAS was firmly based upon two documents,
the 1947 Rio Treaty (Treaty of Reciprocal Assistance) and
the 1947 Charter of Bogotá (the OAS Charter), and provided
the framework within which the 1960 Dominican situation
was handled. While the Inter-American Conference was the
primary governing body of the organization, the essential
work was undertaken by the Council.

The OAS Council is the core of the inter-American system, and in many circumstances it can be the key to OAS
action. Under provisions of both the OAS Charter (Article
52) and the Inter-American Treaty of Reciprocal Assistance
(Article 12), the Council (also known as the Governing
Board of the Pan American Union) may act provisionally as
the organ of consultation.[106] The formal organ of consultation is the meeting of consultation of Ministers of Foreign Affairs. But because haste is often required, and because Foreign Ministers cannot readily be assembled, the
Council may act formally as an ad hoc decision-maker, that
is, as the organ of consultation. The process is fairly
straightforward. When a problem is submitted to the Council, it may act as the Council or it may resolve itself
into the provisional organ of consultation. If the problem
is not settled at this stage, it may call for a meeting of
consultation of Ministers of Foreign Affairs. The ministers, when formally convened for that purpose, constitute
the organ of consultation. The full procedure was followed
in response to the Venezuelan complaint against the Dominican Republic in June 1960.

Before reviewing the specific application, however, a
brief review of Venezuela's role in the process is essential; for it was Venezuela, under President Rómulo Betancourt, that had cause to request invocation of the collective security provisions of the OAS system.

Betancourt once described his country as a "republic
for sale," and his observation doubtless was accurate until the brief spates of democracy experienced by the country under his presidencies.[107] Betancourt and his Acción
Democrática Party (A.D.) initially succeeded in 1945 and

managed to retain office only until 1948, when, after some
convincing, Lieutenant Colonel Marcos Pérez Jiménez took
over. In the interval between Pérez's ascendancy and Betancourt's return in 1959, A.D. members were persecuted and
harassed almost anywhere they obtained refuge in Latin
America. Such treatment ultimately proved disastrous for
both Pérez and Trujillo, for the persecution intensified
Betancourt's resolve to rid the hemisphere of dictators.
Betancourt, of course, was a long-time opponent of dictators and was a member of the Venezuelan "generation of
1928," a title assigned to a group of university students
who revolted against President Juan Vicente Gómez in that
year.[108] Betancourt led the Partido Democrático Nacional
(1935-41) and its successor, the Acción Democrática, both
within Venezuela and in exile.

The Trujillo-Betancourt animosity appears to have
originated with the latter's official and unofficial involvement in the 1947 ill-fated Cayo Confites invasion of
the Dominican Republic. The Venezuelan government was a
major source of financial support for exile groups attempting to overthrow Trujillo; and in 1951, when Betancourt
was again in exile, Trujillo organized an assassination attempt against him in Havana by injection of poison.[109] By
1959, with Betancourt once more in power, the momentum of
opposition to Trujillo was growing. Initially Betancourt
sought to regularize relations between the two countries,
and he even invited Trujillo to his inauguration. By then,
however, Trujillo's obsessive and obdurate hatred had become so great that he responded with a propaganda campaign
against Betancourt and Venezuela. This project reached a
ludicrous climax in November 1959, when a Dominican aircraft mistakenly dropped anti-Betancourt leaflets on Curaçao instead of Caracas.

Meanwhile the Dominican government was conducting a
campaign against both Cuba and Venezuela before the OAS.
In July 1959, the Dominicans had requested convocation of
the OAS Council to consider

> certain charges against the Republic of Cuba and
> Venezuela in respect of two invasion attempts
> against the Dominican Republic verified in June
> 1959, which were allegedly organized in the ter-
> ritory of the Republic of Cuba with the partici-
> pation of the Government of Venezuela.[110]

Unfortunately for the Dominicans, the attempt faltered
when the OAS Council voted, on July 10, to consider the

entire unstable situation that then existed in the Caribbean at the fifth meeting of the Ministers of Foreign Affairs acting as the organ of consultation. Eventually the
Dominican move backfired, for when the fifth meeting was
convened, the two main items on the OAS Council's approved
agenda were the situation creating tension within the Caribbean and the exercise of representative democracy and respect for human rights.[111]

Contrary to Dominican expectations, the fifth meeting
of consultation, August 12-18, 1959, served as the spring-
board for much of Venezuela's counterassault on Trujillo's
regime. A document known as the Declaration of Santiago,
Chile, emerged from the meeting; and it contained references to the "existence of anti-democratic regimes" as violations of the principles on which the OAS was founded.[112]
Resolution IV of the meeting entrusted to the Inter-American Peace Committee the role of investigating "the questions that were the subject of the convocation of this
Meeting."[113] Finally, Resolution VIII of the meeting directed that the Inter-American Council of Jurists prepare
a draft Convention on Human Rights, while Resolution IX entrusted the OAS Council with the duty of preparing a "draft
convention on the effective exercise of representative
democracy."[114]

The fifth meeting of consultation was a severe blow
to Trujillo's diplomacy. For the progressive governments
of Venezuela, Costa Rica, Cuba, and Peru it was quite the
opposite; and the United States appears to have acquiesced
in their victory.

Venezuela's final onslaught against the Dominicans began in early 1960. Employing the Dominican bishop's pastoral letter of January 31, Venezuela requested, on February 5, an OAS investigation into violations of human
rights in the Dominican Republic; on February 8, a special
meeting of the OAS Council was convened to hear the Venezuelan charges.[115] The Council meeting on February 8 heard
both the Venezuelans and the Dominicans; and after some
discussion it referred the matter to its General Committee,
which reported that the Inter-American Peace Committee was
a more appropriate body to consider Venezuela's complaint.
The Peace Committee reported on June 6, 1960, that there
had been substantial violations of human rights in the
Dominican Republic that were the root causes of tensions
within the Caribbean region.[116]

During the period of the Peace Committee's investiga-
tions, Trujillo's campaign against Betancourt increased in
intensity. El Caribe's pages were filled, for example,

with personal attacks on Betancourt, his government, and Venezuela in general.[117] Also during April an unsuccessful military coup in San Cristóbal, Venezuela, was discovered to have been led by Venezuelan military exiles who had entered the country vía Colombia on diplomatic passports issued by the Dominican government. This failure provoked Trujillo into an assassination attempt against Betancourt in Caracas on June 24, 1960, and it was this attack that set off the final series of events leading to the OAS sanctions.

Trujillo's, or at least the regime's, involvement in the attempt against Betancourt was substantially confirmed by the OAS investigating team. The reasons for such a brash act are in some respects explicable, while in other respects they can be classified only as the irrational actions of a man governed by instincts.[118]

Trujillo was caught in a quandary and, unfortunately for him, the complexity of the situation prevented recourse to a habitual simplistic solution. The real death struggle for Trujillo probably should have been with Castro; and had it been a straight two-way fight, he might have succeeded, because he could have relied upon the support of the United States. However, the loose and temporary alliance of Betancourt and Castro added an aspect to the struggle with which Trujillo could not readily contend. Betancourt's popular democratic revolution was appealing to many Latin Americans, for it offered an alternative, besides the Cuban example, to repressive dictatorships.

The anti-Nixon riots of 1958 and the appearance of Castro in 1959 focused U.S. attention on the dual requirement of maintaining Latin American stability while encouraging broad social change. In essence, the United States had to upgrade Betancourt and downgrade Castro, and there simply was no room for Trujillo's involvement. Trujillo became increasingly more expendable as the nature of Castro's revolution attracted Latin American activists. While he was probably correct in finding the State Department culpable in the attacks upon him, Trujillo's error was to lash out against three quite different opponents with the same form of abuse.

Clearly, too, Trujillo's involvement in the attempt against Betancourt was a direct product of his fanatic personal hatred of the Venezuelan. In his almost blind attempt to solve the problem, he employed the conventional technique of an assassination plot. Had the attempt been against Castro, it is possible that the OAS, and certainly the United States, could have tolerated the result. But

when he sought to eliminate the leader of the one social
revolution that the United States was tactically committed
to support, his action was beyond toleration. Latin Americans and Americans knew that Betancourt was not a typical
caudillo; rather, he was a popular image for those who
sought the maintenance of political stability through peaceful social change. The attack on Betancourt's life was too
brazen and too overt to be allowed to go unpunished, and
thus Trujillo's habits and instincts virtually sealed his
fate. Arturo Espaillat was partially correct when he referred to Trujillo's "death struggle" with Castro as one in
which, "except for outside intervention, the Old Man might
have succeeded." However, Espaillat overlooked the obvious
point that the outside intervention was largely a product
of Trujillo's own blunders in his relations with Venezue-
la.119

Although there may have been some doubt about the absolute veracity of all the evidence presented by the government of Venezuela regarding the events of June 24, 1960,
there is little doubt that the OAS Council's committee investigating the assassination attempt believed that this
incident, in conjunction with others to which it drew attention, constituted sufficient evidence to warrant employment of disciplinary procedures against the Dominican Re-
public.120 The incidents in which the Dominican Republic
was involved leading up to June 24, 1960 were the inadver-
tent dropping of leaflets on Curaçao on November 19, 1959
and the military uprising in San Cristóbal between April
20 and 22, 1960.

On the first case the committee of the Council concluded:

> The necessary arrangements to carry out the
> flight from Ciudad Trujillo to Aruba--planned
> for the purpose of dropping leaflets over a Vene-
> zuelan city--and to load those leaflets in Ciu-
> dad Trujillo, could not have been carried out
> without the connivance of the Dominican authori-
> ties [p. 19].

As for the April military uprising, it summarized:

> On March 12, 1960, the Government of the Domini-
> can Republic issued diplomatic passports to the
> Venezuelan nationals former General Jesús María
> Castro León and Juan de Dios Moncada Vidal, and
> on April 16 requested diplomatic visas from the

Embassy of Colombia in Ciudad Trujillo ostensibly
in order to take agriculture courses in Colombia.
These two persons did not use the said passports
for their trip to Colombia,but arrived in Colom-
bian territory on April 17, and on the 20th of
the same month they were in Venezuela heading a
military uprising against the Venezuelan Government. The Government of the Dominican Republic
likewise issued diplomatic passports to Luis M.
Chafardet Urbina and Oscar Tamayo Suárez, Venezuelan nationals and well-known opponents of the
present government of the country [p. 20].

The committee observed that these events, and the background to them, were fairly widely known. Thus when a request was made to the chairman of the OAS Council by the
Venezuelan government "to consider the acts of intervention
and aggression by the Government of the Dominican Republic
against the Government of Venezuela, which culminated in
the attempt upon the life of the Venezuelan Chief of State
on June 24 last" (p. 28), the Council effectively had been
preconditioned to consider the request serious and the
situation dangerous.

The Council met in July 1960 and approved a resolution
that, among other things, put into motion procedures for
convening the organ of consultation, appointed a committee
to investigate the facts, and informed the United Nations
Security Council of measures being taken. By August 8 it
reported:

(1) The attempt against the life of the President of Venezuela perpetrated on June 24, 1960,
was part of a plot intended to overthrow the government of that country.
(2) The persons implicated in the aforemen-
tioned attempt and plot received moral support
and material assistance from high officials of
the Government of the Dominican Republic.
(3) This assistance consisted principally of
providing the persons implicated facilities to
travel and to enter and reside in Dominican territory in connection with their subversive plans;
of having facilitated the two flights of the
plane of Venezuelan registry to and from the
Military Air Base of San Isidro, Dominican Republic; of providing arms for use in the coup
against the Government of Venezuela and the elec-

tronic device and the explosive which were used
in the attempt; as well as having instructed the
person who caused the explosion in the operation
of the electronic device of that explosive and
of having demonstrated to him the destructive
force of the same [pp. 26-27].

The committee's report and its conclusions were an indict-
ment of the Dominican government's complicity in the assassination plot. Such conclusions left little space for the
Dominicans to maneuver, as they doubtless realized. Equally
significant, other members of the OAS realized this; and
even regimes as dictatorial as Haiti's and Paraguay's had
to find the Dominicans guilty despite the former's preference for Trujillo's government over that of Betancourt's.*

Sixth Meeting of Consultation,
San José

The OAS Council, pursuant to its resolution of July
8, met on July 29 and resolved to convoke the organ of consultation, as the sixth meeting of consultation, in San
José, Costa Rica, which began on August 16.[121] Four generalizations can be made about this meeting. First, the
statements by OAS member participants can be categorized
roughly as follows:

1. Attacks on the Dominican Republic and the person
of Trujillo: Venezuela, Peru, Bolivia, Ecuador, Colombia,
and Cuba;
2. Moderate statements in support of the principles
of the OAS and inter-American solidarity: Uruguay, Mexico,
Honduras, El Salvador, Guatemala, Panama, Nicaragua, Chile,
and Costa Rica;
3. Moderate statements, equivocating, compromising,
or virtually noncommittal: United States, Haiti, Paraguay,
and Argentina;
4. In defense of the Dominican Republic and Trujillo:
Dominican Republic.

----

*The actual assassination attempt was fairly straight-
forward and involved nothing more than the detonation of an
explosive-laden vehicle as Betancourt's auto was passing.
Two persons died and Betancourt was injured. The Venezuelans involved were trained in the Dominican Republic by one
of Trujillo's most despicable henchmen, Johnny Abbes García.

Second, many of the statements were liberally endowed with pleas for justice and equity, preservation and promotion of democracy, defense and credibility of the inter-American system and inter-American solidarity, descriptions and interpretations of nonintervention, the moral obligation to assist the Dominican people, and moral commitments to uphold international law. Thus, the meeting served not only as a place of judgment but also as a forum for pronouncements upon, and a reassessment and affirmation of, the ingredients of hemispheric relations.

Third, there were numerous references to the fifth meeting of the consultation, held a year earlier. The significance of these references can be judged in terms of the ease with which the sixth meeting found the Dominican Republic culpable of the offenses alleged, a fact that lends weight to an observation offered earlier that OAS members were predisposed to find Trujillo guilty. The fifth meeting had been convened to consider the unstable situation that existed in the Caribbean region and, although never specifically designated as a source of problems, doubtless the Dominican Republic and Trujillo were in the minds of many delegates. Consequently, by the time of the sixth meeting, and in the face of both the Inter-American Peace Committee's report on the violations of human rights within the Dominican Republic as a source of regional instability and the Council's investigation committee report of August 8, 1960, the sixth meeting was well prepared to consider the Dominican regime intolerable.

Finally, and somewhat related to the third generalization, it was fairly evident from the tone of the statements made at the sixth meeting that most participants anticipated the outcome. There were few statements that could be interpreted as immediate responses to what either disputant said. This suggests that most Foreign Ministers had been briefed before attending the meeting and that conclusions had been derived somewhat independently. The meeting thus formalized a collectivity of reasonably similar conclusions into a single consensus decision and course of action.

Debate at the sixth meeting of consultation began with a statement by the Venezuelans in which Venezuelan democracy was contrasted with Trujillo's tyranny. A request was made that Article 8 (the sanction provision) of the Rio Treaty be invoked and that the Dominican Republic be declared an aggressor as a consequence of its acts of intervention against Venezuela (p. 77). Specifically, Venezuela requested the application of all sanctions "with the exception of the ultimate, intervention by armed force."

The quasi-judicial character of this meeting was evidenced in both procedure and form of approval. For once Venezuela completed its charges, the Dominicans were given the opportunity to reply and to produce counterevidence.*

The Dominican response was comprehensive and detailed, challenging facts in the evidence produced by the OAS investigatory committee (pp. 81, 82), questioning the stability of Betancourt's government (pp. 85-88), and suggesting that the real aggressor--in any case--was Venezuela.** Porfirio Herrera Baez concluded his remarks by raising two significant subjects: the precise nature of the Treaty of Reciprocal Assistance and the relationship between the OAS, the Rio Treaty, and the United Nations. The Dominicans argued that the Rio Treaty was essentially an interhemispheric defense system rather than an intrahemispheric defense mechanism, and it was noted that Article 9 of the Rio Treaty failed to mention defense within the hemisphere.[122] An offer was then made to resolve the Dominican complaint against Venezuela under the terms of Article 7 of the treaty.

Perhaps the most challenging matter raised by the Dominicans was that of the relationship between the United Nations and the OAS and Article 51 (self-defense) in the UN Charter. There is not much point going into the question here; suffice it to note that the Dominican attempt to constrain OAS action failed.[123] For, as noted earlier, decisions appear to have been made; and most representatives employed the occasion to affirm key premises in the inter-

---

*The Venezuelan case was argued by Ignacio Luis Arcaya, a left-wing member of Betancourt's governing coalition. He resigned as Foreign Minister 10 days after his attack on the Dominicans, over Betancourt's failure to support Castro at the seventh meeting of consultation. The Dominicans were represented by Porfirio Herrera Baez, Secretary of State for Foreign Relations.

**Herrera used the term golpismo to describe the possible fate of Betancourt's government. That is, it was on the verge of collapse from within, and the assassination was part of that malaise. He cited instances of Betancourt's expressed animosity toward Trujillo, including a 1947 call (made while Betancourt was visiting Guatemala) for a "prophylactic," or "sanitary cordon" around Trujillo ("un cordon profiláctico contra la República Dominicana") (pp. 98, 99). Also noted was Castro's visit to Caracas in January 1959 to start a fund for the "March of Bolívar to Santo Domingo."

American system. Thus, the words democracy, equity, justice, and solidarity spewed forth with unimaginative regularity.

For the United States this sixth meeting of consultation was a prelude to the seventh, which followed immediately and attempted to grapple with the growing thorn of Cuba. Hence Christian Herter's defense (p. 133) of the inter-American system's capacity to maintain collective security for the members was as much an affirmation of faith in the system as it was a warning against outside intervention.[124] Essentially what happened was that moderate opinion prevailed at the sixth meeting. Panama (p. 143), El Salvador (p. 156), Chile (p. 183), and Guatemala (p. 159) came to the conclusion that,

> If the violations of international law are clear and precise, if the evidence sustains the accusations of one State against another, of intervening in its internal affairs, or of committing acts of aggression that injure its sovereignty, such as there is no doubt of the culpability of the infractor, in conformity with the agreement contained in the Rio Treaty, the Members of the inter-American community have an obligation to impose the sanctions established by Article 8 of the Treaty of Reciprocal Assistance, in accordance with the seriousness of the crime denounced.

An effort was being made, therefore, to establish a clear and indisputable crime-guilt-punishment relationship. Consequently, and despite some digressions into related legal areas, it was toward this conclusion that the sixth meeting of consultation moved.

The meeting concluded on August 21, 1960, with unanimous passage of Resolution I of the sixth meeting of consultation of the Ministers of Foreign Affairs.[125] Resolution I recited the history of Dominican offenses against Venezuela, culminating in the attempted June assassination, and concluded that collective action was justified under Article 19 of the OAS Charter. The meeting then agreed:

> 1. To apply the following measures:
> a. Breaking of diplomatic relations of all the member states with the Dominican Republic;
> b. Partial interruption of economic relations of all the member states with the Dominican Republic, beginning with the immediate suspen-

sion of trade in arms and implements of war of
every kind. The Council of the Organization of
American States, in accordance with the circumstances and with due consideration for the constitutional or legal limitations of each and every
one of the member states, shall study the feasibility and desirability of extending the suspension of trade with the Dominican Republic to
other articles.

    2. To authorize the Council of the Organi-
zation of American States to discontinue, by a
two-thirds affirmative vote of its members, the
measures adopted in this resolution, at such
time as the Government of the Dominican Republic
should cease to constitute a danger to the peace
and security of the hemisphere.

    3. To authorize the Secretary General of
the Organization of American States to transmit
to the Security Council of the United Nations
full information concerning the measures agreed
upon in this resolution.

The sixth meeting was a milestone in OAS history, for
it committed the organization to collective economic and
political action against a perceived threat to hemispheric
security. The conclusion appears to have been arrived at
by OAS members somewhat independently, and thus Trujillo's
value as governing a stable regime was outweighed by his
nuisance value. When this occurred, the OAS and its most
prominent member, the United States, turned. Specifically,
for the United States the sixth meeting was a brief realization that the status quo would not remain indefinitely.

In September the OAS Council appointed a special committee to review the effectiveness of Resolution I and to
make further recommendations as required. In December the
committee reported, and on January 4, 1961, Resolution I
was expanded. The January 4 extension of Resolution I
read:

    1. To state that it is feasible and desir-
able that the member states of the Organization
who signed the Final Act of the Sixth Meeting of
Consultation of Ministers of Foreign Affairs extend the suspension of their trade with the Dominican Republic to the exportation of the following items.

a. Petroleum and petroleum products
b. Trucks and spare parts

2. To request the member states, in connection with the preceding paragraph, to take measures to prevent the re-export of the items mentioned from their territory to the Dominican Republic.

3. To request the governments of the member states to inform the Chairman of the Council of the Organization regarding the measures they take with respect to the resolution, in order that this Council and the Security Council of the United Nations may be kept informed in the matter.

Thus, by January 1961 the profile of OAS sanctions against the Dominican Republic was complete.* The complete sanctions scheme remained in force for exactly one year, and on January 4, 1962, the sanctions were canceled. Before turning to our evaluation of the sanctions, a brief note on U.S.-Dominican relations is essential.

The United States and the
Dominican Republic

It is probably not surprising that Dominican foreign relations during Trujillo's rule were dominated by hemispheric ties that were predominantly related to U.S. influence. For example, a review of Dominican diplomatic representation in 1950-51 (the apex of Trujillo's career) reveals that of the 31 countries with representatives accredited to the Dominican Republic, 18 were fellow OAS members, while of the 29 countries in which Dominicans were accredited, 19 were fellow OAS members.[126]

If the Dominican Republic had an identifiable foreign policy during Trujillo's rule, at best it was opportunistic and appears to have had three bases: nonintervention and intervention to protect the regime; trappings of humanitarianism; and anticommunism. In brief, Trujillo appealed at various times to nonintervention as a means of protecting and solidifying his regime in the face of exiles and

---

*The resolution to extend the sanctions passed with the bare two-thirds required majority. Brazil submitted a dissenting report with the Special Committee's December report and recommendations. By January, therefore, other factors were beginning to come into play.

others supported by Cuba, Haiti, and other countries. Conversely, he was not averse to surreptitious intervention, as typified by the attempt on Betancourt's life in June 1960, to remove opponents of his regime almost anywhere in the Caribbean or United States.[127]

The humanitarian facade was concocted in 1939 when Dominicans announced, at a conference in France on Jewish refugees, that they were willing to accommodate 100,000 refugees. A community was established at Sousa on the north coast, and over the next few years about 800 refugees arrived; the scheme never reached the grandiose proportions envisaged at its proclamation, however.[128] The other on-going aspect was the attacks on racism in South Africa that appeared with some frequency in official newspapers.[129] All of this appears to have been a rather shallow attempt to cloak the regime in respectability, and it had about the same authenticity as Trujillo's anticommunism.

Americans have been duped so frequently by the anti-communist gimmick that it is surprising that it can be trundled out with such appalling frequency.* From 1946 until 1961 it was manipulated by Trujillo to win friends and influence in Washington. On only two occasions did the pace weaken, the first time in 1949, when the Communist Party was legalized long enough to ferret out supporters and then to establish a Committee on Anti-Dominican Acts. Again, very briefly in 1961 the regime allegedly flirted with communism, and Dominican media even quoted Tass news agency reports in an effort to convince Americans that the ill treatment of Trujillo after the San José meeting was driving Dominicans to the political alternative.

Within the United States this type of nonsense, in combination with regular and irregular lobbying activities, paid limited political dividends. Witness the following exchange:

> Mr. Poage: I think it is pretty well known that Mr. Trujillo has made a big point about his opposition to Communism, up until, as you say, the last 2 or 3 months when you forced him into another position. But for the last 30 years he has made a tremendous point of it.

---

*Like the Dominicans before them, Rhodesians recently have promoted the "red scare" as a propaganda technique designed to win sympathy in the United States.

Mr. Dillon: Well I don't know of any organization in the world that is more stanch [sic]
against communism than the Catholic Church, and
they oppose Mr. Trujillo.

Mr. Poage: They did not until we meddled
into the country's affairs and caused the persecution of a number of people. . . .

Mr. Poage: I am not trying to defend Mr.
Trujillo, I think he is ruthless. Sure, I think
he has been our friend. . . . I think when we
are going to go out and persecute somebody we
ought to persecute somebody who has been perse-
cuting us rather than simply basing our action
on some theoretical idea that he is violating human rights. . . .

Mr. Poage: And here we come out and say
that we are going to kick the outfit in the teeth
that has been at least very vocal about opposition to communism. And I think up until the last
few months everybody agreed they had been very active in preventing communism . . . one of the
very few of these stable Latin American governments.[130]

Bilateral Dominican-U.S. relations in the Trujillo era
are summarized in the following chronology compiled from
a number of sources.

1930: The United States reluctantly extends recognition
to Trujillo's government.
1937: United States pressures Trujillo to indemnify Haiti
for victims of the October 1937 Blood River Massacre.
1940 (September): $5 million U.S. Export-Import Bank loan
for improvement of harbors and air bases for joint use.
1941 (August 2): Lend-lease arms agreement.
1941 (December 8-11): Dominican Republic declares war on
the Axis.
1947 (July 17): Trujillo-Hull Agreement settling outstanding debts.
1951 (February 23): Dominican Point Four Agreement signed.
1951 (November 26): Dominicans grant facilities for test-
ing of long-range U.S. guided missiles.
1953 (March 6): Military Assistance Agreement signed (terminated June 20, 1961).
1956 (Summer): Jesús de Galíndez vanishes in New York and
subsequent FBI investigation links Trujillo.

1958 (June 17): Dominican officers and cadets enrolled in U.S. military establishments are ordered home after Trujillo's son Ramfis fails to graduate at Fort Leavenworth.

1958 (June 19): Trujillo rejects U.S. military aid and revokes agreements permitting the United States to operate radar stations.

1959 (July 10): Brazil, Chile, the United States, and Peru propose a fifth meeting of consultation to consider Caribbean unrest.

1960 (July-August): U.S. House of Representatives Committee on Agriculture reviews Dominican sugar quota.

1960 (August 21): The United States votes sanctions against Trujillo's regime.

1960 (September): President Eisenhower imposes a special two-cents-a-pound levy on Dominican sugar imports.

1961 (January): The United States votes to extend OAS sanctions.

1961 (September): President Kennedy's special envoy, J. B. Martin, visits Dominican Republic.

1961 (December) to 1962 (January): The United States takes the initiative for removal of OAS sanctions.

This list does not include, of course, the plethora of semiofficial and private relations maintained between the two countries. It is known that of the total 1961 foreign investment of an estimated $110 million, $107 million was American, including a number of subsidiaries of United Fruit, Pan-Am, Aluminum Company of America, Chase-Manhattan Bank, and First National City Bank of New York.[131]

During the investigation of Galíndez's disappearance, it was revealed that Trujillo had a stable of Washington public relations personnel, including lawyer Frank Rosenbaum, Cholly Knickerbocker (columnist Igor Cassini), former Truman aide Joseph Feeney, and General George Olmstead.[132]

Briefly, formal U.S.-Dominican relations were constrained by propriety and protocol, and there is fairly convincing evidence that in official U.S. circles Trujillo was an acknowledged rogue. The ability to respond to his indiscretion, however, was limited both by his usefulness and by his well-lubricated private U.S. following.* Nevertheless, once official U.S. policy came down from the fence

---

*Tales are plentiful of minor corruption of elected and nonelected U.S. officials. The Dominican embassy in Washington, for example, was known to have provided female companionship to at least one senior Southern Senator.

and sought to restrain Trujillo, his Washington court proved little more than a stumbling block. Moreover, once the United States sketched Trujillo's fate, it became fervent, albeit for a short time, in its desire to see Trujillo's regime considerably modified. It is possible, of course, that if Betancourt's social democracy had been the only alternative, the United States would have made an effort simply to control Trujillo. Castro, however, created the proverbial monkey wrench.

SANCTIONS AND SUGAR

The evaluation of the impact of sanctions really consists of two distinct groups of data. First, available statistical material relating directly to the sanctioned items listed in extended Resolution I is set forth. This is supplemented, as will become clear later, with a discussion of U.S.-Dominican sugar quotas. The second phase of the evaluation draws upon other statistical data (along the lines of the Italian material in Chapter 3), in an attempt to establish a broader perspective upon which to make observations about the state of the Dominican economy during the period August 1960-January 1962.

Reflecting upon Resolution I, J. Slater suggested that the decision clearly emphasized U.S. determination to bring strong pressures to bear on Trujillo.

> First, the Council action grew out of a study made by the United States Department of Commerce at the request of the Department of State to determine what economic measures would most effectively hurt the Trujillo regime. Second, although collective in form, the new sanctions were in essence unilateral, for the United States was the only significant source of those items. Third, the proposed measures met stiff opposition in the Council, and the strong leadership of the United States and Venezuela was required to ensure their approval. . . . Thus, beginning in mid-1960, the United States attempted to force major changes in the Trujillo regime, if not actually to bring it down.[133]

The observations lend credence to the obvious willingness of the United States to respond unilaterally when vital interests were at stake; in some respects, therefore, the

1960-62 Dominican situation was a progenitor of similar
U.S. action in October 1962 and the Cuban missile affair.
A full appreciation of this point is essential to an adequate comprehension of the apparent success of OAS sanctions
in the Dominican case. Of course, this may be really nothing more than another concession that great-power politics
have greater chances of success.

All of this could be verified fairly readily if Slater's
observations were correct in every respect. Thus, while it
is true that the sanctions set forth in extended Resolution
I arose out of a very brief study conducted by the U.S. Department of Commerce, it is not absolutely accurate to assume that the commodities selected were significantly supplied by the United States. It is true that the United
States was the predominant trading partner of the Dominican
Republic (Figure 4.3), but an analysis of Dominican imports
for 1960 under the three major categories of Resolution I
reveals somewhat different results (see Tables 4.5-4.7).
In value ($R.D.) U.S. sources supplied approximately 55.4
percent of trucks, buses, and parts; 13.3 percent of petroleum (71.1 percent of this was lubricants); and 44.4 percent of arms and explosives imported into the Dominican
Republic in 1960. Clearly, because these are Dominican
trade statistics for the year preceding sanctions, there
is much room for inaccuracy.*

Table 4.5 offers nothing very surprising as an overview of truck imports. It is noticeable that even before
sanctions on trucks had been imposed, although after the
San José meeting (the fourth quarter of 1960), the quantity
of vehicles imported from the United States represented
only 20 percent of the total imports from that source.
Conversely, imports from the United Kingdom and West Germany represented 32 percent and 42 percent, respectively,
of the total quantity imported from those sources. Moreover, nonmembers of the OAS account for 53 percent of
trucks, buses, and parts imported. Hence, this type of
sanction was of limited value because the United States
represented only the largest single source of vehicles and

---

*As a matter of fact, it was known that arms were im-
ported from Czechoslovakia, East Germany, and Poland; and
there was a temptation to translate "cotton" and "textile
machinery" imports from these sources into arms. The total
$274,640 for arms is doubtless very inaccurate, for this
figure constitutes only 0.3 percent of the estimated 1960
military budget.

FIGURE 4.3

Dominican Republic: Imports, Exports, and Trade Balances, Main Partners, 1960

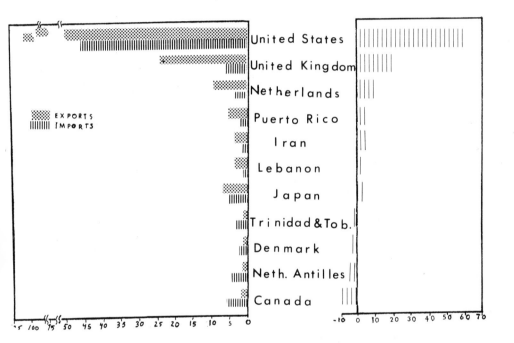

Imports-Exports
millions of $RD

Balances
millions of $RD

Source: República Dominicana, Boletín de comercio exterior 8, no. 12 (1961): 3.

TABLE 4.5

Dominican Imports of Trucks, Buses, and Parts, 1960

Country of Origin	January 1–September 30		October 1–December 31		Total, January–December	
	Number	Percent	Value ($R.D.)	Number	Percent	Value ($R.D.)	Number	Percent	Value ($R.D.)
United States	160	52	579,797	40	34	104,618	200	47	684,415
West Germany	29	9	97,324	21	18	35,468	50	12	132,792
Austria	3	1	13,592	4	3	16,992	7	2	30,584
France	--	--	--	1	1	1,048	1	0.2	1,048
Italy	9	3	29,851	3	3	10,232	12	3	40,083
United Kingdom	103	34	231,989	48	41	111,976	151	36	343,965
Japan	3	1	3,940	--	--	--	3	0.7	3,940
Total	307		956,493	117		280,334	424		1,236,827

Source: República Dominicana, Boletín de comercio exterior 8, no. 12 (1961): 5–6.

212

because the European states were apparently prepared, if the fourth quarter is any indication, to fill the vacuum created by a U.S. suspension of trade.

Table 4.6, aside from pointing out some of the defects of Dominican statistics, provides a challenge to assumptions that the United States was a major petroleum supplier. U.S. supplies of petroleum and petroleum products represented 13.3 percent of the total value of Dominican petroleum imports, a quarterly average of 3.3 percent.* However, 8.9 percent was imported in the first three quarters and 4.4 percent in the final quarter of 1960. Dominican imports of petroleum products from the United States actually increased marginally (1.1 percent) after the San José meeting.**

The most interesting statistics, however, are those of Trinidad and Tobago and the Netherlands Antilles (Aruba and Curaçao) and their respective mother countries. Table 4.7 demonstrates this remarkable statistical switch in trade. The essential point about these figures is that petroleum, as a sanctioned commodity, was well beyond the United States' direct capacity to control.†

The reasons why Britain and the Netherlands apparently felt compelled to reduce colonial exports while increasing

---

*The quarterly average is employed as a rough guide, and was arrived at by simply dividing the total percentage by four.

**This increase also may stem from goods in transit and unexpired contracts. It is obvious that the final quarter does not correspond to the period from August 21, 1960 to January 4, 1961; and it would be impossible to make it correspond. In any case, the quarterly period serves to demonstrate even better some of the points suggested, because it covers the period immediately before the extension of sanctions to petroleum and trucks, and it leaves open the question "If patterns can be discerned within this short period of time, how much more accurately could they be defined if it were possible to include the additional six weeks?"

†This excludes the possibilities that the United States might diplomatically have sought British and Netherlands support for the sanctions, or have sought to exert pressure on American companies that had ties with the British Petroleum Corporation or Royal Dutch Shell, the major exporters from the two colonial territories concerned. There is no evidence that representations were ever made to nonhemispheric states in respect to petroleum.

TABLE 4.6

Dominican Imports of Petroleum and Petroleum Products,
1960
(in $R.D.)

Country of Origin	January 1–September 30	October 1–December 31	Total, January–December
Canada	507,785	--	507,785[a]
United States	793,346	418,345	1,211,691[a]
Cuba	59,925	--	59,925
Trinidad and Tobago	1,300,592	167,643	1,468,235
Netherlands Antilles	3,631,430	4,170	3,635,608
Puerto Rico	115	14	129
Colombia	230,259	--	230,259
West Germany	3,235	4,203	7,438[a]
Denmark	--	1	1
Spain	3,206	--	3,206[b]
Italy	5	--	5
Netherlands	37,671	660,922	698,593
France	200,885	--	200,885
United Kingdom	81,761	482,370	564,131
Switzerland	27	4	31
Indonesia	50,804	19,680	70,484[c]
Japan	10,692	4,307	14,999
Iraq	471,003	13,300	484,303
Panama	130	--	130
Total	7,382,870	1,774,967	9,157,837

[a]The figures given here do not correspond with "Articles by Country" listings: Canada, 505,880 (p. 52); United States, 1,200,416 (p. 55); West Germany, 4,170 (p. 73). In the latter case the total equals that of the first four categories upon which the above were compiled. The remaining countries correspond.

[b]Petroleum (all types) is not listed as an import from Spain in the "Articles by Country" listing.

[c]Indonesia is not included in the "Articles by Country" listing.

Note: Included are crude oils, gasoline, domestic fuels and kerosene, lubricants, and all other types of mineral oils.

Source: República Dominicana, Boletín de comercio exterior 8, no. 12 (1961): 36–37.

TABLE 4.7

Selected Petroleum Imports into the Dominican Republic,
1960

	First Three Quarters	Fourth Quarter	Full Year
Percent of total petroleum imported during year	81.9	18.1	
Trinidad and Tobago, Netherlands Antilles	66.6	9.7	55.7
United Kingdom, Netherlands	1.6	64.4	13.6
Percent total of all sources	68.2	74.1	69.3

Source: Derived from Table 4.6.

domestic exports, if in fact that even happened, is pure
conjecture, although it might be possible to offer some
suggestions.* In any case, whatever the reasons, the European states were clearly in a position to fill any gaps
that might be left by an American suspension of trade in
petroleum.

A final point that warrants only a note here concerns
the absence of recorded petroleum imports from Canada during the fourth quarter of 1960. There is evidence that
during early 1961 tankers loaded petroleum products, for
delivery to all customers in the Dominican Republic, at
the Imperial Esso refinery in Montreal. Imperial Esso is
a subsidiary of Esso-Standard of New Jersey, an American
company. Legally there is nothing wrong with this, in
spite of the probability that the orders originated in,
and certainly the profits accrued to, the United States.

---

*A number of techniques could have been employed: sim-
ple alterations in cargo manifestos; shipment of petroleum
products to the mother country from the colony and reexport
to the Dominican Republic; reexports from Britain and the
Netherlands of petroleum obtained from sources other than
the Caribbean (the Middle East); or shipment from the two
colonies in vessels of British and Dutch registry rather
than under flags of convenience.

215

It is possible, although hardly verifiable, that similar
deliveries were made during late 1960 and, for reasons
known only to Dominican statisticians, remained unrecorded.

Table 4.8 is self-explanatory and because of its
paucity of information need not be considered seriously at
this time.

On the whole, it is reasonable to conclude that any
threat to impose economic sanctions upon the Dominican
Republic was a serious and profound form of warning, and
more so when it included U.S. trade. In these circumstances
it is generally true that a broad threat to restrict trade
virtually amounted to unilateral U.S. action. However,
there are a number of points arising from that observation
that require elaboration.

Given the extent of bilateral trade relations between
the United States and the Dominican Republic, a general
trade embargo by the Americans would have had dreadful
short-term consequences for the Dominicans. But the commodities sanctioned did not constitute a general trade embar-

TABLE 4.8

Dominican Imports of Arms, Weapons, and Explosives, 1960
(in $R.D.)

Country of Origin	Value	Percent of Total	Category
United States	121,943	44.40	Explosives, arms
Puerto Rico	370	.13	Explosives, arms
West Germany	50,634	18.43	Explosives, arms
East Germany	334	.12	Explosives
Belgium	14,349	5.22	Arms and parts
Spain	1,100	.40	Arms
France	189	.06	Explosives, arms
Italy	83,041	30.23	Explosives, arms
Netherlands	144	.05	Arms and parts
Japan	2,536	.92	Explosives
Total	274,640		

Source: República Dominicana, Boletín de comercio
exterior 8, no. 12 (1961): 5-6, 36-37, 52-55, 66-67,
72-76, 79, 81-83, 85-86, 92, 96, 101.

go, nor did they encompass commodities for which the United
States was realistically the major supplier.*

This conclusion raises another series of unanswered
points. The main economic sanctions were those imposed on
January 4, 1961: trucks, buses, and petroleum. These
sanctions, based upon the investigating committee's recommendations, were decided upon by virtue of the U.S. Department of Commerce study. Assuming that the Department of
Commerce had Dominican trade statistics available, of the
same or better quality than those employed here, it is not
unreasonable to suggest that the Department realized that
U.S. trade in petroleum with the Dominican Republic did
not constitute the bulk of that country's supply, and that
a sanction on trucks and buses was of minor consequence.

If those points can be granted on the basis of available statistical material, then it appears reasonable to
suggest that at some point a transition was made from effective economic sanctions to acceptable economic sanctions.
The intermediary in this process was probably the U.S.
State Department, which had commissioned the Department of
Commerce study. The State Department was aware of growing
Latin American opposition to an extension of sanctions but
nevertheless required the extension because Trujillo was
still intractable by December 1960. Moreover, by this time
the United States had made its significant move on the sugar
quotas and, as a result, was deeply committed to oppose
Trujillo. Consequently, OAS support became vital, and
this could be achieved only by proposing a minimum acceptable form of sanctions. When the sanctions were extended
by the bare two-thirds majority, it must have been evident
to the State Department that what it considered to be the
minimum actually amounted to the maximum acceptable sanctions.

It is difficult to imagine what the American reaction
would have been had the proposed extension of sanctions
been defeated in the OAS Council. But it can be surmised
that Washington would have been mildly embarrassed, for it
would have emphasized that the OAS-Dominican confrontation,
in practical political terms, was really a direct U.S.-
Dominican confrontation.

_____

*There is a value judgment here that trucks and buses
were not of as great importance to the Dominicans, in the
short run, as was petroleum. Hence the sanction on trucks
and buses is judged to be of little consequence.

Finally, that the United States was prepared to gamble on less than unanimity for the extension of sanctions has some significance. The failure of the Latin Americans to respond with enthusiasm to the U.S. attack on Cuba at the seventh meeting of consultation made it vividly clear to the United States that it could not afford to permit another Cuba to evolve from within the Dominican Republic. It became a matter of deep interest, therefore, not only to achieve political change in the Dominican Republic but to bring this about with speed and at the expense of Trujillo and his regime. This leads the discussion to the other aspect of U.S. economic pressure on Trujillo.[134]

It is questionable whether U.S. manipulation of Dominican sugar quotas and prices in 1960 and 1961 actually constituted a sanction. It will be demonstrated later, contrary to widely held supposition, that sugar-free manipulations such as those undertaken by President Eisenhower were not really economic sanctions and, therefore, that the special fee did not cause direct economic hardship for the Dominicans, as claimed by a number of observers.[135] Rather, the fee represented, as it was intended, a denial of the windfall at a time when the United States was officially ostracizing Trujillo.[136]

By early 1960 it was becoming quite apparent that Cuba was no longer a source of supply for U.S. domestic sugar requirements, and thus the scramble began among other contenders for the veritable gold mine that was the Cuban quota. In many respects Dominicans had an inside track, for the chairman and vice-chairman of the House Agriculture Committee (Congressmen Cooley and Poage) and their families had been guests of Trujillo. Thus, it is not surprising that a healthy portion of the redistributed quota found its way to the Dominican Republic.[137]

The tables below provide a statistical summary of the state of U.S. sugar quotas prior to and during the period under review. Quota sugar is that percentage of estimated total U.S. requirements in excess of domestic production, prorated on a percentage basis to various suppliers. Nonquota sugar is that quantity purchased in excess of regular quotas as a consequence of excessive demand or failure by a supplier (domestic or foreign) to meet requirements. Authorized sugar quotas and nonquotas refer to formal approval by the Secretary of Agriculture to import sugar (in spite of quota allocations). Nonauthorized sugar may not be imported. Table 4.9 provides information on total U.S. requirements and sources based upon domestic and foreign supplies. Table 4.10 refines the foreign component of

TABLE 4.9

Final Basic Sugar Quotas: U.S. Sugar Act (1948), Selected Years, 1948-62
(in short, raw-value tons)

	1948	1957	1960	1961	1962
U.S. needs	7,200,000	8,975,000	10,400,000	10,000,000	9,800,000
Domestic beet	1,800,000	1,948,357	2,267,301	2,609,170	2,795,769
Mainland cane	500,000	599,528	697,670	715,000	944,231
Hawaii	1,052,000	1,087,373	1,265,375	1,030,000	1,110,000
Puerto Rico	910,000	1,136,987	1,323,111	980,000	1,140,000
Virgin Islands	6,000	15,505	18,043	17,330	15,000
Philippines	982,000	980,000	980,000	980,000	1,050,000
Cuba	1,923,480	2,993,897	2,419,655	--	--
Other foreign	26,520	213,353	432,945	371,305	738,387*
Withheld from Cuba	--	--	995,900	3,297,195	2,206,613

*Includes Argentina, 10,000, and Dominican Republic, 65,000. Deducted from Cuban re-
serve by authority of Presidential Proclamation no. 3485, July 27, 1962.

Source: U.S. Congress, House Committee on Agriculture, Selected Data on Sugar Under
the Sugar Act of 1948, as Amended . . . 1962, 89th Cong., 2nd sess., August 16, 1965
(Washington, D.C.: U.S. Government Printing Office, 1965), p. 12.

TABLE 4.10

Prorated U.S. Sugar Quotas: Latin America, Selected Years, 1948-62
(in short, raw-value tons)

Country	1948	1957	1960	1961	1962
Cuba	1,923,480	2,993,897	2,419,655	--	--
Peru	5,903.2	77,124	138,827	121,507	132,939
Dominican Republic	3,542.2	60,420	130,957	111,157	191,834
Mexico	3,204.1	43,134	115,809	95,409	118,734
Nicaragua	5,429.2	11,588	19,766	17,471	18,193
Haiti	489.5	6,127	9,105	8,105	12,145
Guatemala	177.9	--	--	na	8,325
Honduras	1,823.3	--	--	na	--
El Salvador	4,360.3	--	--	na	4,221
Venezuela	154.0	--	--	na	--
Costa Rica	11.0	3,367	4,202	3,968	12,215
Panama	--	3,371	4,218	3,980	8,116
British Guiana and British West Indies	--	84	84	84	37,447
Brazil	0.7	--	--	na	74,694
French West Indies	--	--	--	na	12,430
Colombia	0.2	--	--	na	12,430
Ecuador	--	--	--	na	10,319
Argentina	7.7	--	--	na	10,000
British Honduras	--	--	--	na	4,104
Paraguay	--	--	--	na	4,104

na = not available

Source: U.S. Congress, House Committee on Agriculture, Selected Data on Sugar Under the Sugar Act of 1948, as Amended . . 1962, 89th Cong., 2nd sess., August 16, 1965 (Washington, D.C.: U.S. Government Printing Office, 1965), p. 13.

Table 4.9 specifically to Latin American suppliers. Table 4.11, final adjusted quotas, is a further and more accurate refinement of Table 4.9. Finally, Table 4.12 provides details on final or actual purchases for the years in question. Together, the four tables illustrate the process of sugar quota purchases and demonstrate the immense increase in Dominican purchases for the period during which OAS sanctions were in effect. It must be appreciated, of course, that sugar was not a sanctioned commodity and, in any case, extended Resolution I referred only to Dominican imports and not exports.

Two other factors to be accounted for are the attractiveness of the U.S. market and the price of sugar in the U.S. market as a factor in the 1960 sugar debate (see Tables 4.13 and 4.14). Prices that are consistently above world market prices doubtless are attractive, and this is especially true when those prices are combined with a fairly stable and assured market. Moreover, the average per-ton U.S. price was almost double the world price--and this was in hard currency. The only caveat was that countries with quotas were expected to purchase U.S. agricultural products and machinery, so the net return was reduced.

The other factor was the rapidly increasing price of sugar for domestic American consumers. One of the principal purposes of the quota system was to control price fluctuations and to assure consistency in supply and price. Table 4.14 illustrates the relatively rapid rise in the price of sugar particularly from July to September 1960.* It is important to realize that these major price changes all occurred during the 1960 U.S. presidential and congressional election campaign. Hence, when the administration proposed to further pressure the market by restricting the Dominican quota, it is understandable that the House Agriculture Committee bucked.

On March 15, 1960, the administration submitted proposed amendments to the 1948 Sugar Act to Congress and requested that the President be delegated authority to reduce quotas of any country, other than the Philippines (quota fixed by treaty), "when he found it necessary to do so in the national interest or to insure adequate supplies of sugar."[138] The reasons, as explained by the Secretary

---

*Raw sugar prices rose by 10 percent between February and September and refined sugar by only 3.7 percent, while the U.S. and world market prices rose by 11.6 percent and 9 percent, respectively.

TABLE 4.11

Final Adjusted U.S. Sugar Quotas: Latin America, Selected Countries and Years
(in short, raw-value tons)

Country	1948	1957	1960	1961	1962
Cuba	2,940,467	3,127,028	2,419,655	0	0
Dominican Republic	15,231	62,454	130,957	111,157	364,158[b]
El Salvador	7,607	0	0	0	14,471[b]
Haiti	1,924	6,333	9,105	8,268	35,695[b]
Mexico	8,351	44,586	115,809	95,409	51,689[a]
Nicaragua	2,122	10,275	19,766	17,471	18,696[b]
Peru	25,385	79,721	138,827	121,507	290,550[b]
Brazil	0	0	0	0	235,865
Colombia	0	0	0	0	36,147
Costa Rica	0	0[a]	4,202	3,968	20,346
Ecuador	0	0	0	0	56,226
Guatemala	0	0	0	0	28,103
Panama	0	3,485	4,218	3,980	1,901
Paraguay	0	0	0	0	4,104
Cuban reserve	0	0	1,435,100[b]	3,297,195	2,206,613[b]

[a]Reflects a reduction because of deficits.
[b]Reflects an increase from allocation of deficits.

Source: U.S. Congress, House Committee on Agriculture, Selected Data on Sugar Under the Sugar Act of 1948, as Amended ... 1962, 89th Cong., 2nd sess., August 16, 1965 (Washington, D.C.: U.S. Government Printing Office, 1965), pp. 2, 3.

TABLE 4.12

U.S. Sugar Quotas and Nonquota Purchase Authorizations, 1959-61
(in short, raw-value tons)

	1959	1960[a]	1961
Domestic beet	2,267,665	2,514,945	2,609,170
Mainland cane	697,783	773,873	715,000
Hawaii	977,970	940,444	1,030,000
Puerto Rico	969,875	893,620	980,000
Virgin Islands (United States)	12,405	8,618	17,330
Philippines	980,000	1,156,426	1,470,731
Cuba	3,215,457	2,419,655	0
Peru	95,527	273,827	636,377
Dominican Republic	81,457	452,814	333,880
Mexico	64,809	400,437	685,000
Nicaragua	14,027	41,766	43,368
Haiti	7,014	35,672	45,273
Netherlands	3,731	10,556	10,000
China (Taiwan)	3,624	10,476	170,028
Panama	3,624	10,476	10,000
Costa Rica	3,616	10,469	30,250
Canada	631	2,288	1,897
United Kingdom	516	1,871	1,550
Belgium	182	660	1,635
Hong Kong	3	11	30
Federation of West Indies and British Guiana	84	92,849	266,007
El Salvador	0	6,000	12,000
Guatemala	0	6,000	17,000
Brazil	0	100,347	306,474
Ecuador	0	0	36,000
Colombia	0	0	46,000
French West Indies	0	0	75,000
Australia	0	0	90,000
Paraguay	0	0	5,000
India	0	0	175,000
Subtotal	9,400,000	10,164,100	9,828,000[b]
Not authorized for purchase	--	235,900	180,000
Total	9,400,000	10,400,000	10,000,000

[a]Includes authorizations of July 14 and 21, August 2, and
September 10, 1960.

[b]Of this quantity approximately 14,900 tons were not imported
by March 31, 1961 and could not be authorized for importation after that date.

Note: 1961 data are as of November 20.

Source: Reproduced from U.S. House of Representatives, Committee on Agriculture, History and Operations of the U.S. Sugar
Program (Washington, D.C.: U.S. Government Printing Office,
1962), p. 28.

TABLE 4.13

U.S. and World Markets: Raw Sugar Prices, Monthly
Averages for Selected Years
(in U.S. cents per pound, New York)

	1948	1953	1957	1960	1961
United States	4.64	5.43	5.30	5.35	5.36
World market	4.23	3.41	5.16	3.14	2.91
Difference	+0.41	+2.02	+0.14	+2.21	+2.45

Source: U.S. House of Representatives, Committee on
Agriculture, History and Operations of the U.S. Sugar Program (Washington, D.C.: U.S. Government Printing Office,
1962), p. 15.

of State, were to safeguard consumers from interruptions
in supply and fluctuations in price. The House Committee
on Agriculture rejected the proposals in early June and
the administration, in response to producer representation,
agreed to a compromise.[139] This activity related directly
to the Cuban situation and probably should have warned the
administration of the hazards of tinkering significantly
with the quota system. The committee agreed that Castro
was a danger, but it would be too much to expect that it
would see Trujillo in the same light. In any case, a
compromise on the legislation was achieved on July 7, and
under provisions of these amendments a series of nonquota
sugar purchases were authorized in late July and early
August to make up for the Cuban deficit.

Of the original Cuban quota 321,857 tons had been
allocated to the Dominican Republic. However, on July 21
it was designated as "not authorized for purchase." It
was under these circumstances, nonauthorization of the nonquota Dominican sugar purchases, that the House Committee
on Agriculture met, from August 24 to 26, 1960, in response
to a special presidential message of August 23 requesting
legislation that would provide

> that amounts which would be purchased in the Do-
> minican Republic pursuant to the July amendment
> need not be purchased there but may be purchased
> from any foreign country without regard to allo-
> cation.[140]

TABLE 4.14

Sugar Prices: New York, Selected Months, 1960
(in cents per pound)

	February	May	June	July	August	September	October	November	Average January–December
Raw sugar (no duty)	5.50	5.65	5.55	5.75	5.95	6.05	6.03	6.05	5.74
Refined sugar (gross)	9.35	9.20	9.20	9.40	9.70	9.70	9.70	9.70	9.50
U.S. market price*	5.06	5.14	5.31	5.54	5.53	5.65	5.58	5.60	5.35
World market price*	3.02	3.05	2.97	3.26	3.31	3.25	3.25	3.25	3.14

*Raw sugar, price to exporter at source.

Source: Compiled and computed from Sugar y Azúcar 55, nos. 2, 5–12 (1960): various pages; and U.S. House of Representatives, Committee on Agriculture, History and Operations of the U.S. Sugar Program (Washington, D.C.: U.S. Government Printing Office, 1962), p. 15.

Undersecretary of State Douglas Dillon, in an appearance before the committee, explained that in the light of the OAS resolution at San José:

> The U.S. Government would be in an extremely equivocal position if it . . . were now to grant to the Dominican Republic an economic benefit by authorizing the additional purchase of nearly four times as much sugar as the United States imported from that country last year [1959], especially when more than one-third of the purchase value would be a windfall resulting from the premium of the U.S. price over the world price.
>
> To reduce the sugar quota of a country with a leftist dictator only to grant a substantial portion of that quota to a dictator whose activities have been formally condemned by all American States would seriously handicap the conduct of our foreign relations throughout the hemisphere.[141]

He then requested authority for the President to suspend the Dominican quota and to purchase the quantity of sugar required from any country, without restraint of quotas.

Fundamentally, the committee rejected the request. Its specific objections appear to have fallen into three categories:

1. That the request constituted a sanction in excess of that approved by the OAS resolution.
2. That the Trujillo government was basically friendly, anticommunist, and stable, and thus was not a serious threat to the United States.
3. That Americans had investments in the country and that these would be in jeopardy if the request was met.

On the first point, chairman Cooley observed that since no other American state had applied sanctions, there was no reason for the United States to be first.[142] The point was even more bluntly stated at the hearing on August 25, when Douglas Debevoise, president of the South Puerto Rico Sugar Company, charged the State Department with being inconsistent. He pointed out that at San José it had argued for caution, and now it was requesting permission to lead the assault. He was not even prepared to concede that sanctions of any type should have been imposed.[143]

Dillon's reply to these arguments was that the government did not consider that it was applying sanctions but, rather, that it sought to prevent a windfall for the Trujillo regime. He added that the request was not in any way more unfair to Trujillo than to Castro, because the matter of reducing the Dominican quota was not an issue.

> We reduced the Cuban quota by about 25 per cent, and we are not talking about reducing the Dominican quota; actually it has been increased by about 55 per cent as a result anyway of this increase in demand that has been certified for the United States. All we are saying is that we don't think it ought to be increased by 400 per cent as a result of this windfall.[144]

The second objection to the request, the anticommunist stance of Trujillo, need not be delved into here; suffice it to note that some rather fascinating exchanges occurred, especially between W. R. Poage and Dillon. Similarly, on the possibility of Trujillo taking over American investments, Poage and Debevoise's exchanges are classic:

> Mr. Poage: It has happened in the Dominican Republic, has it not, as we have shown our animosity for the Dominican Government, they have turned to communism, have they not?
> Mr. Debevoise: I hope not, but that is the danger.
> Mr. Poage: They have not gone all the way, of course, because we have not gone all the way in kicking them down yet. . . . But now . . . the State Department has asked us to make the foreign affairs decision, have they not?
> Mr. Debevoise: That is what it seems to amount to.
> Mr. Poage: And if that decision is made it will definitely confiscate your property, just as effectively as any decision that Castro has made in Cuba, will it not? If that decision is carried out and implemented, it is but the first step in the confiscating of your property?
> Mr. Debevoise: That is what I am afraid of.[145]

This fascinating dialogue probably bordered as much on fantasy as reality, and was premised upon a blatant, and ultimately futile, Trujillo ploy. The Soviet Union had already rebuked Trujillo in favor of Castro and probably had no desire to come to the assistance of Trujillo at the probable cost of alienating the rest of Latin America. And even if Trujillo were overthrown, there was no readily apparent Castro-type leader waiting in the Dominican mountains. Trujillo had absolutely no realistic inclination toward communism, however loosely defined. Nor was there any reason whatsoever to suppose that an increased alienation from the United States would lead to that end. He depended heavily upon the U.S. sugar market and had every reason to avoid pushing his gamble too far. He was, after all, scheduled to benefit from the punishment meted out to Cuba. To confiscate American properties under any guise would have instantly lost him the gamble.[146]

The Agriculture Committee reported on August 29 and recommended such a severe series of restrictions on the President's discretionary authority to limit quotas that when the report came before the Senate the next day, the restrictions were eliminated.[147] It was at this stage that Congress adjourned, leaving the President in limbo on the Dominican quota but with the expectation among sugar brokers that an effort would be made to restrict imports of Dominican sugar. Thus, on September 23 a Dominican nonquota purchase was authorized subject to an "entry fee" of two cents per pound to be paid to the U.S. government. This penalty was designed to reduce the advantage of the U.S. price over the world price. Nevertheless, it was conceded among sugar brokers that despite the fee, it was still to the advantage of the Dominican Republic to export sugar to the United States.

The reasons for this conclusion are quite simple and tend to support Dillon's "denial of a windfall" thesis. Table 4.15 sets forth the estimated revenues for the Dominican Republic for quota and nonquota sugar sales to the U.S. market in 1960 and 1961, and Table 4.16 provides an identical calculation based upon world market value. Taking the years 1960 and 1961 together, it can be seen that the Dominican Republic profited by an estimated $1,093,394 by selling to the United States regardless of the two cents per pound fee. In addition, there was greater consistency and stability in the U.S. price and market, a consistency that offered even larger quotas for Dominicans in later years.

In sum, therefore, U.S. sugar manipulations did not constitute an economic sanction because the benefit of increased quotas had not existed in the first place. However, the treatment meted out to the Dominican Republic by the denial of the bonus had a carrotlike effect on the

TABLE 4.15

U.S. Sugar Purchases and Estimated Dominican Loss of
Revenue, 1960-61
(values in $U.S.)

	1960	1961	Combined Total
Volume of exports (short tons)	409,219	304,226	713,445
Average U.S. price per ton	101.47	103.59	
Estimated value	41,521,000	31,515,000	73,036,000
Minus:			
Two cents per pound fee	16,368,760	12,169,040	28,537,800
Handling, insurance, etc.	2,864,533	2,129,582	4,994,115
Balance	22,287,707	17,216,378	39,504,085

Note: J. B. Martin, Overtaken by Events (Garden City, N.Y.: Doubleday, 1966), p. 52, estimated Trujillo's loss of revenue at $22,750,000. Since some of the Dominican sugar exports for 1960 were shipped before the fee was imposed, Martin's figure is probably more accurate. Lautico Garcia, S. J., "La República Dominicana, vive una revolución de tiempo?" Revista Javeriana 57 (March 1962): 171-77, n. 5, suggests the sum of $R.D.23,247,000 as the amount Trujillo lost.

Sources: U.S. Department of Commerce, Overseas Business Reports, OBR 64-80 (June 1964), p. 6; Sugar y Azúcar 55, no. 11 (November 1960): 7.

situation. With the prospect of such lucrative returns, Dominicans had an incentive to accommodate U.S. and, incidentally, OAS desires. Sugar quotas and fees placed an unusual strain upon the country, thereby adding further to burdens upon Trujillo and Trujilloists.

OAS SANCTIONS: AN EVALUATION

As in the preceding chapter, this evaluation relies upon fairly readily obtainable statistics on the Dominican

TABLE 4.16

Dominican Republic: Estimated Sugar Revenue
on World Market, 1960-61
(values in $U.S.)

	1960	1961	Combined Total
Volume of exports (short tons)	409,219	304,226	713,445
Average world market price per ton	62.80	58.20	60.83
Estimated value	25,698,853	17,705,953	43,404,806
Minus:			
Handling, insurance etc. (estimated $7 per ton)	2,864,533	2,129,582	4,994,115
Balance	22,834,320	15,576,371	38,410,691

Source: Compiled from U.S. Department of Commerce, Overseas Business Reports, OBR 64-80 (June 1964).

economy. The material, in many respects, is self-explanatory and is intended to create an overall impression rather
than deduction of a specific conclusion. Clearly, while
many of the statistics are cited from a reliable source,
they are nonetheless in large part of Dominican origin and
thus absolute reliance should be avoided.

Figures 4.4 and 4.5 display trade indexes for Latin
America (average) and the Dominican Republic.* The indexes

---

*Both the League of Nations and the United Nations ex-
perienced problems with contiguous states and the transshipment of goods to the sanctioned state: Italy (1935-
36) and Rhodesia (1965-). When these tables were compiled,
it was hypothesized that Haiti might have functioned for
the Dominican Republic as Switzerland, Austria, and Albania
did for Italy and as South Africa and Mozambique continue
to do for Rhodesia. However, land communications between
the two ends of the island of Hispañola are not adequate
for the large amount of transshipment that would be re-

were obtained by calculating the percentage change for a
given year over the base year. For example, exports of
the Dominican Republic in 1955 were $115 million and in
1956 were $125 million, an increase of $10 million; therefore, 1956 exports increased by 8.7 percent over 1955 and
the index number for 1956 is 8.7. (Unless otherwise indicated, all monetary calculations are in U.S. dollars.)

The two figures demonstrate that Dominican trade was
considerably more active during the period in review than
average Latin American trade; and while both demonstrate
an impact during the 1958-59 recession, only Figure 4.5
shows a rapid rate of recovery for the Dominican Republic.
This would seem to indicate that imports into the Dominican
Republic were curtailed to a greater degree than would have
been caused by the OAS sanctions. This can be attributed
to one or both of two reasons: hesitancy on the part of
customary exporters to sell goods to the Dominican Republic* or a conscious effort by the Dominican government to
discourage imports in an attempt to preserve foreign exchange reserves. It is also possible that imports declined,
of necessity, because of the increased costs involved in

-----

quired to show an appreciable variation in Haitian trade.
Also, Haitian trading patterns were wildly erratic during
the period 1955-63. In fact, it is virtually impossible to
diagnose even a pattern for Haitian trade without then trying to deduce a relationship with Dominican trade. Finally,
in an effort to obtain a closer and more informed opinion
on the theory, a check was made with a reliable source in
Haiti that provided the following comment: "My impression
is that such transit could hardly have taken place without
the large U.S. military mission still here at the time becoming aware of it. It can safely be assumed that . . .
Haiti could hardly afford to jeopardize the continued flow
of U.S. aid by helping the Trujillo regime with which they
never had better than correct relations." At this point,
and in the absence of any other information, the hypothesis
was dropped.

*This also may have been compounded by formal or in-
formal restrictions upon sales to the Dominican Republic,
and possibly even an absence of initiative in seeking markets in that country because of the ever-increasing domestic tariffs and taxes. This latter factor would have been
particularly true in cases where the imported commodity
was in direct competition with a Dominican equivalent,
such as cigarettes.

FIGURE 4.4

Dominican Republic: Index of Imports, 1955–63
(percentage change over base year, 1955 = 100)

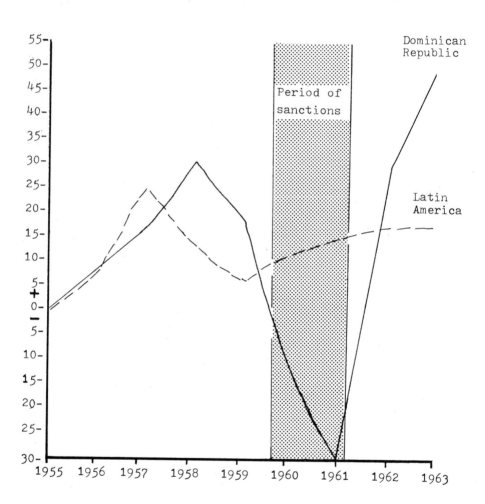

Source: Index calculated from: United Nations, Statistical Yearbook, 1964 (New York: United Nations, 1965),
p. 464.

FIGURE 4.5

Dominican Republic: Index of Exports, 1955–63
(percentage change over base year, 1955 = 100)

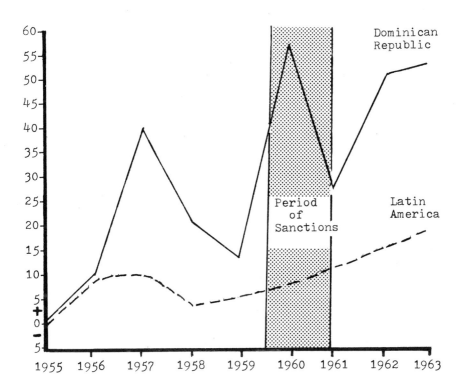

Source: Calculated from: United Nations, Statistical Yearbook, 1964 (New York: United Nations, 1965), p. 465.

importing the same, or even a lesser, volume of goods from alternative and more distant sources. Finally, if information on insurance rates for foreign exports to the Dominican Republic was available, these rates might be higher, and this too would be reflected in increased costs for imports.

The significant point about Figure 4.4 is that while average Latin American imports increased during the period of sanctions, Dominican imports decreased rapidly. Taking the high point (1958) and the low point (1961), Dominican trade varied by 61 points on the index while the same high-low comparison for Latin American average ranged only 17.5 points on the index.

Figure 4.5 confirms that Dominican exports did not suffer as dramatically as did imports. This was so because the official OAS sanctions were levied only upon Dominican imports and because Dominican sugar was exported to the United States (by volume) despite the two cents per pound fee. The export index does permit a view of the probable impact of the withheld U.S. nonquota sugar purchases during 1961, for if these had not been withheld, Dominican exports would have been even higher.[148]

Table 4.17 shows, for comparative purposes, not only the extent to which U.S. trade was part of the Dominican export trade during 1959-62 but also the substantial proportion of that trade consisting of sugar. Sugar represented the following proportions of the total value of Dominican exports to the United States: 1958, 12.1 percent; 1959, 15.1 percent; 1960, 38.9 percent; 1961, 37.5 percent; 1962, 61.6 percent. Any restraint of regular Dominican sugar exports to the United States thus created serious financial problems for Dominicans.

Table 4.18 is a summary of the Dominican Republic's budgetary accounts and public debt for 1958-64.

If it is recalled that in the period from 1944 until 1956 Dominican public accounts had consistently shown a surplus, the deficit for 1961 (slightly more than 20 percent of the total budget) can be appreciated as being of major significance. The deficit becomes even more revealing when the following additional calculations are added: the $R.D.14.8 million deficit for 1960 constitutes 9.5 percent of the total budget; thus the 20 percent budgetary deficit for 1961 constitutes a net deficit of 10.5 percent over 1960. More important, this increased budgetary deficit for 1961 cannot be attributed exclusively to a corresponding loss in import duties, for this source of revenue declined by only 14 percent for 1961 over 1960 and thus

234

TABLE 4.17

Dominican Republic: Total Trade and Sugar Trade with the World and the United States, 1958-62

(in $U.S.1,000 and 1,000 metric tons)

Year	Dominican Imports			Dominican Exports			Dominican Sugar		
	From the World ($U.S.)	From the United States ($U.S.)	Percent United States	To the world ($U.S.)	To the United States ($U.S.)	Percent United States	Total Sugar Production (tons)	Value Sugar Exports ($U.S.)	Value Exports to United States ($U.S.)
1958	129,519	77,392	59.8	136,6.5	68,732	50.3	807.7	54,518	8,317
1959	117,538	69,885	59.5	130,136	68,622	52.7	781.1	45,648	10,381
1960	87,023	45,519	52.3	174,429	106,756	59.2	1,111.7	85,239	41,521
1961	69,489	29,437	42.4	143,148	83,929	58.6	839.7	58,952	31,515
1962	129,083	61,498	47.6	172,434	141,249	81.9	852.0	88,251	87,023

Note: If total value of sugar production were computed, there would be a discrepancy between it and total value of exports due to domestic consumption. Thus, total value of exports does not reflect the total value of production.

Source: U.S. Department of Commerce, Overseas Business Reports OBR 64-80 (June 1964): 7, 18. This publication cites Banco Central de la República Dominicana, Boletín mensual 16, nos. 10-11 (October-November 1963): Dirección General de Estadística, Comercio exterior (Santo Domingo), various years; and American Embassy, Port of Spain, Trinidad and Tobago, as sources.

TABLE 4.18

Dominican Republic: Summary of Budget Accounts and Public Debt, 1958-64
(millions of Dominican pesos)

	1958	1959	1960	1961	1962	1963	1964
Expenditures	163.6	151.3	157.6	147.3	138.5	163.2	178.3
Receipts	154.0	142.7	142.8	117.7	150.0	173.7	189.2
(Import duties)	(55.2)	(48.2)	(42.0)	(36.1)	(59.4)	(60.7)	(61.7)
Balance (+) or (-)	-9.6	-8.6	-14.8	-29.6	+12.5	+10.5	+10.9

Note: Import duties have been included as one of the receipt items to demonstrate that they constitute a large portion of total receipts and also to emphasize the extent of their decline as a source of revenue.

Source: United Nations, Statistical Yearbook, 1964 (New York: United Nations, 1965), p. 593.

236

there was a 6 percent net loss in revenues that cannot be attributed to declining imports. Equally significant is the probability that this net loss would have been even greater if revenues from import duties had not been increased by an expanded range of higher import duties imposed in late 1960. This attempted to offset an anticipated loss in revenue although, as these calculations reveal, the measures were not adequate.[149]

Figure 4.6 provides a graphic view of the Dominican Republic's gold and foreign exchange holdings from 1959 until the first half of 1962. Prior to 1961 the country had managed to maintain an overall favorable balance of payments. However, as indicated in this figure, Dominican gold and foreign exchange reserves dropped quite dramatically. This illustrates that higher prices were being paid for imports; it confirms that exports were down; and it demonstrates that there was a discrepancy between the volume of exports and the financial return obtained from those exports. On this latter point, the figures for 1961 provide an indication that the two cents per pound fee imposed on sugar was having a statistical impact: exports were high but earnings were low.

It is entirely possible that if the United States had not made available an emergency credit of $25 million, on January 22, 1962, to ease the serious balance-of-payments problem, the Dominican Republic would have been forced to adjust the value of the peso from its par value with the U.S. dollar to some much lower level. Had this, and other possible fiscal and monetary measures been necessary, the impact would have been to prolong the deleterious effects of the sanctions. That such drastic measures were not taken appears to indicate either that the sanctions were lifted in sufficient time or that the one-year period of imposition was not excessively dangerous to the economy. It may also reflect an awareness by the Dominicans that, providing political alterations occurred, the sanctions would be suspended before they posed disastrous consequences for the country. It should not be the objective of multilateral sanctions, of course, to totally destroy the target state's economy, for this would border on economic warfare.

The preceding three figures and two tables provide an indication, by conventional means, of the overall financial position of the Dominican Republic as viewed from an external vantage point. With the exception of Table 4.18, on budget and public accounts, the component elements were generally beyond the control of the Dominicans. Hence, the accuracy of the statistics can be verified by sources

FIGURE 4.6

Dominican Republic: Central Bank Gold and Foreign
Exchange Holdings, 1950-62
(quarterly, in millions of U.S. dollars)

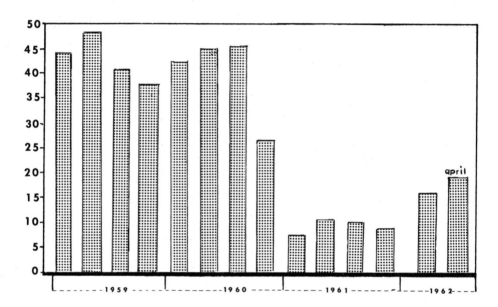

Sources: Chase Manhattan Bank, Latin American Business Highlights 12, no. 2 (Second Quarter, 1962): 19; and
International Monetary Fund, International Financial Statistics 13, 14, various numbers (1960, 1961, 1962), various pages. This latter publication provides annual, quarterly, and monthly totals as desired.

outside the Dominican Republic and the government would
lack the ability to unilaterally offset a decline in trade
or in balance of payments by countermeasures or by adjustment of statistics.

The tables 4.19 and 4.20 are samples of the types of
additional statistics that could be employed to verify and
more accurately assess the impact of the sanctions. Both
categories are fundamentally beyond the capacity of the
individual state's control; for instance, no matter how
much tourist promotion a state might undertake, any adverse
publicity about domestic conditions will generally deter
visitors. Similarly, regardless of the availability of
cargoes, if markets are unavailable, ships simply will not
arrive.

By itself, the information contained in these tables
serves to confirm that by 1960 and 1961 conditions had de-
teriorated for the Dominicans. However, implicit in such
detailed statistics is the probability that declines in
the tourist and shipping industries caused wider repercussions. A 55 percent decline in the number of tourists entering the country, for example, would have an impact, although not necessarily a proportionate one, on the domestic tourist service industry. Similarly, a decline in
shipping would normally have had an adverse impact upon
the stevedoring and warehousing trades, although in this
case total tonnages handled actually increased during 1960
and 1961 over immediately preceding years. The decline in
goods unloaded was offset by the increase in volume of
goods loaded, and this would tend to nullify the degree of
adverse impact on the associated trades and industries.
Any impact on either of the above industries would have
been best quantified in terms of decreased incomes and/or
unemployment. So far, significant statistical material of
this nature has not been uncovered for these industries.

For the above reasons, such indexes serve as limited
clues to the probable level of domestic employment, income,
and internal activity of the economy. They are suggestive
of possible trends and, in analytic terms, function as a
form of economic hyphen between the external and internal
views of the impact of sanctions. In the cases of declines in the tourist service industries and cargo handling
trades, lower-income groups doubtless are most seriously
handicapped. Admittedly, the hypothesis supposes that the
two industries concerned are not affected by the facts
that they may be, as a normal feature, labor-intensive or

TABLE 4.19

Tourists Entering the Dominican Republic, 1958-62
(thousands)

	1958	1959	1960	1961	1962
Arrivals	38.3	31.6	19.9	13.5	42.6

Source: United Nations, Statistical Yearbook, 1964
(New York: United Nations, 1965), p. 427.

TABLE 4.20

Dominican Republic: International Seaborne Shipping,
1957-62

	1957	1958	1959	1960	1961	1962
Vessels entering	1,808	2,061	1,948	1,270	948	1,620
Goods loaded	1,465	1,239	1,936	3,053	2,858	2,794
Goods unloaded	615	650	562	507	502	755
Total	2,080	1,889	2,498	3,560	3,360	3,549

Note: Vessels in 1,000 net registered tons; goods in
1,000 metric tons.

Source: United Nations, Statistical Yearbook, 1964
(New York: United Nations, 1965), p. 324.

subject to overemployment as a usual means for absorbing
excess labor.*

Gross national product (GNP) is one of the most common
economic indicators. Figure 4.7 contains both GNP and per
capita GNP. The figures in parentheses are private consumption expenditures and are included only for the purpose
of information, because they are given in current market
prices (in pesos) rather than in 1967 constant U.S. dollar
prices, as the other figures are.

An adjustment of GNP to current market prices, for
the same years, with private consumption expenditure expressed as a percentage of GNP, provides the results contained in Table 4.21.

A comparison of Figure 4.7 and Table 4.21 supports a
number of possible conclusions about the state of the Dominican economy during 1960-61. First, the decline in overall
GNP in 1961 without a corresponding decline--in fact an
increase--in private consumption expenditure suggests that
a greater percentage of income was devoted to maintaining
normal consumption patterns, and this in turn suggests
either higher prices or lower incomes. Second, because
overall GNP declined but private consumption expenditure
increased, there is a distinct probability that higher-income groups suffered proportionately more from adverse economic conditions than did lower-income groups--or, conversely, that the poor did not become much poorer while the
wealthy were financially in trouble. Third, however, there
was an overall adverse impact on private consumption for
all income sectors that is perceptible in the lag effect
of 1962 private consumption expenditures.**

---

*Conceivably a labor-intensive industry or overemploy-
ment might amount to the same thing in practice. However,
a labor-intensive industry is the result of the absence of
mechanization, while overemployment represents a conscious
effort by a government to maintain an artificially low
level of unemployment (disguised unemployment). It is
possible, therefore, to have overemployment in a labor-intensive industry, although the result would probably be
inordinately low wages.

**Economists refer to this as a lag-income effect. It
is calculated as follows: Consumption (this year) is a
function of income this year plus residue income of previous years; this is generally expressed in the equation
$C_t = f(Y_t, Y_{t-1}, Y_{t-2}, \cdots Y_{t-x})$.

FIGURE 4.7

Dominican Republic: Gross National Product and Per Capita
Gross National Product, Including Private Consumption
Expenditure, 1955-63
(in constant 1967 prices: millions of dollars equivalent)

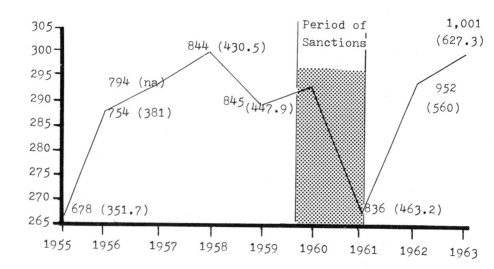

Key: _____ = Per capita GNP (n.a. = not available)
        678   = Total GNP
        (351.7)   = Private consumption expenditure as
                    component of GNP

    Sources: United States, Agency for International De-
velopment, "Gross National Product: Growth Rates and
Trend Data, by Region and Country" (Washington, D.C.:
U.S.A.I.D., mimeographed, April 25, 1969), pp. 8, 9; and
United Nations, Yearbook of National Accounts Statistics,
1964 (New York: United Nations, 1965), p. 77.

TABLE 4.21

Dominican Republic: Private Consumption Expenditures as
a Percentage of Gross National Product, 1955-63
(current market prices in million Dominican pesos)

Year	GNP	Private Consumption Expenditure	Percentage
1955	500.8	351.7	70.2
1956	540.5	381.0	70.4
1957	613.9	403.1	65.6
1958	632.8	430.5	68.0
1959	611.0	447.9	73.3
1960	661.0	451.2	68.2
1961	648.0	463.2	71.4
1962	745.6	560.0	61.6
1963	784.4	627.3	79.9

Source: Calculated from United Nations, Yearbook of
National Accounts Statistics, 1964 (New York: United Nations, 1965), p. 77.

Table 4.22 is included for the purpose of providing
an example of the nature of private consumption expenditure
for a single year, 1959. This year was selected first, because total private consumption expenditure closely approximates the average ($R.D.457.3 million) over the period
1955-63; second, it was the last year (until 1962) in
which reasonably reliable Dominican statistics can be assumed; and third, it represents the last full year (until
1963) in which sanctions were not imposed.

Figures 4.8 and 4.9, price indexes, are designed to
indicate a number of things about different sectors of the
Dominican economy. Thus, the consumer price index reflects
price changes for urban workers and lower- and middle-income salaried workers. Fixed-income, rural, and upper-
income groups, because they usually have different consumption patterns, are not normally as receptive to price variations reflected in the index. The wholesale price index
reflects the general condition of business activity and is
considered to be an important guide to the health of overall commerce. As a general rule, a price index sloping
upward can be interpreted as a sign of increased prices

TABLE 4.22

Dominican Republic: Composition of Private Consumption
Expenditure, 1959
(current market prices, million Dominican pesos)

Expenditure	Total	Percent
Food, beverage, tobacco	228.5	51.0
Clothing, personal effects	18.9	4.2
Rent	52.4	11.6
Fuel, light, furniture, household	34.7	7.7
Personal care and health	44.4	9.9
Transport and communication	40.0	8.9
Recreation and entertainment	7.7	1.7
Miscellaneous services	15.6	3.4
Expenditures abroad	10.1	2.2
Minus:		
Expenditures of nonresidents	4.4	--
Net value of gifts sent abroad	--	--
Total	447.9	100.6

Source: United Nations, Yearbook of National Accounts Statistics, 1964 (New York: United Nations, 1965),
p. 81.

caused by increased economic activity, while a downward
slope is an indication of passiveness in the economy.*
Figure 4.9 divides the consumer price index into two component categories, food and all items, including food.
This indicates the possibility that food prices actually
declined at some point during 1961, particularly on the
basic items.[150]
    Before commenting further upon the impressions sug-
gested by Figures 4.8 and 4.9, various additional statis-

*This also might be described as an upward slope = high
prices = inflation = activity; or a downward slope = lower
prices (and/or increased taxes) = deflation = recession.
Economists may take exception with the simplicity of this
outline, but the fundamental premises are nonetheless sufficient for the purposes of this discussion.

tics will be introduced. The information contained in the tables following Figure 4.9 may be categorized into two groups: statistics relating to capital expenditures and statistics relating to consumer expenditures, employment, and income. The figures within these tables are indicative of information that is required to refine the overall GNP and price indexes for purposes of determining whether any particular income sector within the economy might have been more seriously affected than another.

Tables 4.23 to 4.25 provide an indication of the extent of construction activity. The reason for including this type of information is that if the economy is suffering a strain, this would be reflected in cutbacks in capi-

FIGURE 4.8

Dominican Republic: Wholesale Price Index, 1955-63
(1958 = 100)

Source: United Nations, Statistical Yearbook, 1964 (New York: United Nations, 1965), p. 515.

FIGURE 4.9

Dominican Republic: Consumer Price Indexes, 1955-63
(1958 = 100)

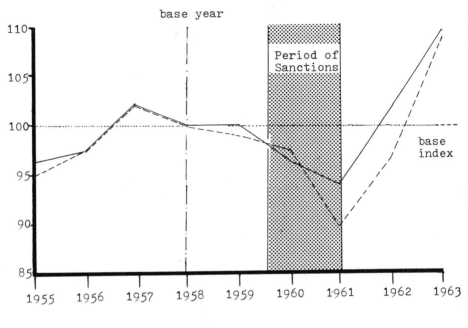

Key: _ _ _ _ = Food
         _____ = All items

Source: United Nations, Statistical Yearbook, 1964
(New York: United Nations, 1965), p. 521.

tal construction expenditures. Such a decline would be
visible in terms of decreased production of construction
materials and a decreased number of building permits applied for and issued.

Table 4.26 is included because motor vehicles, particularly automobiles, were basically luxury items in the
Dominican Republic. Therefore, ownership of automobiles
would tend to be confined to higher-income groups (this
excludes the possibility of a few driver-owned taxis); and
if high-income groups are affected by a decline in economic
activity, the number of motor vehicles in use should sta-

246

TABLE 4.23

Dominican Republic: Estimated Production of Lumber,
Selected Years, 1948-62
(1,000 cubic meters)

1948	1959	1960	1961	1962
74	70	78	57	55

Source: United Nations, Statistical Yearbook, 1964
(New York: United Nations, 1965), p. 268.

TABLE 4.24

Dominican Republic: Domestic Cement Production, 1955-63
(1,000 metric tons)

1955	1956	1957	1958	1959	1960	1961	1962	1963
234	247	280	270	190	170	237	243	228

Source: United Nations, Statistical Yearbook, 1964
(New York: United Nations, 1965), p. 292.

bilize. It cannot be anticipated that figures for motor
vehicles in use would decline, because those groups able
to purchase automobiles have not failed to purchase; rather
they simply would have deferred purchases. Deferment of
purchases is also instructive because it can be interpreted
as a reaction to a depressed economy. Table 4.26 does not
include figures for military vehicles.

There was a 14 percent average increase in the period
1948-66, followed by a somewhat slower, but nevertheless
steady, increase for 1955-62 (average 11.5 percent per
year). The percentage for 1962 indicates a probable small
lag-income effect, while that for 1963 indicates the return
to normalcy and, presumably, prosperity.

Table 4.27, beer production, is included because it
may be anticipated that if there is a decline in lower-income consumption, in response to any cause, it will be
most evident in a corresponding decline in that sector's
purchases of luxury items, such as beer. The figures in

TABLE 4.25

Dominican Republic: Building Permits Issued, 1956-63

	1956	1957	1958	1959	1960	1961	1962	1963
Residential	220	20	--	499	253	195	262	518
Industrial	67	205	33	50	30*	16	7	25
Commercial	290	450	383	243	279*	127	114	137
Other	--	249	113	59	142	46	36	56
Total	577	924	529	851	704	386	419	736

*There is apparently no correlation between industrial and commercial construction and "new businesses started." The governor of the Dominican Central Bank, Alvarez Sánchez, reported 1,409 new businesses started for the first quarter of 1960 and only 167 for the same quarter in 1959. See New York Times, June 11, 1960.

Source: United Nations, Statistical Yearbook, 1964 (New York: United Nations, 1965), p. 321.

Table 4.27 tend to verify that conclusion. If beer production reflects beer consumption, there is little doubt that expenditures on beer dropped substantially (30.5 percent between 1959 and 1961) during the period of sanctions. This decline was much larger than the decline during the recession year of 1959 (5.5 percent between 1958 and 1959).

In the absence of total unemployment statistics, a rather incomplete attempt has been made in Table 4.28 to outline employment in one segment of the Dominican economy, manufacturing. Included in this table is a subsector, employment in electrical and gas industries. Both of these categories demonstrate that wages and salaries declined within both sectors while employment declined in one and remained static in the other. The implication of this table appears to be that there was unemployment in manufacturing industries but that the electrical and gas employees were either occupied in vital sectors of the economy or that the industries employed highly professional personnel who are less susceptible to unemployment when an economy is suffering--or both.

There are two broad conclusions that can be derived without much difficulty: (1) the Dominican Republic was

TABLE 4.26

Dominican Republic: Motor Vehicles in Use, 1948, 1955-63
(1,000 units)

	1948	1955	1956	1957	1958	1959	1960	1961	1962	1963
Passenger vehicles	3.1	6.7	8.1	9.2	9.5	10.8	12.2	13.9	15.5	21.0
Commercial vehicles	2.9	5.3	6.5	6.9	6.9	6.5	6.9	7.1	7.4	8.9
Total	6.0	12.0	14.6	16.1	16.4	17.3	19.1	21.0	22.9	29.9
Passenger cars, per- cent increase over previous year		14*	18	12	3	12	12	13	11	26

*Average over previous seven years.

Source: Compiled from United Nations, Statistical Yearbook, 1964 (New York: United Nations, 1965), p. 394.

TABLE 4.27

Dominican Republic: Beer Production, 1948, 1955-63
(1,000 hectoliters)

1948	1955	1956	1957	1958	1959	1960	1961	1962	1963
49.7	70.9	83.0	105.0	132.5	125.3	93.6	87.1	224.7	285.6

Source: United Nations, Statistical Yearbook, 1964
(New York: United Nations, 1965), p. 247.

TABLE 4.28

Dominican Republic: Employment and Earnings, Manufacturing
Industry and Electrical and Gas Industries, Selected Years,
1953-62
(in 1,000 employees and million $R.D. per year)

	1953	1958	1960	1961	1962
Manufacturing Employees	62.2	83.0	86.1	76.7	79.9
Percent change over previous year		+33	+8	-10	+4
Wages and salaries	28.1	35.8	34.9	34.5	70.9
Average wage per employee (in $R.D.)	452	431	405	450	887
Electricity and Gas Employees	0.9	1.3	1.7	1.7	2.0
Percent change over previous year		+44	+30	0	+17.6
Wages and salaries	1.0	1.6	2.2	2.1	3.8
Average wage per employee (in $R.D.)	1,111	1,231	1,294	1,235	3,801

Source: Compiled and calculated from United Nations,
Statistical Yearbook, 1964 (New York: United Nations,
1965), pp. 214, 336.

in economic trouble from 1959 until 1962; (2) the sanctions contributed measurably to this situation. Although sanctions cannot be credited exclusively with either Trujillo's or the Trujilloists' collapse, they were a significant element. They fulfilled two roles. First, they served to increase pressure upon an already troubled regime by adding to domestic difficulties and then by providing an excuse for Dominicans to blame Trujillo and Trujilloists for many more ills than could have been attributed under more usual circumstances. Second, after Trujillo's assassination, sanctions acquired an importance to Dominican political opposition groups greatly out of proportion to any identifiable economic impact. In this respect sanctions contributed to the accumulation of discontent, assured the presence of an outside guarantor (the United States, under OAS auspices) for opposition groups seeking to promote domestic solutions, and (in combination with the lure of an unrestrained sugar quota) acted as a muted persuader to an impetus for change. Hence sanctions, in practice, were of moral and symbolic value.

In economic terms the sanctions appear to have had differing impacts upon different income sectors of Dominican society. With the simultaneous decrease in income and decrease in availability of imported goods, middle- and upper-income groups probably suffered the greatest alteration in consumption patterns. In addition, increased tariffs and taxes habitually impose the greatest financial burden upon upper-income groups. Referred to as the "demonstration effect," increased wealth for a segment of a developing economy's population leads to substantially altered patterns of taste and effective demand in favor of imported goods. This rejection of traditional consumer consumption patterns tends to generate domestic market instability, and thus consumption patterns founded upon imported goods will be seriously affected by any threat to the continued supply of these goods.[151] And when that threat is united with one against the income that supports the consumption of imported goods, the source of that threat becomes an object of reproach.

For the middle- and upper-income sectors of Dominican society, Trujillo and his regime posed such a threat. However, the sanctions simply confirmed the dangerous nature of the regime to the wealthier segments of the Dominican society; for they had already judged against Trujillo and the Trujilloists on the basis of accumulated internal difficulties. In this sense, the sanctions became the proverbial straw breaking the camel's back insofar as upper-income groups were concerned.

For the lower-income groups the sanctions caused less significant problems. The drop in the consumer price index for 1961 suggests that there was a sharp increase in unemployment.[152] It cannot be clearly ascertained, however, whether unemployment would have been more prevalent in urban than in rural areas. There is reason for concluding that the impact of unemployment, and its consequent hardship, was greater in the urban areas. For example, in addition to the decline in price indexes, there were also declines in service-oriented industries, such as the tourist trade, and these portended impacts on urban employment levels. In addition, urban poor are less self-sufficient than are rural poor, who are more usually able to survive off the land.

In the rural employment sector, for example, Table 4.29 shows a decline in sugar production for 1961, which possibly resulted in some rural unemployment. However, this can be surmised only because, as was noted when discussing the consumer price index, rural subsistence and consumption patterns are not reflected in such an index. Rural subsistence is liberally defined, in this instance, as the ability to survive with or without earned income off self-produced food products.[153]

Yet the conclusion that there was high or higher unemployment among lower-income groups is haunted by one observable feature of Dominican society: the relationship between poverty and the probable impact of sanctions. The people were poor to begin with and subsisted marginally in good times, so unless they starved--and there is no indication that large numbers of people did--increased unemployment would simply add to the difficulties of subsistence survival. Rather than alter their patterns of consumption, they probably reduced the quantity of goods consumed. This would not be considered unusual for most

TABLE 4.29

Dominican Republic: Sugar Production, 1955-63
(1,000 metric tons)

1955	1956	1957	1958	1959	1960	1961	1962	1963
637	780	836	838	809	1,112	873	902	806

Source: United Nations, Statistical Yearbook, 1964 (New York: United Nations, 1965), p. 242.

lower-income people; and hence, unless pointed out to them, would not by itself serve as a rallying point for discontent, particularly of the intensity necessary to succeed against a well-organized and well-armed regime. It is unlikely that lower-income groups would have been in a position, no matter how badly they were affected by the imposition of sanctions, to undertake an assault upon the Trujilloist monolith.

Finally, in terms of the political attitudes of the upper- and middle-income groups, the sanctions were only of marginal impact, tending to affect the luxury aspect of their survival. But it was this feature of their survival, in conjunction with their social status--the latter having been continuously threatened since the rise of Trujillo-- that made it imperative that the Trujilloists no longer be permitted to remain in power.

NOTES

1. Juan Bosch, The Unfinished Experiment: Democracy in the Dominican Republic (London: Pall Mall, 1966), p. xii.

2. Germán Arciniegos, "Preface," in Sumner Welles, Naboth's Vineyard (Mamaroneck, N.Y.: Paul Appel, 1966), I, p. iv. Welles's comprehensive work is definitive up to 1924, the end of the U.S. occupation. It should be consulted for further detailed historical information about the Dominican Republic prior to Trujillo.

3. Juan Bosch, Trujillo: Causas de una dictadura sin ejemplo (Lima: Populibros Peruanos, 1959), p. 112. Bosch refers to events in Dominican history as the points ("punto por punto") that led inevitably to a man like Trujillo. This book, written in 1958-59, reflects his bitterness with Dominicans for their susceptibility (p. 130) to people like Trujillo. He terms this a "national infirmity" (p. 141) that has resulted in a national "inferiority complex" (p. 137). He predicted, however, that while this "national psychology helped Trujillo's designs," his methods would cause a "one hundred and eighty degree turn in the national psychology and at the same time his regime will fall." Some of his later works--Crísis de la democracia de America en la República Dominicana (Mexico, D.F.: Centro de Estudios y Documentación Sociales, 1965), translated into English as The Unfinished Experiment (New York: Praeger, 1965); and El Pentagonismo del imperialismo (Mexico, D.F.: Siglo XXI Editores, 1968)--are less bitter about Domini-

cans and more critical of outside interference in Dominican
affairs. More recently his works, Composición social dominicana (Santo Domingo: Impresora Arte y Cine, 1970) and
especially Dictadura con respaldo popular (Santo Domingo:
Publicaciones Max, 1971), are much more reflective. However, he does argue rather convincingly that the Trujilloists still rule the country. This was confirmed in an extended interview with him in Santo Domingo in August 1971.

4. The era of Trujillo was decreed by Law no. 247 of
April 16, 1940. Law no. 3828 of May 14, 1954 decreed that
1955 would be designated as "Año del Benefactor de la
Patria." Jesús de Galíndez, La era de Trujillo (Santiago
de Chile: Editorial del Pacífico, 1956), pp. 25-26. This
book has been published in English as The Era of Trujillo
(Tucson: University of Arizona Press, 1973).

5. Rafael Vidal, "Introduction," in A. R. Nanita,
Trujillo (5th ed., rev., in English; Ciudad Trujillo: Editorial del Caribe, 1954), p. 18. Nanita was one of Trujillo's trusted sycophants, former Senator, former Cabinet member, and former private secretary. Rafael Vidal was one
of the five "founders" of the Partido Dominicano in 1931-32,
and over the years was in and out of Trujillo's favor with
regularity. Nanita was Trujillo's official biographer, and
his biography is noted with disdain by most commentators.

6. R. D. Crassweller, Trujillo: The Life and Times
of a Caribbean Dictator (New York: Macmillan, 1966), p.
104. For example, Nanita, op. cit., p. 102, in reference
to the 1930 election, said: "Trujillo's election opened
wide the gates of hope. . . . The people changed the course
of destiny by choosing a saviour." Equally dreadful is
Lawrence de Besault, President Trujillo: His Work and the
Dominican Republic (2nd ed.; Washington: Washington Publishing Co., 1936). He alleges immediate faith of the
people in their new (1930) President (p. 75). Besault was
one of Trujillo's early admirers and propagandists.

7. Crassweller, op. cit., pp. 283-91. Also see J.
L. Mecham, Church and State in Latin America (rev. ed.;
Chapel Hill: University of North Carolina Press, 1966),
p. 298.

8. There is a limited quantity of material available
on the regime's philosophy. The classic document is Trujillo's The Evolution of Democracy in Santo Domingo (Ciudad Trujillo: Editorial del Caribe, 1955). Perhaps the
success of this led to the production of his later Fundamentos y Política de un régimen (Ciudad Trujillo: Editorial del Caribe, 1960). Other regime theorists include
Nanita, op. cit.; and Besault, op. cit. Arturo Espaillat

(one of Trujillo's bodyguards), referring to matters of liberty, observed: "I had always considered words like 'human rights' to be something invented by liberals to hinder my operations." See his Trujillo: The Last Caesar (Chicago: Regnery, 1963), p. xii.

9. Trujillo, Evolution of Democracy, p. 4.

10. For a more in-depth discussion, see Howard J. Wiarda, Dictatorship and Development: The Methods of Control in Trujillo's Dominican Republic (Gainesville: University of Florida Press, 1968), pp. 102-23.

11. During the early years of his regime a band of thugs known as "La 42" openly acted on his behalf by terrorizing all internal opposition. "La 42" was named after the notorious 42nd Company of U.S. Marines, the terrorists of the American occupation. See Germán E. Ornes, Trujillo: Little Caesar of the Caribbean (New York: Nelson, 1958), pp. 5-6. Activities of "La 42" diminished once America entered World War II and Trujillo found their activities to be an embarrassment to his profitable relationship with American war aims.

12. On this general subject see E. Lieuwen, Generals vs. Presidents: Neomilitarism in Latin America (New York: Praeger, 1964); and Arms and Politics in Latin America (2nd ed., rev.; New York: Praeger, 1961); Victor Alba, El militarismo (Mexico, D.F.: Editorial Culturo, 1960); J. J. Johnson, The Military and Society in Latin America (Stanford, Calif.: Stanford University Press, 1964); S. E. Finer, The Man on Horseback (New York: Praeger, 1962); Gino Germani and Kalman Silvert, "Politics, Social Structure and Military Intervention in Latin America," Archives européenes de sociologie 2 (1961): 62-81; and Wiarda, op. cit., pp. 42-59.

13. Crassweller, op. cit., Ch. 10, pp. 123-47, at 124.

14. Bosch, Trujillo, pp. 147-48, estimated that 45 percent of the labor force worked for Trujillo directly, while 35 percent were in the bureaucracy. To this can be added another 5 percent employed in military, security, and police agencies, for the total of 80 percent suggested by Juan Isidro Jimenes-Grullón, "Trujillo: More Croesus than Caesar," The Nation 189 (December 26, 1959): 485-86. The dependence upon Trujillo for employment led Bosch to observe (p. 149) that "the country has progressed as the personal estate of the dictator."

15. See Tad Szulc, Twilight of the Tyrants (New York: Holt, 1959). Dominicans were apparently very cautious about people who spoke Spanish. Also see S. Rodman, Quisqueya: A History of the Dominican Republic (Seattle: University of Washington Press, 1964), p. 137.

16. Ornes, op. cit., pp. 178 ff. The Civic Primer is reprinted in Besault, op. cit., pp. 355-64.

17. Nanita, op. cit., pp. 282-83. Taking 260 as a reasonable number of working days during the year, this works out to 35 appointments per working day for the year 1950 (or about one every 15 minutes in an 8-hour workday).

18. Charles Porter and R. J. Alexander, The Struggle for Democracy in Latin America (New York: Macmillan, 1960), p. 147.

19. For additional information see Partido Dominicano, Acción y obra del Partido Dominicano (Ciudad Trujillo: n.p., 1956); and Declaración de principios y estatutos del Partido Dominicano (Ciudad Trujillo: Editorial Mantalvo, 1945).

20. Crassweller, op. cit., p. 119, notes that frequently the spies were domestic servants. Ornes, op. cit., p. 155, adds that a disguised school of domestic science served as a training institution for would-be informers until the P.D. discovered that graduates were being boycotted.

21. El Caribe, April 1, 1960. He became formal ambassador to the United Nations on August 15. Gaceta oficial no. 8499 (August 15, 1960): 3.

22. A fairly accurate account of the period is in: J. B. Martin, Overtaken by Events: The Dominican Republic from the Fall of Trujillo to the Civil War (Garden City, N.Y.: Doubleday, 1966). Martin was President Kennedy's special envoy in the Dominican Republic in 1961-62.

23. The official investigation may be found in Teodoro Tejeda Díaz, Yo investigué la muerte de Trujillo (Barcelona: Plaza y Janes, 1964). The conspiracy theory is in Espaillat, op. cit., pp. 7-22. Also see Norman Gall, "How Trujillo Died," New Republic 148 (April 13, 1963): 19-20; Rodman, op. cit., pp. 152-58; Crassweller, op. cit., pp. 433-39; Martin, op. cit., pp. 53-60; and Wiarda, op. cit., pp. 170-73.

24. A list of the major conspirators and their subsequent fates is in Martin, op. cit., pp. 747-53.

25. Tejeda Díaz, op. cit., p. 87; and Espaillat, op. cit., pp. 7-22. Espaillat's allegations were denied by the State Department, New York Times, September 21, 1962.

26. Martin, op. cit., makes no reference to the possibility of U.S. involvement; Crassweller, op. cit., pp. 435-36, mentions it without comment; Tad Szulc, Winds of Revolution: Latin America Today--and Tomorrow (New York: Praeger, 1965), p. 221, alleges that "the Kennedy Administration, which knew of their plans, had not discouraged [them] from acting"; Rodman, op. cit., pp. 156-57, accepts

Espaillat's version; and Wiarda, op. cit., p. 173, n. 64, asserts, "There is little doubt that the United States was fully informed about the conspiracy in advance, did nothing to prevent it, and most likely collaborated with the conspirators and actively participated in the plot."

27. Tejeda Díaz, op. cit., p. 51.

28. Martin, op. cit., pp. 60-63, provides further details. Crassweller, op. cit., pp. 444-45, describes the strange reactions of various members of the Trujillo family to the sight of Trujillo's body while it lay in state. If Crassweller is correct about these reactions, it seems to rule out the possibility of punishment and vendetta as reasons for the ensuing massacres. Rather, there was effectively a civil war being waged among the Trujillos, and between them and Balaguer, although the latter may not have realized this.

29. In August 1961, Balaguer had requested OAS assistance in drawing up new electoral legislation, and in June he had invited Juan Bosch to return from exile in Costa Rica. See J. Slater, "The United States, the Organization of American States, and the Dominican Republic," *International Organization* 18 (Spring 1964): 227; H. Wells, "The O.A.S. and the Dominican Elections," *Orbis* 8 (1963): 150-63; and New York *Times*, August 25, 1961.

30. Martin, op. cit., p. 66.

31. U.S. Congress, House of Representatives, *Hearings*, 86th Cong., 2nd sess., August 24, 1960, p. 67.

32. U.S. Department of State, *American Foreign Policy: Current Documents, 1961* (Washington, D.C.: U.S. Government Printing Office, June 1965), pp. 326-27.

33. Public Law 86-15 and H.R. 5463, 87th Cong., 1st sess., March 31, 1961, "An Act to Amend and Extend the Sugar Act of 1948." See also House of Representatives, *Report* no. 79, March 14, 1961; Senate, *Réport* no. 125, March 28, 1961; House of Representatives, *Conference Report* no. 212, March 29, 1961; and Senate, *Hearing Before the Committee on Finance (Sugar)*, March 27, 1961, for background information on the disposition of the presidential request.

34. Szulc, *Winds of Revolution*, pp. 106-15, attributed the change to the near-disastrous trip, in May 1958, of Vice-President Nixon to South America. Also J. Slater, *The OAS and United States Foreign Policy* (Columbus: Ohio State University Press, 1967), p. 10.

35. Martin, op. cit., pp. 712-13.

36. Ibid., pp. 67-83.

37. He took an estimated $200 million in cash with him (New York *Times*, November 20, 1961) and his father's body (*Le Monde*, November 21, 1961).

38. New York *Times*, November 20, 1961. Ciudad Trujillo became Santo Domingo again on November 23.

39. *The Times* (London), December 19, 1961.

40. U.S. Department of State, *Current Documents, 1961*, op. cit., pp. 336-37.

41. Material for this discussion was gleaned, generally, from E. Lieuwen, *Arms and Politics in Latin America*, and Generals vs. Presidents; Szulc, *Twilight of the Tyrants*, and The Winds of Revolution; Slater, *The OAS and the United States Foreign Policy*; M. C. Needler, *Political Development in Latin America: Instability, Violence, and Evolutionary Change* (New York: Random House, 1968); and W. C. Soderlund, "The Functional Roles of Intervention in International Politics" (unpublished Ph.D. dissertation, University of Michigan, 1970). Some of the material contained in this dissertation has since appeared in W. C. Soderlund, "An Analysis of the Guerrilla Insurgency and Coup d'Etat as Techniques of Indirect Aggression," *International Studies Quarterly* 14 (1970): 335-60.

42. "Dictatorial," as defined by Needler, has three characteristics. A government could not be an avowedly provisional regime holding office for 36 months or less; had to come to power, or remain in power, after the conclusion of the constitutionally prescribed term of office; or rule in clear disregard of constitutionally guaranteed liberties. Needler, op. cit., p. 171.

43. I am indebted to Walter C. Soderlund for the raw data for this table. The results of his analysis of some of the same data, plus an expanded explanation of how each of the terms employed is defined, is contained in his "Functional Roles of Intervention." I am solely responsible for the conclusions derived from the application of this material. Some of Soderlund's data was also employed in Needler, op. cit.

44. Crassweller, op. cit., p. 213. Another Dominican exile, Sergio Bencosme, was mistakenly murdered in New York in 1935. Ibid., p. 311. There were other attempts against Trujillo and his regime during the first 16 years of his rule: the 1933 Blanco plot; the activities of Enrique Blanco (no relative), "a sort of Robin Hood"; and the 1946 tank detachment conspiracy. See Ornes, op. cit., pp. 145-47. There was also a bomb attempt against Trujillo's life at Moca in 1936, but this was later established to be the work of agents provocateurs. Ibid., p. 129.

45. The Legion was instrumental in José Figueres' rise to the presidency of Costa Rica in 1948. Thereafter Figueres became a staunch foe of Trujillo, to the extent that Trujillo tried to have Figueres assassinated in 1951 and in 1957. Crassweller, op. cit., p. 312.

46. Espaillat, op. cit., pp. 112-25, cites a number of examples of Trujillo's assassins and spies at work. Identifiable political assassinations can be found in the years 1950, 1952, and 1956.

47. Crassweller, op. cit., pp. 347-48, for further details.

48. The degree was awarded posthumously. The dissertation (Galíndez, op. cit.) was published after his death. It is now available in English as The Era of Trujillo (Tucson: University of Arizona Press, 1973).

49. The Dominican official version of Murphy's death may be found in: G. S. Long, El caso de Gerry Murphy y la República Dominicana (Ciudad Trujillo: Oficial, 1957).

50. Rodman, op. cit., p. 154; Crassweller, op. cit., p. 318.

51. These categories are somewhat parallel to Friedrich and Brzezinski's "islands of separateness." C. J. Friedrich and Z. K. Brzezinski, Totalitarian Dictatorship and Autocracy (New York: Praeger, 1961), pp. 239-89. More detail on each subject may be found in C. L. Brown-John, "Economic Sanctions: The O.A.S. and the Dominican Republic, 1960-1962" (unpublished Ph.D. dissertation, University of Toronto, 1971), Ch. 6.

52. Welles, op. cit., pp. 470-93, 620-23; Nanita, op. cit., pp. 175-76.

53. Even as severe a critic as Gérman Ornes (op. cit., p. 172) was led to remark favorably upon Trujillo's financial reforms. He provided the following comparison:

	1930	1956
National income	$7 million	$542.6 million
Exports	$10 million	$126.5 million
Foreign debt	$20 million	0

54. Ornes, op. cit., p. 6, estimated $40 million and Crassweller, op. cit., p. 298, estimated "more than $30 million." El Embajador hotel, perhaps showing the scars of 1965 U.S. mortar fire, has a certain grotesque decor liberally sprinkled with cracked walls. It is only one of two good hotels in Santo Domingo.

55. Lieuwen, Arms and Politics, p. 283. The extent of this depression can be gauged by consulting United Na-

tions, Economic Commission for Latin America, Economic Survey of Latin America, 1960 (New York: United Nations, 1961).

56. New York Times, October 27, 1959, and March 6, 1960. The estimated loss in revenue amounted to $20 million. The average monthly world market price for sugar in 1959 was $2.97 a cwt. Average monthly prices in 1955–61 (each cwt.) were 1955, $3.24; 1956, $3.48; 1957, $5.16; 1958, $3.50; 1959, $2.97; 1960, $3.14; 1961, $2.91. U.S. Congress, House Committee on Agriculture, History and Operations of the U.S. Sugar Program, 87th Cong., 2nd sess., May 14, 1962, p. 15.

57. New York Times, October 27, 1959. The newspaper added: "If economic prosperity deteriorates . . . the regime's political foundations may collapse." For an expanded general analysis of this theme see Crane Brinton, The Anatomy of Revolution (New York: Vintage Books, 1965), p. 65.

58. New York Times, October 28, 1959.

59. Ibid., December 5, 1959.

60. Ibid., June 11, 1960. His statements have been independently confirmed, at least to the extent possible with Dominican statistics, by consulting Gaceta oficial 81 (1960), at the issue closest to the end of each month.

61. See Ornes, op. cit., pp. 131–48; Nanita, op. cit., pp. 183–98; Galindez, op. cit., pp. 306–16; Wiarda, op. cit., pp. 42–59; and A. C. Hicks, Blood in the Streets (New York: Creative Age Press, 1956).

62. New York Times, August 25, 1960.

63. Ibid., July 7, 1959.

64. Ibid., October 27, 1959. The Canadian Banks involved were the Royal Bank of Canada ($32 million) and the Bank of Nova Scotia ($8 million). The loans apparently were secured against the Río Haina (Trujillo's) sugar complex. Whether the banks obtained repayment of the loans after seizure of the estates in 1961 is unknown.

65. A report of missile developments may be found in Hispanic American Report 14 (March 1961): 39.

66. Ornes, op. cit., p. 138. There was also $1 million of U.S. military aid scheduled for the fiscal year. Wiarda, op. cit., p. 46, suggests that this was a conservative figure.

67. The following statistics were obtained by scanning the entire list of Dominican imports by country and by commodity, Comercio exterior 8 (1960): 4–105. It might have been possible to include machinery of various types from this list, but this would have been even more tenuous than the following categories.

68. There is also a strong suspicion that arms were imported from Eastern Europe. The New York _Times_, August 25, 1960, cited Poland as a supplier. Poland's largest export to the Dominican Republic in 1960 was listed as $R.D.40,644 of assorted cotton goods. Czechoslovakia is listed as having exported $R.D.131,210 cotton goods. It is possible that "cotton" and "cotton products" were synonymous with arms and munitions, particularly when it is recalled that the Dominican Republic apparently was self-sufficient in the production of cotton goods as early as 1955.

69. New York _Times_, July 7, 1959 ($36.6 million was reported by the same source on September 25, 1959). Crassweller, op. cit., p. 346, suggests that the $50 million was in addition to a budgetary appropriation of $38 million, for a total of $88 million, or 58 percent of the budget (at least). Crassweller points out, of course, that the Trujillos pilfered most of the money (p. 347).

70. These sums were arrived at by totaling the figures listed under supplementary expense laws made under authority of the Social Improvement Fund. These were published approximately every two weeks in _Gaceta oficial_ (1960). For example: March 12, $72,239.75 (primarily for the air force); March 29, $127,878.92; April 2, $678,759; April 29, $1,390,474.14. The "Foreign Legion" was a special anticommunist force stationed in the Haitian border area, possibly to combat "communists" in Haiti under the terms of the December 1958 Trujillo-Duvalier Agreement of Malpasse. See Crassweller, op. cit., p. 352.

71. New York _Times_, February 26, 1960.

72. Of related interest was Trujillo's announcement on October 17, 1959, that traditional Christmas bonuses to government employees might not be paid that year. He offered, however, $1 million of his own funds to tide the government over in paying bonuses. Ibid., October 27, 1959.

73. Ibid.

74. The following are some examples:

a. A special tax on champagne, whiskey, vodka, and liqueurs of $R.D.11 per liter, for the National Defense Fund. _Gaceta oficial_ no. 8439 (January 9, 1960), pp. 4-5.

b. Price of diesel fuel and kerosene raised throughout the country. Ibid., pp. 14-15.

c. Increased tax on soft drinks produced in the country, for the National Defense Fund. _Gaceta oficial_ no. 8448 (February 16, 1960), pp. 2-3.

d. Gasoline rationed to conserve foreign exchange and to more adequately supply government vehicles. _Gaceta oficial_ no. 8496 (August 3, 1960), pp. 14-15.

        e. Law No. 5412, general tariff increases on a
wide range of imported goods. Gaceta oficial no. 8511 (October 11, 1960), pp. 5-14.
        f. Extension of Law No. 5412 to cover new items.
Gaceta oficial no. 8512 (October 15, 1960), p. 1.

        75. To this list might be added the purchase in 1956
of the West Indies Sugar Company for $35,800,000. "Ten
million was paid in cash and the balance in three annual
installments, in September of 1957, 1958, and 1959." All
three deferred payments were made in advance of their due
dates. Crassweller, op. cit., p. 255; New York Times, October 27, 1959.
        76. Of related interest were the number of military
persons, including General José René Rósman Fernández, Secretary of State for the Armed Forces, involved in Trujillo's assassination. Others included former General Juan
Tomás Díaz (publicly humiliated and stripped of his rank
by Trujillo); General Antonio Imbert Barrera (former governor of Puerto Plato province); Lieutenant Amado García
Guerrero (Trujillo's Corps of Military Adjutants); and former Captain Antonio de la Maza (Corps of Military Adjutants).
There had also been some real and not-so-real military de-
fections. Air Force Captain Otilio Mendez Aguina (El
Caribe, April 3, 1960) was in the former category, while
Air Force Captain Juan de Dios Ventura (April 1959) was a
plant among the June 14 invasion force (El Caribe, April
21, 1959).
        77. Ornes, op. cit., p. 147: "The Dominican Republic
has comparatively more generals than any other army in the
world." Gaceta oficial no. 8472 (April 29, 1960), pp. 8-9,
contains a lengthy list of military personnel receiving
"Orders of Trujillo" at the 30th anniversary celebrations.
        78. Espaillat, op. cit., p. 39.
        79. Lieuwen, Generals, p. 98. For example, the con-
stitutional amendment of November 23, 1960, declaring that
an attack on the government was an attack on the people.
Gaceta oficial no. 8522 (November 23, 1960), p. 1.
        80. Espaillat, op. cit., p. 4.
        81. Mecham, op. cit., p. 417. Also see Angel del Rio,
ed., Responsible Freedom in the Americas (Garden City, N.Y.:
Doubleday, 1955); and F. B. Pike, ed., The Conflict Between
Church and State in Latin America (New York: Knopf, 1964).
        82. Galíndez, op. cit., p. 330.
        83. Ornes, op. cit., p. 330.
        84. Hispanic American Report 14 (March 1961): 39.
        85. Mecham, op. cit., p. 424.

86. Wiarda, Dictatorship, p. 165.

87. As Juan Perón, then in exile in Ciudad Trujillo, knew. Zanini had been Nuncio in Argentina and was instrumental in turning the Church against Perón. See Crassweller, op. cit., p. 382.

88. Some parish priests refrained from reading it that Sunday, apparently out of fear of the consequences. The letter was never published in the Dominican Republic during Trujillo's lifetime, and in fact an unsuccessful effort was made to keep it secret. The text of the letter, dated January 25, 1960, may be found in the New York Times, February 3, 1960. It is mentioned in Hispanic American Report 13 (January 1960): 29; the text is in ibid., February 1960, p. 104.

89. The text is in New York Times, March 4, 1960.

90. Wiarda, Dictatorship, p. 166; New York Times, February 28 and 29, 1960.

91. Mecham, op. cit., p. 298.

92. Crassweller, op. cit., p. 385.

93. Examples may be found in every issue, although some of the better articles are in El Caribe, February 17 and 25; March 2, 15, and 26; April 1, 2, 4, and 16; and May 2, 1960.

94. Mecham, op. cit., p. 298. The text of the reply is in Hispanic American Report 13 (February 1960): 132.

95. Hispanic American Report 14 (March 1961): 39. The last recipient of the title was Holy Roman Emperor Frederick Barbarossa in 1167. Unlike Barbarossa, Trujillo was unable to create his own Pope.

96. A review of the opposition is contained in a letter from Dominican bishops to Balaguer, August 28, 1961. Reprinted in the second report of the OAS investigating subcommittee: OEA/Ser. G/VII/CE/RC-vi-22, November 16, 1961, p. 43.

97. J. S. Nye, "Consumption and Political Development: A Cost-Benefit Analysis," American Political Science Review 61 (1967): 417-27, at 419-20.

98. Ornes, op. cit., p. 238.

99. See New York Times, July 12, 1959, for observations on the extent of corruption.

100. Wiarda, Dictatorship, p. 86, n. 11.

101. To these may be added three other estimates: Espaillat, op. cit., p. 54, rejects the $800 million to $1 billion and suggests $300 million. José Almoina, Trujillo's private secretary (1945-47) and author of Yo fuí secretario de Trujillo (Buenos Aires: Editorial del Plata, 1950), and Una satrapía en el Caribe, writing under the

pseudonym of Gregorio R. de Bustamante, estimated Trujillo's wealth as $250 million in 1949 and increasing annually by $30 million; cited in Galíndez, op. cit., pp. 348-49. (The reference to Almoina as the author of the Bustamante book is in the same source. No other record of this writing has been uncovered.) Crassweller, op. cit., p. 279, estimated the total wealth as $500 million.

102. Ornes, op. cit., p. 237. Lists of specific commodities or enterprises under Trujillo control may be found in Galíndez, op. cit., pp. 349-57; Bosch, Trujillo, pp. 211-26, 234-38, 241, 258; Kraslow, Miami Herald, July 8, 1962; T. P. Whitney, "The U.S. and the Dominicans: What Will Be Done with the Trujillo Properties?" New Republic 146 (February 12, 1962): 13-14; El Caribe, December 5, 1961; Hispanic American Report 12 (February 1962): 1097, and 15 (June 1962): 358. A general discussion is also in R. Grullón, "Antecedentes y perspectivas del momento político dominicano," Cuadernos americanos 121 (1962): 221-52, at 225-26. Some statistics are provided in L. García, "La República Dominicana, vive una revolución de tiempo?" Revista Javeriana 51 (March 1962): 171-80, at 177.

103. A number of businessmen and professionals were rounded up in January 1960. New York Times, January 29 and 30, 1960. Estimates of the numbers arrested ranged from 1,000 to 1,500 persons.

104. See A. V. W. Thomas and A. J. Thomas, The Organization of American States (Dallas: Southern Methodist University Press, 1963); Gordon Connell-Smith, The Inter-American System (London: Oxford University Press, 1966); C. G. Fenwick, The Organization of American States: The Inter-American Regional System (Washington, D.C.: Pan-American Union, 1963); and M. Canyes, The Meetings of Consultation: Their Origin, Significance and Role in Inter-American Relations (3rd ed.; Washington, D.C.: Pan American Union, 1962).

105. The Drago Doctrine (1901) was one very specific Latin American response. See W. H. Collcott, The Caribbean Policy of the United States, 1890-1920 (New York: Octagon Books, 1966).

106. The Pan American Union is the general Secretariat of the OAS and its affiliated agencies. Articles 78-92, OAS Charter.

107. Rómulo Betancourt, Venezuela: Política y petróleo (Mexico, D.F.: Fondo de Cultura Económica, 1956).

108. Robert J. Alexander, The Venezuelan Democratic Revolution (New Brunswick, N.J.: Rutgers University Press, 1964), p. 97.

109. Crassweller, op. cit., p. 410.

110. Pan American Union, Tratado interamericano de asistencia recíproca: Aplicaciones, 1948-1959 (Washington, D.C.: The Union, 1964), I, p. 395. Pp. 395-98 contain a short review of the Dominican case.

111. A broad resolution on "the situation then existing in the Caribbean area" was proposed to the Council on July 10, 1959, by Brazil, Chile, Peru, and the United States. The Council reviewed the proposal at a meeting on July 13, and after a lengthy discussion of the different points of view agreed to convoke the fifth meeting of consultation. Also see O.A.S. Official Records, Fifth Meeting of Consultation of Ministers of Foreign Affairs: Final Act (Santiago, Chile, August 12-18, 1959), OEA/Ser.C/11.5. The matter of respresentative democracy and human rights was not contained in the resolution proposed on July 10. However, the U.S. representative, John C. Drier, did note that one matter affecting the Caribbean situation was "the desire of the people of this Hemisphere for an increasingly effective exercise of representative democracy." O.A.S., C-a-332 (July 10, 1959), p. 23.

112. OEA/Ser.C/11.5, pp. 4-6. It also pronounced for the "rule of law," the "separation of powers," and "control of the legality of governmental acts by competent organs of the state" (p. 5).

113. Ibid., p. 7. This included (p. 8) the "relationship between violations of human rights" and "the political tensions that affect the peace of the hemisphere."

114. Ibid., p. 10-12.

115. The relevant OAS documents at this initial stage are OEA/Ser.G/III/C-sa-357, February 8, 1960; C-sa-358, February 10, 1960; C-sa-359, February 15, 1960; C-sa-360, February 17, 1960.

116. The Peace Committee's report is OEA/Ser.B/III/CIP-d-60, June 6, 1960. Its report to the Council is OEA/Ser.G/III/C-sa-373(1), June 8, 1960. Proceedings of the Council on that date are OEA/Ser.G/III/C-sa-373.

117. The newspaper carried a daily column of "news" on Venezuela. For example, El Caribe, July 1, 1960, p. 24, "Se desmorona en Venezuela Partido Acción Democrática" (The crumbling of the Venezuelan Democratic Action Party). Increasingly Venezuela and Cuba were lumped together as communist with the U.S. State Department charged with acting as the promotional dupe. For example, an editorial in El Caribe, April 3, 1960, p. 5, accused the State Department of collaborating with Castro and Betancourt, and a cartoon on p. 4 depicted a figure of the State Department

rolling out a red carpet for the two with Castro shouldering a sign labeled "Sovietization of the Americas."

118. Crassweller, op. cit., p. 413, where he suggests, "Trujillo's instincts told him to kill."

119. Espaillat, op. cit., p. 143.

120. The report submitted by an investigating committee to the OAS Council, acting provisionally as the organ of consultation, is in Pan American Union, Inter-American Treaty of Reciprocal Assistance: Applications, 1960-1964 (Washington, D.C.: The Union, 1964), II, pp. 17-57. Page references in the text are to this report.

121. Information obtained from Pan American Union, Sexta reunión de consulta de ministros de relaciones exteriores: Actas y Documentos, OEA/Ser.F/III.6 (Washington, D.C.: The Union, 1961). Parenthetical page references are from this document. Previous meetings of consultation were held in Panama (1939), Havana (1940), Rio de Janeiro (1942), Washington (1951), and Santiago de Chile (1959). The seventh meeting was held immediately after the sixth, also in San José. See Canyes, op. cit., pp. 3-27, at p. 11.

122. See J. L. Kunz, "The Inter-American Treaty of Reciprocal Assistance," AJIL 42 (1948): 120. Following the Dominican reasoning would have led to a curious anomaly: Latin American states surrounded by other states (such as Paraguay) would not have been protected by the Rio Treaty because a nonhemispheric invader would have to cross a third state's territory first.

123. The most useful discussion on this subject is in I. L. Claude, "The O.A.S., the U.N. and the United States," International Conciliation 547 (March 1964). Also G. Connell-Smith, The Inter-American System (London: Oxford University Press, 1966).

124. The principles of nonintervention are set forth in Articles 15, 17, 19 of the OAS Charter. (These are Articles 18, 20, and 22 of the revised Charter.)

125. Venezuela and the Dominican Republic, as parties, were excluded from voting. The full text of Resolution I is in PAU, Applications, II, pp. 8-9.

126. Compiled from M. L. Horwitz, ed., The Diplomatic Year Book (New York: Funk and Wagnalls, 1951), pp. 143-772.

127. Dominican intervention in domestic Haitian affairs is well documented. For example, see Pan American Union, Tratado interamericano de asistencia recíproca: aplicaciones, 1948-1959 (Washington, D.C.: The Union, 1964), I, pp. 65-71, 75-143.

128. The Brookings Institution, Refugee Settlement in the Dominican Republic (Washington, D.C.: The Institution, 1942).

129. For example, *El Caribe*, April 8, 1960. Frequent reports on the fate of American blacks also were given as the civil rights movement gained momentum in the United States.

130. U.S. House of Representatives, Committee on Agriculture, *Hearings, Before the Committee on Agriculture*, 86th Cong., 2nd sess., August 24, 25, and 26, 1960, pp. 36, 47. Congressman W. R. Poage (D-Texas) was vice-chairman of the committee and Douglas Dillon was Undersecretary of State for Economic Affairs. Somewhat similar views can be found among the comments by the committee's chairman, Congressman Harold Cooley (D-North Carolina). Not until 1962 was it clear just how close Cooley and Poage were to Trujillo's interests.

131. A replacement cost estimate. U.S. Department of Commerce, *Survey of Current Business*, August 1963, p. 2; and *Overseas Business Reports*, OBR 64-80 (June 1964), pp. 6-16.

132. Espaillat, op. cit., pp. 181-83. Robert James, "Report Trujillo Paid Off U.S. Aides Probed," Indianapolis *Star*, January 22, 1963; Peter Maas, "Boswell of the Jet Set," *Saturday Evening Post* 236 (January 19, 1963): 28-37.

133. J. Slater, "The United States, the Organization of American States, and the Dominican Republic, 1961-1963," *International Organization* 18 (Spring 1964): 268-91, at 273-74.

134. On specific U.S. goals see Slater "The United States, the Organization of American States, and the Dominican Republic," p. 271, where he views the goals vis-à-vis Castro's presence.

135. Martin, op. cit., p. 52; and Espaillat, op. cit., p. 91, for example.

136. Douglas Dillon before the House Agriculture Committee, August 24, 1960, *Hearings*, p. 28.

137. See D. Cater and W. Pincus, "Our Sugar Diplomacy," *The Reporter* 21 (April 13, 1961): 24-28. For background on the origins and reasons for U.S. sugar quotas; House of Representatives, Committee on Agriculture, *History and Operations of the U.S. Sugar Program* (Washington, D.C.: U.S. Government Printing Office, 1962).

138. Materials for this discussion were obtained from U.S. House of Representatives, Committee on Agriculture, *Hearings: Extension of Sugar Act of 1948 as Amended*, 86th Cong., 2nd sess., June 22, 1960; *Report No. 1746*, June 6, 1960; *Report No. 2090: Conference Report*, July 3, 1960; *Hearings*, August 24, 25, 26, 1960; and *Report No. 2200*, August 29, 1960. Citations will be made in short forms.

267

See also "Facts About Sugar," Sugar y Azúcar 55 (1960):
various issues and pages.

139. "Facts About Sugar," Sugar y Azúcar 55, no. 3
(March 1960): 32.

140. House Committee on Agriculture, Report No. 2200,
August 29, 1960, p. 4.

141. House Committee on Agriculture, Hearings, August
24, 1960, p. 28.

142. Ibid., p. 32.

143. Ibid., p. 73. Debevoise's position before the
committee was quite clear. The South Puerto Rico Sugar
Company (established 1900) began operations in the Dominican Republic in 1912. The replacement value of its inves-
ments there were estimated at $70 million (1960). He
stated that his company was entitled to 32.33 percent of
total Dominican sugar sales (ibid., p. 80), which amounted
to 48,000 tons of the quota and 104,000 tons of the nonquota sugar. He estimated (ibid., p. 76) that this 152,000
tons could be sold at an average price of $6.40 a cwt. or
$128 a ton, for an approximate total worth of $19,456,000.
In the light of his company's direct material interest in
U.S. sugar purchases, his comment that (ibid., p. 81) "a
fair share of quota, I have always thought, would tide them
[the Dominicans] over during this difficult period and lead
to the right result" smacks of sheer hypocrisy. In any
case his estimate of the value of the sugar is considerably
higher than the reported 1960 average price of $107 a ton
(House Committee on Agriculture, History and Operations of
the U.S. Sugar Program, p. 15), which would have provided
an approximate return of $16,264,000. At this $107-a-ton
rate, Dominican earnings for 1960 (exclusive of shipping
charges) from sales to the U.S. market would have been approximately $14,012,399 (quota) + $34,438,699 (nonquota) =
$48,451,098.

144. House Committee on Agriculture, Hearings, August
24, 1960, pp. 32, 33. Cooley (p. 33) raised a valid point
concerning the activity, to that date, of other OAS members
in suspending trade relations. This point has been re-
searched only marginally, largely because of the magnitude
of the task. However, the following may be helpful in respect of Cooley's point: Mexico imposed an arms embargo
on August 31, 1960, Diario oficial 243(11) (September 13,
1960): 1; Venezuela had an ~mbargo on trade dating from
its break in diplomatic relations in late 1959 but did decree specific regulations relating to foreign-owned oil
companies and their trade with the Dominican Republic,
Gaceta oficial 88 (26.373) (October 3, 1960): 549-50.

Cooley had queried Venezuelan oil sales to the Dominicans (Hearings, p. 33). Peru and Colombia had severed diplomatic relations before the San José meeting. And the New York Times, August 27, 1960, reported the U.S. break in relations. It carried a further report on August 31, "Diplomatic Missions Leaving the D.R."; reported on September 7 that Argentina and Uruguay had broken relations; September 9, Haiti; and September 10, Brazil. Whether any countries besides the United States left residual missions in Ciudad Trujillo is unknown.

145. Hearings, pp. 97-98. There is a great temptation to label this exchange as a Laurel and Hardy routine. Debevoise's comments should be viewed in the face of his earlier comment (ibid., p. 79): "Believe me, we have stayed out of politics." Debevoise stated (p. 81) that his company accounted for $70 million of an estimated $120-130 million U.S. investment in the Dominican Republic.

146. Debevoise's entire testimony was a challenge to his claim that "I have presented the facts as objectively as I know how." House Committee on Agriculture, Hearings, August 25, 1960, p. 76. Equally interesting, as a digression, is the manner in which the publication Sugar y Azúcar reported the respective key statements. Lawrence Myers, head of the Sugar Division, U.S. Department of Agriculture, who testified on August 26, "was reported to have said [emphasis added] that the U.S. would have no trouble getting enough sugar next year even if Cuba and the Dominican Republic were cut out entirely." Debevoise "warned that there would be a scarcity of sugar in the U.S. and a rise in prices if U.S. purchases of Dominican sugar were cut." "Facts about Sugar," Sugar y Azúcar 55, no. 10 (October 1960): p. 40. Myers' comments were echoed on September 1 by Robert Shields, president of the U.S. Beet Sugar Association, ibid. no. 11 (November 1960): 42.

147. House Committee on Agriculture, Report No. 2200, August 29, 1960, pp. 1-2; Sugar y Azúcar 55, no. 10 (October 1960): 40.

148. U.S. Department of Commerce, Overseas Business Report: Market Indicators for Latin American Republics, OBR 65-41 (Washington, D.C.: U.S. Government Printing Office, June 1965): 13, provides an incomplete value-volume-price index for imports and exports. The more complete import information is provided here, in order to indicate what would have to be done to develop comprehensive indexes for measuring the impact of sanctions on trade.

Index Numbers of Foreign Trade: Imports to
United States
(1958 = 100)

	Dominican Republic	Latin America
Value		
1959	91	93
1960	67	96
1961	54	99
1962	100	103
Volume		
1959	83	93
1960	64	98
1961	53	101
1962	109	101
Price		
1959	109	100
1960	105	98
1961	101	98
1962	91	98

In value and volume, the Dominican Republic had the lowest indexes of any Latin American state during 1961.

149. See Law No. 5412, Gaceta oficial no. 8511 (October 11, 1960): 5-14; and as amended in ibid., no. 8512 (October 15, 1960): 1. Also of interest, as an overview of the Dominican tariff structure, is U.S. Department of Commerce, Import Tariff System of the Dominican Republic, pt. 2, 60-71 (Washington, D.C.: U.S. Government Printing Office, December 1960), 2 pp.

150. The German Overseas Bank reported a lowering of prices during July 1961. It referred to these as "further price reductions." The reductions included meat by 25 percent; electricity by 20 percent; sugar by 25 percent; refined flour by 10 percent; sisal bags of coffee by 12 percent; and bulk cocoa by 12 percent. See Deutsche Uber-seeische Bank, Wirtschaftsbericht über die Lateinamerikan-ischen, December 1961, pp. 29-31. Also see various issues of the Dominican Gaceta oficial, especially nos. 8550-8565 (1961).

151. See R. Nurske, Problems of Capital Formation of Underdeveloped Countries (Oxford: Oxford University Press, 1953), pp. 58, 63, 67.

152. Without passing judgment upon the merits or de-merits of the Phillips curve, this is the suggestion upon which the curve is premised: decreasing prices = increased

unemployment. See A. W. Phillips, "The Relation Between Unemployment and the Rate of Change of Money Rate in the United Kingdom, 1861-1957," *Economica* 25 (1958): 283-99. There is apparently still some disagreement among economists about the utility of the Phillips curve.

153. Commenting upon this period, the U.S. Department of Commerce said:

> Economic growth slowed during the 1959-61 period, the last years of the Trujillo regime. The rate of inflow of foreign equity capital slowed almost to a stop; unemployment grew, especially in the cities, and created one of the most serious problems in the Dominican Republic today.

Overseas Business Reports, OBR 64-80 (June 1964), p. 4.

PROLOGUE TO THE UNILATERAL
DECLARATION OF INDEPENDENCE

There is a considerable temptation to view the Rhodesian situation as something akin to a civil war rather than
an international crisis. True, it has become an international event; and certainly the nature of Rhodesian society,
like that of South Africa, is an affront to human dignity
throughout the world. The point is simply that in the two
preceding cases, the international organizations responded
to some form of readily perceptible aggressive act by one
state against another. In the Rhodesian situation, however,
the nature of the aggression is far less perceptible and
does not fall within any of the conventional views of what
constitutes aggression. Clearly it is essentially a question of degree; and the world, albeit at British insistence,
has declared that Rhodesia's unilateral declaration of independence (UDI) on November 11, 1965, constituted international aggression because the continuation of a situation
in which a racially supressed majority was dominated by a
minority constituted a threat, over time, to international
peace.

That is the judgment upon which this discussion is
based, and therefore it is not the purpose of this analysis
to offer an opinion upon the legality of either Rhodesia's
UDI or the international organization's judgment. Nor is
it the purpose to editorialize upon the morality of the
situation, beyond noting that racial discrimination is objectionable wherever perpetrated.

For all intents and purposes, the prologue to Rhodesia's 1965 UDI can be traced back to a 1922 Rhodesian re-

jection of association with the Union of South Africa and its opting for responsible government. Running throughout the entire period from 1922 to 1965 was an assumption that Rhodesia would achieve Dominion status within the Commonwealth. In fact, so widely was this view held that officials in the Canadian External Affairs Department were uncertain of the status of Rhodesia at the July 1938 Imperial Economic Conference in Ottawa. Rhodesians were never able to understand how their situation could have been different from that of South Africa in 1910, for, unlike South Africans, Rhodesians had not fought a war against Britain; their Land Appointment Act was not as blatant a form of apartheid; and their loyalty was beyond question.[1]

Rhodesia, like America, is a pioneer land, as Kipling put it, of "great spaces washed with sun." A frontier zeal and mentality that permeates white society led colonizers to assume a dominant role vis-à-vis native peoples in the tradition of Livingstone and Rhodes. But apartheid, such as has flourished under the stringent morality of South Africa's Dutch Reformed Church, was anathema to the English-based white Rhodesian. The parallel between adamantly racist South Africa and white-dominated Rhodesia should not be so glibly drawn. Agreed, they seek to achieve somewhat similar ends; and since 1965 necessity and proximity have been as much the progenitors of a "mutual sentiment problem" as has a fundamental belief in white racial dominance. In fact, it has been only with some difficulty that the Rhodesians' traditional distrust of South Africa has altered. And, it should be noted, South Africa has moved into the Rhodesian business with much trepidation and very softly, for that country's own survival could have been in jeopardy at any time during the Rhodesian affair.[2]

Ian Smith informed Rhodesians on October 1, 1965 that he would journey to London to make a final appeal to the British Prime Minister to acknowledge that unless a constitutional settlement was achieved a unilateral declaration of Rhodesian independence would follow. Behind Smith's announcement was a history of aggravated relations between Britain, Rhodesia, the ill-fated Rhodesian federation, and the growing intensity of nationalism in Africa.

In 1922, when Rhodesians voted to reject union with South Africa, they opted for a fate that was to lead them to closer ties with Britain. In September 1923 the territory was annexed to Britain, and a year later Sir Charles Coghlan became Southern Rhodesia's first Prime Minister. From the general election of September 11, 1933, until his resignation in favor of a federation position in September

1953, Sir Godfrey Huggins and his United Party governed
Rhodesia.[3]

Meanwhile, beginning in 1949, moves toward a federation of Northern Rhodesia, Southern Rhodesia, and Nyasaland were under way, culminating in a White Paper on June
18, 1952. A final conference on federation was held in London in January 1953, and a referendum in April voted almost
two to one in favor of federation. Thus, shortly after
Garfield Todd became Premier of Southern Rhodesia, upon
Huggins' resignation, the latter as head of the Federal
Party, succeeded to the position of Federal Prime Minister.

Between 1954 and 1959 growing black nationalism, especially in Northern Rhodesia and Nyasaland, made the federation an unpalatable situation for the larger white population of Southern Rhodesia. This nervousness was highlighted
in June 1957, when Todd's United Rhodesia Party revolted
and forced him out in favor of Sir Edgar Whitehead, the
Federation's representative in Washington. Meanwhile,
Huggins (now Lord Malvern) retired and was succeeded as
Federation Prime Minister by Sir Roy Welensky. However,
African nationalism was gaining momentum; and in 1958 Hastings Banda returned to Nyasaland, after 40 years' absence,
to assume leadership of the African National Congress
(ANC) Party. Early in 1959 Banda was arrested and detained
in Southern Rhodesia, and the ANC was banned. These events
led Britain to appoint the Moncton Commission to consider
the future of the Federation. Despite African boycotts,
the commission recommended that individual territories be
given the right of secession. From 1961, therefore, until
the official dissolution of the federation on December 31,
1963, numerous constitutional changes were made. Among
them was an enlargement of the Southern Rhodesian Parliament to include African representation on a "B" or second
electoral roll; the secession from the Federation and ultimate independence of Nyasaland as Malawi in 1962; and
secession by Northern Rhodesia in 1963 under Kenneth Kaunda.

Consequently, by January 1, 1964, Southern Rhodesia
remained as the only nonindependent entity of the former
Federation. In addition politics had changed directions
within the country, and the impending collapse of the Federation had led to the defeat of the United Front (Rhodesia) Party. Actually, the defeat began in a federal
general election of April 1962, when Sir Roy Welensky called
for support for the Federation. In response the opposition Rhodesian Front (formerly the Dominion Party) boycotted the election; and in a Southern Rhodesian election
in December 1962 the Rhodesian Front, under Winston Field,

defeated the United Front. Thus Southern Rhodesians had
rejected the discredited federalists in favor of a party
of white, anti-African nationalism. In April 1964 Winston
Field resigned and was succeeded by his Minister of the
Treasury, Ian Smith.

Throughout 1964 Smith's government moved to quash African nationalism, including banning the Salisbury Daily
News and a number of African nationalist groups, such as
the Zimbabwe African National Union (ZANU). In November
1964, a Rhodesian independence referendum was conducted,
and 55.7 percent of the eligible voters approved. From
this referendum on, the issue was no longer "if" independence but "when" independence and under what circumstances:
majority (black) or minority (white) plus the "B" roll
rule. In February 1965 Arthur Bottomley and Lord Gardiner
visited Rhodesia from London to discuss independence.

Smith, in order to bolster his bargaining position,
called a general election for May 7. His Rhodesian Front
Party swept all 50 seats contested, while the Rhodesia
Party was reduced to obscurity and ultimately dissolution
in June. The only opposition Smith faced was from independent blacks elected on the "B" roll.

From May 1965, therefore, Rhodesia became more vociferous in its insistence on independence. After being
shunned by the July Commonwealth Prime Ministers' Conference, Smith spoke of independence outside the Commonwealth.
British Prime Minister Wilson warned Rhodesia of dire consequences if it acted unilaterally. During July, Cledwyn
Hughes, British Minister of State for Commonwealth Affairs,
conducted talks in Salisbury with Rhodesian leaders and
affirmed the British view that unrestrained minority rule
was unacceptable. Independence, Smith was assured, would
be impossible without constitutional guarantees of majority rule; Smith rejected this in September, when he informed Parliament that independence was imminent. Consequently, the October 1 broadcast announcing Smith's negotiating expedition to London served as an expression of
intent to bargain. During October events moved quickly
and in accordance with an almost predefined script toward
UDI.[4]

Smith had been preceded to London by his Minister of
Internal Affairs, W. J. Harper, and his Minister of Finance,
J. J. Wrathal. Both were vocal advocates of UDI, and the
latter's visit to London was to test the financial community's reaction to a possible UDI.

Meetings between Smith and British Prime Minister Wilson were held at two levels between October 5 and 11.

First private (unrecorded) conversations were held, and these were interspersed with more formal sessions on October 7, 8, and 11.[5] Smith also used the visit to test possible reaction by other states.* At the meeting on October 8, Wilson indicated to Smith that while Britain was on record against the use of economic sanctions in the South African situation, Rhodesia was regarded differently and, moreover, pressure for military intervention might become irresistible. Smith replied that any such action would do more harm to Africans than to Europeans.[6] Generally, however, the tone of the meetings was that Britain appeared to ask all the questions while Rhodesia supplied almost prepared answers. A scrutiny of the proceedings certainly suggests that Rhodesia's decision on UDI had been taken and that leeway for a negotiated settlement was slim indeed.

In fact, at a Cabinet meeting on October 8, Wilson presented draft regulations relating to sanctions and associated measures to be imposed by Britain in response to a Rhodesian UDI. Doubtless the Commonwealth Relations Office (CRO) must have anticipated a breakdown in the Smith-Wilson talks and began preparations to organize a response.

By mid-October 1965 the British government had concluded that a UDI was inevitable, and all that remained was to plan a strategy for the event. Such a strategy would need to encompass every possible field of action, such as the United Nations and Commonwealth, and would require certain mechanics to bring it into operation: the actual cessation of relations with an illegal regime, plus constitutional and legislative responses. Finally, the British government would have to make some form of provision for Zambia and then decide what measures could be taken against Rhodesia without seriously impairing Zambia's viability. Moreover, from the British viewpoint, the use of direct military force would be ruled out.

In the United Nations, unquestionably it was to Britain's advantage to initiate action, despite the probably justifiable assertion that Rhodesia was not really the business of the United Nations. Such initiative would be preferable to being led, no doubt unwillingly, into some half-baked scheme with which the Committee of 24 had be-

---

*It is known that the American and German ambassadors visited Smith on October 7. The German Embassy issued a statement later that day warning of consequences with UDI. An American statement was contained in a USIS press release on October 8.

come associated. But the danger of bringing the matter before the United Nations at too early a stage was that it might result in a Security Council resolution involving the use of force.[7]

The matter of severing relations with Rhodesia involved the withdrawal of British diplomatic staff from Salisbury and the return of Rhodesian personnel from attached duty at British embassies in Washington, Bonn, and Tokyo.

Constitutional and legislative action would include the de jure dismissal of the Rhodesian government and modification of British laws applying to Rhodesia, such as the Import Duties Act of 1958, under which Rhodesia was included within the Commonwealth Preference Area.[8] Problems might have arisen, for example, in regard to the Commonwealth Sugar Agreement and the contractual arrangements made thereunder. Of course, such difficulties could have been handled by a UN decision in accordance with the League of Nations (Coordinating Committee) Legal Subcommittee's view that contractual arrangements of all types cease when sanctions are imposed. In addition, Rhodesia would be excluded from the London money market, thereby curtailing its capacity to obtain credits for tobacco crops and other transactions. As well, Britain could impose exchange controls, thus excluding Rhodesia from the sterling area; it could block overseas balances; and it could provide assistance to loyal Rhodesian public servants. Of course, it was clear that many of these activities would cost Britain money; hence the burden of sanctions was two-sided.

Rhodesian trade in 1964 was roughly as follows: 25 percent to Britain; 26 percent to Zambia; 12 percent (indirectly) to Eastern Europe; 8 percent to South Africa, and 29 percent elsewhere. Tobacco constituted 53 percent of the total value of Rhodesian exports to Britain in 1964 and represented 33 percent of all Rhodesian exports. It was reasonable to estimate by October 1965 that Rhodesian exports would decline by about 60-70 percent, or about £100 million if major commodities were embargoed. It was clear that South Africa and Portugal would not cooperate, that France and Japan* would be uncertain participants in

---

*France's position seemed to be premised upon a desire to keep the issue of French Somaliland (Territory of Afar and Issas) out of the United Nations' hands. As well, French commercial interests were deeply involved in Rhodesian tobacco. Japan was negotiating a massive iron ore

any sanctions program, and that East European states probably would maintain an indirect trade with Rhodesia in much the same manner as that carried out with South Africa.

For the British, restrictions on exports to Rhodesia clearly would involve careful monitoring of trade with South Africa (Britain's third largest export market) and restrictions against Portugal (a NATO and EFTA ally). In addition, British oil companies were involved to the extent that they supplied about 40 percent of Rhodesia's needs, with the balance being of American, French, and Kuwaiti origin. For example, of the 4.5 million tons of oil imported by South Africa in 1964, Rhodesia imported 500,000 tons, of which 180,000 tons went to Zambia.

For Britain, Zambia was a particularly vexatious problem, as were, to a lesser degree, the "captive" states of Bechuanaland (Botswana), Swaziland, and Basutoland (Lesotho).[9] There was the obvious fear that Rhodesia would retaliate against Zambia by cutting off the Rhodesian railway system, Rhodesian coal, and Kariba Dam power. For Britain the difficulties were numerous, and included the facts that 40 percent of British industry's copper originated in Zambia and Zambian tobacco was processed in Rhodesia. In anticipation of Rhodesian pressures, Britain contemplated an airlift and consulted Canada and the United States about possible participation. The Zambian "rescue operation" became a major preoccupation in ensuing months and involved three phases: a special dispensation for Zambia in the face of sanctions; development of indigenous sources of supply where feasible; and provision of alternative means of communications.

President Kaunda was under immense internal and external political pressure to intervene against Rhodesia, yet the precarious nature of Zambia's existence vis-à-vis Rhodesia precluded rash action. The prospect of bringing into use alternative sources of power and resources was feasible only to the extent that studies and capital were available. Thus, for Kariba power, development of the Kafue hydroelectric scheme might prove possible; Rhodesian coal from Wankie mines might be replaced by development of coal resources at Nkandabwe and Siankandoba; and the Rhodesian railroads might be supplanted by the Bas-Congo au Katanga and Benguela Railways, as well as by development of roads

---

deal, and in fact a Japanese delegation was in Rhodesia on the day of UDI.

and highways.* In the short run, however, the position of
Zambia was delicate; and as the inevitability of UDI became
apparent, the crisis facing Zambia became clearer.

It was under these circumstances that events immediately leading to UDI on November 11, 1965 proceeded. Much
of what transpired during this period was jockeying for
position via media while gestures were made simultaneously
toward negotiated solution.

On October 11 the United Nations' Fourth Committee en-
tertained a joint U.S.-British resolution that was intended
to serve more as a deterrent to UDI than an attempt to involve the United Nations in the situation. It was clear
to the British and others that the problem of Rhodesia was
essentially British; but that if international involvement
was to ensue, then it was best undertaken under the auspices of the Commonwealth.**

In a television address on October 12, Wilson reiterated his government's views and warned of the disastrous
consequences for Rhodesia and racial harmony in Africa if
UDI were undertaken. He emphasized the Commonwealth responsibility and suggested a mission to Rhodesia on behalf
of the Commonwealth to talk with Smith.[10] Meanwhile, Wilson kept Commonwealth leaders informed, by personal letters, of the evolving situation. Britain was prepared even
to discuss the possibility of independence before majority
rule, but with constitutional guarantees for the majority.
From the Rhodesian side came a national address to Rhodesians, and on October 14, Harry Reedman, head of the Rhodesian mission in Lisbon, informed Portugal via radio that
he had a mandate to place the case for independence before
all people interested in justice.[11] It should be recalled
that throughout this period of bargaining, the Wilson government was a minority in Parliament, and hence Smith had
a psychological upper hand. Smith rejected the possibility
of Commonwealth intervention on October 18, and two days
later he proposed independence based upon the 1961 constitution with an accompanying treaty undertaking not to amend

---

*Roads, railroads, airports, and harbor facilities had
been explored in a classified report on transportation of
import and export traffic of the Republic of Zambia (July
1965), prepared by Canadian consultants.

**It was apparently agreed among some Commonwealth lead-
ers that the creation of a Rhodesian government in exile
would be self-defeating, for it would effectively acknowledge independence de facto.

the constitution after independence. This Britain rejected,
and with rejection the respective positions of the two parties became consolidated while they simultaneously endeavored to bluff the other into altering its position. However, a confrontation did exist by mid-October, and there
were not many valid alternatives available.

Britain was now faced with the task of endeavoring to
internationalize a probable UDI while simultaneously maintaining the maximum amount of individual flexibility and
control. This tightrope meant that by internationalizing
the event, Britain effectively limited its capacity unilaterally to conclude a settlement. One move in the United
Nations had been successfully made to expand the dispute
while still retaining British initiative. The Commonwealth,
however, was another cauldron; and Commonwealth leaders
were becoming increasingly vociferous about British responsibilities.[12]

On October 20 and 21, Smith and Wilson exchanged correspondence that certainly led Britain to believe that a
last-ditch effort to find a solution to the problem was being attempted by Smith. In hopes of forestalling the apparently inevitable, Wilson flew to Salisbury where meetings were held on October 26 and 29, with Wilson taking
time in between to meet with loyal Rhodesians. These meetings ended in failure except for the recommendation that a
royal commission be appointed to consider the independence
of Rhodesia.[13] On October 30 and 31 meetings were held in
Salisbury to prepare a proposal for a royal commission.
The report was dated October 31, 1965. In accordance with
procedure customary to royal commissions, Wilson announced
both to Parliament and in a letter to Smith that his government would reserve its decision on whether to accept or
reject findings of the proposed royal commission.[14] Smith
responded on November 8 to the effect that unless Wilson
agreed that the proposed royal commission had some validity,
"We are back in the position we reached at the end of our
talks in London, when we both agreed that the views of our
respective Governments were irreconcilable."[15] Wilson
made another attempt to find a basis for agreement in a
letter to Smith on November 10, but by then events had
reached a conclusion and Smith replied with UDI.[16]

Before turning to the consequences of and response to
this action, it is useful to backtrack slightly to consider
the political dilemma facing Britain. Julius Nyerere,
President of Tanzania, in reviewing the developing situation, referred to the impetus of Africans toward independence and the determination of African people in Rhodesia

to obtain freedom. Further, he warned, generally, that
Africans might be forced to abandon peaceful attempts if
the West failed to understand.[17] Harold Wilson, aware of
the strength of this belief in Africa, had held talks with
African leaders on his way to and from the talks in Salisbury in late October. Hence, much of what Wilson did in
response to Smith in the interval between conclusion of the
Salisbury talks and UDI appears to have been premised upon
the extent to which his options had been restricted by the
growing internationalization of the situation. For example,
reserving decisions on recommendations of a proposed royal
commission may have been prompted by an aide-mémoire given
to Wilson by Ghanaian President Nkrumah on October 31. In
it, and a subsequent statement, Nkrumah vigorously rejected
the proposed commission.[18] In other Commonwealth states,
perhaps reflecting an unusual level of Commonwealth unity,
Smith was condemned and Wilson's efforts to achieve a
solution were cautiously approved.[19]

     Wilson's reasons for turning the prospect of UDI into
an international event were obvious. First, he lacked real
choice because the racial and constitutional problem was
evident to Commonwealth members from at least 1963. Second, Wilson doubtless anticipated that world opinion would
strengthen his bargaining position vis-à-vis Smith. Third,
by internationalizing the situation, Wilson could lend
greater credence to his threat of dire consequences should
UDI be proclaimed; the consequences were specifically economic, and undoubtedly Wilson sought to blunt the more extreme of Smith's supporters (W. J. Harper and D. Lardner-
Burke) who were pushing him to UDI. Finally, Wilson might
have been attempting to reduce his options, thereby empha-
sizing the limited range within which he could negotiate.
In any case, by November 11 the positions were quite clear.[20]

                THE IMMEDIATE INTERNATIONAL RESPONSE

     In this section two somewhat unrelated but mutually
interacting components of the Rhodesian case will be discussed. First, the response by the United Nations is outlined during the most vigorous period, November 1965 to
April 1966. Next, there is an incomplete but broadly representative compilation of responses to both Rhodesian UDI
and the UN Security Council decision, especially operative
paragraph 8 of Resolution 217.[21] It should be obvious, of
course, that responses to a UN decision to impose sanctions
were not universally forthcoming; and thus no attempt is

made to view members' responses in any manner but that there was an almost unanimous adverse reaction to UDI. In addition, it must be recalled that UN members were called open more than once over an extended period of time to affirm faith in the prescribed organizational goals. Finally, these components in the Rhodesian case have been linked for one significant reason.

The UN response to Rhodesian UDI was by far the most complete and universal international involvement in a situation. Even a casual look at the number of member states of the three international organizations under discussion illustrates that the 100-plus members of the United Nations surpassed both the League and the OAS combined. Consequently, as British Prime Minister Wilson gambled, world opinion was a crucial factor in the Rhodesian case through sheer volume. Unlike the League or OAS, there were no major world powers outside the organization that could function as "sanctions-busters." Instead, the only apparent problem facing unanimity in world opinion were two already discredited members, Portugal and the Republic of South Africa. Superficially, therefore, Rhodesian sanctions had potential for attracting more widespread and deeply felt international support than any other internationally organized situation. Further, it will be apparent in the following discussion that world opinion and intentions were profound. Given this observation, it is essential that world opinion be viewed as supportive of the direction taken by the international organization. Hence, because the UN response seems to closely reflect international indignation, it is included as a related component.

The United Nations had been cognizant of the situation in "Southern" Rhodesia at least as early as the 15th session of the General Assembly in 1960. In 1963, however, the General Assembly explicitly called upon the British government "not to accede to the request of the present minority government of Southern Rhodesia for independence until majority rule based on universal adult suffrage is established in the Territory."[22] Britain was then called upon to hold a constitutional conference to make arrangements for independence under majority rule at the earliest possible date.

At a General Assembly meeting on September 24, 1965, agenda item 23, "Implementations of the Declaration on the Granting of Independence to Colonial Countries and Peoples," again was assigned to the Fourth Committee. By October 11 the Fourth Committee reported on its deliberations and recommended adoption of a draft resolution on Rhodesia that was approved by the General Assembly on October 12.[23] This resolution clearly reflected the extent to which an antici-pated Rhodesian declaration of independence was imminent. In the preamble it was stated that a unilateral declaration of independence was an act of rebellion and that giving effect to it would constitute treason. The resolution con-tinued by condemning the Smith regime and calling upon Brit-ain "to take all possible measures to prevent a UDI and, in the event of such a declaration, to take all steps nec-essary to put an immediate end to the rebellion." The resolution concluded with an acknowledgment that the situa-tion was urgent.

There is little doubt that the October 12 resolution reflected British and American preferences in the situation. Clearly Britain sought as stern a UN statement as possible without at the same time unduly restricting either Brit-ain's capacity to negotiate or its ability to press Smith with every means at its disposal. As noted earlier, oper-ative paragraph 8 contained no references to the use of force, a clear concession to Britain's quietly expressed unwillingness to consider the use of force and the Ameri-cans' desire to avoid racial conflict in Africa.*

The Fourth Committee's activities on Rhodesia, which began again on November 1, ultimately saw fruition as a General Assembly resolution on November 8, 1965.[24] In the week during which this resolution was hammered into being, the situation was moving rapidly to a climax. In Rhodesia, Smith's Cabinet was pressing for independence, with Lardner-Burke leading the charge for an immediate declaration of independence. Smith, however, was in the process of reject-ing the royal commission proposal while Wilson struggled to gain time. In Ghana, Nkrumah, probably stunned by his set-back on his African unity scheme at the just-concluded Or-ganization of African Unity meeting (October 21-25), de-nounced Wilson in most vitriolic terms and clamored for military intervention. More stable African Commonwealth leaders, such as Milton Obote (he had met with Arthur Bot-tomley in Kampla on the royal commission issue), Hastings Banda (Malawi), Kenneth Kaunda (Zambia), and Julius Nyerere (Tanzania), more or less acknowledged that Wilson was at-tempting to stall UDI until a time less favorable to Smith.

---

*It is important to realize that Britain, as a party to the dispute, was limited in its capacity to participate in overt UN activities. Thus, carrying the ball was left to its most influential friend.

In the middle of this vying for positions, Rhodesia declared a state of emergency on November 4, thereby increasing the frenzy that was being concocted by Smith's government.[25] In Britain opposition Conservatives were beginning to scream "bungle"; and in desperation Wilson, despite the probability of intense opposition from within his Cabinet, suggested another meeting with Smith, possibly on Malta. The United States, meanwhile, affirmed its support for Britain and opposition to UDI in a letter from President Johnson to Smith on October 30.* Given the buildup of tensions, it is not surprising that the resolution of November 8 acknowledged that the tone of the dispute had changed dramatically since October 12.

British and American influence over the November 8 resolution was considerably less than had been the case a month earlier. The number of abstentions alone indicated that the impetus for UN action was beyond complete British control.** Consequently the resolution strongly shows its origins as a reflection of African frustration with what was occurring. It took into account Britain's failure to implement independence under majority rule; noted increased cooperation between Rhodesia, South Africa, and Portugal designed "to perpetuate racist minority rule"; solemnly warned all parties that the United Nations would oppose any declaration of independence not based on universal adult suffrage; and outlined a number of related points in anticipation of a Rhodesian move.

The November 8 resolution clearly recognized that UDI was imminent; and consequently its sternness--besides being another warning to Smith--was intended to create the atmosphere of crisis while outlining the measures to be taken. Thus, the operative paragraphs condemned support or assistance by any state to the minority regime, and appealed to all states to use all their powers (a term not clearly enunciated but doubtless reflecting a compromise on specifics) against UDI and not to recognize any government not representative of a majority of the people. The resolution also acknowledged Smith's warnings of retaliation and thus drew to the attention of the Security Council

----

*Details of this message were not publicly known until November 7.
**Countries such as Austria, Brazil, Costa Rica, Denmark, Ecuador, El Salvador, Finland, Guatemala, Honduras, Ireland, Italy, Mexico, Norway, Panama, and Sweden suggest a certain homogeneity in the desire to abstain.

(a necessary preliminary to a Chapter VII resolution) the "explosive situation in Southern Rhodesia which threatens international peace and security."

The November 8 resolution also entered a somewhat impractical area in operative paragraphs 7(a)(b)(c), 8, and 12. In brief, Britain was called upon as administering power to "effect immediately" the release of all political prisoners and detainees, to repeal all repressive and discriminatory legislation, and to remove all restrictions on African political activity and rights. In addition, Britain was requested to suspend the 1961 Rhodesian constitution and to call a representative constitutional conference immediately. Finally, Britain was called upon to employ all necessary means, "including military force," to implement these measures.

While the intent of these directives was specific, the impractical quality stemmed from the reality of the situation. For while it is true that Britain could have constitutionally subscribed to the directives set forth in paragraphs 7 and 8, practical compliance would have involved a direct physical presence in Rhodesia--which, explicitly, seems to have been the intent in any case. This realization was conceded in the prescription to employ military force.[26] Thus the logic was quite simple: direct the administering state to undertake impossible tasks and provide it with tools to fulfill the task while simultaneously quashing a rebellion. The logic was straightforward, despite the obvious difficulties involved.

The African case for military force was based upon sound principles:

1. Each African state achieved independence after a long and difficult struggle.
2. Many African leaders knew from personal experience the bitterness of subjugation to a racial minority.
3. Britain frequently had used force against Africans seeking democratic freedoms; now it faced a regime seeking to enforce nondemocratic rule.
4. Smith's declaration of independence would constitute the indictable crime of treason, for which he should be arrested, tried like any other rebel, and sent to prison (like numerous Africans and Indians who had committed treason in the past).
5. Economic sanctions would probably fail because South Africa and Portugal would again connive to thwart world opinion.

6. A failure to use force in pursuit of world community goals would leave Africans with no recourse but to bloody revolution.[27]

It is suspected, but difficult to substantiate, that Britain actually had undertaken a study of factors involved in the introduction of force into the Rhodesian situation. Such a contingency study doubtless would have opposed such recourse for two broad reasons: military and political. Under the former heading there was the possibility that the well-equipped and well-trained Rhodesian forces would have opposed the British; and they would have had an advantage from a strategic viewpoint, for British troops would have had to be flown in from Aden, the nearest air base. Such a confrontation also would have pitted white Britons against their fellow Englishmen. This problem of "kith and kin" was an issue with considerable emotional, and hence political, appeal in Britain.[28] Conservatives, for example, who opposed the minority Labour government's challenge to Smith, played upon the kith-and-kin theme with great vigor. In sum, therefore, the use of military force was a politically unrealistic--although valid--option. In any case, on November 10 Rhodesian troops were deployed to strategic positions throughout the country while in London the Rhodesian High Commissioner delivered a message to the Queen reaffirming Rhodesian loyalty to the Crown.

Reaction at the United Nations to Smith's UDI on November 11 was swift and included introduction of an African states' provisional draft resolution before the Fourth Committee and at plenary sessions of the General Assembly. The draft resolution called upon Britain to apply all pertinent UN resolutions and to take all necessary measures to end the Rhodesian rebellion. The African states also endeavored to force the Security Council into session on November 11 but eventually settled for approval of the draft resolution in the Fourth Committee, and later in the General Assembly, the following day.[29]

While Britain's ability to influence the Fourth Committee and General Assembly was miniscule, it still retained influence in the Security Council. Consequently the Security Council met at British insistence on November 12 and passed an initial condemnatory resolution.[30] Britain then introduced a second resolution calling upon UN members to take effective economic measures similar to those promulgated by Britain (trade prohibition, exchange controls). This second resolution was countered by an African draft sponsored by Ivory Coast. Neither resolution

was particularly attractive, the British because of its
vagueness and the African because it was too direct.* The
resulting statement and apparent irreconcilability of the
two resolutions led the Security Council to meet briefly
on November 15 and adjourn until the following day. Meanwhile, meetings continued between African and Western delegations, most notably the Americans. Moderates among the
African states, especially those in the Security Council,
began work on a compromise resolution that would have included specific economic sanctions, but under provisions
of Chapter VI of the Charter (pacific settlement of disputes). Throughout this period Britain was pressing for
creation of an expert Sanctions Committee to review the
feasibility of specific economic sanctions and to report
back to the Security Council.

As a further counter to strong African pressure, the
United States and the Netherlands produced another draft
resolution, which encompassed the British preference for a
committee of experts to report before the end of 1965.
The draft also called upon states to consider additional
"effective" economic measures, but it was not specified
whether these would precede or follow the experts' report.
The Security Council was scheduled to meet on November 18
but did not convene until the following day, in order to
provide crucial time for a final compromise attempt. When
it did convene, it had a Bolivian-Uruguayan resolution before it and a reminder that this was an attempt to overcome
differences reflected in two distinct earlier draft resolutions. It was this Latin American resolution that was
approved (10-0-1) on November 20, 1965 and thereby placed
the United Nations in the sanctions business.[31]

Resolution 217 essentially reflected the Ivory Coast's
and African preferences. However, it was a Chapter VI
resolution, thereby reflecting the British preference for
a more flexible approach and contrary to what would have
resulted from a mandatory Chapter VII resolution, the African states' preference. However, while in large part it
harbored a minimum African sentiment, Resolution 217 nevertheless contained major concessions to Britain. Thus, in

---

*The first draft of the African resolution contained a
reference to Charter Articles 42 and 43. This was not in
the second draft. The draft resolution also contained a
vague reference to "breaking all economic relations,"
which led to confusing results.

operative paragraph 1 the Rhodesian situation's "continuance in time" constituted a threat to international peace. This was a modification of the original African proposal, which made Rhodesian UDI a threat to international peace and security. The "continuance in time" phrase was double-edged, for it provided a legal basis for the United Nations to intervene in a matter fundamentally described as internal or domestic. However, it also modified the international organization's involvement to the extent that it provided Britain with facility to argue that the time was not ripe for full-scale international involvement.

Operative paragraph 8 was also modified significantly from the original African draft. This is the operative sanctions component of Resolution 217 and hence was crucial for the United Nations. The African draft had called upon UN members to break all economic relations with Rhodesia, including an embargo on oil and petroleum products. At British insistence this was modified, and members were requested "to do their utmost" to break economic relations. Doing one's utmost to prevent something and outright banning clearly are quite distinct. Equivocation in this point emphasized that Britain was not yet prepared to abandon hope for a settlement. Obviously these modifications tended to blunt the probable impact of economic sanctions, thereby permitting some additional turning of the screw should subsequent negotiations collapse. It should be understood that Resolution 217, despite the directive in paragraph 8, made no reference to Articles 41 and 42 of the Charter. That is, there was nothing mandatory.

In the period between November 1965 and April 1966, at least three major events occurred that had a significant impact upon the UN sanctions program. First, the OAU Council of Ministers met in Addis Ababa on December 3-5, 1965 and passed a major resolution, one provision of which directed OAU members to sever diplomatic relations with Britain if the Rhodesian rebellion were not crushed by December 15.[32] Second, British Prime Minister Wilson announced imposition of a British oil embargo against Rhodesia. In Wilson's statement to Parliament, he observed that France and Italy had indicated a willingness to cooperate with restraints on Rhodesia, as had the United States.[33] Finally, there was a Commonwealth Heads of Government meeting in Lagos, Nigeria, on January 11 and 12, 1966, which affirmed that the principle of "one man, one vote" was absolute in terms of Rhodesia.[34] In addition, world reaction to UDI, with a few exceptions, was universally condemnatory; and some states immediately undertook

to implement Resolution 217 with special laws and regulations.[35] Generally, therefore, states reacted in support
of Britain and the United Nations; and although there were
several instances of criticism directed at Britain for its
failure to move decisively in crushing Smith's rebellion,
some were predictable while others were well-intentioned.[36]

In some countries, while official policy supported
British and UN efforts, unofficial reaction was diverse and
often emotional. Australia and New Zealand offered the
clearest examples of equivocation. On November 16 Sir
Robert Menzies, Australia's Prime Minister, in a statement
to the Australian House of Representatives indicated that
Australia rejected any notion of the use of armed force
while simultaneously urging support for Britain. However,
a spokesman for the Australian Labour Party (then in opposition) argued that there might be circumstances in which
armed force would be conceivable and that Australia should
be prepared to respond.[37]

In New Zealand, a rather substantial search of conscience was under way, for there was widespread sympathy
for Smith and white Rhodesians. Prime Minister Keith Holy-
oake referred to UDI as a distressing decision with grave
consequences for Rhodesia, Africa, and the Commonwealth.[38]
Meanwhile, his government began preparations to restrict
relations with Rhodesia, although there were stumbling
blocks (apparently such as GATT commitments) that precluded
a rapid move in support of Britain. New Zealand newspaper
opinion clearly reflected the division in opinion, with
some urging support for Rhodesia--"Give Smith a Chance"
or the spectacle of the world's "gutless bullying" of Rhodesia.[39] Others opposed Smith's move as "stubbornness
taken to stupidity" or slated that New Zealanders should
make it clear that they opposed racism.[40]

Direct opposition to Britain and the United Nations,
as anticipated, came from South Africa and Portugal. In
a statement on November 11, South African Prime Minister
Hendrik Verwoerd argued that Rhodesia clearly was an internal British matter; and in recognition of that, the Republic would deliberately refrain "from any intervention
in, or comments on, the negotiations."[41] The South African press, especially the Afrikaanse element, either reported events, urged detachment, or expressed clear hostility to Britain.[42]

Portugal's position was outlined by Foreign Minister
A. M. Nogueira at a press conference on November 25. Nogueira argued that Portugal's votes in the United Nations
did not mean identification with a racist regime and that,

like Britain, Portugal saw the Rhodesian situation as a parallel to Portugal's with its dependent territories. Finally, he argued that Portugal's study of sanctions showed that more harm would befall Zambia, Malawi, and Katangu (Congo) than Rhodesia.[43]

Other states that warrant special comment at this time are the United States, Germany, Japan, and France. The French attitude to the Rhodesian affair was totally pragmatic, and was based essentially upon an unwillingness to concede that colonial issues were within UN purview. Thus, France expressed disapproval of Smith's actions, and in accordance with British representations--not a UN resolution --the Quai d'Orsay agreed to withdraw its Consul from Salisbury. There was also a commitment to refrain from buying Rhodesian tobacco (valued at 6 million francs in 1964), although there is no indication that France was overly willing to cut back on imports of Rhodesian copper (valued at 185 million francs in 1964) or restrict Rhodesian access to accounts held in French banks. However, there was no evidence at this stage that the French government would attempt to control Compagnie Française des Pétroles sales of petroleum products through the company's total retail network. For France, therefore, the Rhodesian matter was exclusively British; and while it was not to be allowed to get out of hand, certainly the United Nations had no role.

Japan was another problem, so much so that British Foreign Secretary Michael Stewart had visited Tokyo just before UDI to seek Japanese support for British policy. When UDI occurred, it was referred to as "regrettable" in Tokyo and the possibility of sanctions apparently was put under consideration.[44] By the time Resolution 217 was approved, the Japanese were prepared to implement any "effective" measures, provided this effectiveness was related to broad implementation by a majority of UN members. However, the Japanese were prepared to honor trade contracts concluded before UDI. There were two issues at stake in this Japanese reluctance to rush into sanctions. First, Japanese industry depended heavily upon Zambian copper; hence there was a reluctance to upset supplies. Second, a Japanese trade and investment mission was in Rhodesia when UDI was declared, and it was in the process of negotiating a major deal for the development of Rhodesian mineral resources. In addition, major Japanese industry was putting pressure upon the government to do as little as possible in order not to disrupt this vast source of materials. Japan, therefore, required a considerable amount of pushing to become involved in sanctions; consequently it followed world opinion reluctantly and bailed out as quickly as possible in succeeding years.

Hints of fluidity in Japanese policy were evidenced on numerous occasions, and on December 17 the British Ambassador in Tokyo called upon Prime Minister Sato, presumably to seek support for an oil sanction but possibly also to draw to Sato's attention the problems posed by Japan. An estimated 50,000 tons of Rhodesian sugar and $500,000 worth of Rhodesian pig iron entered Japan between mid-November and mid-December 1965. Thus, even when Japan did attempt to move in late December, its regulations affected only about 5 percent of total imports from Rhodesia. By far the largest percentage was pig iron, and this traffic was controlled by a joint Japanese-American company operating in Rhodesia. Consequently, despite Foreign Minister Etsusaburo Shiina's apparent desire that Japan adopt an Asian approach to Rhodesia, the business interests prevailed.

Germany was also in a rather interesting position, and in mid-November 1965 Foreign Minister Gerhard Schröder visited London to inform the British of severe opposition within the German Cabinet to any form of sanctions. Consequently, when events unraveled, the Foreign Ministry was under immense pressure not to become involved. It took until December 8 before any positive steps were taken by Germany; and on that date, after a Cabinet meeting, it was announced that the government intended to introduce licenses and that a decree would be issued after a subsequent Cabinet meeting. Meanwhile, Germany's Ambassador in London, Herbert Blankenhorn called upon British officials to explain the difficulties and mechanics of the proposed system. The German licensing system was intended to have the effect of an embargo, although importers were permitted considerable leeway in making application for import licenses. Among other things disturbing Germany about the Rhodesia situation, aside from its low priorities, was the world shortage of copper (about $3 million annually imported from Rhodesia) as well as the obstructed flow of long-grained Rhodesia asbestos to a German industry tooled up for that commodity.*

---

*Germany could have obtained sufficient supplies of asbestos from Canada at equivalent prices, except that Canadian asbestos is short-grained and not suited to German production.

Eventually the licensing decree was introduced as a provision of the Foreign Trade Law covering "disturbances of the peace." German industrialists and importers objected, for they did not see Rhodesia as a threat to world peace. East Germany accused the Federal Republic of dragging its heels because of a basic sympathy to the Smith regime. There is no doubt that Germany did not rush into sanctions, but to interpret that response as sympathy with Smith was ridiculous. Both Germanys were in strong competition for African favor, and the Federal Republic was not inclined to sacrifice hard-won support in black Africa for a regime even its allies found objectionable. The German reluctance to enter an economic war with Rhodesia stemmed from the simple fact that German industry depended (as did Japan) upon Rhodesian and Zambian resources; and in turn Rhodesia purchased about $12 million annually of German chemicals, electronic equipment, and reinforcing steel. Britain was reduced to dealing with Germany one product at a time.*

About the only major step German authorities took on their own initiative was to refuse (December 9) an instruction by the former governor of the Rhodesian Reserve Bank to transfer Rhodesian funds in the Bundesbank to a Hamburg agency. The bank declined on the ground that it could only do so on instructions from the Reserve Bank's new board in London.

The Swiss National Bank, it should be noted, followed instructions from Rhodesia. The Swiss apparently had made it clear to Rhodesia that it would not be permitted to use Switzerland as an intermediary for circumventing sanctions. To this end, exchange controls were established and known credits of the Rhodesian Reserve Bank were blocked in Swiss banks (less than $1 million).

The U.S. role at the early stages was unobtrusive and diligent. U.S. diplomats worked with vigor behind the scenes at the United Nations to win support for the British

_____

*For example, a spokesmen for the German government announced at a press conference in Bonn (December 13, 1965) that the Cabinet was prepared to approve an ordinance establishing licensing procedures for tobacco. On December 14 it was reported that the freighter _Pericles_ was arriving in the free port of Hamburg with $1.1 million of Rhodesian sugar. A license was not granted for import of the sugar into Germany. Payment for the cargo was eventually made into a blocked Rhodesian account in London.

draft sanctions resolution. Specific U.S. actions began with UN Ambassador Goldberg's announcement on November 12 of an embargo on arms, restrictions on travel for U.S. citizens, suspension of the Rhodesian sugar quota, and a discouragement of U.S. private investments. Later, these actions were followed by withdrawal of the U.S. Consul General from Salisbury and suspension of action on Rhodesia's application for export loans and credit guarantees. Beyond this the United States seemed content to follow Britain's lead, to the extent that strategic considerations did not arise.

There were a horde of other individual state activities under way in the period between November 1965 and April 1966; but generally, with the exceptions noted above, they followed predictable patterns. Before concluding this section, note is required of three other major events of the period: the OAU meeting, the British petroleum embargo, and the Commonwealth meeting in Lagos.

This brief look at the role of the OAU will be fixed on the period November 11 to December 15, the latter being the date on which OAU members agreed to sever relations with Britain. Aside from individual African state reactions, the significant multilateral African efforts were as follows. The OAU Committee of 11, at a meeting in Dar es Salaam on November 13 called on the people of Zimbabwe (Rhodesia) to rise against Smith. Further, the committee called upon independent African states to facilitate the passage of men and materials to reinforce an armed Zimbabwe liberation movement. On November 16, at a meeting of East African Presidents in Nairobi, it was agreed that every effort would be made to support Rhodesian nationalists, including facilitating exile activity.* At about the same time the United Arab Republic had announced that orders had been issued to officials at Port Said and Suez to bar any ship flying a Rhodesian flag or hired by Rhodesia.[45] Simultaneously, Haile Selassie lodged a formal request with the Secretariat for an OAU summit meeting.

---

*Prime Minister Wilson apparently had written personal letters to each President prior to the Nairobi meeting, at which he argued that UDI could have been avoided if the British government had been prepared to compromise its principles. He expressed concern about the dangers of the use of force and urged support for his efforts to have Rhodesians rally about the Governor.

During this entire period Kwame Nkrumah was actively
at work organizing a vague African armed force and, in that
connection, a number of African states indicated that they
considered themselves to be in a state of war with Rhodesia.
This condition of war was noticeably vague, for if it had
actually been a state of war, then presumably it implied
an acknowledged international personality against which war
could exist--that is, a de jure status for Rhodesia. Thus,
while this may be a fine point in law, it is nevertheless
true that a state of war implies recognition of the entity
against which war is to be conducted.[46] In any case, it
is doubtful whether an African force could have been successful against well-trained and well-armed Rhodesians,
and defeat would have been disastrous for Africa.

Between November 19 and 22 a five-member special OAU
Committee on Rhodesia met in Dar es Salaam. Among other
things the committee was to consider the possibility of
bringing the two Rhodesian nationalist groups together as
one government in exile.[47] During the meetings three members visited Lusaka to assess Zambian reactions to proposals
being contemplated. The OAU Committee of Five recommended
a full-scale meeting of OAU Foreign Ministers and Defense
Ministers for December 3, 1965. It was becoming evident
by this time that African patience with Britain was expir-
ing rapidly. Only Julius Nyerere and Tomo Kenyatta appeared to have retained some grasp of the difficulties facing Africans, especially those in Zambia, although Nyerere's
appeal for moderation in October had reached its limits.[48]
There was a growing and perceptible disbelief in the veracity of British intentions, and this was nurtured by confusion and frustration about the appropriate African response. Realistic Africans, whether they liked the situation or not, seemed to have been reduced to the role of
noisemakers, in hopes of cajoling Britain into living up
to its responsibilities.

An extraordinary session of the OAU Council of Ministers was held in Addis Ababa December 3-5, 1965. The tone
of the sessions was largely established by OAU Secretary
General Diallo Telli, who, with the help of extreme African nationalists, argued through a resolution that for all
practical purposes sacrificed Zambia's interests. Briefly,
the OAU resolution called upon African states to terminate
all forms of trade and economic and financial relations,
as well as to sever all means of transportation and com-

294

munication.* The resolution also called upon all countries
to deny petroleum to Rhodesia and for friendly states to
use "radio and other information media" to serve African
needs.** Finally, the resolution tested African unity with
a call to all OAU members to sever diplomatic relations
with Britain by December 15 if the rebellion were not
crushed. The Committee of Five, by separate resolution,
was then empowered to coordinate African measures.

The next 12 days was a fascinating period of African
soul-searching. For, as Julius Nyerere described the situation, "the honour of Africa" was at issue.

> We are not proposing to break diplomatic relations
> with Britain because we wish to do so; we shall do
> it only if it becomes necessary for our own honour,
> for the honour of Africa, and as a means of show-
> ing our determination never to falter in the cam-
> paign against racialism on this continent.[49]

Nyerere required a demonstration of British determination
to bring Smith down; and while he understood Britain's
preference for economic sanctions, he argued for a more
positive act, such as a British guarantee for Zambian security through occupation of the Kariba Dam and power station. This, he suggested, would be acknowledged by Africans as an expression of willingness to act swiftly against
Smith.[50]

Britain, realizing that African prestige and credibility were at issue, sought ways to obtain a compromise.
There were suggestions of a Commonwealth Foreign Ministers
meeting, considerable talk about the multiracial Commonwealth, quiet correspondence with Commonwealth leaders,
and visits to African states by Commonwealth Secretary-
General Arnold Smith and assorted British officials. It
was never quite clear, for example, whether the OAU resolve to sever relations was mandatory or simply a recommendation; consequently, under pressure exerted by Britain,

---

*Aside from the obvious problems this posed for Zambia,
there were also instances where the Congo (Brazzaville)
supplied extra fuel to regularly scheduled aircraft on
Paris-Brazzaville-Salisbury-Johannesburg runs, to compen-
sate for reduced supplies in Salisbury. Nor, by late November, had Brazzaville imposed any restrictions on imports
of Rhodesian tobacco.
**A reference to Radio Free Europe facilities in Africa.

some states were prepared to reconsider their position. It was not surprising, therefore, that on December 12 Prime Minister Abubakar Tafawa Balewa of Nigeria, apparently running directly counter to the views of his newly appointed (December 1) Foreign Minister, Alhaji Bamdi, announced his interest in convening a Commonwealth Heads of Government meeting in Lagos. Balewa was perceptibly disturbed by the apparent irresponsibility of Francophone African states, and he was sensitive to the situation and isolation of Zambia.*

By December 10, therefore, it was becoming clear that many African states would not comply with the OAU resolution of December 3. Consequently, despite a plea by Sékou Touré of Guinea on December 14, only nine states had broken formal diplomatic relations with Britain by December 18;** and it was becoming clear that many African states would not comply.

In brief, the failure of African solidarity over the December 3 resolution cannot be attributed to a lack of desire by African states. Rather, some states had far too much to lose by a break with Britain, and consequently economic and political necessity seemed to outweigh Africa's honor. Besides, Sclassie's call for an OAU Heads of State meeting and Belawa's call for a Commonwealth Prime Ministers meeting provided a sufficient basis for most African states to defer action on the resolution. To the extent, therefore, that Africans could visualize British pressure increasing on Smith, most were prepared to concede that opportunities should be given to Britain before decisive action (force) was undertaken.[51]

Britain, either responding to the pressure or in an attempt to defuse the situation, promulgated an Order in Council on December 17, 1965, prohibiting oil imports into Rhodesia. This action followed a visit by Wilson to the United Nations (December 16), Ottawa, and Washington, where he outlined British intentions and sought cooperation for his government's policy, especially provision of an oil airlift for Zambia.[52] He had received assurances

---

*It should be noted here that Commonwealth Asian states were not enthusiastic about the OAU resolution, and both India and Malaysia expressed regret that Africans were considering a break in relations.

**Mali, Mauritania, Algeria, Congo (Brazzaville), Tanzania, Sweden, UAR, Ghana, and Guinea. The Somali Republic had broken relations in 1963.

of support for the airlift from Washington and Ottawa. In a statement to the House of Commons, he conceded, in response to a question, that the British oil embargo might escalate into a mandatory Chapter VII resolution.

The decision by Britain to impose a petroleum embargo was based upon the dual assessment that an airlift could supply Zambian needs in the short run and that if other states volunteered support, Smith's regime would collapse by Easter 1966.* Actually, Rhodesian petroleum needs were fairly limited; consequently it had not proved excessively difficult to obtain the cooperation of major oil producers, although there were enough small suppliers to meet Rhodesian needs in any case. By late December 1965, a number of countries (including France) had agreed to voluntary restraints on oil sales to Rhodesia. However, as will become evident shortly, this voluntary approach did not prove sufficient.** Before turning to this point, some explanation is required about the Commonwealth Prime Ministers meeting.

The January 1966 Commonwealth Prime Ministers meeting in Lagos, Nigeria, was unquestionably one of the most significant meetings in Commonwealth history. In the shadow of the OAU debacle, British prestige in Africa was at a low point, although the Africans now had a proven inability to organize any effective alternative thrust against Rhodesia. It was perhaps with this quandary in mind that Nigerian Prime Minister Sir Abubakar Tafawa Balewa went to London

---

*It also may have had something to do with an attack on Wilson's government by his own back-benchers in the House of Commons on December 7 over the government's failure to stop a British Petroleum-owned tanker from delivering oil to Beira, Mozambique, for Rhodesia.

**By 1965, 85 percent of Rhodesia's lubricating oils were supplied by Shell Oil and Shell (South Africa) through a subsidiary, Consolidated Oil. Mobil Oil Corporation was supplying oil to Rhodesia through a pipeline at Lourenço Marques, Mozambique. France published an order in the official journal forbidding export of oil to Rhodesia, and letters were sent to oil companies requesting that reexports be controlled. The United States advised Americans to comply with the British oil embargo on December 17 and simultaneously announced a U.S. airlift of petroleum products for Zambia from Leopoldville and Elizabethville in the Congo. The United States embargoed oil shipments to Rhodesia on December 28.

(December 13-16) to argue for convening of a Prime Ministers meeting. Balewa was an African moderate who apparently
favored a realistic African approach to the Rhodesian situation, including training and educational opportunities for
Rhodesian Africans. His efforts were not universally approved, either in Africa or in his country.[53] The ambiva-
lence of African leaders perhaps was best illustrated by
Nkrumah, who, when he announced severance of relations with
Britain on December 16, added that this in no manner affected British technical and professional assistance to
Ghana's armed forces. Nkrumah clearly distinguished between diplomatic relations and the Commonwealth tie, and
apparently saw advantages in retaining some semblance of a
relationship with Britain despite blustering adherence to
the OAU resolution.[54]

It was clear as momentum gathered for the meeting that
not all Commonwealth members approached the prospect of
confrontation with Africans in Africa with enthusiasm.
About December 21, for example, Australian Prime Minister
Menzies informed Balewa that "under existing circumstances
Australia is not in favour" of convening a Prime Ministers
meeting.[55] The Australians undoubtedly feared a military
escalation and opposed "the giving of any Commonwealth orders to Britain" as to how it should exercise authority
and discharge responsibilities. This type of response
added fuel to speculation that the Commonwealth was on the
verge of an "old boy-new boy" split, and in the week or so
before the meeting a scenario pessimism was played.

It was obvious, for example, that such a meeting would
be plausible only if Prime Minister Wilson attended. Yet
it is reasonable to presume that he would not have attended
if a respectable number of other heads of government had
not assured him of their presence.* It was also apparent
that Britain was not enthusiastic about discussing the
"post-UDI" future of Rhodesia, for statements that might
be made in Lagos in that connection would stand to jeopardize prospects for settlement emanating from Rhodesia. One
of the advantages of Commonwealth meetings is the opportunity to conduct "in camera" international discussions,
and these proved crucial to British policy.

---

*It should be noted that in the middle of all this the
OAU called an OAU heads of state meeting for January 19,
and by January 1, 1966, 19 affirmative replies had been
received. There was also a meeting scheduled in Tannana-
rive on January 15 of the Organisation Commune Afrique et
Malagache.

On January 11-12, 1966, with the exception of Tanzania, Ghana, and an Australian observer, the Commonwealth Prime Ministers met in Lagos. British objectives were numerous:

    1. To gain time for sanctions to work,
    2. To affirm their determination to Africans that the Smith regime would be brought down,
    3. To blunt African pressure for the use of force,
    4. To create support for Zambia and Malawi if necessary,
    5. To offer Africans some indication of good faith on the matter of indigenous Rhodesian development.

The final communiqué suggests that in almost every respect the meeting was a success for Britain.[56] The Prime Ministers reaffirmed their faith in the intolerable nature of a racially discriminatory society. On the matter of force, they "accepted that its use could not be precluded if this proved necessary to restore law and order." On a Canadian initiative two continuing committees were created, one on assistance to Zambia and the other on assistance in training Rhodesian Africans. Finally, the newly created Commonwealth Sanctions Committee was directed to maintain a continuing review of the Rhodesian situation and to recommend additional Prime Ministers meetings as required.* From this meeting until April 7 the process became one of tightening sanctions while efforts continued to achieve a bilateral Rhodesian-British basis of settlement.[57] It must be reiterated at this point that such sanctions as were being imposed--either voluntarily or under the November 20 UN resolution--were not sanctions under the provisions of Chapter VII (Articles 41 and 42) of the UN Charter. This voluntary nature was acknowledged at the Lagos meeting, for the communiqué indicated that some Prime Ministers reserved the right, "if need arises," to propose mandatory sanctions under Articles 41 or 42 of the Charter. Thus the meeting affirmed that sanctions, while under authority of the Security Council, were still voluntary.

By the middle of January 1966, 90 percent of Rhodesia's traditional trade in tobacco had been restricted; and Brit-

---

*This committee, existing under the auspices of the newly created Commonwealth Secretariat, consisted of representatives from Commonwealth High Commissions in London who met regularly in London.

ain anticipated that farmers would desert Smith by July, when large British purchases of tobacco normally would have been made. The major breaks in sanctions thus far included Rhodesian sales of pig iron to Japan (£4 million); of asbestos and copper to Germany (£2.5 million); of chrome and tobacco to the United States (£2.4 million); and of meat, tobacco, and asbestos to Switzerland (£1.5 million). In addition, South African, Swiss, Belgian, and Italian insurance companies were writing new policies in Rhodesia, much to the annoyance of the British Insurance Association. In an effort to plug these holes, Britain endeavored through press leaks, statements, and en clair communications to embassies, to use African and Commonwealth representatives in various capitals to pressure the major offenders.*

The other major gap was petroleum, and on January 15 Rhodesian Radio announced that the regime had concluded an "agreement" with Venezuela for the supply of crude oil in Panamanian ships.[58] This agreement reflected Rhodesian concern for the future of crude petroleum supplies, for very little crude was delivered to Rhodesian refineries during January, although refined and semirefined products were still entering the country.[59] On January 31 and February 3, meetings were held in Cape Town between representatives of the oil companies and South Africa's Commerce and Economic Affairs Minister N. Diederichs in which discussion focused upon voluntary limitations of oil sales to Rhodesia. The route from South Africa to Rhodesia was by railroad across the Limpopo River at Beitbridge, at which point the British apparently established a surreptitious monitoring system, as well as along the Transvaal-Mozambique railroad.[60] In addition a group of private Rhodesians had purchased complete stocks from filling stations in the South African Transvaal. This activity prompted the British and American governments to encourage B.P., Shell, Esso, and Mobil to restrict supplies to the Transvaal to 1965 levels plus 15 percent for petroleum and 10 percent for other products.**

---

*In the Congo, Union Minière warned General Joseph Mobutu that they would have to close down their plants if the Congo imposed sanctions, for Rhodesia would cut off Wankie coal. Zambia also faced flooded mines if Rhodesian coal were cut off.

**An estimated 700,000 gallons of petroleum products flowed across Beitbridge in February 1966. This was considerably below Rhodesia's normal requirement of about 3.5 million gallons.

Because of the increased prospects of petroleum traffic to Rhodesia, Britain, with the agreement of the Malagasy
Republic, established an air surveillance base for the
Mozambique Channel at Majunga, Malagasy Republic. The reason for this surveillance became increasingly clear during
March 1966, for it was reported on March 5 that two tankers
were on course to Beira with petrol for Rhodesia. In addition, private companies were engaged in the construction
of storage tanks at Beira.[61] By midmonth it was reported
that Rhodesia was being supplied with 200,000 gallons of
petroleum daily by South African trains over the Laurenço
Marques railway line. In addition the Norwegian tanker
Benguela was destined for Beira with 1.5 million gallons
of kerosene for Rhodesia.[62] Throughout March reports of
oil shipments being made or en route to Rhodesia were plentiful; they culminated with the arrival on the scene of the
Joanna V in late March.[63] On or about April 3 the British
government committed itself to the interception of this
Greek-registered vessel, for there was no doubt that it
(and another tanker, Manuela) were carrying cargo for Rhodesia.[64] The Joanna V was intercepted and boarded by British naval officers, then permitted to proceed to Beira.

This clear violation of Britain's efforts to maintain
sanctions against Rhodesia, combined with various other
violations, often very overt, and the increased frustrations
of African states, particularly those of the Commonwealth,
during the almost weekly Sanctions Committee meetings in
London, led Britain into a new more decisive (it was hoped)
venture.[65]

Preparations were launched, therefore, to move into
the United Nations with the problem.* In a paper prepared
for a meeting of heads of government of East and Central
Africa in Nairobi at the end of March 1966, Julius Nyerere
quoted British Foreign Secretary Michael Stewart as saying
that Britain would support mandatory oil sanctions against
Rhodesia and that Britain would press to get "the mandatory sanctions extended to other goods besides oil."[66]
Presumably in this vein, therefore, Britain requested an
emergency meeting of the Security Council for April 7, and
the following day a draft British resolution was submitted.[67]

It was intended that the Security Council meeting
would be held on the evening of April 7, but the President

---

*There were unconfirmed rumors that New Zealand might
be prepared to sponsor a Chapter VII resolution in the
Security Council calling for a mandatory oil embargo.

of the Council that month, Moussa Leo Keita (Mali), was
chairing a meeting of African representatives at the Mali
mission in New York. Thus, instead of the Council meeting,
eight non-African states met in private and apparently
there was no contact between the two groups. The Security
Council finally did convene on April 9, 1966,[68] and the
British draft resolution was submitted. After consideration
of amendments proposed by African states, the Security
Council approved Resolution 221 on April 9, 1966 (10-0-5).[69]

Resolution 222 was directed specifically at Portugal,
calling upon it to prevent petroleum transshipments to
Rhodesia. Further, the resolution called upon all states
to ensure that their vessels did not convey oil to Rhodesia
via Beira, and Britain was empowered to arrest the Joanna V
if it left Beira harbor without its cargo.

Portugal, as the object of the April 9 resolution,
struggled to clarify its position and in a Foreign Ministry
communiqué of April 6 it rejected all responsibility for
the Joanna V's presence in Beira. It also raised the issue
of supplies to Malawi and Zambia, over which it had some
control.[70] Lord Walston, British Minister of State for
Foreign Affairs, had been in Lisbon to discuss the broad
sense of the then-draft British Security Council resolution. Again Portugal rejected contentions that it was responsible for the oil deliveries to Beira, and in support
mentioned details of the ownership of the vessel and the
banking arrangements involved in the shipment, then charged
that "big international companies" could have stopped the
supply at the source if they had wished. When this approach
apparently failed, the Portuguese challenged the validity
of the April 9 resolution.[71] Portugal questioned the
genuineness of the "threat to or breach of the peace" that
arose from the conditions set forth in the April 9 resolution. The legal validity of the resolution itself was contested on the basis of abstentions of permanent members,
constituting null votes. A request followed that the issue be submitted to the UN Office of Legal Affairs for an
opinion.*

---

*One minor sidelight warranting note is the activity
of the Panamanian government. Obviously under pressure
from Britain, Panama issued a decree on April 13, 1966,
prohibiting ships under Panamanian registry from transport-
ing petroleum products to Rhodesia: On April 10 the Joanna
V had changed from Greek to Panamanian registry; on April
12 this registration was revoked. Meanwhile, in German

The limited oil embargo resolution was significant because it gave Britain time to continue its extensive diplomatic offensive and avoided the possibility of Britain's
being forced to veto a Chapter VII resolution. It also
avoided a more direct confrontation with South Africa over
the latter's increasing support for Rhodesia. Thus the
British options were limited:

    1. Continuation of the present slow process of eco-
nomic attrition,
    2. Greater confrontation with Portugal and South Af-
rica,
    3. Negotiations with Rhodesian whites who opposed
Smith,*
    4. Military intervention to quash Smith.

In late April, Oliver Wright, Prime Minister Wilson's
private secretary, visited Cape Town and Salisbury, where
he met with Sir Humphrey Gibbs. This visit was followed by
an announcement by Wilson on April 27 that Britain and Rhodesia would resume talks. The initiative for the talks
was probably Smith's, for apparently he was under increasing domestic political pressure to arrive at a solution.[72]
Reaction to the announcement was generally positive, and
it would appear that perhaps the April resolution was beginning to pay dividends.[73]
During May, therefore, Britons and Rhodesians conducted
talks in London; and when they ultimately failed (the shock
to Rhodesians of the April 9 resolution had worn off), Britain settled in for the long haul.

THE LONG-TERM INTERNATIONAL RESPONSE

Throughout the remainder of this chapter no effort
will be made to cover in detail the extensive negotiating
efforts of British and Rhodesian officials that culminated
in the H.M.S. Tiger talks of December 2-4, 1966.[74] Nor
will there be as much detail as set forth in the preceding
section, with the exception of Security Council Resolution

---

courts the fate of a Rhodesian sugar cargo on the Pericles
was under review.
    *A number of persons are identifiable as probable op-
ponents of Smith, but discretion suggests that names be
avoided.

232 of December 30, 1966, imposing mandatory Chapter VII sanctions.

It probably was becoming clear by May and June 1966 that if the sanctions were to be successful, they would require constant and sustained vigilance. Stanley Uys, one of South Africa's better-informed correspondents, reported on June 19:

> The sanctions campaign against Rhodesia has taken time to gather momentum. One reason is that some of Rhodesia's major trading partners did not impose sanctions until some weeks after U.D.I. . . . Rhodesian officials and business circles admit now that sanctions are having an increasingly serious effect in the economy. . . . The president of the Associated Chambers of Commerce of Rhodesia, Mr. John Hughes, has declared that it would be "dishonest and dangerous" to say that sanctions were not having an effect on Rhodesia's economy.[75]

Of course there were still serious problems and gaps and continuing calls for the use of force;[76] but presumably Britain's favorable assessment of the prospects for sanctions, combined with Rhodesia's ad hoc efforts to grapple with sanctions (and the resulting dislocation of the economy), provided a mutual impetus for renewed negotiations. Commonwealth Secretary Arthur Bottomley, however, warned the Commonwealth Sanctions Committee in London that the talks had been fruitless and might soon be broken off;[77] and on June 25 a member of the British negotiating team returned from Salisbury, apparently with that suggestion. However, throughout June and July officials of the British government's Commonwealth Relations Office carried out continuous discussions in Salisbury, in an effort to find a basis for altering the 1961 Rhodesian constitution in order to accommodate both sides. The discussions regularly ran afoul on the same two points: guarantees of unimpeded progress toward majority rule and guarantees against retrogressive amendment of the constitution.

Rhodesians feared that majority rule would come about before Africans (in their opinion) were ready, and as a result they sought to maintain complete control over African progress toward majority rule, a policy totally unacceptable to Britain. In addition, Britain was intent on a return to constitutionality before formal negotiations could begin, and this Rhodesians were unwilling to consider.

Rather, Rhodesia sought a settlement formula that would include a grant of independence on their conditions. The
fact that neither side broke the talks may be deemed indicative of the extent to which an authentic settlement was
sought. One other factor that was beginning to emerge was
the possibility of postponing the scheduled Commonwealth
Prime Ministers meeting from the original July date to
September.[78]

Increasingly, of course, the two parties were being
locked into untenable and irreconcilable positions. Consequently, when Wilson announced in the British House of Commons on July 5 that talks had been recessed temporarily,
he added, "There would be no purpose in reaching agreement
on the constitutional future of Rhodesia if that agreement
did not at the same time win for Rhodesia acceptance in
international society."[79] Unfortunately, Rhodesians appear
to have viewed the internationalization of what they had
considered to be a personal matter between Britain and Rhodesia as a betrayal of faith. Yet this remark by Wilson
was certainly consistent with attempts to maintain a controlled international character for the UDI issue during
October-November 1965. Moreover, if Rhodesians were still
under the illusion that they could arrive at an arrangement
with Britain without heed to world, and particularly African, opinion, that illusion suggests the degree to which
they had insulated themselves from the world.

It must also be noted that during this period Rhodesian attitudes began to harden, as the country adjusted to
the impact of sanctions, and support remained relatively
solid for Smith and his regime. For Wilson, however, other
complications existed, including a 47-day seamen's strike
that ended on July 1, pressure on the pound that resulted
in an increased bank rate on July 14, and balance-of-payments difficulties that caused the government to announce
inflationary controls on July 20. Consequently, as Wilson
began to look more and more like a man in serious trouble,
Smith and his Rhodesian Front were beginning to exude
greater confidence. Thus, after the Rhodesian budget of
July 21, it was fairly evident that while the country was
operating below its 1965 level, it was surviving. In fact,
much of the loss of foreign exchange was offset by a decline
in the need to import--that is, increased self-sufficiency.
Hence, the diversion of financial and economic resources
to other sectors of the economy was permitting major read-
justments to combat the effects of santions.*

---

*For example, an announcement by the Ford Company that
it would have to lay off workers because of shortages was

For Britain the situation was again becoming delicate; and by late July and early August, African states (notably Ghana) were beginning to call for renewed consideration of a Chapter VII mandatory sanctions resolution. Wilson, perhaps to head off this mounting pressure and to affirm British good intentions, announced the resumption of British-Rhodesian talks on August 8.[80] Meanwhile, the Commonwealth Sanctions Committee began preparation of its report to the Commonwealth Prime Ministers Meeting scheduled for September 6-15 in London.

The September 1966 Prime Ministers meeting was a serious test of British intentions and sincerity, and there is no doubt that Wilson devoted considerable effort to preparing his case. There was a general disillusion with the sanctions plan agreed upon at Lagos in January, and thus pressure existed for more direct steps.* Clearly a move into a Chapter VII situation would be profound; but the alternatives for Britain were becoming fewer because British, Commonwealth, and UN prestige would suffer considerably if Smith's regime were permitted to get away with its defiance of the international community. Doubtless Wilson was also faced with a dilemma concerning his Cabinet colleagues, for they were notably split into a group favoring strict Chapter VII sanctions and those who feared that such a resolution inevitably would have to be extended to include South Africa and Portugal. Thus the alternatives facing the Prime Ministers were becoming numerous:

1. Providing more negotiation time but with a specified and clear recourse,

_____

responded to by government action to prevent dismissal. Hence unemployment was low. The tobacco crop was largely protected when the government purchased crops at a reserved price (about 70 percent of the 1965 price). Finally, of course, the white Rhodesian had a fairly high standard of living and, considering the stakes, apparently was prepared to take some cut in living to protect his future.

*This included more pressure for the use of force to crush Smith. India's line, for example, started to toughen in July, when Swaran Singh (Foreign Minister), in the Lok Sabha, urged Britain to take "sterner measures" on July 25. By August 16, in response to an official visit to India by Zambian Vice-President Reuben Kamanga and Foreign Minister Simon Kapwepwe, Dinesh Singh (Minister of State for Foreign Affairs) called upon Britain "to crush white rebellion in Rhodesia by force if necessary."

2. An intensification of existing voluntary sanctions,
3. Limited mandatory sanctions restricted to petroleum products,*
4. Selective mandatory sanctions, including commodities usually exported by Rhodesia,
5. General mandatory sanctions on both imports and
exports,
6. The use of force.

It would be interesting to surmise to what extent vociferous views expressed on other occasions were toned down.
If the final communiqué is any indication, there is reason to believe that the meeting was a mellowing experience.[81]
Thus when the communiqué records, "Though sanctions had undoubtedly depressed the Rhodesian economy, they were unlikely at their present level to achieve the desired political objectives within an acceptable period of time," it
probably reflects skepticism and exasperation with the efficacy of sanctions, viewpoints probably expressed by Hastings Banda (Malawi) and Milton Obote (Uganda). Moreover,
while there was unanimity on the move toward mandatory
Chapter VII sanctions, the communiqué certainly reflects a
major divergence in views (total versus selected mandatory
sanctions) between, for example, Ghana and Malta. Doubtless selective sanctions consumed a great deal of the discussion, because the meeting had before it the report of
the Commonwealth Sanctions Committee, which summed up the
almost weekly meetings of that committee in London. The
issue of mandatory selective sanctions was the key to British strategy. (See Table 5.1 for a summary of British
trade in Southern Africa.)
One interesting aspect of the communiqué is the reference to an acceptable period of time within which sanctions
were anticipated to be effective. Time is a key factor in
economic sanctions and, as will be discussed in the con-

---

*Cape Town newspapers reported (September 1) that Brit-
ish Ambassador Sir Hugh Stephenson had called on Foreign
Minister H. Muller as part of "secret approach to Verwoerd"
to point out the dangers mandatory sanctions would hold for
South Africa, especially on petroleum. The Ambassador
also may have been seeking assurances for the Simonstown
agreement on British naval facilities in Cape Town. The
International Court of Justice decisions on South West Africa (Namibia) on July 18, 1966, probably gave the Republic cause for renewed strength in dealings with Britain.

TABLE 5.1

British Trade with Southern Africa, 1964-65
(£ million)

	1964	1965	Percent Total British Trade 1964	1965
Exports				
Total Africa	4,500	4,800	100	100
South Africa	240	265	5.2	5.4
Commonwealth Africa (Zambia, Malawi, Trust Territories)	184	197	4.0	4.1
Rhodesia	26	32	0.6	0.6
Angola and Mozambique	11	15	0.2	0.2
Imports				
Total Africa	5,696	5,763	100	100
South Africa	182	181	3.2	3.1
Commonwealth Africa (Zambia, Malawi, Trust Territories)	256	285	4.5	5.0
Rhodesia	27	30	0.5	0.5
Angola and Mozambique	36	37	0.6	0.6

Source: Commonwealth Relations Office.

cluding section of this study, trade embargoes cannot be maintained indefinitely. If a target state can withstand the initial impact of sanctions--especially over long periods of time--it may gradually achieve de facto recognition. It will be suggested later, in fact, that time, in conjunction with weak, poorly conceived, early decisions, was the major handicap of the Rhodesian sanctions.

Clearly the "talks about talks" that had gone on for most of June, July, and August were not sufficient either to meet the desire of Commonwealth members to see a speedy end to the Rhodesian affair or to solve the issue itself. Thus, following the Commonwealth meeting, Commonwealth Secretary Herbert Bowden was sent to Salisbury and met with Governor Sir Humphrey Biggs and Smith on September

13-28.* Clearly Bowden's position and the proximity of the visit to the Commonwealth meeting suggests that this was considered to be Smith's "last chance." The communiqué clearly committed Britain to take decisive action should the talks fail, and hence Wilson was locked into a fairly specific course of action.

Smith, of course, was also in a delicate position; and while he did ignore Bowden's arrival in order to attend a Rhodesian Front meeting in Bulawayo, he could not ignore the consequences of a failure to at least go through the motions. Time again became a factor on Smith's side, and any stall was useful. Obviously it would have served Smith's domestic needs if he had been able to force Britain into breaking negotiations, for he still had to contend with white liberal opposition. As for world opinion, he could afford to be disdainful but he could not permit it in any manner to affect his dependent relationship with South Africa. Consequently, Smith was not free to move at will, for he had to insure that world attention was not deflected any more directly from Rhodesia to South Africa.

When the Bowden mission returned empty-handed to London, it was made clear to Smith that the door was still open for a constructive response. Smith responded with a counteroffer.[82] There followed another British counter-proposal of October 15, 1966, and a Rhodesian reply on November 4.[83] However, the futility of the exercise was perhaps highlighted by Smith's remarks to Rhodesians on November 11, 1966, the first anniversary of UDI, when he accused Britain of "merely playing a game of tactics--dragging this thing monotonously on and on." He concluded:

> Time is on our side, and time is the substance of achievement. To this end, we are honestly and sincerely prepared to follow the present exercise to its conclusion.[84]

Rhodesia and Britain were obviously poles apart; and as the former became adamant in opposition to "one man, one vote," Britain's flexibility became increasingly reduced to the NIBMAR acronym (No Independence Before Majority African Rule).

---

*Bowden had been preceded to Salisbury, during the Commonwealth meeting, by Morrice James, Deputy Undersecretary of State, Commonwealth Office.

Meanwhile, at the United Nations, meetings of the Fourth Committee had been held to consider the question of Rhodesia; and on October 21 the committee proposed a draft resolution to the General Assembly.[85] The resolution, as amended, was adopted by the General Assembly on October 22 (Resolution 2138). It noted "with grave concern" the "talks about talks" and condemned any arrangement that failed to recognize "the inalienable rights of the people of Zimbabwe to self-determination." It concluded with an affirmation of the "one man, one vote" theme.

This resolution was significant insofar as the international community was concerned because it affirmed that Britain's obligations were now subject to review by world opinion, thereby forewarning Britain that a deal with Smith (whereby they would both avoid recourse to mandatory sanctions) was out of the question. The resolution also reflected the high degree of suspicion that centered upon the then-ongoing Salisbury talks. The October 22 resolution, therefore, was interim; hence, when the talks did appear to have collapsed totally, the Fourth Committee resumed action. Thus, at a series of meetings in early November a new, much stronger draft resolution was hammered out.[86] It is interesting that during Fourth Committee consideration, the Latin American block identifiably emerged as not being enthusiastic about either extensive mandatory sanctions or the use of force (see Table 5.2).

The draft resolution (G.A. no. 2121) was approved on November 15, 1966 (94-2-17). Briefly, the General Assembly again condemned the possibility of a private British-Rhodesian arrangement; condemned Portugal and South Africa; and condemned financial interests that supported and assisted the Smith regime. Britain was then called upon "to take prompt and effective measures to prevent any supplies," including petroleum products, from reaching Rhodesia; to take all necessary measures "including in particular the use of force" to end the illegal regime; and to account for this stewardship to the Committee of 24. States generally were called upon to render moral and material support to the people of Zimbabwe, including refugee assistance through international agencies. The resolution thus placed the onus and direction for action entirely upon Britain, thereby opening the way either for Britain to seek mandatory sanctions or (more likely) for the Security Council to make such a decision.

Wilson's options were narrowed even more, and in another desperate move he despatched Herbert Bowden on a second visit to Salisbury on November 23. The announcement

TABLE 5.2

Draft General Assembly Resolution No. 2121 (XXI),
November 15, 1966: Abstentions and Votes Against,
Where Recorded

	Latin America	Common- wealth	Euro- pean	Other
Operative paragraph 4 (88-2-23)				
Abstentions	11	3	7	2
Against	--	--	1	1
Operative paragraph 8 (78-18-17)				
Abstentions	12	--	4	1
Against	--	5	13	--
Draft resolution (94-2-17)				
Abstentions	--	4	12	1
Against	--	--	1	1

Sources: UNGA Doc. A/C.4/L.836, November 5, 1966;
UNGA Resln. A/C.4/2.486, November 8, 1966; UNGA Doc.
A/6482/Add.1, November 15, 1966.

of the mission was couched in terms of a response to an
appeal from Rhodesian Governor Sir Humphrey Gibbs, who,
Britain doubtless feared, might resign, thereby removing
the focal point of loyal resistance to Smith's regime.
Bowden's time was limited because Wilson was committed to
a timetable that included a major policy statement in Parliament (and issuance of a White Paper) on November 29,
meetings in Washington on November 29 and 30, and a request
for a Security Council meeting on December 2. Thus, several exchanges and moves were made in the period between
November 23 and December 1, when Wilson announced that in
accordance with the Commonwealth communiqué, he would meet
with Smith.[87] Hence on December 2, 1966, Wilson and Smith
met on board H.M.S. Tiger and "hopes soared" for a settlement.[88]
    Much of the groundwork for the Tiger talks appears to
have been done by Sir Morrice James, Undersecretary in the
Commonwealth Office, who probably carried a proposal for
such a meeting with him when he arrived in Salisbury on

the evening of November 28. It is very doubtful that Wilson was excessively optimistic about prospects for the talks, but he had to make every possible effort before severing the exchanges. Only the prospect of mandatory sanctions and pressure from South Africa favored Wilson in his dealings with Smith.[89]

On the whole the meetings appear to have been "gentlemanly," with decorum maintained. Much of the discussion hinged upon the representation provisions of the 1961 constitution (Section 37 of Chapter III, the number of constituencies and electoral districts); a proposal for a Senate (Smith's proposal) and representations therein; and the return to constitutional rule. On this latter subject Wilson warned Smith:[90]

> A more serious problem was the timetable set at the Commonwealth Prime Ministers' Meeting, which did not permit any further delay before restoration of lawful government in Rhodesia, if mandatory sanctions, with all their consequences for Rhodesia and other countries, were not to be imposed. Mr. Smith and his colleagues should be under no illusion on this score.

Smith replied:

> The current discussions showed that there was a real chance of solving the constitutional problems involved; it was hard to believe that international pressure for action could not be held off for another month or two to enable a negotiated settlement to be reached.

Finally, they discussed matters relating to constitutional safeguards, majority rule, and those other matters generally referred to as Britain's Six Principles (majority rule, guarantees against retrogressive constitutional amendment, improved political status of Africans, progress toward ending racial discrimination, acceptability of any proposed settlement to all Rhodesians, no oppression of any groups). The meetings concluded on December 4 with a draft agreement on settlement. Each party agreed to submit the proposed agreement to their respective Cabinets and to indicate with a simple "Yes" or "No" (without amendment) by 10 a.m. GMT December 5 whether the proposals were acceptable. After a Rhodesian request for a few hours' extension (perhaps indicative of Smith's attempts to surmount

extremist oppositions in his Cabinet), the proposed settlement was rejected by Rhodesia.[91] Thus, on the evening of
December 5, 1966, Wilson announced his government's intention to appeal to the Security Council and the Foreign Secretary, George Brown, flew to New York to begin the process.*

Initially Britain was intent on establishing the principle of mandatory sanctions and then, when necessary, extending them in a manner appropriate to achieve greater effectiveness. Hence the mandatory sanctions were designed
to produce a maximum impact on Rhodesia while sparing its
neighbors the full brunt. The problem, of course, was that
African states (including Commonwealth members) were faced
with the dilemma of reconciling their inability to have an
impact upon Rhodesia with their intense desire to pressure
Britain. The dilemma was heightened by a basic conflict
between mainly African states that sought comprehensive
mandatory sanctions in order to avoid discrediting the concept, and mainly Western and European states that saw in
extensive sanctions just so many more opportunities to circumvent them and thus bring sanctions into disrepute.

Aside from the omission of oil from the British draft
--an omission corrected in the final Security Council res-
olution--Britain basically could count upon substantial
support because the question of honesty was now resolved.
Thus Britain had made every effort to negotiate with Smith
--the record was public; and it was now prepared to proceed
in accordance with the September commitment, in the face
of a very unhealthy domestic economy that surely would not
benefit from sanctions.[92] This prospect naturally ended
the domestic British political support that Wilson had received after UDI.

Opposition Conservative Party support for Wilson remained intact until about 50 Conservatives, led by M. P.
Julian Amery, voted against the December 1965 oil embargo
order. Edward Heath, then opposition leader, had directed
party members to abstain, which most did. However, while
Amery went one direction, Sir Tufton Beamish (opposition
defense spokesman) and 30 other Conservatives voted for
the oil embargo. Throughout the summer of 1966 Wilson
skillfully carried the momentum in debate with Heath; how-

---

*Britain's representative at the United Nation, Lord
Caradon, had already met with friendly delegations and was
circulating a draft British resolution. Herbert Bowden
reported to the Commonwealth Sanctions Committee at its
meeting in London on December 5.

ever, in the post-Commonwealth meeting period Conservative opposition mounted. Moreover, even some Labour Party M.P.'s began to tire of African diatribes directed at Britain and the government (for example, the "Britain is a toothless bulldog" remark of Zambia's High Commissioner in London). Finally, there was the growing fear in Britain that the contest could easily be expanded to include South Africa, Britain's fourth largest trading partner (January-September 1966, £171.6 million, U.K. Trade and Navigation Accounts, Her Majesty's Stationery Office, October 1966). In this light it must be noted that on December 6, the day after the appeal for mandatory sanctions was announced, the pound sterling slipped so badly on the London money market that it required Bank of England support and the stock market dipped significantly.* The split of the two major parties was clearly evidenced in the House of Commons debate that followed Wilson's announcement of mandatory sanctions, and consequently the government resolution seeking support for efforts under way was generally voted against by the Conservative Party (the vote in the Commons was 353 to 244, but in the House of Lords Wilson's proposals were defeated 100 to 84).

On December 8 British Foreign Secretary George Brown introduced a draft British resolution to the Security Council.** Brown argued against a confrontation with all of Southern Africa and in favor of limited sanctions over which effective control could be maintained by fellow UN members. On the question of a mandatory oil sanction he stated:

> I appreciate the strong measure of support that exists for inclusion of oil in mandatory sanctions. If an amendment in this sense was to be made in acceptable terms my delegation would not oppose it. I say this on the basis of a full understanding, which it is clear also exists among delegates here, of the importance of not allowing sanctions to escalate into economic confrontation with third countries.[93]

---

*Wilson may have been faced with the possibility of resignations from his Cabinet. Both Barbara Castle and Anthony Greenwood were known to oppose any deal with Smith short of complete capitulation.

**This draft apparently was an enlarged version of that circulated by Caradon.

On December 13 African amendments were proposed to the British draft resolution.[94] The proposed amendments included oil, coal, and manufactured goods. Apolo K. Kironde (Uganda) described the amendments as being designed to fill gaps in the British draft resolution by offering the African states a minimum acceptable basis for mandatory sanctions. On the matter of oil and confrontation with South Africa he argued that all members were bound by Article 25 of the UN Charter (obligatory nature of Security Council decisions).[95] Chief S. O. Adebo (Nigeria) referred to Rhodesia as a "great moral issue"--a sentiment that should not have been overlooked.

Resolution 232 of December 16, 1966, finally imposed mandatory sanctions against Rhodesia in accordance with Articles 39 and 41 of the UN Charter.[96] Table 5.3 sets forth some aspects of the vote on the resolution and notes varying degrees of enthusiasm for each section (France abstained on everything).

Because of the significance of Resolution 232, extracts from the operational sanctions paragraphs follow:

> Reaffirming that to the extent not superseded in this resolution, the measures provided for in resolution 217 (1965) of November 20, 1965, as well as those initiated by Member States in implementation of that resolution, shall continue in effect,
>
> Acting in accordance with Articles 39 and 41 of the United Nations Charter,
>
> 1. Determines that the present situation in Southern Rhodesia constitutes a threat to international peace and security;
>
> 2. Decides that all States Members of the United Nations shall prevent:
>
> (a) the import into their territories of asbestos, iron ore, chrome, pig-iron, sugar, tobacco, copper, meat and meat products and hides, skins and leather originating in Southern Rhodesia and exported therefrom after the date of this resolution;
>
> (b) any activities by their nationals or in their territories which promote or are calculated to promote the export of these commodities from Southern Rhodesia and any dealings by their nationals or in their territories in any of these commodities originating in Southern Rhodesia and exported therefrom after the date of this resolu-

TABLE 5.3

Resolution 232:   Votes by Sections

	In Favor	Against	Abstain
Preamble Paragraph 2	14	0	1
Operative Paragraph 1	14	0	1
Proposed Operative Paragraph 2(a)[a]	6	0	9
Proposed Operative Paragraph 2(b)[b]	7	0	8
Proposed Amendment Operative Paragraph 2(a)[c]	8	0	7
Operative Paragraph 2(f)	14	0	1
Proposed Amendment Operative Paragraph 4[d]	7	0	8
Proposed Amendment Operative Paragraph 5[e]	7	0	8
Operative Paragraph 6	14	0	1
Operative Paragraph 4	12	0	3
Operative Paragraph 5	14	0	1
Operative Paragraph 9	14	0	1
Operative Paragraph 10	14	0	1
Resolution 232	11	0	4[f]

Note: Four proposed amendments were defeated through failure to obtain the required two-thirds majority.

[a]The defeated amendment deplored Britain's failure to use force to bring Smith's regime down.

[b]The proposed amendment required action to force Portugal and South Africa to refrain from action in contravention of Resolution 217 (1965).

[c]The amendment would have added coal and manufactured goods to the resolution.

[d]The proposed amendment required Britain to withdraw all previous offers to Smith and declare NIBMAR as the only basis for independence.

[e]The proposed amendment invited Britain to use any means to prevent oil transport to Rhodesia.

[f]USSR, Bulgaria, Mali, and France.

Source: UNSC, Doc.S/PV.1340, December 16, 1966.

tion, including in particular any transfer of
funds to Southern Rhodesia for the purposes of
such activities or dealings;

(c) shipment in vessels or aircraft of their
registration of any of these commodities originating in Southern Rhodesia and exported therefrom
after the date of this resolution;

(d) any activities by their nationals or in
their territories which promote or are calculated
to promote the sale or shipment to Southern Rhodesia of arms, ammunition of all types, military aircraft, military vehicles, and equipment and materials for the manufacture and maintenance of arms
and ammunition in Southern Rhodesia;

(e) any activities by their nationals or in
their territories which promote or are calculated
to promote the supply to Southern Rhodesia of all
other aircraft and motor vehicles and of equipment
and materials for the manufacture, assembly, or
maintenance of aircraft and motor vehicles in
Southern Rhodesia; the shipment in vessels and aircraft of their registration of any such goods destined for Southern Rhodesia; and any activities by
their nationals or in their territories which promote or are calculated to promote the manufacture
or assembly of aircraft or motor vehicles in Southern Rhodesia;

(f) participation in their territories or
territories under their administration or in land
or air transport facilities or by their nationals
or vessels of their registration in the supply of
oil or oil products to Southern Rhodesia;

notwithstanding any contracts entered into or licences granted before the date of this resolution;

3. Reminds Member States that the failure or
refusal by any of them to implement the present
resolution shall constitute a violation of Article
25 of the Charter.

It must be noted that Resolution 232 required UN members to apply law extra-territorially paragraph 2(a) and
(e). For the wording "any activities by their nationals or
in their territories" clearly distinguished between nationals and territory, thereby implying activities of nationals irrespective of territory. Also, the resolution
went some distance beyond what might have been anticipated

317

from the Prime Ministers' September communiqué. Finally, the insertion of the words "notwithstanding any contracts entered into or licences granted before the date of this resolution" was a strategic move to include all items in the preceding paragraphs within the purview of the entire resolution.

For all practical purposes Resolution 232 brings to a conclusion the discussion of the process by which multi-lateral sanctions were imposed against Rhodesia. There have been subsequent resolutions, of course, and UN reports and studies;[97] some of these will be referred to in due course. In addition, there are other relevant documents that have emerged since Resolution 232; and where necessary, reference will be made.[98] However, for purposes of this discussion the basic sanctions framework was not estab-lished; and some effort may now be given to assessing the impact. At the end of this discussion a brief note on some events since December 1966 is included in order to tie to-gether the loose ends.

SANCTIONS: AN EVALUATION

Unlike the Italian and Dominican cases, there is no shortage whatsoever of statistical material on Rhodesia and various aspects of its economic performance. In addi-tion there exists a wealth of comments and observations about the real or imagined impact of sanctions. Conse-quently, the problem is really that of grappling with the torrent of information and attempting to reduce it to pro-portions reasonable for illustrative purposes. The sources of information have been diverse and include UN publica-tions, Rhodesian Information Service materials, and such other information as is deemed to have originated from re-liable sources. Finally, in an attempt to organize the ma-terial and place it into some perspective, statistical in-formation is grouped into two major categories: trade or economic activity of other states (vis-à-vis Rhodesia) and material directly reflecting the state of the Rhodesian economy for the period since November 1969. It should also be recalled that a wide variety of voluntary sanctions had been imposed. These too have significance in terms of assessing impact but, generally, are not included here be-cause of their repetitive volume.

Basically Rhodesia is a primary producer of agricul-tural and mineral commodities, and therefore most emphasis is placed upon these items.[99] In addition, insofar as the four stages of sanctions are concerned--voluntary sanctions (November 1965 to April 1966), voluntary and mandatory petroleum sanctions (April 1966 to December 1966), selective mandatory sanctions (December 1966 to May 30, 1968), and comprehensive mandatory sanctions (May 30, 1969 to present, as reaffirmed)--the activities of five states stand out: West Germany, Japan, Portugal, South Africa, and Zambia.[100] The extent of trade with these countries, especially in selected commodities, is set forth in Table 5.4.

West Germany appears to have been one of the major violators of sanctions. It should be recalled, however, that for most of the time since Rhodesia's UDI in 1965 Germany was not a member of the United Nations and thus its adherence to voluntary and mandatory sanctions was essentially voluntary. Moreover, while the British launched a major diplomatic offensive in Bonn to encourage German support for sanctions the German Cabinet was apparently divided (largely over a fear of losing friends in Africa). German industry placed immense pressure upon the government that resulted in the peculiarities of a licensing system and some apparent doctoring of statistical information. Thus, as the figures in Table 5.5 suggest, total German imports do not appear to have been significantly affected by sanctions.[101] The character of the imports does appear to have changed dramatically however: a rapid drop in tobacco imports and an increase in copper. Late in 1966 the German copper industry was successful in having statistics for copper omitted from the monthly reports; hence we can only assume that the trade continued to be significant.

Japan doubtless found the imposition of sanctions immensely inconvenient and difficult, and it was only under constant prodding that the Japanese government maintained the fiction of adherence.[102] Moreover, it has never been much of a secret that Japanese businessmen and ships were involved in trade with Rhodesia (often through Singapore).[103] As noted earlier, Japan reimposed sanctions only under duress, because of the countervailing pressures of large industry, which was heavily engaged in developing trade and investment patterns with Rhodesia at the time of UDI.

It is clear, of course, that Japanese trade with Rhodesia did decline by almost 45 percent (at least for reported statistics); however, there are so many defects in reported Japanese trade statistics that broad conclusions are highly dubious. Even available UN statistics (which seem to be significantly inaccurate) show Japan as one of the major trading partners of Rhodesia even after UDI.

TABLE 5.4

Rhodesia: Main Exports by Country, 1965
(percentage)

	Asbestos	Copper	Chrome	Iron Ore	Pig Iron	Tobacco	Meat	Sugar
Britain	17.7	10	--	--	--	--	48	28
West Germany	11.4	64	--	--	--	14	--	--
United States	9.6	--	58	--	--	--	--	--
Italy	--	--	--	--	--	--	12	--
Spain	7.8	--	--	--	--	--	1	--
South Africa	6.7	--	16	--	--	--	9	--
Switzerland	--	--	--	--	--	7	--	--
Japan	4.7	--	6	100	96.4	--	--	--
Czechoslovakia	7.7	--	--	--	--	--	--	--
Poland	--	10	--	--	--	--	--	--
Netherlands	--	--	--	--	--	6	--	--
Belgium	--	5	--	--	--	--	--	--
France	--	--	6	--	--	--	--	--
Sweden	--	--	5	--	--	--	--	--
India	--	4	--	--	--	--	--	--
Zambia	--	--	--	--	3.6	--	11	30
Malawi	--	--	--	--	--	--	--	28
Canada	--	--	--	--	--	--	--	9
Other	34.4	7	9	--	--	28	19	5
Total (£ million)	10.7	6.5	3.8	0.321	2.5	47.0	7.0	3.5

Source: Financial Mail (South Africa), December 23, 1966.

TABLE 5.5

West Germany: Selected Imports from Rhodesia,
1965-67
(1,000 DM)

	Tobacco	Asbestos	Copper	Chrome	Total
1965	72.621	13,370	46.934	1.452	140.461
1966	38.272	11.059	70.000[a]	na	122.096
January	7.191	.908	4.511	na	13.001
February	2.553	1.034	1.972	na	6.453
March	2.104	.982	.533	na	4.484
April	2.629	.954	8.910	na	13.286
May	2.636	1.871	13.007	na	18.552
June	1.884	.741	10.321	na	13.958
July	4.197	1.733	8.141	na	14.366
August	3.492	.742	3.162	na	7.742
September	2.379	.832	6.709	na	10.471
October	3.139	.395	4.200	na	8.663
November	3.066	.438	na[b]	na	6.257
December	3.002	.429	na[b]	na	4.863
1967					
January	3.304	.525	na[b]	na	4.415

[a]Estimated total for 1966.
[b]These figures were not available, apparently through
effective lobbying by the copper industry.

Source: Federal Republic of Germany, Federal Office
of Statistics, Monthly Reports.

Portugal's trade with Rhodesia is governed by the
Beira Convention of June 17, 1950, which covers trade with
Mozambique and Angola as well as Portugal.[104] As noted
earlier, Portugal and its colony of Mozambique were key
elements in the UN sanctions program. Oil has continued
to flow into Rhodesia over pipelines from Lourenço Marques
(owned by Mobil Oil Corporation) and Beira (to the Rhodesian refinery at Umtali) as well as over the Lourenço Marques railway.

Moçambique, since U.D.I., has supplied Rhodesia
with enough refined fuel to enable the Smith Government to stockpile against a two-year sanctions
siege.

TABLE 5.6

Japan: Imports from Rhodesia, 1965-66
(£ million)

	1965, January to December	1966 January to October	1966 January to December
Tobacco	9.273	3.474	na
Asbestos	1.647	2.285	na
Mineral substances	.277	--	.498
Iron (ore and concentrates)	5.193	4.620	na
Copper (ore and concentrates)	.208	.063	na
Copper matte	.531	--	.653
Copper ingots	.358	na	na
Nickel (ore and concentrates)	.724	--	.851
Pig iron	9.359	1.203	na
Brass and bronze waste	na	na	.127
Wattle extract	na	na	.724
Skins (alligator)	na	na	.034
Other	.882	.896	.140
Totals	28.452	12.541	3.027
		15.568	

Source: Compiled from Japan, Ministry of Finance,
Trade of Japan.

This is the minimum estimate of foreign observers who have kept a close watch on "clandestine" petrol and oil trains from Lourenço Marques
to Rhodesia since the initiation of the fuel run
14 months ago.

The observers calculate that at least
70,000,000 gallons of petrol alone have reached
Salisbury and Bulawayo from the Sonarep refinery
here in Lourenço Marques in the past 12 months.
. . . Output of the Sonarep refinery is almost 180 million gallons of refined fuel a year.
. . . Rhodesia's pre-rationing consumption
of petrol was approximately 50,000,000 gallons
a year but this has dropped to about 35,000,000
gallons a year.

> . . . In Rhodesia, the petrol issue is a
> closed secret and information as to possible stor-
> age points is almost impossible to come by.
>   The estimate for Moçambique does not take
> into account the supply from the South African
> life-line.[105]

The trade from Rhodesia to Mozambique may have followed the
1965 patterns.[106] (See Table 5.7.) Table 5.8 contains
some information on general Portuguese-Rhodesian trade for
1966.

Portuguese exports to Rhodesia, at least on paper, declined dramatically in volume but not in value in 1966,
while Portuguese imports increased by 48.9 percent by volume but decreased 43.4 percent by value. (The distinction
here is between value and volume. True, volume doubled,
but value was cut in half.) This suggests that Portugal
was prepared to take advantage of Rhodesia's situation to
overvalue its exports while purchasing Rhodesian products
at cut-rate prices. Of course, this still gave Rhodesia a
surplus of almost 38 million escudos (about $1,363,000), a
place to export its surpluses, and some money to pay for
the petroleum imports.

Information on South Africa, while available, has
tended to obscure its trading relations with Rhodesia, presumably to avoid drawing attention to the interrelationship
referred to by one South African commercial publication as
a "South African common market."[107] In the area of petro-

TABLE 5.7

Mozambique: Imports from Rhodesia, 1965
(£ sterling)

Vegetable oils	317,000
Electrical energy	255,000
Lumber	232,000
Cottonseed husks	142,000
Railway ties	77,000
Fresh fruit	68,000
Fish	65,000
Total	1,156,000

Source: Commonwealth Relations Office.

TABLE 5.8

Portugal: Trade with Rhodesia, 1965-66
(1,000 escudos)

	Tons	Value
Exports		
1965 total	3,366.2	14,494
1966		
Tinned fish	21.7	400
Sardines	17.4	266
Cork (articles)	154.9	2,814
Cork (pressed)	146.1	2,630
Textiles	8.7	1,217
Undyed cotton	16.3	1,115
Industrial machines	28.8	2,265
Total	393.9	10,707
Imports		
1965 total	4,466.1	93,413
1966		
Fresh and frozen meat	776.3	14,460
Sugar	7,079.1	11,013
Tobacco	524.9	14,972
Natural rubber	51.3	650
Hides	158.7	2,016
Raw cotton	165.8	3,311
Total	8,756.1	46,422

Source: Portugal, National Institute of Statistics,
Boletín de estatístico (January and December 1966).

leum there is no doubt that South Africa made facilities
available to Rhodesia, usually under the guise of private
citizens' activities.[108] This included construction of a
Rhodesian refinery at Messina just across the Limpopo from
Rhodesia.[109] Consequently, official information is not
readily obtainable. In addition, because Rhodesia and
South Africa tend to trade in similar products and commodities, and Rhodesian trade would be only a small fraction
of the South African total, it is relatively easy to lose

the Rhodesian component of South African trade. Thus, we can assume only that similar patterns have prevailed since 1965. (See Table 5.9.)

Zambia undoubtedly has the most complex relationship with Rhodesia; and probably under any other circumstance, the two territories would not exist as separate countries. Zambia and Rhodesia share a railway and a hydroelectric dam; Zambia has problems exporting its copper without Rhodesian railway facilities; Zambia cannot mine its copper without Rhodesian coal to provide the power to run the pumps to prevent the mines from flooding. In fact, Zambia was forced in late 1966 to give priority to coal shipments over the limited railway facilities in order to prevent a disaster in the mines.[110] Zambia's precarious existence was emphasized in September 1966, when 100,000 gallons of diesel fuel were lost after saboteurs destroyed tanks near Lusaka.[111]

Zambian copper exports were also in serious jeopardy throughout 1966; and had it not been for massive injections of British money, the economy would have collapsed.* Rhodesia placed pressure upon Zambia to pay all transportation costs in advance, and Zambia refused to ship copper over the Rhodesian railroads (Zambia produced 61,000 tons of copper per month for export in 1966). This forced Zambia to seek alternative routes; and as a consequence of talks in Kinshasa (July 12-15, 1966), the Congo agreed to permit 40,000 tons of Zambian copper to move via the Benguela railway. Unfortunately this proved unsatisfactory; and on July 27, 1966, Zambia resumed copper shipments via Rhodesian railways, providing purchasers paid transportation charges in advance. This solution enabled Rhodesia to receive more foreign cash.[112]

Generally, therefore, Zambian trade with Rhodesia was a matter of necessity, as was acknowledged at the Commonwealth Prime Ministers meeting at Lagos in January 1966. The Zambian airlift, the Great North Road, and the Tan-Zam railway were all designed to alleviate Zambian dependence; yet these remedies overlooked the obvious point that unless additional supplies of coal were obtained, electricity developed, and petroleum supplied (to say nothing of the host of manufactured goods), Zambia and Rhodesia

---

*By July 1966 Britain had spent £10 million (double Zambia's expenditures) for work on Dar es Salaam and Mtwara harbors, the Kandabwe coal development, and the Great North Road.

TABLE 5.9

South Africa: Selected Exports, January-June 1965
(£ million)

Asbestos	5.7
Iron ore and concentrates	2.4
Tobacco	2.0
Ferrochrome	2.3
Unrefined copper	7.8
Refined copper	1.7
Pig iron	4.4
Chrome ore	1.0
General reexports	25.0
Total	260

Source: Afrikaanse Handelinstituut, Volkshandel, August 1966.

TABLE 5.10

Rhodesia: 1965 Exports
(million £ sterling)

Zambia	36	
South Africa	12.8	
Malawi	7.7	
Congo (Kinshasa)	2.05	
Bechuanaland	1.6	
Mozambique	0.95	
Japan	0.48	(asbestos)
United States	1.0	(mainly chrome)
Switzerland	1.8	(meat, tobacco, asbestos)
Portugal	0.19	(tobacco, meat, sugar)
Total	142.5	

Source: Commonwealth Relations Office.

are functionally interdependent. (Rhodesia's 1965 exports are shown in Table 5.10.)

The Zambian portion probably could have been broken down as set forth in Table 5.11. Clearly, Zambia was not importing Rhodesian goods in the sense of violating sanctions, for its special status was acknowledged. However, Zambia's situation and Rhodesia's commanding position permitted the latter to obtain valuable foreign currencies, and thus Zambia's hostage status became a vital feature of the UN and British sanctions campaign--a feature that helped Rhodesia immeasurably.

While a number of other countries might be viewed in terms of limited but continuing trade with Rhodesia, it is not really necessary to pursue the point. It should be obvious by now that Rhodesia's position as a major supplier of minerals and food products to Europe and Asia made its ability to withstand sanctions rather formidable. To the extent that it was assisted by South Africa and Portugal, its ability was accentuated, for clearly if Mozambique and the Republic of South Africa had cut off oil supplies, Rhodesia would have been in serious trouble.

Rhodesia is predominantly a primary-products country with a small, but relatively wealthy, white population. In substantial measure the wealth of this population has depended upon the export trade and related commerce. Sanctions, when initially imposed, severely upset traditional trading patterns with Britain and Zambia that had accounted for more than half of all Rhodesian exports. Added to this was another 10 percent of Rhodesian exports to African and Commonwealth countries; thus the first sanctions in November 1965 affected at least 60 percent of Rhodesia's traditional markets. These same areas accounted for 42-43 percent of Rhodesia's imports, although one distortion was South Africa, from which Rhodesia received almost 25 percent of its imports.[113] Generally, there is little doubt that the initial imposition of sanctions was a severe blow. In fact, throughout 1966 the Rhodesian economy was in serious trouble and discontent, particularly in the white business community, was rampant. The reason, of course, was that traditional commercial patterns were upset and overseas markets and suppliers were confused. Complaints from within Rhodesia were widespread, and by mid-June 1966 the following types of reports were commonplace.

. . . 85% of the business people I spoke to about sanctions thought their effects increasingly disastrous [Sunday Telegraph, June 19, 1966].

327

TABLE 5.11

Zambia: Imports from Rhodesia, January-August 1966
(1,000 £ Zambian)

	January	February	March	April	May	June	July	August	Total
Food and live animals	742.9	319.6	302.5	317.8	193.2	205.1	153.4	213.6	2,448.3
Beverages and tobacco	68.9	526.7a	38.5	58.9	24.9	53.5	.14	66.6	838.4
Crude materials, inedible (except fuels)	24.3	64.2	41.0	34.0	29.9	137.7	51.8	89.0	476.2
Mineral fuels, lubricants, related materialsb	562.8	513.3	552.2	501.7	554.6	519.7	473.4	487.2	4,164.9
Animal and vegetable oils and fats	4.7	3.1	3.3	.003	9.3	30.2	--	15.5	66.2
Chemicals	89.3	96.0	51.0	49.154	122.1	169.7	153.8	145.9	877.2
Manufactured goods, classified chiefly by material	389.7	618.6	581.5	412.3	433.1	483.6	452.7	417.8	3,789.4
Machinery and transport equipment	159.7	379.0	276.7	226.6	279.9	279.1	252.3	368.42	2,221.8
Miscellaneous manufactured articles	130.1	282.2	289.9	207.4	223.8	272.2	160.7	140.4	1,707.0
Miscellaneous transactions and commodities (not specified elsewhere)	.02	--	--	--	--	.4	--	--	--
Total	2,176.8	2,803.0	2,136.7	1,808.0	1,870.9	2,151.4	1,698.4	1,944.6	16,589.6

aMainly tobacco
bMainly electricity

Source: Zambia, Central Statistical Office.

Most businessmen feel it is essential for a
settlement to be reached before the economy is
committed to planting another tobacco crop while
the fate of the bulk of the current crop is still
uncertain [Times (London), June 20, 1966].

Major economic sanctions . . . cannot fail to
have severely detrimental effects on the Rhodesian
economy by depriving the country of its major
sources of foreign exchange earnings and undermining the basis of future economic development. The
effect of these sanctions may be concealed for a
short time by artificial devices such as stockpiling of tobacco, credit creation, and employment
orders. But such policies will only serve to ag-
gravate basic problems and will cause a more violent disruption of the economy in the long run
[Professor Taylor, Head of Economics Department,
Salisbury University College, in the Manchester
Guardian, June 29, 1966].

Rhodesian businessmen urged Smith and his "hard-liners"
(John Wrathall, the Finance Minister, for example) to re-
lent and seek a negotiated settlement. John Hughes, President of the Rhodesian Associated Chambers of Commerce, in
a public speech predicated increased unemployment, much
less credit for farmers, and a need for government support
for the 1967 tobacco crop:

His speech is interpreted as a blunt warning to
the Smith regime by Rhodesian Big Business that a
settlement of the political crisis must be reached
soon.

Close study of his remarks also yields hints
that the secret sales of tobacco, Rhodesia's principal source of foreign exchange, have gone badly.[114]

The President of the Rhodesian Motor Trade Association,
Joe Sager, warned that petrol rationing was jeopardizing
the industry.[115] Sir Roy Welensky (former Federation
Prime Minister) stated that "every sane person should
strive for agreement; my mind boggles at the cost of failure."[116] And even some sympathetic (business-oriented)
observers urged Smith's regime to reconsider. Referring
to Rhodesia in general and Smith in particular, the Johannesburg Financial Mail editorialized:

Your economy is in a mess, although many of your
countrymen don't yet realize it.

South African aid has enabled you to test
the belief (about which some of us have admittedly
been sceptical) that you had merely to weather the
initial storm (your claim that U.D.I. would be a
three day wonder in the city) in order to establish
de jure independence and to regain the foundation
of economic development and prosperity.

Now you must face the painful truth that this
hope has proved unfounded. We beg you to. It is
no use pretending that Wilson desperately wants to
throw in the towel, as most Rhodesians have pre-
tended in recent weeks. It is no use believing
that other international trading partners will step
in as Britain and Zambia step out, as many of your
supporters appear to believe now.

The harsh fact is that the Rhodesia you know
and love will not survive the blows it is not sus-
taining--whatever South Africa may decide to do.[117]

So apparent was the portent of successful sanctions that
some could speak of Britain having "time on its side because the cumulative effect of economic sanctions will affect the Rhodesians' negotiating position in the long run.[118]
The year 1966, and specifically June 1966, after talks
had collapsed, was perhaps the nadir of the Rhodesian resistance to sanctions and the apex of British tactics.
Thereafter, things began to improve, as Rhodesia began to
diversify its economy and find new markets.[119] Once the
shock had been felt, therefore, Rhodesia began to construct
its recovery. This was considerably assisted once the
problems of the mandatory April petroleum embargo were successfully circumvented. This was done, as noted earlier,
in various ways: construction of the processing plant at
Messina in South Africa, the increase of tanker traffic
over the Lourenço Marques and Botswana railways (the precarious position of Seretse Khama's Botswana precluded
closure of the latter line), and a requirement that the
five major oil companies supplying Rhodesia increase their
facilities.[120]
In October 1966, Rhodesia floated another £4.5 million loan at 6.5 percent as part of its campaign to become
self-sufficient financially. This move indicated the extent to which the country was consolidating its financial
efforts to overcome sanctions.[121] It is comprehensible,
in retrospect, why Smith's colleagues could gamble on re-

jecting the H.M.S. Tiger formula, because by December 1966
the country's economy was on the upswing. Consequently,
by the time the selective mandatory sanctions were imposed,
it was beginning to be too late. Table 5.12 is instructive
in this regard, for while the sanctioned commodities were
significant in total Rhodesian trade for 1965, they were
barely consequential in terms of the country's immediate
neighbors, who proved to be crucial in the sanctions
scheme (4.4 percent), while they constituted 59 percent of
commodities traded outside the region. There is one other
factor, frequently disregarded in this case, the basis for
policy decisions on possible consequences of sanctions.
The figures in Table 5.12 are for 1965, and thus conclusions about the impact of sanctions were predicated upon
the assumption that trade patterns--especially in commodi-
ties--would remain relatively static indefinitely. This
assumption cannot be supported in the long run, for, as
has been suggested here, once Rhodesia began to alter patterns of commerce and enterprise--and in the process to
circumvent sanctions--the impact was weakened.

In effect, therefore, the mandatory selective sanctions in December 1966 were too late, for new patterns were
already en courant.[122] Moreover, by the time sanctions
were extended on May 29, 1968, by Security Council Resolution 253 (1968) Rhodesian recovery momentum, or at least
momentum from states prepared to supply the country, was
well under way. The 1968 extension of mandatory sanctions
did little but impel Britain to seek another round of negotiations that culminated in the H.M.S. Fearless talks of
October 9-13, 1968.[123] This is the way it more or less
continued until the November 1971 visit of Alec Douglas-
Home (British Foreign Secretary) to Salisbury and the
agreement reached on November 24, 1971; proposed terms for
a Rhodesian settlement were followed by the failure of the
Pearce Commission.[124] Whether a return of Harold Wilson
to the job of Prime Minister in March 1974 will renew impetus toward settlement remains to be seen.

Both the national income and industrial production
indexes (Tables 5.13 and 5.14) show rapid rates of increase
from 1967 on, with scarcely any sign of problems during
1968. In fact, industrial production increased at an average of 9.9 points from 1967 to 1972, which quite obviously
compensated for the 1966 decline.* The same pattern follows in other areas, such as construction (Table 5.15).

_____

*Naturally the veracity of Rhodesian statistics is
open to query, especially when they were not available dur-

TABLE 5.12

1965 Rhodesian Exports Included in British Draft Resolution on Selective Mandatory Sanctions, December 1966

(£ million)

	Tobacco (unmanufactured)	Sugar (raw)	Chrome, Ferrochrome	Asbestos Fiber	Pig Iron, Iron Ore	Copper	Meat, Meat Products	Hides, Skins	Total	Other Exports	Grand Total
South Africa	0.5	--	1.3	0.7	--	0.3	--	0.1	2.9	9.9	12.8
Zambia	--	1.3	--	0.1	0.1	--	0.6	--	2.1	34.0	36.1
Malawi	--	0.8	--	--	--	--	--	--	0.8	6.9	7.7
Botswana	--	--	--	--	--	--	--	--	--	1.6	1.6
Mozambique	0.2	--	--	0.1	--	--	--	--	0.3	0.6	0.9
Portugal	0.1	--	--	0.1	--	--	--	--	0.2	--	0.2
Total	0.8	2.1	1.3	1.0	0.1	0.3	0.6	0.1	6.3	53.0	59.3
United Kingdom	21.4	1.0	0.9	3.1	--	0.5	3.3	--	30.2	0.9	31.1
All other countries	24.8	0.4	3.3	6.7	2.7	6.0	2.8	1.0	47.7	4.5	52.2
Grand total	47.0	3.5	5.5	10.8	2.8	6.8	6.7	1.1	84.2	58.4	142.6

Source: Commonwealth Relations Office.

TABLE 5.13

Rhodesia: Index of National Income, 1963-72

1963	1964	1965	1966	1967	1968	1969	1970	1971	1972
100	104	114	113	123	132	152	167	188	210

Source: Economic Survey of Rhodesia, 1973 (Salisbury: Government Printer, 1973), p. 12.

TABLE 5.14

Rhodesia: Index of Industrial Production, 1963-72
(with percent change over previous year)

1963	1964	1965	1966	1967	1968	1969	1970	1971	1972
92.1	100.0	109.0	101.2	109.0	118.1	134.6	149.3	164.0	178.6
	+8.5	+9.0	-7.1	+7.7	+8.3	+13.9	+10.9	+9.8	+8.9

Source: Economic Survey of Rhodesia, 1973 (Salisbury: Government Printer, 1973), p. 14.

TABLE 5.15

Rhodesia: Construction Output Index, 1963-72

	1963	1964	1965	1966	1967	1968	1969	1970	1971	1972
Total	100	99.7	103.9	96.4	109.8	146.0	166.0	190.3	229.1	258.2
Public	100	90.4	101.7	95.4	104.6	115.5	129.6	140.3	155.9	188.1
Private	100	117.2	111.0	99.4	126.2	242.0	280.6	347.5	459.3	478.6

Source: Economic Survey of Rhodesia, 1973 (Salisbury: Government Printer, 1973), p. 15.

In Tables 5.16, 5.17, and 5.18 other patterns emerge. However, it is possible to see statistically what has been obvious in any case: Rhodesia is surviving economically. Thus, in Table 5.16 the index dropped in 1966 for tobacco, petroleum products, nonmetallic minerals (asbestos), metals, and total industrial production. The same pattern did not emerge in 1968, however, after comprehensive mandatory sanctions were imposed.

Similarly, in the consumer price indexes we note inflationary trends in food prices during the period 1965-66 and from 1969 on, the former probably due to shortages and economic dislocation during the 1966 severe sanctions period, while the latter appears to be related more to economic recovery. The same trends show up in the (white) transport index.*

Finally, we can view the Rhodesian economy from the vantage point of government expenditures. Table 5.19 sets out government expenditures in broad terms and for selected (major) areas of expenditure. It seems fairly apparent that Rhodesia is spending considerable sums on defense, which would fit in with Smith's approach to consolidation of the white regime's dominance. In addition, propaganda has been produced both for internal and external consumption. For internal consumption Rhodesian propagandists have played up "terrorist attacks"** as a means of consolidating white fears of what will befall them should Africans take over--and, of course, every African political upheaval on the continent becomes further proof. On the

---

ing 1966 because of invocation of the Official Secrets Act. However, they are really the only comprehensive statistics available and are certainly far more useful than those available through the United Nations.

*This division of consumer price indexes into European and African reflects the condition of that pathetic country. While it is difficult to maintain the distinction here, it has been done so as not to distort the picture further.

**For example, in a chronological table contained in a mimeographed official Rhodesian publication, "The Years Between, 1923-1973," events are listed with reasonable accuracy until UDI. Thereafter, facts are omitted (for example the H.M.S. Tiger talks, or the April 1966 UN oil embargo). Instead, a slowly increasing stream of reports of terrorist attacks is listed. Thus, in Rhodesian history, an important event on April 24, 1974 was that a farmer and his wife repulsed a terrorist attack on their homestead.

TABLE 5.16

Rhodesia: Index of Industrial Production, 1964-72

Period	Food-stuffs	Drink and To-bacco	Tex-tiles	Cloth-ing and Foot-wear	Wood and Fur-ni-ture	Paper and Print-ing	Chem-ical and Petro-leum Prod-ucts	Non-metal-lic Min-eral Prod-ucts	Metals and Metal Prod-ucts	Trans-port Equip-ment and Work-shops	Other Manu-fac-turing Groups	All Manu-fac-turing Groups	Elec-tri-city Pro-duc-tion	Min-eral Pro-duc-tion	Total Indus-trial Pro-duc-tion
1964	100.0	100.0	100.0	100.0	100.0	100.0	100.0	100.0	100.0	100.0	100.0	100.0	100.0	100.0	100.0
1965	110.0	95.2	114.1	105.4	111.8	112.8	118.9	103.2	109.1	111.1	82.5	108.7	108.7	110.5	109.0
1966	113.3	90.7	115.1	104.8	118.2	97.6	93.1	97.1	100.1	75.9	78.9	98.6	111.2	105.3	101.2
1967	116.2	90.6	142.0	122.9	121.7	103.5	98.1	110.6	117.8	71.3	82.2	107.2	130.6	113.4	109.0
1968	123.6	90.8	151.7	122.0	125.5	108.2	112.8	154.4	133.2	84.1	91.3	117.2	146.6	108.9	118.1
1969	132.3	96.4	217.4	125.1	136.2	117.8	126.5	162.0	153.6	98.2	92.1	132.2	158.2	132.4	134.6
1970	155.3	107.1	200.7	130.1	156.6	141.9	155.2	195.5	185.5	100.3	114.7	148.0	169.1	145.1	149.3
1971	171.1	112.2	233.6	138.6	172.9	150.6	168.9	225.8	213.0	117.1	131.4	163.8	179.4	157.5	164.0
1972	184.3	123.6	254.8	154.7	179.9	171.2	188.1	248.4	239.1	115.5	153.9	180.6	159.0	175.1	178.6

Source: Economic Survey of Rhodesia, 1973 (Salisbury: Government Printer, 1973), p. 14.

TABLE 5.17

Index of European Consumer Prices, 1963-72

(1964 = 100)

Period	Food-stuffs	Drink and Tobacco	Clothing and Footwear	Rent and Taxes	Fuel and Light	House-hold Goods	Ser-vants' Wages	Trans-port	Mis-cella-neous	All Items
1963	98.5	91.8	98.4	100.4	96.9	98.8	95.1	99.7	93.0	97.3
1964	100.0	100.0	100.0	100.0	100.0	100.0	100.0	100.0	100.0	100.0
1965	102.5	105.1	100.5	99.5	100.9	101.6	101.9	101.0	102.5	101.7
1966	106.1	115.4	101.7	99.4	101.2	102.9	102.6	108.5	104.3	104.3
1967	107.7	118.1	102.8	100.2	101.5	103.9	103.5	116.3	107.0	106.4
1968	110.4	118.4	102.9	102.1	101.5	103.5	106.0	120.1	111.5	108.7
1969	111.5	122.7	104.0	106.1	101.8	104.1	110.0	124.1	117.4	111.7
1970	115.1	128.9	107.3	111.4	102.9	106.2	110.9	127.7	121.9	115.6
1971	118.0	128.6	110.1	117.6	102.5	108.7	114.7	129.6	127.1	119.1
1972	123.9	128.4	113.2	122.9	101.9	111.0	122.0	134.0	135.9	124.3

Source: Economic Survey of Rhodesia, 1973 (Salisbury: Government Printer, 1973), p. 24.

TABLE 5.18

Index of African Consumer Prices, 1963–72

(1964 = 100)

Period	Foodstuffs	Drink and Tobacco	Clothing and Footwear	Rent and Taxes; Fuel and Light	Household Goods	Servants' Wages	Transport	Miscellaneous	All Items
1963	97.8	94.4	99.0	99.0	98.8	--	99.9	65.8	95.3
1964	100.0	100.0	100.0	100.0	100.0	--	100.0	100.0	100.0
1965	103.3	102.9	100.1	100.4	103.3	--	100.0	99.7	102.5
1966	107.4	107.5	100.1	101.7	107.1	--	103.8	99.8	105.7
1967	109.4	1C7.4	102.5	101.9	107.7	--	106.6	101.3	107.2
1968	113.9	107.4	102.6	101.9	108.0	--	108.5	101.4	109.7
1969	113.8	110.1	103.5	101.8	109.4	--	111.3	102.1	110.1
1970	116.1	113.4	105.1	103.7	114.3	--	113.6	104.1	112.4
1971	118.8	119.4	105.7	109.5	120.2	--	115.9	106.5	115.8
1972	122.1	127.8	108.9	111.6	124.7	--	117.6	107.7	119.1

Source: Economic Survey of Rhodesia, 1973 (Salisbury: Government Printer, 1973), p. 24.

other side of the propaganda deluge is the "red menace" (often tinted Chinese yellow). Thus Rhodesian propagandists depict their white-minority-ruled state as a barrier to the encroachment of communism* (a theme that sounds suspiciously like Trujillo).

As for the material contained in the various UN studies on Rhodesia, most of it is useful, although much appears to have originated with British sources that grabbed with glee at any and every sign that sanctions were succeeding. The statistical material is far from complete, and certainly cannot be taken as accurate insofar as all UN members are concerned. As has been suggested on a number of occasions above, trade in various commodities continued--albeit with some hesitation in 1966--almost from the day UDI was declared. Table 5.20 provides a summary up to mid-1968 of Rhodesian exports to reporting countries. Even when the tables are expanded to include trade with South Africa, as they are in the UN documents, the picture is no better. One is faced with an inevitable and recurring theme:

> The trade of Southern Rhodesia remained quite substantial in mid-1968, despite the Security Council resolutions of 1965 and 1966, as resolution 232 (1966) called on States to cease trade with that territory only in certain commodities and as some States continued to trade with Southern Rhodesia in contravention of that resolution.[125]

And, of course, while various UN reports[126] have named South Africa and Portugal as the principal violators of the sanctions, this appears to have done little but impel a further resolve by these states to continue to support Smith's regime.

The extent to which the sanctions have been violated, usually by a major international corporation having an office in South Africa (that is, the branch in Rhodesia is a subsidiary of the South African affiliate of a parent British, European, or American company) is quite extensive.

---

*Two pamphlets, Zambezi-Red-Frontier, with appropriate photographs of "captured" Chinese and Russian weapons and security forces at work, and Red for Danger, contain attacks upon African leaders (Nyerere) and liberation movements in Angola and Mozambique. Rhodesia, it appears, is the bastion against such insidious plots.

TABLE 5.19

Rhodesia: Government Expenditures, 1964-72, Percent Change by Year and by Sector

	1964	1965	1966	1967	1968	1969	1970	1971	1972
Total current expenditure ($U.S. million)	137.0	146.3	145.5	158.0	181.7	194.4	212.5	226.9	270.2
Percent change in total		+6.7	-0.5	+8.5	+15.0	+6.9	+9.3	+6.7	+19.0
General administration and defense	0	+16.7	+1.3	+1.7	+13.1	+13.8	+6.8	+13.3	+25.6
Education and health	0	+7.4	+8.6	+5.1	+7.7	+9.4	+9.6	+9.2	+18.5
Economic services	0	+13.1	-0.6	+24.3	+29.5	-3.6	+13.0	-4.6	+29.5
Percentage of expenditures									
General administration and defense	28.6	31.3	31.9	29.9	29.4	31.3	30.6	32.5	34.3
Education and health	24.4	24.6	26.8	26.0	24.3	24.9	25.0	25.6	23.9
Economics services	18.9	20.0	20.0	22.9	25.8	23.2	24.0	21.4	23.3
Public debt service	20.0	16.7	12.5	13.4	13.2	12.9	13.1	13.2	11.4

Source: Economic Survey of Rhodesia, 1973 (Salisbury: Government Printer, 1973), p. 18.

TABLE 5.20

Imports from and Exports to Rhodesia by Reporting
Countries, 1965-68
(in $ U.S.)

	1965	1966	1967	January–June 1968
Imports				
Bovine meat	8,562	6,743	4,559	--
Meat products	6,118	1,600	360	41
Sugar	9,524	4,075	1,690	2,906
Tobacco	106,644	40,013	8,730	765
Hides and skins	2,797	1,837	124	--
Asbestos	23,059	11,315	3,343	1,661
Iron ore and concentrates	4,836	4,303	--	--
Chromium ore and concentrates	9,316	4,274	3,470	--
Leather	65	6	0	--
Pig iron	14,352	9,615	840	--
Copper	35,231	6,367	598	--
Exports				
Petroleum	--	--	--	--
Petroleum products	1,410	153	95	21
Motor vehicles and parts	33,707	5,865	3,352	27
Aircraft and parts	1,173	142	44	48

Source: Security Council, S/8954, December 30, 1968.

A glance through publications such as Industry and Commerce
of Rhodesia for any recent year reveals names such as
Scripto pens, Parker pens, Lever Brothers, Chrysler, Rootes,
Citroen, Datsun, BMW, Toyota, Peugeot, Mercedes-Benz, Ben-
son & Hedges, Barclays Bank, Netherlands Bank of Rhodesia,
Standard Bank, Polymer (a Canadian-government-owned corporation), Dunlop Rubber, Exide, Schweppes, Bata Shoes--and
on the list goes to encompass virtually every necessary
commodity.

Moreover, the fact that mineral output actually increased during the 1965-67 period (Table 5.21), although
the value index declined, suggests that those major foreign
corporations (Japanese, German, French, American) with
large investments in Rhodesian primary production of minerals were not significantly deterred from continuing surreptitious trade. Thus, German and French requirements
for long-grained Rhodesian asbestos, an American market
for Rhodesian chrome, and a Japanese commitment to long-
term development of iron ore and copper deposits all conspired to aid the Rhodesian economy in retaining a semblance of buoyancy. As one British newspaper observed:
in respect of a report that several European firms had
been cooperating with Rhodesia to break sanctions and
boost Rhodesia's steel industry:[127]

TABLE 5.21

Rhodesia: Mineral Output, 1964-72
($U.S. million)

	Value	Value Index
1964	53.5	100.0
1965	63.9	110.5
1966	65.2	105.3
1967	66.7	113.4
1968	67.4	109.0
1969	87.7	132.6
1970	98.7	145.4
1971	101.2	158.1
1972*	97.1	175.8

*Does not include information for December 1972.

Source: Industry and Commerce of Rhodesia, 1973
(Salisbury: Commercial Publication, 1973), p. 103.

341

In spite of international sanctions and the repeated assurances that they were being tightened
the economy has ticked over, if not prospered.
In the steel deal, specific German and Austrian
companies are quoted in a dossier as supplying
equipment and buying the finished product. Their
involvement is a matter for discipline of the
countries concerned. Germany and Austria are not
the only countries to harbour sanctions breakers;
they and the others must decide whether they regard sanctions as now no more than a formal exercise or whether they meant what they said in
subscribing to United Nations' resolutions.

SUMMARY

There is no particular reason why the Rhodesian sanctions should have fallen upon difficult times. It should
be noted that the designation "failure" has been avoided,
because the sanctions have not failed. In fact, the con-
tined existence of the UN sanctions and the periodic and
very necessary reinforcements (for example, S/Res/333
[1973] of May 22, 1973) are essential. In one manner or
another the official UN sanctions will continue to embar-
rass states that maintain trade relations with Rhodesia
either directly or through South Africa and Mozambique.
In addition, the existence of the sanctions will continue
to emphasize that Rhodesia is not a desirable place to
emmigrate, thereby undermining the continuing official campaign to encourage white professionals to come to Rhodesia.
Further, the existence of the sanctions--as in the Dominican case--will legitimize to some extent the continued
pressures upon the white Rhodesians.[128] Increasingly,
Rhodesia will have to become an armed garrison, because
it will become increasingly more isolated, especially when
Portugal either withdraws or is forced out of Mozambique.
Thus, despite minor setbacks, such as the lifting of U.S.
embargoes on Rhodesian chrome (a clear payoff for the
Rhodesian Information Office in Washington), African states
can probably derive some consolation in the long run. Rhodesia will always be under pressure, and the sanctions
legitimize that pressure in one form or another.[129]
It is doubtful whether Britain had ever seriously believed that sanctions would bring the Smith regime down.
In fact, while Britain consistently argued for a return to
legality, there is little reason to believe that this would

342

have meant that Smith should step down immediately. For
one thing, he was more pliable, as evidenced during the
H.M.S. Tiger talks, than were extremists in his Cabinet;
and presumably the British hoped to drive his fanatics into
a political corner. As for the sanctions, they were a
tool; and it would be naive to assume that Britain imposed
them in November 1965 without having turned at least some
expertise loose on the question. The British Board of
Trade had always been skeptical of the probable efficacy
of sanctions; but Wilson, when faced with the petulance
and intransigence of Smith, had no alternative. The cycle,
once begun, has proved impossible to reverse; and as the
Smith regime tightened its economic belt, Britain was
forced by its own commitments to narrow its maneuvering
position.

Meanwhile, as the Rhodesian economy adjusted to the
sanctions and began to recover, Smith's options vis-à-vis
Britain became more viable and numerous. Thus, by the
time the H.M.S. Tiger talks collapsed, the two governments
were on totally divergent paths. Therefore, mandatory
sanctions in December 1966 really stood to contribute little to the economic impact upon Rhodesia, for the nature
of Rhodesia's economy was already beginning to change.
British voluntary sanctions, with concomitant diplomatic
pressures, had made their contribution by the end of June
1966; and beyond the broad international respectability
accorded by UN resolutions, the British had little to gain
at the United Nations.

British policy, clearly, had been to impose voluntary
sanctions, convince white Rhodesians that UDI was a serious
blunder, discredit Smith, and demonstrate the strength of
British resolve. Success depended heavily upon the trau-
matic impact of sanctions; and when Britain failed to move
with sufficient severity and alacrity, the shock--while
severe--was not fatal. After the collapse of the H.M.S.
Tiger talks, British policy became that of achieving the
same ends through a policy of attrition. This could conceivably work in the very long run, as the mandate for
achieving a solution in Rhodesia shifts from Britain more
directly to African shoulders.[130] The NIBMAR commitment
was basically an untenable position for Britain by the
time Commonwealth Prime Ministers extracted it, but it is
still a valid option for Africans. It seems highly plausible that within the next few decades it will become a
reality in Rhodesia, as impetus and responsibility for a
solution to the Rhodesian problem shift to African shoulders.[131]

1. A number of these points are raised in a front page editorial in the South African newspaper Vaderland, October 11, 1965. The paper observed: "Independence was given to South Africa on the basis of majority government measured by standards which at that time were still worth something to the British Government." (All Afrikaanse newspapers have been translated.) In his address to Rhodesians on November 11, Prime Minister Ian Smith made much of "our loyalty to the Queen."

2. One of the Die Burger's regular columnists, known as "Dawie," feared, on October 30, 1965, that an outbreak between Britain and Rhodesia could precipitate a crisis of such proportions as to drag South Africa "willy-nilly" even into the center. In retrospect the ability to avoid being dragged in is a credit to a cautious, almost imperceptible move toward a virtual alliance with Rhodesia.

3. A comprehensive treatment of Rhodesian politics may be found in L. W. Bowman, Politics in Rhodesia (Cambridge, Mass.: Harvard University Press, 1973). Other useful works on Rhodesia include James Barber, Rhodesia: The Road to Rebellion (Oxford: Institute of Race Relations, 1967); Philip Mason, The Birth of a Dilemma (Oxford: Institute of Race Relations, 1958); Sir Roy Welensky, Welensky's 4000 Days (New York: Roy Publishers, 1964); and Kenneth Young, Rhodesia and Independence (New York: Heineman, 1967).

4. Many documents relating to the prologue to UDI may be found in United Kingdom, Southern Rhodesia: Documents . . . November 1963-November 1965, Cmnd. 2807 (London: Her Majesty's Stationery Office, 1965).

5. Ibid., pp. 69-95.

6. United Kingdom, Documents . . . 1965, p. 84.

7. As a matter of fact, Rhodesia already had been a matter before the United Nations. In 1962 it was acknowledged to have nonself-governing status within the terms of Article 73 of the Charter. G.A. Res. 1747 (XVI).

8. Actually the Commonwealth preference was not a serious issue. See two articles by R. W. Green, Board of Trade Journal, June 11 and December 31, 1965. Also, the preference was criticized in the report of the Confederation of British Industries, Britain and Europe: An Industrial Appraisal, I (London: The Confederation, 1966), p. 9. In the legislative field such matters as passports, nationality, and extradition were problems.

9. For an idea of the difficulties faced by these states, see Zambia, First National Development Plan: 1966-1970 (Lusaka: Office of National Development and Planning, 1966), pp. 22, 24, 235; and Botswana, Transitional Plan for Social and Economic Development (Gaberones: Government Printer, 1966), pp. 43-44, paras. 255-56.

10. Cmnd. 2807, p. 95.

11. Rhodesia Herald, October 19, 1965, and Reuters, Lisbon, October 14, 1965.

12. Much of the factual material contained in this section was obtained from Commonwealth Survey, published fortnightly by the British Information Services, London. Where doubt existed about interpretation of fact, other sources have been consulted.

13. The Wilson-Smith correspondence and records of Salisbury meetings are in Cmnd. 2807, pp. 92-102, 102-32. A report on the proposed Royal Commission is at pp. 132-35.

14. Ibid., pp. 136-38.

15. Ibid., p. 142.

16. Ibid., pp. 142-43.

17. Julius Nyerere, speech at a state banquet in the Netherlands, April 21, 1965, in Nyerere, Freedom and Unity (Dar es Salaam: Oxford, 1966), pp. 330,331.

18. Ghana, Statements on Southern Rhodesia (Accra: n.p., January 10, 1966), contains a series of six related documents dated from October 31, 1965 to January 10, 1966.

19. See Times of Zambia, October 28, 1965; Evening News (Accra) and Daily Graphic (Accra), October 31, 1965; Otago (New Zealand) Daily News, November 2, 1965. The only disconcerting notes emerged from either Izvestia, October 26, 1965, which referred to efforts by Smith and Wilson to make a deal, or South African newspapers, such as Transvaler, November 8, 1965, which thanked Wilson for "action which had united the whites in Southern Africa."

20. Both the London Times and the Manchester Guardian carried Smith's UDI statement on November 12, 1965.

21. United Nations, Security Council Resolution 217 (1965) of November 20, 1965, S/Res./217 (1965).

22. A/Res/1889 of November 6, 1963, para. 5. Other relevant resolutions are A/Res./1514 (December 14, 1960); A/Res/1747 (June 28, 1962); A/Res/1760 (October 31, 1962); A/Res/1883 (October 14, 1963); and A/Res/1956 (December 11, 1963).

23. The report is A/6040 (October 11, 1965). The final resolution is A/Res/2012 (October 12, 1965). Approved: 95-2 (South Africa, Portugal)-1 (France).

24. A/Res/2022 (November 8, 1965).

25. Rhodesia *Gazette*, November 5, 1965; Manchester *Guardian*, October 13, 1965.

26. London *Times*, November 6, 1965, "U.N. Urge Use of Force--British Objections Swept Aside"; Montreal *Gazette*, November 2, 1965.

27. In large part these points were derived from a fine article on the December Commonwealth Prime Ministers conference in Christchurch (New Zealand) *Star*, December 4, 1965.

28. Also see William Gutteridge, "Rhodesia: The Use of Military Force," *The World Today* 21 (December 1965): 499-503.

29. A/Res/2024 (November 12, 1965). Vote in Fourth Committee 101-2-1 (France). Vote in General Assembly 107-2-1 (France). Britain did not participate in either vote.

30. S/Res/216 (November 12, 1965). Later one word was changed; hence this resolution is also S/Res/216 Rev. 1 (November 15, 1965).

31. S/Res/217 (November 20, 1965).

32. OAU, Council of Ministers, *Resolutions* (Addis Ababa: OAU, n.d.), pp. 91-92.

33. United Kingdom, *Hansard* (December 20, 1965), cols. 1690-1703.

34. The full communiqué is in *Commonwealth Survey* 12, no. 2 (January 21, 1966): 84-87.

35. For example, Central Bank of Cyprus, *Travel and Exchange Control Regulations*, December 14 and December 20, 1965, circulars nos. EC29/65/6300 and EC28/65/6300; Congo (Leopoldville), House of Representatives, Foreign Affairs Committee, resolution of November 19, 1965, on sanctions; Jamaica, House of Representatives, resolution of November 16, 1965. For further details on the responses of 61 countries, see *Commonwealth Survey* 11, no. 26 (December 21, 1965): 1282-95.

36. In the former category Moscow Radio, on December 12, 1965, referred to British connivance, as did official Czechoslovak sources--see *Rude Pravo*, November 12, 1965. *Izvestia*, November 12, 1965, accused the Labour government of being the representative of new imperialism, while *Pravda* (November 13, 1965) labeled UDI as an "organized imperialist plot." As for the latter, a statement in the Indian Lok Sabha by Foreign Minister Sardar Swaran Singh is typical. Singh placed full responsibility upon Britain and then criticized Britain for failing to use force to bring Smith down. India, *Foreign Affairs Record* 11 (November 1965): 349-51. The statement by Singh may also

have reflected a reaction to British criticism of India's crossing the Kashmir truce line days earlier. In Trinidad, The Nation, unofficial mouthpiece of Eric Williams People's National Party, referred to the British failure to use force as "plain racial prejudice" (December 9, 1965).

37. Australia, "Official Text" (November 16, 1965), p. 4; Australian Labour Party, information release no. 15/65 (November 19, 1965): 5, statement by A. A. Caldwell.

38. New Zealand, "Official Release," November 12, 1965.

39. Sunday News (New Zealand), November 28, 1965; Taranak Daily News (New Zealand), November 28, 1965 and November 22, 1965.

40. Otago Daily Times, November 2, 1965; Auckland Star, November 23, 1965.

41. South Africa Information Service (New York) release, November 18, 1965, reprinted in Commonwealth Survey, December 21, 1965, pp. 1291-92.

42. The Johannesburg Sunday Express, November 14, 1965, reported that "a sympathetic South Africa" would find "no difficulty in leaking imports into Rhodesia"; the Johannesburg Star, December 21, 1965, noted the urgency of South Africa remaining uninvolved in the Rhodesian affair; while Vaderland and Transvaler (both nationalist newspapers) editorialized support for maintaining the white barrier between South Africa and African nationalists.

43. Reuters, Lisbon, November 25, 1965.

44. Asahi Shimbun (Tokyo), November 12, 1965. Nissho Ltd. and Kobe Steel were jointly involved in developing a Rhodesian iron ore smelter.

45. El Ahram, November 15, 1965. It also should be noted that Britain had sent a squadron of RAF Javelins to Ndola in Zambia and the aircraft carrier H.M.S. Eagle was at Dar es Salaam in case of need.

46. On this point see Ivan Bernier, International Legal Aspects of Federalism (London: Longmans, 1973), p. 79. Nasser used the term "state of war" when he referred to the UAR's view of Rhodesia in an address to the Arab Student Union on November 18. El Ahram, November 19, 1965.

47. The groups were Zimbabwe African People's Union (ZAPU) and Zimbabwe African National Union (ZANU). Al Gumhuriya (Cairo), November 18, 1965. The Commonwealth Secretary-General, Arnold Smith, arrived in Dar es Salaam for meetings with President Nyerere just after the OAU completed its discussions. Clearly, Commonwealth connections were being utilized to soothe frustrations.

48. Washington Post, October 17, 1965.

49. Julius Nyerere, "The Honour of Africa," speech to the National Assembly (Dar es Salaam, December 14, 1965), p. 11. (Mimeographed.)

50. Ibid., p. 8. Also see Kwame Nkrumah's speech to his National Assembly of November 25, 1965, in Ghana, Statements on Southern Rhodesia, pp. 10-19.

51. Montreal Gazette, December 9, 1965.

52. Great Britain, Hansard, December 20, 1965, cols. 1690-1703; Economist, December 20, 1965, p. 865.

53. The West African Pilot (Lagos), a left-wing paper, was very critical of Balewa and called for an immediate break with Britain. The Daily Times (Lagos), moderately independent, opposed Balewa's visit to London.

54. Nkrumah's speech to the National Assembly, December 16, 1965, in Ghana, Statements on Southern Rhodesia, pp. 20-22. Also see The Nation (Trinidad), December 10, 1965, for views on the same theme.

55. Australia, official press release, December 28, 1965.

56. Commonwealth Prime Ministers Meeting, "Communiqué," Commonwealth Survey 12 (1966): 84-87.

57. The Secretary of State for Commonwealth Relations, Arthur Bottomley, for example, attempted to visit Salisbury as a "private citizen" in mid-January 1966. The non-visit was prevented by Smith, who refused to talk with non-officials. London Times, January 15, 1966. Also see a report on Selwyn Lloyd's visit to Rhodesia and Zambia (on behalf of the Conservative Party), London Times, February 22, 1966.

58. Rhodesia Herald, December 16, 1966. The overthrow and assassination of Nigerian Prime Minister Balewa during the week January 15-22 was a major boost to the morale of white Rhodesians--in a negative sense--by confirming fears of African irresponsibility.

59. There is reason to believe that Britain had to resort to the threat of prosecution of Shell and B.P., for violation of the Order in Council, in order to obtain compliance. The Rand Daily Mail, February 2, 1966, under the headline "B.P. Refuse to Supply Oil for Rhodesia," tried to counteract British Government pressure on B.P. via embarrassment. The Times of Zambia (Lusaka), February 25, 1966, reported that all Shell's tanks in Salisbury were full and that the Feruka refinery was preparing to handle Venezuelan crude.

60. Rumors circulated in London and Cape Town that Rhodesia had concluded a 30,000-tons-a-month deal with Iran. Rand Daily Mail, February 17, 1966. The French company, "Total," was also involved in supplying Rhodesians.

61. _Anovincia_ (Luanda), March 5, 1966; and Reuters dispatch, Johannesburg, March 4, 1966.

62. _Cape Argus_, March 11, 1966. The kerosene was purchased in the Netherlands from funds transferred there in January 1966 by the Rhodesian government. The _Benguela_ eventually unloaded the kerosene in Durban, South Africa.

63. A Liberian-registered ship, _Enterprise_, was intercepted near Durban; the British tanker _Denby Grange_ left Lourenço Marques for Beira on March 24; the Norwegian tanker _Aurelia_ discharged cargo at Durban on March 27. Rand _Daily Mail_, March 25, 1966; _Sunday Express_ (Cape Town), March 20 and 27, 1966.

64. The _Joanna V_ was Greek-registered and owned by a Panamanian company whose executive officers resided in New York. Some members of the board of directors were Canadian residents in Montreal. _Globe and Mail_ (Toronto), April 14, 1966; Montreal _Gazette_, April 5, 1966; and Canada, House of Commons, _Debates_, April 5. The ship had been chartered by Rafaellia Sons of Johannesburg. _Joanna V_ owned by Varnicos Corporation, incorporated in Panama; Panama, Public Registry, vol. 543, folio 458, entry 117813 of March 18, 1966; and Varnima Corporation, ibid., vol. 543, folio 299, entry 117563 of February 18, 1966. Directors of both companies were identical. _V_ stood for Venizelas.

65. Asbestos and chrome were major problems. The Rhodesian asbestos companies had formed a marketing company in South Africa known as the Southern Asbestos Co., registered December 7, 1965, and located in the Commercial Exchange Building, Johannesburg. An obviously industry-inspired article appeared in _Frankfurter Allegmeine_ (February 15, 1966) arguing against the boycott. The article claimed that a British firm, Turner and Newall, had built up large stocks of Rhodesian asbestos in Mozambique and South Africa. _Le monde_, February 20-21, 1966, indicated that French authorities had advised industrialists to find new sources of chrome. But General Jean-Pierre Maire, Secretary of the France-Rhodesia Association, visited Salisbury to promote trade (_Le monde_, March 3, 1966); Union Carbide of the United States had purchased Rhodesian chrome by making payments in dollars to South Africa that were then transferred to S.A. Rand; Rothmans purchased tobacco in this manner; and a Canadian industrialist, George Weston, announced his intention to invest £250,000 in Rhodesia (London _Times_, January 31, 1966).

66. Paper submitted by Tanzania to heads of state meeting, Nairobi, March 1966, p. 8.

67. UN S/7235 (April 7, 1966) and S/7236/Rev. 1 (April 8, 1966).

68. PV. 1277 (April 9, 1966). The African amendments were S/7243 (April 9, 1966) and sought to expand Britain's draft to include South Africa and to include other merchandise under Articles 41 and 42 of the Charter.

69. S/Res/221 (April 9, 1966). Greece explained to the Council meeting that Joanna V had been deleted from the register of the Greek Mercantile Marine and her master was to stand before a disciplinary council.

70. Portugal, press communiqué, April 6, 1966. On April 28 the Portuguese Mission at the United Nations issued a communiqué that stated that meetings took place between Portuguese, Zambian, and Malawi representatives in Mozambique on at least two occasions. The meetings were to arrange rail and road supplies of petrol to these countries. In addition, "increasing quantities of copper coming from Zambia are permitted to be taken abroad through the railway at Lobito."

71. S/7271 (April 28, 1966). President Salazar, in an address to the Portuguese National Assembly on April 13, had argued for settlement with Britain by Rhodesia. Wilson apparently sent Salazar a personal message the following day in appreciation of his remarks.

72. It is also possible he was under pressure from South Africa and that Verwoerd and Wilson had been in correspondence. L'opinion (Rabat), April 28, 1966, covered Oliver Wright's secret visit to Salisbury.

73. The Nationalist (Dar es Salaam), April 29, 1966, welcomed the talks but cautioned about Smith's motives. The Rand Daily Mail referred to the talks as a "return to sanity" (April 28, 1966). Vaderland, April 28, 1966, noted that one of the pressures on Smith was that he was beginning to involve his friends in difficulties. Die Transvaler, April 29, 1966, discussed Verwoerd's role in the process.

74. The record of these talks are in United Kingdom, Rhodesia: Documents Relating to Proposals for a Settlement 1966, Cmnd. 3171 (London: Her Majesty's Stationery Office, December 1966), Appendix J, pp. 38-103.

75. Sunday Times (Johannesburg), June 19, 1966.

76. See Die Welt (Bonn), June 28, 1966, where the possibility of the German licensing system for asbestos is apologetically excused from its failures. On the same subject see Financial Times, July 7, 1966. Continued calls for the use of force appeared in, for example, The Nation (Port of Spain), June 10, 1966.

77. Globe and Mail (Toronto), June 23, 1966; Financial Times, June 24, 1966.

78. The Lagos *Pilot*, June 28, 1966, referred to this as Britain "wriggling out of its commitment." Zambia apparently preferred Delhi to London for a meeting.

79. United Kingdom, *Hansard*, July 5, 1966, cols. 252-58. The Pretoria *News*, July 6, 1966, responded that Wilson's remark "may well alarm white Rhodesians into continued stubborn resistance."

80. United Kingdom, *Hansard*, August 8, 1966, cols. 1017-18.

81. Text of the communiqué is in Commonwealth Survey 12, no. 20 (September 30, 1966): 978-86.

82. The British-Rhodesian exchange on the points for negotiation is in United Kingdom, *Rhodesia: Documents*, Appendix B, pp. 16-21.

83. Ibid., Appendixes C and D, pp. 21-29. A series of other detailed exchanges occurred throughout November. Ibid., pp. 30-37.

84. Rhodesia *Herald*, November 12, 1966.

85. A/6482 (October 21, 1966). Meetings held were 1606 to 1619 (October 11-31, 1966); 1621 (November 2); and 1629 to 1633 (November 8-10). The Committee of 24 (Special Committee on the Situation with Regard to the Implementation of the Declaration on the Granting of Independence to Colonial Countries and Peoples) had also been meeting over the months.

86. A/6482/Add.1 (November 15, 1966). This became General Assembly Resolution A/Res/2151 (XXI), November 17, 1966, and was sent to the Security Council under cover of a letter from the Secretary-General on November 21, 1966 (S/7595), in accordance with operative paragraph 6.

87. Details are in Commonwealth Survey 12, no. 25 (December 9, 1966): 1228-34. Wilson's announcement to Parliament is in *Hansard*, December 1, 1966, cols. 621-28.

88. Toronto *Star*, December 1, 1966.

89. The public record of the H.M.S. *Tiger* talks are in United Kingdom, *Rhodesia: Documents*, Cmnd. 3171, pp. 38-103. This document does not contain records of private meetings held during the three-day period or of messages exchanged between Smith and his Cabinet.

90. Ibid., p. 51.

91. Smith's reply to Wilson argued that it would be "irresponsible" to abandon the 1965 constitution under which the regime was operating. There was also the issue of Smith's dislike of Wilson's "socialist" government (Smith's wedge into domestic British politics). Smith rejected socialism as synonymous with racial equality and argued, "We are individuals, supporting the capitalist sys-

tem with the accent on individual initiative and enterprise."
Rhodesia Herald, November 12, 1966. Mrs. Ian Smith is
South African and a known racist, so presumably she had
some influence on her husband.

92. Britons had been reminded of the dangers of sanctions against South Africa. See Financial Times, November
22, 1966, "S. African Sanctions--What Britain Stands to
Lose."

93. The Nationalist (Dar es Salaam), in its editorial
of December 12, argued that if Britain was not prepared to
propose effective oil sanctions herself, "She is being
hypocritical, dishonest or falsely motivated."

94. S/7630 (December 13, 1966). Sponsored by Uganda,
Mali, and Nigeria.

95. South African Transport Minister B. J. Schoeman
had indicated that South Africa would not respect mandatory
sanctions on December 10. Cape Argus, December 12, 1966.
The new South African Prime Minister, Bathasar Vorster,
had also issued a statement on December 6 in which he said
that the Republic would not comply with mandatory sanctions.
Agriculture and Waters Minister J. J. Fouché repeated the
sentiment in a speech on December 14. Vorster apparently
also wrote to Wilson on December 12 to convey a similar
message.

96. S/Res/232 (1966), December 16, 1966, reissued on
December 30, 1966. For details of the vote see S/PV. 1340,
December 16, 1966.

97. Resolutions S/Res/253 (1968); S/Res/277 (1970);
and S/Res/333 (1970). Also, for example, Secretariat working paper A/AC.109/L.393 (April 7, 1967); General Assembly
report A/6700/Add.1 (September 27, 1967); document
A/6868/Add. 1 (October 1967); S/7781/Add. 5 (June 13, 1968);
S/8786 (August 28, 1968); up to S/10920 (April 15, 1973).

98. For example, United Kingdom, Rhodesia: Report on
Exchanges with the Regime Since the Talks Held in Salisbury
in November, 1968, Cmnd. 4065 (London: Her Majesty's Stationery Office, 1969).

99. Rhodesians have proved willing to become self-
sufficient to a large extent in manufactured goods. See
Sunday Times (Cape Town), April 9, 1967, "Made in Rhodesia
Boom for Manufacturers."

100. This should not be interpreted to mean that these
states alone were responsible for sanctions violations
(voluntary or mandatory); for example, Libya exported £635
of manufactured goods to Rhodesia in 1967, a small but
typical example of what frequently occurred. Kingdom of
Libya, Statistical Abstract, 1967 (Tripoli: n.p., 1967),
p. 225.

101. _Die Welt_, June 27 and July 6, 1966; _Financial Times_ (London), July 7, 1966.

102. Note the trip by British Foreign Secretary George Brown to Tokyo in early 1968 to "tighten sanctions." _Irish Times_, January 11, 1968.

103. The Manchester _Guardian_, January 19, 1967, mentions the use of false certificates of origin by the United States, Britain, and France to deliver "through Rhodesia's back door goods that they were sworn not to send in the front entrance." Dutch, Danish, Japanese, and Portuguese ships "have helped to violate sanctions against the export of Rhodesian tobacco and chrome." Rhodesia _Herald_, September 23, 1967.

104. The text is in Ministério dos Negócios Estrangeiros, _Boletím de informação_, March-April 1965, pp. 1-6.

105. _Cape Argus_, March 8, 1967. Also see Johannesburg _Star_, January 26, 1966; _Times of Zambia_, February 26, 1966; _Cape Argus_, March 4, 1966.

106. Rhodesia, _Statistical Bulletin_, September 1966. Issued in Cape Town by the Rhodesian Mission to South Africa.

107. _Commercial Opinion_ (South Africa), October 1967.

108. The Firends of Rhodesia Association solicited funds for gifts of petrol. See advertisement in _Cape Argus_, January 28, 1966.

109. Details of the refinery's 500,000 gallons-a-week production are in _Sunday Express_ (South Africa), March 12, 1967.

110. _Financial Times_ (Johannesburg), October 25, 1966.

111. _Times of Zambia_, September 12, 1966. The loss was about 4,000 tons, or about 25 percent of Zambia's total petrol requirements for a month.

112. Union Minière tried to help Zambia by moving copper from Katanga through Rhodesia at 15,000 tons per month, thereby freeing Congo routes for more Zambian copper. Communiqué (Kinshasa Meeting), July 15,1966; _Financial Times_, June 21, 1966; Manchester _Guardian_, June 21, 1966; _Financial Times_, August 11, 1966.

113. These figures were extracted from R. B. Sutcliffe, _Sanctions Against Rhodesia: The Economic Background_ (London: Africa Bureau, January 21, 1966). (Pamphlet.)

114. The _Sunday Citizen_ (Salisbury), June 12, 1966; Manchester _Guardian_, June 14, 1966. There had been a memorandum to Smith in early 1965 from the business community on the disadvantages of UDI.

115. Salisbury Radio, June 17, 1966; Manchester _Guardian_, June 18, 1966.

116. _The Scotsman_, June 21, 1966.
117. _Financial Mail_, June 24, 1966.
118. _Daily Mail_, June 20, 1966.
119. The _Cape Times_, January 30, 1967, reported that about 160 million pounds of tobacco was held in secret stores (Belvedere Airport hangar), and thus only about 80 million pounds of the 1966 crop had been sold. The _Irish Times_ (Dublin), March 8, 1967, reported that Rhodesia would continue to support tobacco farmers and on March 29 reported a second secret tobacco auction. The Rand _Daily Mail_, January 30, 1967, reviewed the "secret" textile barter deal between the French firm Marcel Boussac and the Rhodesian firm of John Landau of Salisbury. "The tobacco is to be sent to depots in Europe where Boussac's agents hope to dispose of the consignment at considerable profit." The _Financial Gazette_ (South Africa), February 10, 1967, noted that a spokesman for Peugeot in Paris had confirmed that they had been approached to establish a motor vehicle plant in Rhodesia. Rhodesia also sold pig iron and chrome to Union Carbide (United States) throughout 1966.
120. _Financial Mail_ (Johannesburg), September 9, 1966 (a reliable source), estimated Rhodesian consumption at 60-70 percent of pre-embargo levels (about 4 million gallons per month).
121. The Rhodesian Post Office Savings Bank, in its report for the year ended June 30, 1966, suggested a high degree of liquidity in financial transactions during the first seven months of sanctions. Bank withdrawals exceeded deposits by only £430,000. _Financial Mail_, February 3, 1967.
122. Lord Alport did attempt another series of negotiations from June 22 to July 13, 1967. See Wilson's comments in _Hansard_, July 25, 1967, cols. 325-27.
123. United Kingdom, _Rhodesia, Report on the Discussions Held on Board H.M.S. 'Fearless', October 1968_, Cmnd. 3793 (London: Her Majesty's Stationery Office, 1968). Also see Wilson's remarks to Parliament, _Hansard_, October 15, 1968, cols. 207-23. Wilson felt that changes in Smith's government, including "the disappearance of intransigent racialists," had been a factor leading to these talks. For a record of the British-Rhodesian discussions after _H.M.S. Fearless_, see _Rhodesia: Report on Exchanges with the Regime Since the Talks Held in Salisbury in November 1968_, Cmnd. 4065 (London: Her Majesty's Stationery Office, June 1969).
124. The Settlement terms are in United Kingdom, _Rhodesia: Proposals for a Settlement_, Cmnd. 4835 (London:

Her Majesty's Stationery Office, November 26, 1971). The
Pearce Commission arrived in Salisbury on January 11, 1972,
in order to assess the acceptability of the terms of the
November proposed settlement. In his report Lord Pearce
stated: "The Commission reject the suggestion that the
African answer should be construed as 'Yes.' . . . The
majority of Africans rejected the proposal." See Rhodesia:
Report of the Commission on Rhodesian Opinion Under the
Chairmanship of the Rt. Hon. Lord Pearce, Cmnd. 4964 (London:
Her Majesty's Stationery Office, May 23, 1972).

125. S/8954, December 30, 1968, p. 5.

126. S/7781/Add.5, June 13, 1968; S/7781/Add.4, November
30, 1967; A/6700/Add.1, September 27, 1966, A/AC.
109/L.393, April 7, 1967; A/6868/Add.1, October 30, 1967.

127. Manchester Guardian, April 16, 1974.

128. In March 1974 it was announced that Rhodesia was
clearing a 10-mile-wide strip of land along its borders
with Mozambique and Zambia to provide a no-man's zone to
assist in combating terrorists. Windsor Star, March 5,
1974. It is also relocating border residents. See International
Herald Tribune (Paris), August 28, 1974.

129. It is difficult to imagine that Rhodesia would
have time on its side, simply because African opinion will
continue to focus upon racism on the continent while world
opinion goes on to more pressing issues, thereby leaving
Rhodesia to its fate. On U.S. chrome imports, see General
Assembly resolution A/Res/2765 (XXVI), November 17, 1971.
U.S. President Gerald Ford apparently favors reimposition
of restrictions on Rhodesian chrome imports into the United
States. International Herald Tribune (Paris), August 15,
1974.

130. Richard Falk has pointed out that under certain
circumstances, such as racial situations, violence has
been given a certain amount of legitimacy by international
organizations (the UN General Assembly). In R. Falk, "The
Beirut Raid and the International Law of Retaliation,"
AJIL 63 (1969): 415 ff., at 425.

131. The "News Release" from the Commonwealth Secretariat
of May 31, 1974, covering a meeting of the Commonwealth
Sanctions Committee for that date, contains a reference
to African states taking initiatives to promote
self-determination in Africa. Commonwealth Secretary-
General Arnold Smith also reported on talks with Portugal's
new Foreign Minister, Mario Soares, concerning the fate
of Mozambique vis-à-vis Rhodesia. The Scotsman (Edinburgh),
May 12, 1974, warned that white Portuguese settlers might
follow Ian Smith's example in Rhodesia.

6

APPLIED SANCTIONS
AND CONCLUSIONS

During the period in which this study was being written, the world was faced with the Middle East oil embargo;
and periodically there was cause to ponder whether the
nature of the general conclusions might be affected by that
embargo or style of economic warfare. The difficulties of
viewing sanctions in the light of the Arab oil boycott
would have been reduced significantly if nagging doubts
about the contrived nature of reaction to the oil embargo
could have been eliminated. Unfortunately, the embargo
and North American energy crisis have had earmarks of a con-
coction, and thus to suggest that limited rationing in the
United States is a consequence of the Arab oil boycott
smacks of contrivance of a most sophisticated quality.
However, there may very well have been significant lessons
in the Arab oil boycott for practitioners of sanctions in
pursuit of international legal norms. Such lessons as the
value of petroleum embargoes and concerted action are instructive, for, as was noted above, petroleum and unity
were key factors in each of the cases under review.

The failure to impose an effective sanction on petroleum supplies to Italy was one of two key defects in the
League sanctions scheme. Petroleum was on the OAS list
of sanctioned commodities to the Dominican Republic, and
petroleum received special attention from the UN Security
Council in the Rhodesian case. Thus, an Arab oil boycott
would appear to be an effective component of international
sanctions.

A second significant ingredient appears to have been
transportation routes. Thus, a British (or League) hesitancy or failure to close the Suez Canal meant unhindered
Italian supply for invasion forces. UN failure to control

supply routes from Mozambique and the Republic of South
Africa meant unhindered supply routes to Rhodesia.

> The Rhodesians' thanks could be extended to the
> many governments who turned a blind eye when their
> nationals broke sanctions by trading directly or
> indirectly with Rhodesia. The British Government
> did make a genuine effort to impose sanctions,
> but its policy of continuing them against Rhodesia
> while refusing to take steps against the Republic
> [of South Africa] was plainly self-defeating.[1]

As for the Dominican Republic, the significance of transportation was diminished by the island status of the country and, with the exception of Haiti, to which only limited
land communications existed, its geographical isolation.

Geography is an obvious factor in any sanctions scheme
and, again with the exception of the Dominican Republic,
played a major part in the three international organizations' attempts to isolate target states. Thus, a failure
to take into account--from the very beginning--the geographical location of the target state can be significant.
This "contiguous factor" is important because in two cases
special, long-standing trading patterns existed. Perhaps
the rule that emerges here is that future considerations
of sanctions programs must devote considerably more effort
to reconciling interests of contiguous states, especially
if they claim neutrality or are hostile to the intent of
sanctions. Switzerland's crumbling in the Italian case
and Portugal's and South Africa's overt hostility to UN
sanctions clearly were factors to be reckoned with. However, before continuing into an expanded brief on sanctions
guidelines, we must first review the context of the enforcement process.

SANCTIONS AND INTERNATIONAL
ORGANIZATIONS

There seems to be little doubt that international organizations require some form of sanctioning capacity because logically there are very few alternatives. If the
organization lacks the capacity to impose sanctions of
some type against its members (or, in the case of Rhodesia,
a member's dependency), it is little more than voluntary
in nature. In addition, if states are to contemplate seriously the advantages of lawlike behavior in international

relations, there must be some attempt, even if it is scarcely better than a facade, at chastizing a state responsible for an act in contravention of the principles of international law. Unfortunately, there exist some very fundamental difficulties.

First, there is the magnitude of the crime and, second, there is no reason to expect that every state views a law violation as a crime or as a crime warranting sanctions as severe as might be proposed by states directly affected by the offender. On the former point, international organizations until recently have tended to conceptualize offenses in law that might warrant sanctions as major, fairly well-defined, forms of aggression--be it aggression against a single state or an entire race. Hence, the massive crime was responded to with massive sanctions. Consider, for example, Articles 3 and 6 of the Rio Treaty and the relevant provisions of the UN Charter (Articles 51 and 53) as reflections of the concept.

The OAS has the capacity to respond to two situations, an aggression that is an armed attack (Article 3) and an "aggression which is not an armed attack" (Article 6). Thus, in the former instance, if the OAS responds to a clearly defined armed aggression, Article 51 (self-defense) of the UN Charter applies and, without prejudice to the rights and responsibilities of the Security Council, OAS members may continue to resist aggression until the issue is resolved. However, if the aggression is not an armed attack (Article 3 of the Rio Treaty and Article 51 of the UN Charter do not apply) and the OAS organ of consultation decides to respond, then the OAS is involved in an enforcement action and Article 53 of the Charter would apply (presumably in conjunction with Article 54, informing the Security Council).

The problem is that in either instance the OAS can only fall back upon Article 8 of the Rio Treaty: "The measures on which the Organ of Consultation may agree will compromise one or more of . . . " a list of economic and political sanctions. Clearly the options are numerous if a direct correlation could be drawn between offense and sanction. But all evidence suggests that even the most minor offense would be responded to with massive sanctions in order to achieve results. Yet how many states are prepared to impose universal economic and political sanctions against a state that may have served as a haven for a contingent of guerrillas? We lack, therefore, both organizational and constitutional capacities to correlate international offenses with punishments. This is a further argument against drawing parallels too closely to municipal law.

The second difficulty relates to the variety of views of what constitutes an offense. Thus we are faced, for example, with the anomaly of very clear violations of the Tokyo Convention on Offenses on Board Aircraft and the Montreal Convention on Hijacking; but the international community has been frustrated in its ability to punish offenders because the offenders do not constitute persons in traditional international law terms (even in terms of piracy on the seas), and the states that provide refuge for offenders have not been held liable because of the vagueness of the concept of political offenses in international law. These two factors involved here are the inability of the international community to respond to microcrimes, particularly given the absence of an individual's status in international law, and the fundamental disagreement about what constitutes a crime. It would seem appropriate, therefore, for international organizations to give consideration to a broader definition of the capacity of individuals to be subjects of international law. In addition, it would seem appropriate for international organizations to delegate authority to respond to minor crimes to nonstate entities. This would mean, effectively, that the International Civil Aviation Organization would be given greater responsibility by the UN Security Council (for example, under a Security Council resolution rather than an ICAO resolution) for the punishment of states harboring individuals responsible for crimes against humanity. Of course this does not solve the problem of differing views of what constitutes a crime. However, employing the reasoning of the German-American Mixed Claims Commission in the Lusitania case (1923) (7 RIAA 32), an aggrieved state could hold the state of nationality of the offenders responsible or accountable for damages. This would be especially true in circumstances where parties that are not directly parties to a dispute (however vaguely defined) suffer damages.

All of the preceding discussion overlooks one very basic and essential point. The discussion to this point has hinged upon a presumption that a correlation must exist between crime and punishment. Or that, at best, the sanctions employed should be introduced in regularized stages (diplomatic, then economic, either voluntary or mandatory), thereby permitting both leeway to tighten the sanctions should the offending state fail to respond and leeway to permit negotiations pursuant to a settlement. It is the latter point wherein both the weakness and the intrinsic merit of sanctions emerge.

In each of the preceding cases the respective international organization imposed sanctions with varying degrees of severity over time, in an effort to force the target state to negotiate. This is the essential worth of sanctions. They impress upon the target state the seriousness of the international community's view of the offender's behavior, but they do not create conditions (war) where negotiations become virtually impossible. Sanctions, therefore, can be considered only as one tactic in the international organizations' strategy to correct offensive behavior. In both the Rhodesian and Italian cases, far too much reliance was placed upon sanctions as a total solution. Thus, sanctions were viewed in much the same manner as the robber with the gun. "If you don't hand over the money, I'll shoot" provides the victim with two choices: either hand over the money or call the bluff. If the victim calls the bluff, then the robber must shoot or show himself as a coward. If he shoots, he may do so reluctantly and may seek to frighten, wound, or kill his victim. In the latter instance the crime is complete and the result sought is achieved. However, in either of the other situations the victim may again call the robber's bluff; and if the latter continues to shoot only to frighten or wound, the victim may continue to resist until the robber runs out of bullets or gives up the robbery attempt.[2] The point is that for the robber to succeed, the victim must be convinced of the seriousness of the robber's intentions and his capacity to carry them out. Anything less leads to a series of negotiations.

In summary, therefore, unless the international organization is prepared to respond quickly and severely to law violations, the sanctions will fail or must be accounted for as only another, very limited, tactic. In the following section we shall take a somewhat anatomical look at sanctions to see why this conclusion is inevitable.

SANCTIONS: AN ASSESSMENT

As was noted earlier, overexpectation concerning the capabilities of sanctions in international law has been a recurring feature of their employment. The reasons appear to be threefold: the experience of economic warfare; the parallel of municipal law; and the impression that sanctions, almost singularly, could in some mystical manner achieve the prescribed results. Ironically, the experience of war has provided a practical foundation upon which a theory in pursuit of peace has been constructed; and the adaptation of the war practice, by international organizations in time of peace, has served as a basis for conceptualization of sanctions programs. But war, and the total commitment that it involves, is an illusory format. Decisions involving sanctions, reached by international agencies, have lacked the depth of emotional involvement that total war evokes. Consequently, peacetime sanctions have not, and probably cannot, command the physical commitment of men and materials required to enforce wartime embargoes and blockades. Economic warfare is a corollary to a heavy commitment of materials to battle, while peaceful multilateral sanctions require no such involvement.

International agency sanctions only require acquiescence and, unless directly involved as the victim of an alleged aggression, states have sought the minimum obligation that would entail the least cost to themselves. States will determine the intensity of their commitment to sanctions in proportion to the perceived danger that the offending state poses to their individual national interests. For example, did it really matter to Great Britain that Rafael Trujillo organized an assassination plot against Rómulo Betancourt?

It could be argued that in all cases it matters that international law is being violated, and that it is in the common interest of all parties in the political system to see the transgressor punished. Such a Rousseauian view may explain the origins of common interests, but it does not suffice to impel states into an unlimited acceptance that common interest should prevail over particularistic interests. The defects are too readily apparent.

First, states frequently find it difficult to agree upon the precise status of a particular law or principle invoked at any given time. This is simply another way of saying that, given the same facts and the same precepts of law, two Foreign Offices will probably arrive at different conclusions.

A second factor militating against unswerving support for law and principle relates to the price that must be paid. States have demonstrated a reluctance to upset existing markets, trading patterns, and other bilateral relations in order to undertake a sanctions scheme. In part, this hesitancy stems from the realization that whenever one state retreats from a market, another state or individual entrepreneur will rush in to fill the void. Political ties, particularly if they are close, are likewise difficult to terminate abruptly. Economic sanctions are usually considered to be of a short-term nature; and where economic and political ties have developed over a long period, states will tend to act pragmatically. Thus, they will endeavor to minimize costs and maximize the gain to the international organization (and incidentally to international law), while simultaneously attempting to retain a semblance of harmonious relations.

A third factor detracting from a total commitment to sanctions originates with the decision process. An organizational decision to impose sanctions tends to represent a consensus, although not necessarily a compromise, of the attitudes of the states party to that decision. There is bound to be disagreement over the methods by which the decision is to be implemented. Some states, lacking an interest in the dispute at issue or sympathizing with the target state, may view the minimum form of sanctions as adequate. Other states may seek the maximum form of sanctions, including armed intervention. The outcome probably will not wholly satisfy any state, but it will offend even fewer.

These reasons and the factors related to them should serve as a warning of the dangers inherent in any extended equation of international agency sanctions with economic warfare. The two are very distinct and generate quite different degrees of response by individual states.

The second analogy, resulting in overexpectation of the efficacy of sanctions, is that of municipal law. It is perhaps unfortunate that international law has become overburdened by, and indebted to, the legalistic approach. No doubt lawyers and their juridical logic have made a healthy contribution to the development and codification of international law. But the mistake of the student of jurisprudence is that once he codifies the law, he is led to assume, barring subsequent formal change or radical judicial interpretation, that the law will remain immutable and subject to relatively rigid observance. Implicitly he bases this reasoning upon experience with domestic law; and thus, when the law is violated, his juridical inclinations seek recourse to juridical solutions. It is also unfortunate that the student of jurisprudence apparently fails to appreciate that the translation of municipal jurisprudence to the international milieu abstracts that body of legal norms from the environment within which it has habitually functioned. Consequently, any societal consensus on the fundamental premises of a municipal legal system, be it A. V. Dicey's rule of law or otherwise, is lost in the transition. Since there is no universal agreement on

the origins and nature of the precepts of international
law, it is often difficult to determine whether "the law"
has in fact been violated. Municipal law generally does
not face that dilemma. The municipal law analogy has been
the model, therefore, that has contributed most to the development of elaborate illusions about the capacities of
sanctions in international law and relations.

International law is not law in the all-pervasive domestic sense, nor is it law that remains beyond reproach.
There is no doubt that there are international laws that
are generally subscribed to by states without equivocation;
but these are laws of necessity, that is, laws that facilitate the process of international relations and the guaranteed mutual survival of most of the system's participants.
Subscription to such laws provide the benefits of mutual
survival, and the sanction is the absence of such benefits.

Finally, and in a somewhat similar vein, there appears
to have been a tendency to simplify sanctions, to view
them as something like a legal remedy to be imposed from
which benefits will flow. This simplification overlooks
two fundamental precepts: that states that violate international law will have contemplated the consequences in
advance (a sort of applied rebus sic stantibus in state
behavior) and that a state or, in particular, a government
that is exposed to international castigation will seek to
survive. Clearly, in each of the three cases discussed
here the survival of the incumbent regime was in some manner contingent upon the behavior that triggered sanctions.
Thus, because sanctions are perceived by the target state
(and/or regime) to be a challenge to survival of the state
(regime), they will be resisted in every possible manner.
Naive assumptions that states (regimes), once sanctioned,
will repent and rectify deviant behavior are dangerous for
an effectively planned sanctions program.

Before turning to the theory that emerges in a very
loose form from this study, the pattern of each case will
be reviewed.

In the Italian-Ethiopian situation the essential ingredients for a lack of successful sanctions are fairly
obvious. Sanctions take time to succeed, and Italy's
armies moved relatively rapidly (about eight months from
the time Ethiopia was invaded to the fall of Addis Ababa).
Petroleum, a key factor, was not included in the League's
sanctions scheme; and the major transportation route (the
Suez Canal) remained open. Neutrality--or at least pre-
tenses of neutrality--were disastrous, for not only did
the open neutrality of the United States effectively sup-

port Italian aggression, but the more devious neutrality of Switzerland and the back-door neutrality of a number of Latin American states gave Italy implied support for its resistance to, or disregard of, League sanctions.

Then there was the straight and simple matter of major states' politics. For France, Italy was less offensive in Africa than a revitalized Germany in Europe; and the Hoare-Laval agreement reflected the assignment of priorities. Italy was a major power; Italy and France had common interests in the African and Ethiopian region; they had common interests in North Africa and on their common European boundary. Ethiopia was expendable to the French, and the British were not prepared (probably justifiably, under the circumstances) to go alone in support of vague notions of collective security.

Finally, Italy was strong, by most standards, in late 1935. Mussolini's preparations for war meant that, relative to other European states emerging from the depression, Italy was economically vibrant. Moreover, its mixed agricultural-industrial economy meant greater economic stability, not only internally but vis-à-vis neighboring states. Italy would have been a tough nut to crack under the most favorable of League circumstances, unless League members were prepared to add military force to their organization's clout. The enforced closure of the Suez Canal and a blockade of the entrance to the Red Sea, combined with military pressure in the Mediterranean, might have challenged Italy considerably more, especially if simultaneous military support of Ethiopia had been included. However, given the League's composition, the burden of collective security probably would have fallen directly upon Britain and France; and with the latter so reluctant, the burden would have been Britain's. Thus, once League sanctions were reduced to an almost bilateral British confrontation with Italy (and possibly the United States), the benefits of collective security paled before the more specific benefit of European security. The Hoare-Laval pact may have been a reprehensible action at the time; but in the absence of a more universal involvement in sanctions, it was the only alternative. Sanctions in the Italian case were reduced to a weak bargaining ploy.

In the Dominican case we have an apparent success for international organization sanctions. But exaltation over the success must be tempered by an appreciation of the peculiarities of the Dominican situation: the strictly hemispheric nature of the exercise and U.S. dominance in the hemisphere, the geographical and ideological isolation of the Dominican Republic, the general decay of the regime, the availability of political alternatives within the state, and the nature of the crime committed.

That the Dominican economy suffered during the period of sanctions cannot be doubted. However, such difficulties can be attributed as much to the factors set forth in Chapter 4 as to OAS sanctions. In addition, the economic problems of the country during the period of sanctions might be attributed in part to two other factors.

First, the political chaos of the post-Trujillo period. The existence of the private armies of Ramfis and Pétan, and the state of almost civil war, were not conducive to any long-term economic plans. Clearly such an environment precluded significant domestic or foreign capital investment. Political uncertainty, to the extent chronicled earlier, prevented sophisticated Dominican fiscal and monetary management of public and private funds.

Second, the drain on the economy by misappropriation of public--or even private--funds abroad is unknown. For example, when the Venezuelan dictator Marcos Pérez Jiménez fled his country, he absconded with over $400 million; the result was virtual bankruptcy of the Venezuelan treasury. Similarly, when members of the Trujillo family fled, they did not arrive in exile in dire poverty. Between June and November 1961, members of the family had ample opportunity to contemplate exile and the possibility of converting Dominican holdings into numbered Swiss bank accounts. If it could be demonstrated, for example, that a total as small as $100 million (12.5 percent of the estimated Trujillo personal wealth) had slipped out of the country, the economic implications would be immense. A figure approximately equivalent to one year's Dominican public budget is substantial. All other economic pressures, economic sanctions included, would pale into insignificance when compared with the conversion of 100 million Dominican pesos to hard currency. This factor, perhaps more than anything else, explains why there was a rapid decline in gold and foreign exchange holdings between September 1960 (over $45 million) and September 1961 (less than $10 million). It also explains the sudden pressure, in late 1961, upon the Dominican balance of payments, a pressure that was temporarily eased by the $25 million U.S. credit in January 1962.

In view of the statements by Dominican politicians that the sanctions were largely of moral worth, it would appear that the major causes of Dominican economic difficulties were of domestic origin. This must be qualified, of course, by two general observations. First, the OAS, by drawing attention to the country, was significantly responsible for the atmosphere of uncertainty that would have dissuaded foreign trade with, and investment in, the Dominican Republic. Second, OAS Resolution I provided an umbrella-like mandate for fairly massive U.S. intervention in the domestic affairs of the country. What was important, therefore, was not the economic sanctions but the breadth of interpretation placed upon Resolution I, the progenitor of those sanctions. The economic sanctions, while of limited economic utility, were of essential political value because they made plausible political change within the country. They also made acceptable OAS and, more importantly, U.S. direct involvement in the nature and direction of that change.

Sanctions therefore became part of the varied response to a dangerous political situation. Furthermore, because this response was largely political, although law was employed to strengthen the political stance, sanctions became only one aspect of the OAS strategy. If the members of the OAS had simply condemned the Dominican Republic and imposed the provisions of Resolution I in isolation from political pressure, it is improbable that economic sanctions would have succeeded. The OAS in the 1960 Dominican situation was under no illusion about the intentions of Resolution I. The economic sanctions were the most simplistic form of coercion imaginable, and they contrast vividly with elaborate schemes worked out by the League of Nations for Italy.

The OAS members were straightforwardly requested to sever diplomatic relations and to suspend shipments of arms, petroleum, and trucks and parts to the Dominican Republic. In retrospect it would appear that there never was a profound belief that the sanctions would have a significant economic impact. That the sanctions might have had an impact was fundamentally incidental to the broad political fiat that the OAS voted to itself.

The formality of imposing the sanctions, and their later removal, served as points of reference for the Dominicans and warned them, in the former instance, that their government's activities were disapproved and, in the latter instance, that they were once again welcomed into the fold of Latin American society.

In the Dominican case, sanctions became another component of the process of causing political change within the Dominican Republic. For the Dominicans they were both a reminder of the OAS presence and a ploy to be bantered about among Dominican politicians. For the OAS, and more particularly for the United States, sanctions were a useful weapon in the processes of negotiation, persuasion, and coercion. Sanctions, therefore, were an addition to the conventional techniques of negotiation; and for the United States they were the mandate for outright intervention. They were used to impress upon the Dominicans the seriousness of the situation and the consequent requirement for renewed and more substantive negotiations. In this political context the OAS and U.S. sanctions were quite effective.

The Rhodesian case, finally, offers some rather interesting variations because the sanctions initially appeared to be succeeding. That is, they were affecting the Rhodesian economy to such an extent that negotiations toward a settlement of the dispute were undertaken in an almost crisis atmosphere. However, the Rhodesian case emphasized one vital aspect of any sanctions program: that to achieve results, they must undermine the confidence of the target state and its population. Specifically, the failure by Britain to employ a "hammer blow" to undermine white confidence was fatal.[3] Rhodesia, as a primary-goods producer, is fairly susceptible to world economic fluctuations; and complete mandatory UN sanctions in November 1965, combined with a limited show or employment of force, would probably have brought the Smith regime down. Such a move at that time might very well have alienated white Rhodesians and many Britains in the short run, but would have added immeasurably to a satisfactory solution in the long run.

Instead, presumably in a spirit of misguided fairness, Britain vacillated and Wilson became the buffoon for Smith's militants. In addition, the failure by Britain to request UN support from the beginning, irrespective of the domestic constitutional issue, served both to undermine British credibility insofar as Africans were concerned and to provide Rhodesia with time to get back on its feet. Thus, by July 1967, when the regime's Finance Minister, John Wrathall, introduced his budget, the country was recovering. That budget included a 9 percent rise in expenditures, with an increase in short- and long-term borrowings designed to mitigate deflationary effects of sanctions. In addition, through subsidies for diversification of crops to replace tobacco, increases in old-age pensions, increased contributions to medical services, and export tax incentives, Wrathall was able to exude the sort of optimism that bolstered white Rhodesian morale.

The man-in-the-street whose morale is at a new high point is also likely to take the view that

Rhodesia can get along "very nicely thank you"
without a settlement that involves making substantial concessions to Mr. Wilson, the Commonwealth
and the United Nations.[4]

Consequently, as Rhodesian morale increased, the frequency
of sanctions violations became greater and more blatant.
By early 1968 cargoes of Rhodesia tobacco and cigarettes
(usually picked up in Cape Town) were popping up all over
Europe.[5]

What occurred, therefore, was that the Rhodesian case
lost its crisis essence and became a face-to-face match or
standoff. Then, as the unity of purpose in Britain began
to waver and domestic political support crumbled (as Rhodesia became a domestic political issue), the British bargaining strength diminished. Consequently, when the British government began to reconsider the use of force (in
March 1968), it was too late. One South African newspaper
commented, "Taking up arms against Rhodesia would be the
most outrageous folly of the century, far eclipsing all
other errors of judgement perpetrated by Mr. Wilson and
his colleagues."[6] In Britain the Manchester _Guardian_
(Liberal) advocated the use of force in editorials, while
the _Daily Mail_ (Conservative) retorted that to send British
soldiers to fight white Rhodesians in the name of morality
was "smooth hypocrisy."[7] The arguments opposing force in
1968 were the same as those in 1965, the only difference
being that they were probably more valid in 1968 than they
would have been in 1965.

In brief, therefore, Rhodesian sanctions have not succeeded in the short run because they were not decisively
and efficiently imposed. However, it would seem highly
probable that they will ultimately succeed because they
will provide a constant focus on Rhodesia and implicitly
legitimize violent African attempts to overthrow racism
in the country. Moreover, this process will be facilitated
if Portugal withdraws from Mozambique, as seems to be a
distant possibility.[8] Time, in this circumstance, is on
the side of Africans, for they have to eternity to continue
the process of attrition.

SANCTIONS: A THEORY

Four broad assumptions underlie this discussion.
First, that sanctions impose some discernible alteration

in the target state's regular patterns of trade, production, and internal consumption, and that these patterns are readily visible.

Second, that while imported goods can be quite varied, the greatest initial impact of sanctions will be found in decreased imports of luxury goods. This will be followed by a leveling-off period and, in the absence of additional sanctions (including military sanctions), a recovery will occur. This may be worked out by a ratio between value of imports and volume of imports: for example, $200 (value) = 1 ton (volume) of chrome, or $200 (value) = 1 ounce (volume) of refined gold. However, in luxury items the value-to-volume ratio tends to be higher in favor of value (perfume, wine, liquors, consumer durables). Thus, a rapid initial decline in the value of imports may be only an indication that high-value luxury items are being sacrificed (this was certainly the case for Rhodesian imports). This is of limited utility, aside from propaganda value, to the achievement of the objectives of a particular sanctions scheme. (It was suggested in the Dominican case, of course, that the sanctions had an impact on luxury consumption by wealthy and upper middle-class Dominicans, thereby creating incentive for them to find a basis for accommodation with the OAS. This seemed particularly true after Trujillo's assassination, when domestic political solutions were being sought.) It is also very possible that a rapid decline in value of imports may include sophisticated capital-investment goods, although an accurate judgment upon this point would require a detailed knowledge of the nature of the target state's economy and its plans for development. In real terms, the rapid value decline of imports can be deceptive to exponents of economic sanctions because of the tendency to see the sudden decrease as confirmation that sanctions are working. The impact of a rapid volume decline would normally be much more significant to the bulk of the population because it would tend to affect normal private consumption patterns and income sources. In the short run, the sacrifice of luxury items will simply cause annoyance, whereas what is required is long-run economic stagnation and unemployment.

The third assumption relates to the ability of the target state to control and/or combat the impact of some, but not all, sanctions. For example, the target state cannot significantly increase the number of tourists who enter the country of their own volition. However, it can control, within limits, the patterns of domestic production and consumption.* Hence, statistics on the probable impact of sanctions must be divided into external and internal categories, as determined by the target state's ability to respond effectively to the adverse implications of any particular set of statistics.

The fourth assumption is that a target state will require support, especially from contiguous states. Clearly, if statistics demonstrate that the target state is suffering from inflationary trends (rapid rises in price indexes) while employment is dropping (declines in activity in service trades, or decreases in per capita productivity), then the target state will have to take countermeasures. Such measures can be facilitated greatly if the target state has third-party assistance for currency conversions, surreptitious trade and barter transactions, and transportation facilities. In addition, if the status of the contiguous states is of the quality of hostages, either overtly (Rhodesia and Zambia and Malawi) or covertly (Italy and Austria, Hungary, and, to some extent, Switzerland), then the capacity to resist sanctions is dramatically improved.

Finally, two incidental points that should be mentioned are that if the bulk of the target state's population is poor** to begin with, then the marginal increase of poverty due to sanctions may prove to be negligible; and that a long-term imposition of sanctions may be so long as to permit diversification of the economy, including substitution of products, development of alternative sources of supply, and arrangement of barter deals for provision of necessities. These two factors can significantly distort the projected impact of sanctions and must be accounted for in advance planning.

Advance planning, even hastily undertaken, seems to be a key ingredient of any sanctions scheme. Such planning should not be confined simply to those commodities in which the target state is overtly vulnerable (Rhodesian tobacco),

---

*It can also control statistics on domestic matters, but not externally determined statistics (trade statistics from usual trading partners) unless a de facto conspiracy exists to deceive through statistical manipulation (German copper imports from Rhodesia during late 1966 and 1967).

**Here a problem occurs vis-à-vis Rhodesia, for there is no doubt that the bulk of the population (blacks) is poor. However, the ruling minority appears to be fairly well off, so in this context only bulk refers to the white minority, for Africans are functionally apolitical.

although this is certainly necessary. Advance sanctions planning should look at five elements: political stability (or lack of it) of governing leaders; broad characteristics of the target economy (ratio of agriculture to industry); the possibilities of agricultural and industrial diversification (thereby gearing sanctions to anticipate change); the target state's relationship with contiguous states and/or other friendly states and neutrals (if, in fact, the latter can be considered acceptable from the international agency's viewpoint); and the levels of income of functional participants in the political system (this would include fringe participants, such as members of a street mob). This latter element becomes significant if politically functional citizens are living on low incomes, that is, if subsistence living is the norm rather than the exception.

Of the above five elements involved in advance sanctions planning, subsistence living and a dominant agricultural society are vital primary considerations for the economic impact of sanctions. Political stability of the target state's regime becomes significant only when the possibility exists that indigenous opposition can be generated and supported toward supplanting the incumbent. Diversification of the economy and contiguous states are related to political stability when these two elements assist the target state's governing regime to thwart sanctions and remain in office (Rhodesia and, to a lesser extent, Italy). In summary, however, the success (or political impact) of sanctions will be inversely related to the rapidity with which the target state can respond to overcome sanctions. Consequently, the real task of sanctions is not just to cause short-term economic and political fluctuations; rather, the sanctions scheme must be geared to undermine the foundation upon which a governing regime functions. Sanctions, regardless of the type, must be viewed as a political rather than an economic function. The error in the past has been to view sanctions from the perspective of whether or not they caused economic problems when, in fact, they should have been viewed politically and directed toward specifically political goals. It is further suggested here that this narrow view is a consequence of conceptualizing sanctions as simply the enforcement portion of a juridically perceived international legal system. In the following pages the point is enlarged upon by viewing the impact of sanctions from a predominantly economic viewpoint. From this position it should be apparent that the strict economic consequences of sanctions will achieve goals only under very limited and exceptional circumstances.

The first phase of the concluding hypothesis is that the period immediately after the imposition of economic sanctions, there will be a rapid decline in trade.* If all contracts are immediately suspended, excluding goods in transit, this decline will be most noticeable within the first two or three months. This is the approximate amount of time required to process and transport cargo by sea; and it will vary, for example, within a highly developed regional trading system such as Latin America. A hypothetical outline of this impact is shown in Figure 6.1. If the economic sanctions included complete imports and exports (they did not include the latter in the Dominican case), the following would occur.

Exports would decline less rapidly than imports at first, because the sanctioned state has more control over its exports and because it has a greater impetus to obtain and retain foreign currencies gained from export earnings, in order to meet the impending strain on its existing foreign currency and gold reserves.

At some point, but not necessarily six months or the "level" of 1.5 indicated in Figure 6.1, the target state's economy would reach a low, or stabilization, point.** This would be the level at which the economy proved itself capable of meeting its own needs with its own resources: limited self-sufficiency. This has been designated as the "mean economic subsistence level," but it actually would not represent a static level, as suggested in Figure 6.1. More precisely, it is a compromise of a number of subsistence levels as determined by an aggregation of subsistence levels for all functionally political income groups. In cases, for example, of a limited import embargo (the Dominican case), the mean economic subsistence level probably would be reached over a much more extended period of time. The absence of an export embargo would preclude a rapid overall economic decline in the short run. In the very long run, as the necessity for imports eroded the financial return on exports, a mean subsistence level probably would be reached. Clearly, other adverse economic factors, which would generally debilitate the health of the state's economy, would spur the rapidity of the decline, subject

---

*This could be refined into value and volume, but for these conclusions such a distinction is unnecessary.

**These "levels" are simply convenient for this discussion. In practice they could depict individual commodity or aggregate commodities indexes.

FIGURE 6.1

Impact of Economic Sanctions
(import and export embargoes and partial import embargo)

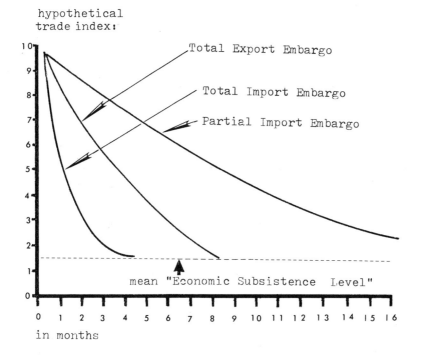

hypothetical
trade index:

Total Export Embargo

Total Import Embargo

Partial Import Embargo

mean "Economic Subsistence Level"

in months

Source: Compiled by the author.

to such countervailing measures as price supports, subsidies, rationing, and forced overemployment (overemployment
was certainly forced upon the Ford Motor Company in Rhodesia by decree in early 1966).

The mean economic subsistence level could be obtained
by compiling information on two separate features of the
target state's society. First, each income group will
find that its economic subsistence level is relative to
its normal pattern and standard of living. For example,
the wealthy might consider a 10-year-old automobile to be
bare subsistence, while the poor, lacking automobiles,
might consider one bowl of rice a day, rather than two,
to be bare subsistence. The second feature of the mean

economic subsistence level is that when one minimum subsistence level has apparently been reached, circumstances may force a slight reduction in it. For example, the wealthy person may be forced to place his auto temporarily in storage, while the poor person may be forced to survive on half a bowl of rice per day.

The precise level of mean economic subsistence will vary in relationship to the demands of the population (their accustomed standard of living) and the ability of the economy to meet those demands--industrialization versus agriculture versus mixed economy. Over time the level will adjust slightly upward and downward, but it will tend to remain relatively static unless the sanctioned economy is able to respond favorably to the pressure. This latter observation serves as an introduction to the second phase of the hypothesis.

Once a mean economic subsistence level has been reached, the economy will not become much more depressed in the short run. In the long run the maintenance of this level will depend upon the sanctioning states' abilities to counteract the target state's resistance and/or upon a tightening of the sanctions to plug gaps and to adjust defects. All of this is premised, of course, upon the continuation of the target state's objectionable policies or the absence of significant political change. It might be suggested, for example, that in the Dominican case the OAS apparently tightened the sanctions by the extension of Resolution I in January 1961. Two things should be recalled, however, about this extension. First, the sanctions of August 1960 had been of no particular economic consequence by December 1960. Second, the January extension initiated the first real OAS economic sanctions. Thus, while the Dominican Republic's objectionable behavior continued into 1961, the OAS's major economic response began only in January of that year.

In the Rhodesian case, while sanctions have been tightened periodically, the most serious moves were made (in December 1966) after the initial and most devastating impact had been felt. Thus, Security Council resolutions on mandatory sanctions have been too late, in most respects, to achieve the desired effect. Finally, in the Italian case the mechanical processes of arriving at a sanctions program took longer to put into effect than the Italians took in winning their war and intimidating Britain and France.

If target states have fairly diverse economies, it is probable that they will be able to recover much more rapidly. This would be the result of substitution, diversification of the economy, and the development of clandestine sources and markets. Basically, at this stage the impetus would rest with the target state. For once it stabilized its economy, it could prudently find new sources and markets, as was done by Rhodesia and, to a lesser extent, Italy.

Of equal significance is the time factor, because the longer the sanctions are imposed, the more diverse become the opportunities to circumvent them. It is strange, but nevertheless true, that sanctioned states do not sit idly awaiting the outcome of an international onslaught. Once the events immediately surrounding the offense fade from public view or are replaced by new crises elsewhere, the target state may begin its quiet return to the world scene. The sanctioning states may begin to mellow in their positions and, as happened in the Dominican case, may remove the sanctions at the earliest possible moment.* It also might be suggested in this case that, because of the limited nature of the import embargo, and had other economic and political factors not intervened, time was certainly on the side of the Dominicans. This suggestion is implicit in the "partial import embargo" curve in Figure 6.1.

In other situations, where opinions mellow but policy is fixed, it may happen that relations between the sanctioned and sanctioning states return to informal normalcy, with many parties--including the target state--agreeing not to press for a formal normalization of relations (Rhodesia's representatives in Lisbon, Cape Town, and Washington). Finally, the target state may benefit from crises generated elsewhere and, for various reasons, the imperative of maintaining the sanctions will become less than the imperative that the target state be reintegrated into the world or regional community. For example, the burgeoning United States-Cuba confrontation was a significant factor favoring early removal of the sanctions against the Dominicans; and the emergence of a militant Germany certainly aided Italy's hasty rehabilitation in 1936.

In the long run, the target state thus acquires a political and emotional advantage. Its position can be strengthened further by the extent to which it proves capa-

---

*In the Dominican case there is a temptation to suggest that a certain amount of symbolism was involved. Or was it just coincidence that the Council voted to extend sanctions on January 4, 1961, and to remove them on January 4, 1962?

ble not only of resisting the sanctions but also of recovering, by its own wiles, from their impact. Once this advantage is gained, it remains only for the target state to gain the upper hand by demonstrating that the sanctions are more costly to the sanctioning states than to the object of their action.[9]

The ability of the target state to maneuver into this position appears to be related to a number of factors, both political and economic. Initially, the economic factors are of primary importance, because they are the means by which the target state most effectively and immediately responds to the sanctions. However, as noted earlier, both domestic and international politics are crucial, and time generally favors the target state.

There is apparently a correlation between the nature of the target state's economy and its ability to resist sanctions. If the economy is diverse and/or highly industrialized, it should recover much more rapidly than a primarily agricultural economy. Figure 6.2, therefore, builds upon Figure 6.1 and sets forth three hypothetical rates of economic recovery from economic sanctions imposed and maintained. The notations a, b, and c represent what may be termed "recovery take-off stages,"[10] that is, those points where an economy increases indigenous productivity beyond the mean economic subsistence level, and meets and surpasses its minimum requirements in the face of sanctions. In general the Dominican Republic would be at the c level, although, because of the limited nature of the OAS economic sanctions, the decline was not as rapid as indicated in Figure 6.2, nor is it probable that any approximation to a mean economic subsistence level was reached. The recovery rate, while approximately the same inclination as c, would begin at a higher level, c^1. Italy, and to a large extent Rhodesia, could be depicted at the approximate b level, although it could be argued quite persuasively that Italy would have the more rapid take-off rate.

The hypothetical rates of recovery suggested in Figure 6.2 do not include any additional assistance that might be obtained by target states from contiguous states in the form of collaboration or facilities for transshipped goods. For this discussion it relates exclusively to the indigenous capacity to recover.

Whether the Dominican Republic could, or could not, have recovered from the imposition of sanctions is unknown, although if the hypothesis advanced in Figure 6.2 has merit, the country's economy would have survived handily. However, Trujillo's assassination and the subsequent polit-

FIGURE 6.2

Economic Sanctions:

Impact and Recovery Rates

hypothetical
trade index:

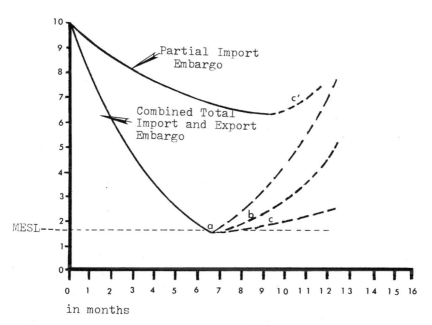

a = Diversified, highly industrial economy.
b = Diversified economy: agriculture and primary
     and secondary industry.
c = Primarily agricultural economy, some industry.
c^1 = Mean recovery rate for all economies subject to
     partial import embargo.

Source: Compiled by the author.

ical events followed much too rapidly, and culminated too
suddenly, to permit any extended projections. Had Trujillo
survived, and had the sanctions been restricted to those
contained in Resolution I, and had the United States not
intervened, then it would have been quite possible for the
regime to have survived somewhat longer. Yet most of the
ingredients for the collapse existed in one form or another
by the time the OAS became involved; and these, in combination, undoubtedly would have caused the regime to disinte-
grate eventually.

In the Italian case Mussolini's regime was solidly en-
trenched, and sanctions do not appear to have threatened
its existence in any manner. Obviously, if the sanctions
had prevented Italy from completing its Ethiopian conquest,
they would have struck a serious blow against the foundation of Mussolini's appeal. For that reason, therefore,
Mussolini could not have permitted the sanctions and any
related short-term intimidation to dissuade him from his
objective. In addition, because his regime and its African adventure posed no perceptible threat--in fact, perhaps
the contrary was true--to the primary interests of Britain
and France (especially the latter), there was no imperative
reason for these countries to alienate Mussolini to the
extent required by the concept of collective security.
Sanctions were scarcely more than a passing, and embarrassing, nuisance to Italy and did little more than provide
Ethiopians with broad public sympathy. The fact that the
Hoare-Laval agreement so closely resembled the 1906 European tripartite agreement on spheres of influence in Ethiopia suggests that Mussolini lost little, and the League
gained nothing, from the imposition of sanctions. Of
course, that conclusion is subject to one qualification:
that states did learn that collective multilateral sanctions
in international law demand a high commitment price.

Finally, in the Rhodesian situation we are faced basically with an "if only" situation. If only Britain had
sought complete mandatory sanctions in November 1965; if
only a modest show of force had been employed; if only
South Africa and Portugal had been placed under more careful and rigid scrutiny; if only African states had possessed
a greater capacity to act, rather than talk, in an economic
and political manner. Rhodesia appears to have survived
the structure of sanctions that has been developed during
the past years; the Smith regime gambled with its political future and appears largely to have been successful in
the short run. However, should the Smith regime fail to
arrive at a negotiated solution with Britain that is sat-

378

isfactory to Africans, then presumably the de facto status of Rhodesia will continue indefinitely. This limbo existence, providing it is periodically reaffirmed at the United Nations and states are reminded of their obligations, will only cause inconvenience for the regime and some minor embarrassments for those governments that would associate with Rhodesia. However, as suggested earlier, the impetus eventually lies with Africans, for in the absence of a negotiated settlement, Rhodesia will be doomed in perpetuity to a fortress existence and will bear the brunt of continued and prolonged violence. Sanctions in the Rhodesian case therefore legitimize the extralegal activities of those states and groups concerned to see the objectionable behavior rectified. In a few words, therefore, these three cases emphasize the role of sanctions as a facilitator or expediter of negotiations.

Little has been done in the available literature to assess the actual utility of economic sanctions and their capacity to influence political events in international relations. Most of the opinions and studies that exist begin with the supposition that sanctions will succeed if properly applied and if good intentions exist.[11]

A detailed and comprehensive scheme of economic sanctions, prepared and approved by an international organization, might bring about desired organizational objectives, although this cannot be certified absolutely. The sanctions appeared to be effective in the Dominican case because they were imposed at a time when the regime was already in serious difficulties. In most respects they were a salutary gesture by the OAS that served only to exacerbate an already difficult domestic plight. They were unsuccessful elsewhere because similar weakened conditions did not exist.

A comprehensive scheme of economic sanctions unquestionably denotes more than a moral commitment. An essential ingredient of economic warfare is a form of physical blockade, and it would seem most appropriate that a comprehensive scheme of sanctions also include a similar physical involvement. That the OAS did not find it necessary to employ a blockade might support the view that regional agency application of economic sanctions is qualitatively different from that of its universal counterpart, although the Cuban "quarantine" raises another perspective. The regional organization has the advantage, for the reasons that led members to create and maintain the organization are the same reasons that permit it successfully to discipline transgressors of the rules, ethics, and law of the regional subsystem. From the regional organization's vantage point, the result is fairly evident. If the individual state values its regional ties, the regional organization has a psychological, and at times practical, advantage in its relations with any deviant member state. However, the multilateral universal agency is less specific-goal-motivated, and hence the ability to identify individual state goals with those of the organization are reduced considerably. This leads to loose law enforcement.

Bluntly stated, sanctions are not by themselves the answer to the problem of enforcing the decisions of international organizations by nondestructive coercion, although they are a potential component of any solution to a problem and therefore cannot be dismissed outright. Sanctions have a role when not blindly rushed into; and each political situation that might suggest recourse to sanctions must be judged in terms not of whether the sanctions might work but of whether the sanctions will work in conjunction with other means and in the face of the target state's capacity to resist. Moreover, such a judgment must include an assessment as to whether the sanctions can usefully contribute anything toward achieving the objectives of the organization. International organizations cannot continue to afford the embarrassment of ill-conceived sanctions, no matter how well defined their intentions.

GUIDELINES TO IMPLEMENTATION

In the preceding section a number of broad elements inherent in any international sanctions scheme were suggested: political stability; agricultural versus industrial versus mixed economy; diversification; contiguous states; and standard of living of functional participants in the political system. However, two other major guidelines emerge, and both should be explored in greater detail by international organizations. One essential theme is delegation; that is, international organizations are faced with two possibilities--deviant state behavior and, more recently, deviant group behavior--and hence they should be more prepared to delegate primary responsibility to those states or organizations that have the greatest direct involvement in the immediate goals of the organization. In order to handle deviant groups more effectively, international organizations must delegate much broader authority, as often as possible, to functional organizations that would be responsible for directly imposing sanctions. For example, this would mean a broader mandate to the International Civil Aviation Organization to impose sanctions relating to air travel under authority of a Chapter VII mandatory sanctions resolution. In this type of case ICAO would be authorized to employ the provisions of Article 41 of the Charter to enforce condemnatory resolutions upon states responsible for violations of air law. The international organization always should be prepared to reinforce delegated authority while retaining primary responsibility when the need arises. In dealing with deviant states the same type of principle is applicable. Consequently international organizations should delegate primary authority as well as responsibility to regional organizations and probably to major powers—or, in lieu of that, to the state(s) in the organization most directly affected by the target state's offensive behavior (for example, Britain and Zambia in the Rhodesian case). Again, of course, responsibility must be retained by the delegating agency, but the locus of solution of international enforcement problems must be more clearly identified with those states and agencies directly involved.

This does not mean that other states and organizations may willfully neglect their responsibilities, or that we are returning to the status of bilateral power politics. Rather, it acknowledges simply that international law enforcement is a question of primary interests and procedures; and therefore procedures must be created to recognize that fact. Collective security through international law enforcement is unrealistic when the premises upon which it is constructed are ephemeral and unrealistic. In conclusion, to be an effective international law enforcement technique, international sanctions must be applied by those with primary interest in the solution being sought—that is, to apply a bit of marketing jargon, as close to the "point of sale" as possible.

NOTES

1. James Barber, South Africa's Foreign Policy, 1945-1970 (London: Oxford University Press, 1973), p. 283.
2. Thomas Schelling, Strategy of Conflict (New York: Oxford, 1963), has developed this in a much more elaborate form.
3. Barber, op. cit., p. 283.
4. Financial Gazette (South Africa), July 28, 1968.

5. The case of the ship <u>Swellendam</u>, which loaded a
cargo of Rhodesian cigarettes in Cape Town on January 11,
1968, was only one example. On the general subject of loopholes, see <u>Christian Science Monitor</u>, March 28, 1968. The
cigarettes in question were probably made by the British-
American Tobacco Company. Some of the cigarettes were unloaded in Antwerp and Rotterdam.

6. <u>Sunday Mail</u>, March 17, 1968.

7. Manchester <u>Guardian</u>, March 21, 1968; <u>Daily Mail</u>,
March 22, 1968.

8. António de Spínola, <u>Portugal e o futuro</u> (Lisbon:
Arcadia, 1974). Spínola returned a hero from Portuguese
Guinea to the position of Deputy Chief of Staff. On March
15, 1974, he was removed from this post, apparently because
of his views in this book. He then headed the coup that
overthrew Premier Marcello Caetano on April 25, 1974. Since
then Portugal's African territories have been moving rapidly
toward a new status and this poses serious consequences for
Rhodesia.

9. Rhodesia has done this in a little brochure,
<u>Sanctions--The Cost to Britain</u> (Salisbury: Ministry of In-
formation, November 1967).

10. This expression is used without prejudice to anything Rostow, or those who agree or disagree with him,
would say about the phrase "take-off stage." In the unencumbered form presented here, the term adequately describes
the intention sought to be conveyed. See W. W. Rostow,
<u>The Process of Economic Growth</u> (New York: Norton, 1962),
pp. 247 ff.

11. For example, see O. Bruck, <u>Les sanctions en droit
international public</u> (Paris: Pédone, 1933); E. Clark, ed.,
<u>Boycotts and Peace: A Report by the Committee on Economic
Sanctions</u> (New York: Harper and Bros., 1932); H. Feis,
<u>Seen from E. A.: Three International Episodes</u> (New York:
Norton, 1966); Royal Institute of International Affairs,
<u>Sanctions: The Character of International Sanctions and
Their Application</u> (London: Chatham House, 1935); and some
of the essays in R. Segal, ed., <u>Sanctions Against South
Africa</u> (Harmondsworth: Penguin Books, 1964).

SELECTED BIBLIOGRAPHY

General Books

Asamoah, O. Y. The Legal Significance of the Declarations of the General Assembly of the United Nations. The Hague: Nijhoff, 1966.

Berliner, J. S. Soviet Economic Aid. New York: Praeger, 1958.

Briggs, H. W. The Law of Nations. 2nd edition. New York: Appleton-Century-Crofts, 1962.

Brinton, C. The Anatomy of Revolution. New York: Vintage, 1965.

De Visscher, C. Théories et réalites en droit international public. 3rd edition. Paris: Pédone, 1960.

Doody, F. S. Introduction to the Use of Economic Indicators. New York: Random House, 1965.

Dror, Y. Crazy States. Lexington, Mass.: Lexington Books, 1971.

Dulles, A. The Craft of Intelligence. New York: Harper & Row, 1963.

Easton, D. A Framework for Political Analysis. Englewood Cliffs, N.J.: Prentice-Hall, 1965.

Ebenstein, W. Totalitarianism: New Perspectives. New York: Holt, Rinehart, 1962.

Eden, A. Facing the Dictators. London: Cassell and Co., 1962.

Finkelstein, M. S., and L. S. Finkelstein. Collective Security. New York: Chandler, 1966.

Fishel, W. R., ed. Vietnam: Anatomy of a Conflict. Itasca, Ill.: Peacock, 1968.

Friedrich, C. J., ed. Totalitarianism: Proceedings of a Conference. Cambridge, Mass.: Harvard University Press, 1959.

_____, and Z. Brzezinski. Totalitarian Dictatorship and Autocracy. New York: Praeger, 1962.

Goodrich, L. M. The United Nations. New York: Crowell, 1959.

_____, and E. Hambro. Charter of the United Nations: Commentary and Documents. Boston: World Peace Foundation, 1946.

Gross, L., ed. International Law in the Twentieth Century. New York: Appleton-Century-Crofts, 1969.

Hobbes, T. Leviathan. Everyman's edition. London: J. M. Dent, 1957.

Horowitz, I. L. Three Worlds of Development: The Theory and Practice of International Stratification. New York: Oxford, 1966.

Hurwitz, M. L., ed. The Diplomatic Yearbook. New York: Funk and Wagnalls, 1951.

Ikle, F. C. How Nations Negotiate. New York: Harper & Row, 1964.

Kahng, T. J. Law, Politics, and the Security Council. 2nd edition, rev. The Hague: Nijhoff, 1969.

Kaplan, M. A. System and Process in International Politics. New York: Wiley, 1964.

_____, and N. deB. Katzenbach. The Political Foundations of International Law. New York: Wiley, 1961.

Kelman, H. C. International Behavior: A Social Psychological Analysis. New York: Holt, Rinehart, 1965.

Livingstone, Dame A. The Peace Ballot: The Official History. London: Victor Gollancz, 1935.

Lowenstein, C. Political Power and the Governmental Process. Chicago: University of Chicago Press, 1957.

Maine, Sir Henry. Ancient Law. Everyman's edition. London: J. M. Dent, 1960.

McDougal, M. S., and associates. <u>Studies in World Public Order</u>. New Haven, Conn.: Yale University Press, 1960.

_____, and F. P. Feliciano. <u>Law and Minimum World Order</u>. New Haven, Conn.: Yale University Press, 1961.

McNair, Lord A. <u>The Law of Treaties</u>. Oxford: Clarendon Press, 1961.

Morgenthau, H. J. <u>Politics Among Nations</u>. 4th edition. New York: Knopf, 1967.

Mueller, J. E., ed. <u>Approaches to Measurement in International Relations: A Non-Evangelical Survey</u>. New York: Appleton-Century-Crofts, 1969.

Nurske, R. <u>Problems of Capital Formation of Underdeveloped Countries</u>. Oxford: Oxford University Press, 1953.

Organski, A. F. K. <u>The Stages of Political Development</u>. New York: Knopf, 1965.

Pfluger, F. <u>Die einseitigen Rechtsgeschäfte im Volkerrecht</u>. Zurich: Schulthess, 1936.

Pruitt, D. G., and R. C. Snyder. <u>Theory and Research on the Causes of War</u>. Englewood Cliffs, N.J.: Prentice-Hall, 1969.

Pye, L. <u>Aspects of Political Development</u>. Boston: Little Brown, 1965.

Rostow, W. W. <u>The Process of Economic Growth</u>. New York: Norton, 1962.

Russett, B. M. <u>World Handbook of Political and Social Indicators</u>. New Haven, Conn.: Yale University Press, 1965.

Scheinman, L., and D. Wilkinson. <u>International Law and Political Crisis: An Analytic Casebook</u>. Boston: Little Brown, 1968.

Talmon, J. L. <u>The Origins of Totalitarian Democracy</u>. New York: Praeger, 1960.

Von der Mehden, F. R. <u>Politics of Developing Nations</u>. Englewood Cliffs, N.J.: Prentice-Hall, 1969.

Whitaker, U. G. <u>Politics and Power: A Text</u>. New York: Harper & Row, 1964.

Wise, D., and T. B. Ross. <u>The Invisible Government</u>. New York: Random House, 1964.

Wright, Q. <u>International Relations</u>. New York: Appleton-Century-Crofts, 1955.

General Articles

Beaufré, A. "Le côntrole et la manoeuvre des crises," <u>Stratégie</u> no. 11 (1967): 5-16.

Bowman, I. "The Strategy of Territorial Decisions," <u>Foreign Affairs</u> 24 (1946): 177-94.

Danelski, D. J., ed., et al. "Law and Conflict Resolution," <u>Journal of Conflict Resolution</u> 11 (1967): 1-116.

Grisez, G. G. "Moral Objectivity and the Cold War," <u>Ethics</u> 70 (1960): 291-305.

Jones, C. O. "Representation in Congress: The Case of the House Agriculture Committee," <u>APSR</u> 55 (1961): 358-67.

Lissitzyn, O. J. "Western and Soviet Perspectives in International Law," <u>Proceedings: ASIL</u> 53 (1959): 21-30.

_____. "International Law in a Divided World," <u>International Conciliation</u> 542 (March 1963): 3-69.

Masters, N. A. "Committee Assignments in the House of Representatives," <u>APSR</u> 55 (1961): 345-57.

Nye, J. S. "Corruption and Political Development: A Cost-Benefit Analysis," <u>APSR</u> 61 (1967): 417-27.

Phillips, A. W. "The Relation Between Unemployment and the Rate of Change of Money Rate in the United Kingdom, 1861-1957," <u>Economica</u> 25 (1958): 283-99.

Tucker, R. C. "The Dictator and Totalitarianism," _World Politics_ 17 (1965): 555-83.

Williams, G. L. "International Law and the Controversy Concerning the Word 'Law,'" _BYIL_ 22 (1945): 146-53.

Books on Sanctions

Arnold-Forster, W. _The Blockade, 1914-1919_. Oxford Pamphlets on World Affairs no. 16. Oxford: Oxford University Press, 1939.

Aroneau, E. _La définition de l'aggression_. Paris: Editions Internationales, 1958.

Atwater, E. _American Regulation of Arms Exports_. Washington, D.C.: Carnegie Endowment, 1941.

Bailey, T. A. _The Art of Diplomacy_. New York: Appleton-Century-Crofts, 1968.

Barros, J. _The Corfu Incident: Mussolini and the League of Nations_. Princeton, N.J.: Princeton University Press, 1965.

_____. _Betrayal from Within: Joseph Avenol_. New Haven, Conn.: Yale University Press, 1969.

Beveridge, Sir W. H. _British Food Control_. New Haven, Conn.: Yale University Press, 1928.

Bowett, D. _Self-Defence in International Law_. Manchester: Manchester University Press, 1958.

Brownlie, I. _International Law and the Use of Force by States_. Oxford: Clarendon Press, 1963.

Bruck, O. _Les sanctions en droit international public_. Paris: Pédone, 1933.

Childs, H. L. _Public Opinion_. Toronto: Van Nostrand, 1965.

Clark, E. _Boycotts and Peace_. New York: Twentieth Century Fund, 1930.

_____, ed. Boycotts and Peace: A Report by the Committee on Economic Sanctions. New York: Harper & Bros., 1932.

Colbert, E. S. Retaliation in International Law. New York: King's Crown Press, Columbia University, 1948.

Consett, W. W. P. The Triumph of Unarmed Forces, (1914-1918). London: Williams and Norgate, 1923.

Eckel, E. C. Coal, Iron and War. New York: Henry Holt, 1930.

Emery, B. The Strategy of Raw Materials. New York: Macmillan, 1934.

Feis, H. Seen from E.A.: Three International Episodes. New York: Knopf, 1947; Norton, 1966.

Fisher, R. International Conflict and the Behavioral Sciences. New York: Basic Books, 1964.

Franck, T. A., ed. "Policy Paper on the Legality of Mandatory Sanctions by the United Nations Against Rhodesia." New York: New York University, Center for International Studies, n.d. [1969]. Mimeographed.

Freedman, R. O. Economic Warfare in the Communist Bloc. New York: Praeger, 1970.

Gordon, D. L., and R. J. Dangerfield. The Hidden Weapon. New York: Harper & Bros., 1947.

Gorge, C. Une nouvelle sanction du droit international. Lausanne: Payot, 1926.

Hawtrey, R. G. Economic Aspects of Sovereignty. New York: Longmans Green, 1930.

Heckscher, A., et al. Sweden, Norway and Denmark in the World War. London: Oxford University Press, 1930.

Hennessy, R. C. Public Opinion. Belmont, Calif.: Wadsworth, 1965.

Higgins, R. The Development of International Law Through the Political Organs of the United Nations. London: Oxford University Press, 1963.

Hindmarsh, A. E. Force in Peace. Cambridge, Mass.: Harvard University Press, 1933.

Hogan, A. Pacific Blockade. Oxford: Oxford University Press, 1908.

Hudson, M. O. By Pacific Means: The Implementation of Article 2 of the Pact of Paris. New Haven, Conn.: Yale University Press, 1935.

Jack, D. T. Studies in Economic Warfare. London: P. S. King & Son, 1940.

Lawrence, J. C. The World's Struggle with Rubber, 1905-1931. New York: Harper & Bros., 1931.

Leith, C. K. World Minerals and World Politics. New York: McGraw-Hill, 1931.

Liska, G. The New Statecraft: Foreign Aid in American Foreign Policy. Chicago: University of Chicago Press, 1960.

McKenna, J. C. Diplomatic Protest in Foreign Policy. Chicago: Loyola University Press, 1962.

Medlicott, W. N. Economic Blockade. 2 volumes. London: His Majesty's Stationery Office, 1946-47.

Mitrany, D. The Problem of International Sanctions. New York: Oxford University Press, 1925.

Montgomery, J. D. The Politics of Foreign Aid. New York: Praeger, 1962.

Oppenheim, L. International Law: A Treatise. Volume I: Law of Peace. 8th edition. Edited by H. Lauterpacht. London: Longmans Green, 1961.

Parmelee, M. Blockade and Sea Power. New York: Crowell, 1924.

Phillipson, C. The International Law and Custom of Ancient Greece and Rome. London: Macmillan, 1911.

Rawles, W. P. The Nationality of Commercial Control of World Minerals. New York: Institute of Mining and Metallurgical Engineers, 1933.

Royal Institute of International Affairs. <u>Sanctions: The Character of International Sanctions and Their Application</u>. London: Chatham House, 1935.

_____. <u>International Sanctions: A Report</u>. London: Oxford University Press, 1938.

Ruzié, D., <u>Organisations internationales et sanctions internationales</u>. Paris: Armand Colin, 1971.

Segal, R., ed. <u>Sanctions Against South Africa</u>. Harmondsworth: Penguin Books, 1964.

Slater, Sir A. <u>Allied Shipping Control</u>. New York: Oxford Press, 1921.

Smith, G. O. <u>The Strategy of Minerals</u>. New York: Appleton & Co., 1919.

Snyder, G. H. <u>Stockpiling Strategic Materials: Politics and National Defense</u>. San Francisco: Chandler, 1966.

Stone, J. <u>Legal Controls of International Conflict</u>. London: Stevens & Sons, 1959.

Surface, F. M. <u>The Grain Trade During the World War</u>. New York: Macmillan, 1928.

Teyssaire, J. <u>Le blocus pacifique</u>. Paris: Beauvais, 1910.

Thorneycroft, E. <u>Personal Responsibility and the Law of Nations</u>. The Hague: Nijhoff, 1961.

Von Delbruck, C. <u>Die wirtschaftliche Mobilmachung im Deutschland</u>. Munich: Verlag fur Kulturpolitic, 1924.

Wright, Q., ed. <u>Neutrality and Collective Security</u>. Harris Foundation lectures. Chicago: University of Chicago Press, 1936.

Wu, Yuan-li. <u>Economic Warfare</u>. New York: Prentice-Hall, 1952.

Yepes, J. M., and P. de Silva, <u>Commentaire du pacte de la Société des nations et des statuts de l'Union panaméricaine</u>. 3 volumes. Paris: Pédone, 1935. Especially II, 256-301.

Articles on Sanctions

American Society of International Law. "Pacific Settlement," AJIL (special supplement) 20 (1926): 368-73.

Anderson, C. P. "The Power of Public Opinion for Peace," AJIL 16 (1922): 241-43.

Atwater, E. "British Control over the Export of War Materials," AJIL 33 (1939): 292-317.

Basdévant, J. "L'action coercitive anglo-germano-italienne contre le Venezuela, 1902-03," RGDIP 11 (1904): 362-458.

Berenstein, A. "Le mécanisme des sanctions dans l'Organisation international du travail," RGDIP 3rd ser., 11 (1937): 446-64.

Boeg, N. V. "Legal Problems of a U.N. Force," Proceedings: International Law Association 49 (1960): 96-152.

Borchard, E. "Arms Embargo and Neutrality," AJIL 27 (1933): 293.

_____. "Enforcement of Peace by Sanctions," AJIL 27 (1933): 518-25.

_____. "Sanctions vs. Neutrality," AJIL 30 (1936): 91-94.

Brierly, J. L. "International Law and Resort to Armed Force," Cambridge Law Journal 4 (1932): 308-19.

Brown, W. G. "The Use of Foreign Aid as an Instrument to Secure Compliance with International Obligations," Proceedings: ASIL 58 (1964): 210-17.

Buell, R. L. "Are Sanctions Necessary for International Organizations?" Annals 162 (1932): 93-99.

Calageropolas-Stratis, S. "La Souveraineté des états et les limitations au droit de guerre," Revue héllenique de droit international 2 (1949): 153-67.

_____. "La légitime défense," Revue hellénique de droit international 6 (1953): 217-30.

Castleberg, F. "Le droit international et la défense," Acta scandinavica 1 (1930): 1-18, 81-87.

Cavaré, L. "L'idée des sanctions en droit international public," RGDIP 3rd ser., 11 (1937): 385-445.

Chakste, M. "Justice and Law in the Charter of the United Nations," AJIL 42 (1948): 590-600.

Chamberlain, J. P. "Enforcing Economic Sanctions," International Conciliation 220 (1926): 287-91.

Contini, P. "International Commercial Arbitration," American Journal of Comparative Law 8 (1959): 283-309.

"Contraband and Blockade," Congressional Digest 9 (January 1930): 13-14.

Coudert, F. R. "The Sanctions of International Law," University of Pennsylvania Law Review 61 (1913), 234 ff.

_____. "Law versus Force in the Solution of International Controversies," Living Age 340 (1931): 587-94.

Deener, D. R. "Comment," Cornell Law Quarterly 36 (1951): 505-33.

De Fiedorowicz, G. "Historical Survey of the Application of Sanctions," Transactions of the Grotius Society 22 (1937): 117-31.

De Visscher, C. "L'interpretation du pacte au Lendermain du différend Italo-Grec," Revue de droit international 51 (1924): 328 ff.

Dulles, J. F. "Should Economic Sanctions Be Applied in International Disputes?" Annals 162 (1932): 103-08.

Dupuis, C. "Les sanctions du droit international," Hague recueil 1 (1924): Pt. III, 407-36.

Eckel, E. C. "Economic Sanctions, Blockades and Boycotts," Asia 32 (1932): 276-83.

Eden, A. "Future of Sanctions," Vital Speeches 2 (1936): 620-23.

Editor. "Binding Force of International Law," _The Solicitor_ 5 (1938): 124.

Falcke, H. P. "Die Friedensblockade," _Niemeyers Zeitschrift für internationales Recht_ 28 (1919-20): 36-182.

Fenwick, C. G. "Intervention: Individual and Collective," _AJIL_ 39 (1945): 658 ff.

_____. "The Legal Aspects of 'Neutralism,'" _AJIL_ 51 (1957): 71-74.

Fisher, R. "Bringing Law to Bear on Governments," _Harvard Law Review_ 74 (1961): 1130-40.

Fitzmaurice, G. G. "Some Aspects of Modern Contraband Control and the Law of Prize," _BYIL_ 22 (1945): 73-95.

_____. "The Definition of Aggression," _International and Comparative Law Quarterly_ 1 (1952): 137-44.

_____. "The Foundations of the Authority of International Law and the Problem of Enforcement," _Modern Law Review_ 19 (1956): 1-13.

Fox, W. T. R. "Collective Enforcement of Peace and Security," _APSR_ 39 (1945): 934-42.

Galina, A. "Neutrality in Contemporary International Law," _Soviet Yearbook of International Law_ (1958): 13-21.

Garner, J. W. "Violation of Maritime Law by the Allied Powers During the World War," _AJIL_ 25 (1931): 31-34.

Giraud, E. "La théorie de la légitime défence," _Hague recueil_ 49 (1934): Pt. II, 687-868.

Giraud, M. "Memorandum on Pacific Blockade up to the Time of the Foundation of the League of Nations," in League of Nations, _Official Journal_ (1927), Appendix II.

Gonsiorowski, M. "The Interpretation of the Covenant in the Sino-Japanese Dispute," _New York University Quarterly Law Review_ 13 (1935-36): 216-43.

Goodrich, L. M. "Pacific Settlement of Disputes," _APSR_ 39 (1945): 956-70.

Greene, J. D. "Economic Sanctions as Instruments of National Policy," Annals 162 (1932): 100-02.

Gross, L. "The Charter of the U.N. and the Lodge Reservations," AJIL 41 (1947): 531-54.

Hajdu, G. "La neutralité dans le système des Nations
Unies," Acta juridicae Academiae scientiarum Hungariae
1 (1959): 205-28.

Hill, D. J. "The Janina-Corfu Affair," AJIL 18 (1924):
98-104.

Hindmarsh, A. E. "Self-Help in Time of Peace," AJIL 26
(1932): 315-26.

Hoffman, S. "U.N. and the Use of Force," New Republic 146
(1962): 11-13.

Holland, Sir T. H. "Minerals and International Relations,"
International Conciliation 266 (January 1931): 9-51.

Hyde, C. C. "Boycott as a Sanction of International Law,"
Political Science Quarterly 48 (1933): 211-19.

_____. "International Co-operation for Neutrality,"
University of Pennsylvania Law Review 85 (1937): 344-
57.

Jackson, B. W. "Foreign Aid: Strategy or Stopgap?" Foreign Affairs 41 (1962): 9, 100.

Jackson, Hon. R. H. "Some Problems in Developing an International Legal System," Temple Law Quarterly 22 (1948-
49): 147-58.

Jenks, C. W. "Some Constitutional Problems of International
Organizations," BYIL 22 (1945): 11-72.

Jennings, R. Y. "The Progress of International Law," BYIL
23 (1946): 334-55.

Johnson, D. H. N. "The Judicial Settlement of International Disputes," Blackfriars (September 1959): 364-
74.

Kebedgy, M. S. "Contribution à l'étude de la sanction du droit international," Revue de droit international et de législation comparée (1897): 113-46.

Kelsen, H. "Collective Security and Collective Self-Defence Under the Charter of the United Nations," AJIL 42 (1948): 783-96.

Kirk, G., et al. "Enforcement of Security: A Symposium," Yale Law Journal 55 (1946): 910-1096.

Kuhn, A. K. "Economic Sanctions and the Kellog Pact (Editorial)," AJIL 30 (1936): 83-88.

Kunz, J. L. "Individual and Collective Self-Defence in Article 51 of the Charter of the U.N.," AJIL 41 (1947): 872-79.

_____. "Sanctions in International Law," AJIL 54 (1960): 324-48.

La Pradelle, A. de. "La sécurité collective et la non-ingérence," New Commonwealth Quarterly 2 (1936): 295-308.

Lauterpacht, H. "Boycotts in International Relations," BYIL 14 (1933): 124-40.

Leonard, J. L. "The Effect of the Employment of Economic Sanctions on National and World Prosperity," Proceedings: Institute of World Affairs (U.C.L.A.) 13 (1936): 221-25.

Levinson, S. O. "Sanctions Mean War," Christian Century 51 (1934): 806-09.

Liang, Y-li, "Regional Arrangements and International Security," Transactions of the Grotius Society 31 (1945): 216-31.

Maccaley, S. "Reprisals as a Measure of Redress Short of War," Cambridge Law Journal 2 (1924): 60-73.

Matsubara, K. "Self-Defence and Reprisals," Journal of International Law and Diplomacy 1-10 (1958): 241-59.

McDougal, M. A., and F. P. Feliciano. "The Initiation of Coercion: A Multi-temporal Analysis," AJIL 52 (1958): 241-59.

McNair, Lord A. "The Legal Meaning of War and the Relation of War to Reprisals," Transactions of the Grotius Society 11 (1926): 29-51.

_____. "The Stimson Doctrine of Non-Recognition," BYIL 14 (1933): 65-74.

_____. "Collective Security," BYIL 17 (1936): 150-64.

Middlebusch, F. A. "Non-Recognition as a Sanction of International Law," Proceedings: ASIL 27 (1933): 40-55.

Mo, Hsu. "The Sanctions of International Law," Transactions of the Grotius Society 35 (1949): 4-14, 22-23.

_____. "The Sanctions of International Law," Transactions of the Grotius Society 36 (1950): 8.

Moncharville, M. "Le conflit franco-turc de 1901," RGDIP 19 (1902): 1 ff.

Moore, J. B. "Fifty Years of International Law," Harvard Law Review 50 (1937): 395-448.

Morse, O. "Methods of Pacific Settlement of International Disputes: Difficulties and Revision," Brooklyn Law Review 25 (1959): 20-32.

Morse, W. L. "International Justice Through Law," Oregon Law Review 26 (1946): 7-38.

Munro, L. K. "Recent Developments in the Role of the General Assembly in the Maintenance of Peace," Proceedings: ASIL 53 (1958): 34 ff.

Nincic, D. "Legitimate Defence in the New International Law," Jugoslovenski revija sa medunardno pravo 2 (1955): 180-90.

Nogueira, A. "Naçoes-Unidas e a definição de agressão," Revista de Faculdade de direito (São Paulo) 54 (1959): 76-91.

Nurick, L. "The Distinction Between Combatant and Noncombatant in the Law of War," AJIL 39 (1945): 680-97.

Parry, C. "British Practice in Some 19th Century Pacific Blockades," Zeitschrift für auslandisches offentliches Recht und Volkerrecht 8 (1936): 496-537.

Peczenik, A. "O definicji sankeji prawxej," Panstwo i prawo 3 (1965): 450-53.

Pélloux, R. "Mesures d'embargo et neutralité," RGDIP 3rd ser., 8 (1934): 58-75.

_____. "L'embargo sur les exportations d'armes," RGDIP 3rd ser., 9 (1935): 146-55.

Politis, N. "Les représailles entre états membres de la Société des Nations," RGDIP 2nd ser., 31 (1924): 3-24.

Potter, P. B. "Sanctions and Guarantees in International Organizations," APSR 16 (1922): 297-305.

_____. "Is the Establishment of Peace . . . Perfection of International Law and Organization? (Editorial)," AJIL 27 (1933): 129.

_____. "The U.N. Charter and the Covenant of the League of Nations," AJIL 39 (1945): 546-51.

Rawles, W. P. "Provisions for Minerals in International Agreements," Political Science Quarterly 48 (1933): 513-33.

Riedl, C. A. "How Can International Legislation Best Be Improved?" Marquette Law Review 31 (1947-48): 259-71.

Root, E. "The Sanctions of International Law," AJIL 2 (1908): 451.

Rowson, S. W. D. "Modern Blockade: Some Legal Aspects," BYIL 23 (1946): 346-53.

Roxburgh, R. F. "Sanctions of International Law," AJIL 14 (1920): 26-37.

Sachs, D. "America's Foreign Funds Control," The Banker (November 1941): 9.

Sayre, P. "U.N. Law," Canadian Bar Review 25 (1947): 809-22.

Schacter, O. "The Enforcement of International Judicial and Arbitral Decisions," AJIL 54 (1960): 1-24.

Schick, F. B. "Council and Court of the United Nations," Modern Law Review 9 (1946): 97-104.

Schwarzenberger, G. "Some Aspects of the Principle of Self-Defence in the Charter of the U.N.," International Law Association: Report of Conference 48 (1958): 550-628.

Shawcross, Sir H. "The Place of Law in International Affairs," George Washington Law Review 15 (1947): 121-30.

"Ship Certificates," New York Times, October 25, 1962, 20.

Sloane, F. B. "Comparative International and Municipal Law Sanctions," Nebraska Law Review 27 (1947): 1-29.

Smith, G. O., et al. "Raw Materials and Their Effect upon International Relations," International Conciliation 226 (January 1927): 7-13.

Sohn, L. B. "U.N. Charter Revision and the Rule of Law: A Program for Peace," Northwestern Law Review 50 (1956): 709-24.

Strinson, J. W. "International Sanctions and American Law," AJIL 19 (1925): 505-16.

Strupp, K. "L'incident Janina entre la Grèce et l'Italie," RGDIP 31 (1924): 255 ff.

Taubenfeld, H. J. "International Armed Forces and Rules of War," AJIL 45 (1951): 671-79.

"Tightening the Embargo on Cuba," Business Week, January 6, 1963, 45.

Von Bulmerincq, A. "Le blocus pacifique et ses effets sur la propriété privée," Journal du droit international privé, 11 (1884).

Wagner, W. J. "Is Compulsory Adjudication of International Legal Disputes Possible?" Northwestern Law Review 47 (1952): 21-54.

Waldock, C. H. M. "The Regulation of the Use of Force by Individual States in International Law," Recueil des cours 81 (1952): 451-514.

Warren, C. "What Are the Rights of Neutrals Now in Practice?" Proceedings: ASIL 27 (1933): 128-35.

_____. "Troubles of a Neutral," Foreign Affairs 12 (1934): 377-90.

_____. "Prepare for Neutrality," Yale Law Review 44 (1935): 467.

_____. "Belligerent Aircraft, Neutral Trade and Unpreparedness," AJIL 29 (1935): 203-11.

Weightman, M. A. "Self-Defence in International Law," Virginia Law Review 37 (1951): 1095-1115.

Wild, P. S. Treaty Sanctions," AJIL 26 (1932): 488-501.

_____. "Sanctions of International Commodity Agreements," AJIL 30 (1936): 664-73.

_____. "Neutrality," International Law Situations (U.S. Naval War College), 1939, 1-154.

_____. "Documents--Blockade," International Law Documents (U.S. Naval War College), 1940, 44-46.

_____. "Contraband of War," International Law Documents, 1944-45, 1-99.

Wilk, D. "International Disputes and the Limitations of the U.N.," Arbitration Journal 3 (1948): 16-21.

Wilson, G. G. "Sanctions for International Agreements," AJIL 11 (1917): 387-89.

_____. "Economic Factors of International Law," AJIL 25 (1931): 503-04.

_____. "Neutrality," International Law Situations, 1931, 1-93.

_____. "Boycott," International Law Situations, 1932, 89-135.

_____. "Neutrality," International Law Situations, 1934, 28, 66, 93-95.

_____. "Neutrality," International Law Situations, 1936, 82-135.

Wright, Q. "International Law and Its Relations to Constitutional Law," AJIL 17 (1923): 234-44.

_____. "Permissive Sanctions Against Aggression," AJIL 36 (1942): 103-06.

_____. "Intervention, 1956," AJIL 51 (1957): 257-76.

Zimmern, A. "The Notion of Collective Security," Proceedings: ASIL 27 (1933): 25-31.

Books on Italy

Aloisi, P. Journal, 25 juillet 1932-14 juin 1936. Paris: Librairie Plon, 1957.

Badoglio, P. The War in Abyssinia. London: Methuen, 1937.

Baer, G. W. The Coming of the Italian-Ethiopian War. Cambridge, Mass.: Harvard University Press, 1967.

Barker, A. J. The Civilizing Mission: The Italo-Ethiopian War, 1935-36. London: Cassell, 1968.

Bastin, J. L'affaire d'Ethiopie et les diplomates, 1934-1937. Brussels: Librairie Universelle, 1937.

Beloff, M. The Foreign Policy of Soviet Russia, 1929-1941. 2 volumes. London: Oxford, 1947-49.

Boca, A. del. The Ethiopian War, 1935-1941. Translated by P. D. Cummins. Chicago: University of Chicago Press, 1969.

Bonnet, G. Le quai d'Orsay sous trois républiques. Paris: Fayard, 1961.

Caioli, A. L'Italia di fronte a Ginevra. Rome: Giovanni Volpe, 1965.

Ciano, G. The Ciano Diaries: 1939-43. Edited by H. Gibson. Garden City, N.Y.: Doubleday, 1946.

_____. Ciano's Diary 1937-1938. London: Methuen, 1952.

Coon, C. S. Measuring Ethiopia and Flight into Arabia. Boston: Little Brown, 1935.

Deakin, F. W. The Brutal Friendship: Mussolini, Hitler and the Fall of Italian Fascism. London: Weidenfeld and Nicolson, 1962.

De Bono, E. Anno XIIII: The Conquest of an Empire. London: Cresset, 1937.

Dell, R. The Geneva Racket, 1920-1939. London: Robert Hale, n.d.

Devine, R. A. The Illusion of Neutrality. Chicago: University of Chicago Press, 1962.

Edwards, C. Bruce of Melbourne: Man of Two Worlds. London: Heinemann, 1965.

Flandin, P. E. Politique française, 1919-1940. Paris: Nouvelles, 1947.

Great Britain, Foreign Office. Documents on British Foreign Policy, 1918-1939. 3rd series. London: His Majesty's Stationery Office, 1950-53.

Harris, B. The United States and the Italo-Ethiopian Crisis. Stanford: Stanford University Press, 1964.

Heald, S., ed. Documents on International Affairs, 1935. 2 volumes. London: Oxford University Press, 1936.

Herriot, E. Jadis II: D'une guerre à la'autre, 1914-1936. Paris: Flammarion, 1952.

Hess, R. L. Italian Colonialism in Somalia. Chicago: University of Chicago Press, 1966.

Hiett, H. Public Opinion and the Italo-Ethiopian Dispute: The Activity of Private Organizations in the Crisis. Geneva Special Studies VII, no. 1 Geneva: Geneva Research Centre, 1936.

Hull, Cordel. Memoirs. 2 volumes. New York: Macmillan, 1948.

Jesman, C. The Russians in Ethiopia: An Essay in Futility. London: Chatto and Windus, 1958.

Jones, A. H. M., and E. Monro. A History of Ethiopia. Oxford: Oxford University Press, 1960.

Kelen, E. Peace in Their Time: Men Who Led Us in and out of War, 1914-1945. New York: Knopf, 1963.

Lagardelle, H. de. Mission à Rome: Mussolini. Paris: Pilon, 1955.

Laurens, F. D. France and the Italo-Ethiopian Crisis, 1935-1936. The Hague: Mouton, 1967.

Laval, Josée, ed. Diary of Pierre Laval. New York: Scribner's, 1948.

La Vradelle, A. de Le conflit italo-éthiopien. Paris: Editions Internationales, 1936.

Leroux, E. L. Le conflit italo-éthiopien devant la S.D.N. Paris: Librairie Technique et Economique, 1937.

Livingstone, Dame A. The Peace Ballot: The Official History. London: Victor Gollancz, 1935.

MacCullum, E. P. Rivalries in Ethiopia. Boston: World Peace Foundation, 1935.

Mandelstam, A. Le conflit italo-éthiopien devant la Société des Nations. Paris: Sirey, 1937.

Margueritte, V. The League Fiasco. London: Hodge, 1936.

Martelli, G. _Italy Against the World_. London: Chatto and Windus, 1937.

Mennevee, R. _Les origines du conflit italo-éthiopien et la Société des Nations_. Paris: Documents Politiques, 1936.

Monti, A. _Gli Italiani e il canale di Suez_. Rome: Vittoriano, 1937.

Nemours, A. _Craignons d'être un jour l'Ethiopie de quelqu'un_. Port-au-Prince: Collège Vertières, 1945.

Neufeld, M. F. _Italy: School for Awakening Countries: The Italian Labour Movement_. Ithaca, N.Y.: Cornell University Press, 1961.

Nicolson, H. _Peacemaking, 1919_. New York: Grosset & Dunlop, 1965.

Oprea, I. M. _Nicolae Titulescu_. Bucarest: Editura Stiintifica, 1966.

Ortega y Gasset, E. _Etiopia: El conflicto italo-abisinio_. Madrid: Puezo, 1935.

Paul-Boncour, J. _Entre deux guerres: Souvenirs sur la III République_. 3 volumes. Paris: Plon, 1945-46.

Potter, P. _The Wal-Wal Arbitration_. Washington: Carnegie Endowment for International Peace, 1938.

Rousseau, C. _Le conflit italo-éthiopien devant le droit international_. Paris: Pédone, 1938.

Schaefer, L. F. _The Ethiopian Crisis: Touchstone or Appeasement_. Boston: Heath, 1961.

Schonfield, H. J. _Italy and Suez_. London: Hutchinson, n.d.

Templewood, Viscount (Samuel Hoare). _Nine Troubled Years_. London: Collins, 1954.

Toscano, M. _Francia ed Italia di fronte al problema di Gibuti_. Florence: Studio Fiorentino di Politica Estera, 1939.

_____. L'Italia e la crisi europea del luglio 1914.
Milan: Giuffre Editore, 1940.

Toynbee, A. J. Survey of International Affairs, 1935.
2 volumes. London: Oxford University Press, 1936.

Vansittart, Lord R. The Mist Procession: The Autobiography
of Lord Vansittart. London: Hutchinson, 1958.

Villari, L. Italy, Abyssinia, and the League. Rome:
Dante Alighiere Society, 1936.

Walder, D. The Chanak Affair. London: Hutchinson, 1969.

Walters, F. P. A History of the League of Nations. London: Oxford University Press, 1960.

Wilson, H. R. For Want of a Nail: The Failure of the
League of Nations in Ethiopia. New York: Vantage,
1959.

Zimmern, A. The League of Nations and the Rule of Law,
1918-1935. London: Macmillan, 1936.

Selected Articles on Italy

Aloisi, P. "America Plays with Fire: What Italy Thinks
of Sanctions," Forum 94 (1935): 326-30; 95 (1936):
11-12.

Askew, W. C. "The Secret Agreement Between France and
Italy on Ethiopia, January 1935," Journal of Modern
History 25 (1953): 47-48.

Avenol, J. "The Future of the League of Nations," International Affairs 13 (1934): 143-58.

Braddick, H. "A New Look at American Policy During the
Italo-Ethiopian Crisis, 1935-36," Journal of Modern
History 34 (1962): 64-73.

Conti Rossini, C. "L'Etiopia è incapace di progresso
civile," Nuova antologia 303 (September 16, 1935):
171-77.

Dean, V. M. "The League and the Italian-Ethiopian Dispute,"
   Geneva Special Studies VI, no. 8. Geneva: Geneva
   Research Council, 1935: 1 ff.

Gathorne-Hardy, G. M. "The League at the Cross-Roads,"
   International Affairs 15 (1936): 485-505.

Geraud, A. "British Vacillations," Foreign Affairs 14
   (1936): 584-97.

Hiett, H. "Public Opinion and the Italo-Ethiopian Dispute:
   The Activity of Private Organizations in the Crisis,"
   Geneva Special Studies VII, no. 1. Geneva: Geneva
   Research Council, 1936: 1-28.

Hoskins, H. "The Suez Canal in Time of War," Foreign Affairs 14 (1935): 93-101.

Koren, W. "The Italian-Ethiopian Dispute," Geneva Special
   Studies VI, no. 4. Geneva: Geneva Research Council,
   1935: 145.

Leonard, J. "The Effect on Employment of Economic Sanctions on National and World Prosperity," Proceedings
   of the Institute of World Affairs (Los Angeles) 13
   (1936): 221-25.

Magistrati, M. "La Germania e l'impresa italiana di Etiopia (Ricordi di Berlino)," Rivista di studi politici
   internazionali 17 (1950): 562-606.

Martilli-Chautard, M. "L'expansion japonaise en Afrique,"
   L'Afrique française (August 1934): 499.

Melly, J. M. "Ethiopia and the War from the Ethiopian
   Point of View," International Affairs 15 (1936): 103-
   21.

Nicolson, H. "British Public Opinion and Foreign Policy,"
   Public Opinion Quarterly 1 (1937): 53-63.

Ottlik, G. "Paix ou sécurité collective," Nouvelle revue
   de Hongrie (1935): 461-65.

Pétain, M. H. P. "La sécurité de la France," Revue des
   deux mondes 8th ser., 27 (1935): i-xx.

Serra, E. "Mussolini, l'Etiopia e un segreto di Sir Samuel Hoare," _Nuova antologia_ 477 (1960): 481-88.

United Kingdom, Department of Overseas Trade, "Economic Conditions in Ethiopia." London: His Majesty's Stationery Office, 1932. (Pamphlet.)

Vare, D. "British Foreign Policy Through Italian Eyes." _International Affairs_ 15 (1936): 80-102.

Watt, D. C. "The Secret Laval-Mussolini Agreement of 1935 on Ethiopia," _Middle East Journal_ 15 (1961): 69-78.

Zimmern, A. "The League's Handling of the Italo-Abyssinian Dispute," _International Affairs_ 14 (1935): 751-68.

Books on the Dominican Republic

Alfau, V. J. _Trujillo and the Roman Catholic Church in Santo Domingo._ Ciudad Trujillo: Editorial Handicap, 1960.

Almoína, J. _Yo fuí secretario de Trujillo._ Buenos Aires: Editorial del Plata, 1950.

Alvarez, A. _La política social de Trujillo._ Ciudad Trujillo: Impresora Dominicana, 1955.

Ariza, S. _Trujillo: The Man and His Country._ New York: Orlin Tremaine Co., 1939.

Atkins, G. P., and L. C. Wilson. _The United States and the Trujillo Regime._ New Brunswick, N.J.: Rutgers University Press, 1972.

Aybar, S. _Génesis y evolución del estado._ Ciudad Trujillo: Editorial Hermanos, 1953.

Balaguer, J., ed. _El Pensamiento vivo de Trujillo._ Ciudad Trujillo: Impresora Dominicana, 1955.

Baquero, G. _Cuban-Dominican Relations._ Ciudad Trujillo: Diario de la Marina, 1956.

Besault, L. de. _President Trujillo: His Work and the Dominican Republic._ 2nd edition. Washington, D.C.: Washington Publishing Co., 1936.

Bosch, J. *Trujillo: Causas de una dictadura sin ejemplo.*
Lima: Populibros Peruanos, 1959. Also published as
Trujillo: Causas de una tirania sin ejemplo. Caracas:
Grabados Nacionales, 1959.

_____. *Crisis de la democracia de América en la Repúb-
ica Dominicana.* Mexico, D.F.: Centro de Estudios y
Documentación Sociales, 1965; also Mexico: B. Costa-
Amic, 1964. Published in English as *The Unfinished
Experiment: Democracy in the Dominican Republic.*
London: Pall Mall Press, 1966; New York: Praeger,
1965.

Briggs, E. *Farewell to Foggy Bottom: The Recollections
of a Career Diplomat.* New York: David McKay & Co.,
1964.

Brookings Institution. *Refugee Settlement in the Dominican
Republic: A Survey.* Washington, D.C.: The Institution, 1942.

Castillo de Aza, Z. *Trujillo: Benefactor de la iglesia.*
Ciudad Trujillo: Editorial del Caribe, 1955.

_____. *Trujillo y otros benefactores de la iglesia.*
Ciudad Trujillo: Editorial Handicap, 1961.

Cestero Burgos, T. *Filosofía de un régimen.* Ciudad Trujillo: Editorial Montalvo, 1951.

Clark, J. A. *The Church and the Crisis in the Dominican
Republic.* Westminster, Md.: Newman Press, 1966.

Cooper, P. *Sambumbia: A Discovery of the Dominican Republic: The Modern Hispaniola.* New York: Caribbean
Library, 1947.

Crassweller, R. D. *Trujillo: The Life and Times of a
Caribbean Dictator.* New York: Macmillan, 1966.

Cruz y Berges, F. *Trujillo, gobierno y pueblo dominicano
frente al comunismo internacional.* Ciudad Trujillo:
Editorial Babeque, 1957.

Damiron, R. *Nostros: Volumen publicado como contribución
a la celebración del 25 aniversario de la era de Trujillo.* Ciudad Trujillo: Impresora Dominicana, 1955.

Diaz, V. _In Praise of an Era_. Ciudad Trujillo: Editorial del Caribe, 1955.

_____. _La política exterior de Trujillo_. Ciudad Trujillo: Impresora Dominicana, 1955.

Dominican Constitution of 1955. Washington, D.C.: Pan American Union, 1958.

Espaillat, A. _Trujillo: The Last Caesar_. Chicago: Regnery, 1963.

_____. _Les dessous d'une dictature: Trujillo_. Paris: Colmann-Levy, 1966. Reprint of _Last Caesar_ with new introduction.

Franco, F. J. _República Dominicana: Clases, crisis y comandos_. Havana: Casa de las Américas, 1966.

Galíndez, Jesús de. _La era de Trujillo_. Buenos Aires: Editorial Americana, 1956; Santiago de Chile: Editorial del Pacífico, 1956. Also published in English. Tucson: University of Arizona Press, 1973.

Gallegos, G. _Trujillo en la historia: Veinticinco años en la ruta de un glorioso destino_. Ciudad Trujillo: Editorial del Caribe, 1956.

Garcia, J. E. _Las obras públicas en la era de Trujillo_. Ciudad Trujillo: Impresora Dominicana, 1955.

Goldwert, M. _The Constabulary in the Dominican Republic: Progeny and Legacy of United States Intervention_. Gainesville: University of Florida Press, 1962.

González, P. _Trujillo: The Rebirth of a Nation_. Ciudad Trujillo: Editorial del Caribe, 1953.

_____. _La era de Trujillo_. Ciudad Trujillo: Editorial del Caribe, 1955.

Guerro, G. _La muerte de 2 dictadores y la del Presidente Caceres_. Santo Domingo: Editorial La Nación, 1962.

Henríquez, N. _La verdad sobre Trujillo: Capítulos que se la olvidaron a Galíndez_. Havana: Imprenta Económica en General, 1959.

Here Is Our Answer. Summary of the reply of the government
of the Dominican Republic to the report of the Inter-
American Peace Committee submitted to the OAS on June
6, 1960. Ciudad Trujillo: Oficial, 1960.

Hicks, A. C. Blood in the Streets: The Life and Rule of
Trujillo. New York: Creative Age Press, 1956.

Hoepelman, A. Era y obra de Trujillo. Ciudad Trujillo:
Impresora Dominicana, 1954.

Jimenes-Grullón, J. I. La República Dominicana: Una fic-
ción. Mérida, Venezuela: Talleres Gráficos Univer-
sitarios, 1965.

Jiménez, R. E. Trujillo y la paz. Ciudad Trujillo: Impresora Dominicana, 1952.

Knight, M. M. The Americans in Santo Domingo. New York:
Vanguard Press, 1928.

Kurzman, D. Santo Domingo: Revolt of the Damned. New
York: Putnam, 1965.

Logan, R. W. Haiti and the Dominican Republic. Oxford:
Oxford University Press, 1968.

Long, G. S. El caso de Gerry Murphy y la República Dominicana. Ciudad Trujillo: Oficial, 1957.

Machado, M. A. La dominicanización fronteriza. Ciudad
Trujillo: Impresora Dominicana, 1955.

Martin, J. B. Overtaken by Events: The Dominican Republic from the Fall of Trujillo to the Civil War. Garden City, N.Y.: Doubleday, 1966.

Mejía, M. A. Las clases sociales en Santo Domingo. Ciudad Trujillo: Librería Dominicana, 1953.

Miolan, A. La revolución social frente a la tiranía de
Trujillo. Mexico, D.F.: Fondo Cultura, 1938.

Monclus, M. A. El caudillismo en la República Dominicana.
Ciudad Trujillo: Impresora Dominicana, 1948.

Mota, F. A. Un estadista de América: Obra socio-política de Trujillo--filosofía, historia, estadística. Ciudad Trujillo: Editorial Montalvo, 1945.

Nanita, A. R. Trujillo. 5th edition, rev., in English. Ciudad Trujillo: Editorial del Caribe, 1954.

Ornes, Germán. The Other Side of the Coin: A Collection of Articles. Washington, D.C.: Embassy of the Dominican Republic, 1958.

_____. Trujillo: Little Caesar of the Caribbean. New York: Nelson, 1958.

Ortiz, S. S. Dominican Taxation During the Trujillo Era. Ciudad Trujillo: Editorial del Caribe, 1953.

Pacheco, A. O. La obra educativa de Trujillo. Ciudad Trujillo: Impresora Dominicana, 1955.

Pagán, D. Por qué lucha el pueblo dominicano: Análisis del fenómeno dictatorial en América Latina. Caracas: Imprenta Caribe, 1959.

Partido Dominicano. Declaración de principios y estatutos del Partido dominicano. Ciudad Trujillo: Editorial Montalvo, 1945.

Patin, M. A. Dominicanismo. Ciudad Trujillo: Librería Dominicana, 1947.

Peña, M. A. Política de Trujillo. Ciudad Trujillo: Impresora Dominicana, 1954.

Penson, J. E. El Partido dominicano. Ciudad Trujillo: Imprenta Arte y Cine, 1958.

Penzini, J. Las acusaciones contra Trujillo: Assault by Slander. Ciudad Trujillo: Sociedad Dominicana de Prensa, 1956.

Pérez, M. R. Décimas sobre la era de Trujillo. Ciudad Trujillo: Editorial Montalvo, 1955.

República Dominicana. Documentos para la historia de la República Dominicana. 3 volumes. I, Ciudad Trujillo: Editorial Montalvo, 1944. II, Santiago: Editorial

Diaria, 1947. III, Ciudad Trujillo: Editorial Montalvo, 1959.

_____ . 1er Plan nacional de desarrollo (version pre-
liminar). Santo Domingo: Oficina Nacional de Plani-
ficación, March 1970.

Roberts, T. D., et al. Area Handbook for the Dominican Republic. Washington, D.C.:   Foreign Area Studies,
American University, 1966.

Rodman, S. Quisqueya: A History of the Dominican Republic. Seattle: University of Washington Press, 1964.

Rodríguez, F. T. Código civil de la República Dominicana:
Leyes que le modifican y lo completan. Ciudad Trujillo: Editorial Montalvo, 1950.

Rodríguez, E. Cronología de Trujillo. Ciudad Trujillo:
Impresora Dominicana, 1955.

_____ . La dificultad de gobernar. Ciudad Trujillo: Impresora Dominicana, 1955.

_____ . Trujillo and Cordell Hull. Ciudad Trujillo:
Editorial del Caribe, 1956.

_____ . De política dominicana-americana: Discurso ante
la estatua de Cordell Hull. Ciudad Trujillo: Editorial Montalvo, 1957.

_____ . United States Military Intervention. Ciudad
Trujillo: Oficial, 1958.

Roman, M. A. Trujillo: El libertador dominicano. Ciudad
Trujillo: Editorial del Caribe, 1956.

Schoenrich, O. Santo Domingo: A Country with a Future.
New York: Macmillan, 1918.

Sociedad Dominicana de Prensa. Trujillo and the Communist
Threat. Ciudad Trujillo: Oficial, 1956.

_____ . Germán Ornes: A Self Portrait. Ciudad Trujillo: Oficial, 1958.

411

_____. The American People Condemn a Move Against a Caribbean Friend. Ciudad Trujillo: Oficial, 1960.

_____. Timesman Edward C. Burks--Deliberate Misrepresentation. Ciudad Trujillo: Oficial, 1960.

Szulc, T. Dominican Diary. New York: Dell, 1965.

Tejeda, T. Yo investigué la muerte de Trujillo. Barcelona: Plaza y Janes, 1964.

Trujillo, Hector B. Strengthening Relations Between the Dominican Republic and the United States. Washington, D.C.: Embassy of the Dominican Republic, 1958.

Trujillo, Rafael. Discurso pronunciado por el Excmo. Sr. Pres. de la República Dr. Rafael L. Trujillo Molina al inaugurar el barrio de mejoramiento social el día 20 de abril de 1946. Ciudad Trujillo: Impresora Dominicana, 1946.

_____. The Evolution of Democracy in Santo Domingo. Ciudad Trujillo: Editorial del Caribe, 1955.

_____. Latin Unity: Two Momentous Addresses. Ciudad Trujillo: Editorial del Caribe, 1955.

_____. Obras de Trujillo. Ciudad Trujillo: Impresora Dominicana, 1956.

_____. The Other Side of the Galíndez Case. New York: Dominican Republic Cultural Society of New York, 1956.

_____. Address by Generalissimo Rafael L. Trujillo at the Cathederal of Santiago de los Caballeros, 17 May 1960. Ciudad Trujillo: Dominican Press Society, 1960.

_____. The Basic Policies of a Regime. Ciudad Trujillo: Editorial del Caribe, 1960.

_____. Fundamentos y política de un régimen. Ciudad Trujillo: Editorial del Caribe, 1960.

_____. Patriotismo y educación. Ciudad Trujillo: Editorial del Caribe, 1960.

_____. *Trujillo Speaks*. A series of four articles published by the Miami *Herald*, April 3-6, 1960, and reprinted by the Dominican government, Ciudad Trujillo: Dominican Press Society, 1960.

Trujillo and the Church. Statements made by senior Roman Catholic Church officers. Ciudad Trujillo: Oficial, 1956.

Uribe, M. *Función del Partido dominicano en la era de Trujillo*. Ciudad Trujillo: Impresora Dominicana, 1961.

Valldeperes, M. *Acción y pensamiento de Trujillo*. Ciudad Trujillo: Editorial del Caribe, 1955.

Vega y Pagán, E. *Historia de las fuerzas armadas*. 3 volumes. Ciudad Trujillo: Impresora Dominicana, 1955.

_____. *Military Biography of Generalissimo Rafael Leonidas Trujillo Molina, Commander in Chief of the Armed Forces*. Translated by Ida Espaillat. Ciudad Trujillo: Editorial Atenas, 1956.

Vegueriza, T. *Acción y doctrina de un régimen político*. 2nd edition. Ciudad Trujillo: Editorial del Caribe, 1959.

Verges, P. L. *Biografía del General Héctor B. Trujillo M.* Ciudad Trujillo: Editorial del Caribe, 1957.

_____. *Trujillo: Prócer anticomunista*. Ciudad Trujillo: Editorial del Caribe, 1958.

Wallich, H. C., and R. Tiffin. *Monetary and Banking Legislation of the Dominican Republic, 1947*. New York: Federal Reserve Bank, 1953.

Welles, Sumner. *Naboth's Vineyard: The Dominican Republic, 1844-1924*. Mamaroneck, N.Y.: Paul Appel, 1966. Reprint of New York: Payson & Clarke, 1928.

White Book of Communism in the Dominican Republic. Ciudad Trujillo: Editorial del Caribe, 1958.

Wiarda, H. J., ed. *Dominican Republic: Election Factbook*. Washington, D.C.: Institute for the Comparative Study of Political Systems, 1966.

_____. Dictatorship and Development: The Methods of Control in Trujillo's Dominican Republic. Gainesville: University of Florida Press, 1968.

_____. The Dominican Republic: Nation in Transition. New York: Praeger, 1969.

Wipfler, W. L. The Churches of the Dominican Republic in the Light of History. Cuernavaca, Mexico: Centro Intercultural de Documentación, 1966.

Wydrzynski, A. Ciudad Trujillo. 2 volumes. Warsaw: Iskry, 1974.

Articles on the Dominican Republic

Alba, V. "República Dominicana: La herencia del 'Benefactor,'" Cuadernos (Paris) (1962): 67-72.

Alexander, R. J. "Dictatorship in the Caribbean," Canadian Forum 28 (May 1948): 35.

Allen, D. A. "Santo Domingo: The Empty Showcase?" The Reporter (December 5, 1963): 28.

Arredondo, A., and C. M. Campos. "Las condiciones de vida del campesino dominicano," Panoramas no. 4 (July-August 1964): 81-110.

Augelli, J. P. "The Dominican Republic," Focus 10, no. 6 (1960): 1-6.

Beals, C. "Caesar of the Caribbean," Current History 48 (January 1938): 31-34.

_____. "Strange Victories," Independent (March 1962): 4.

_____. "Gunboat Diplomacy and the Dominican Crisis," National Guardian 14 (December 11, 1961): 1-7.

Bergquist, L. "The Legacy of a Dictator: Nightmare Island," Look (June 19, 1962): 28-33, 34, 37-38, 41.

Bocca, G. "A Dictator's Legacy," This Week (September 19, 1965): 3.

Bochkaryov, Y. "The Dominican Crisis: Highlights and Sidelights," New Times (Moscow) (January 10, 1962): 11-13.

Bosch, J. "Trujillo y su ambición de poder," El dominicano libre (November 1959): 2.

Burr, R. N. "International Interests of Latin American Nations," in L. J. Cantori and S. L. Spiegel, The International Politics of Regions. Englewood Cliffs, N.J.: Prentice-Hall, 1970.

Castaneda, C. M. "Hacia donde va la democracia dominicana?" Bohemia libre puertorriqueña (Caracas) (May 27, 1962): 40-43.

Clark, J. A. "The Church and the Dominican Crisis," Thought 41 (Spring 1966): 117-31.

Cordero, A. "Significación de la nueva realidad dominicana," Renovación (Ciudad Trujillo) 7, no. 24 (1960): 63-73.

Crist, R. E. "Cultural Dichotomy on the Island of Hispaniola," Economic Geography 28 (1952): 105-21.

Deutsche Uberseeische Bank. "Dominikanische Republik," Wirtschaftsbericht über die Lateinamerikanischen (December 1961): 29-31.

Díaz Valdeperes, J. "La cuestión de 'El Caribe,'" El Caribe, December 29, 1961, 5.

Dominican Republic. "Actualidades sobresalientes" and "La República Dominicana acusa a Betancourt ante la OEA," Boletín de la Secretaría de estado de relaciones exteriores no. 91 (April-June 1960): 9-106.

Dominican Republic Information Center, New York. "A Message from Your Friend in the Dominican Republic," Editor & Publisher (May 5, 1956): 36-37.

Draper, T. "Trujillo's Dynasty," The Reporter 5 (November 27, 1951): 20-26.

Dyer, D. R. "Distribution of Population on Hispaniola," Economic Geography 30 (1954): 337-46.

Editorial. "Que hacer en Santo Domingo," Política 15 (1961): 7-13.

Editorial. "La sombra de Haiti sobre Santo Domingo," El Universal, April 8, 1962, 10.

Editorial. "Strong Free Labor Movement Emerges," Inter-American Labor Bulletin, November 1961, 3.

Estrella, J. C. "La posición dominicana frente a los proyectos de intergración económica en Europa y en América Latina," Revista de la Secretaría de estado de industria y comercio 48 (1958): 15-22.

Gacio, G. J. "Sanciones al régimen de Trujillo," La República (San Jose), August 13, 1960, 3.

Galíndez, J. de. "Un reportaje sobre Santo Domingo," Cuadernos americanos 80 (March-April 1955): 37-56.

Gall, N. "How Trujillo Died," New Republic 148 (April 13, 1963): 19-20.

García, L. "La República Dominicana, viva una revolución de tiempo?" Revista Javeriana 51 (March 1962): 171-80.

Grant, F. R. "Hemisphere Repudiates Trujillo," Hemispherica 9 (October 1960): 1-2.

Gruening, E. "Dictatorship in Santo Domingo: A Joint Concern," The Nation 138 (May 23, 1934): 583-85.

Grullón, R. "Antecedentes y perspectivas del momento político dominicano," Cuadernos americanos 120 (January-February 1962): 221-52.

Halper, S. "The Dominican Upheaval," New Leader 48 (May 10, 1965): 3-4.

Hardy, O. "Rafael Leonidas Trujillo Molina," Pacific Historical Review 15 (1946): 409-16.

Herring, H. "Scandal of the Caribbean: The Dominican Republic, Achievements and the Savagery of the Trujillo Dictatorship," Current History 38 (March 1960): 140-43, 164.

Hicks, A. C. "Election Day in Santo Domingo," The Nation
    164 (May 10, 1947): 543-44.

Holden, D. "Dominican's Uneasy Freedom," Manchester Guar-
    dian Weekly, May 3, 1962, 7.

"How One-Man Rule Works on Doorstep of U.S.," U.S. News
    and World Report 40 (June 15, 1956): 76-80.

James, D. "Castro, Trujillo and Turmoil," Saturday Even-
    ing Post 239 (January 16, 1960): 63 ff.

Jimenes-Grullón, J. I. "Trujillo: More Croesus Than Cae-
    sar," The Nation 189 (December 26, 1959): 485-86.

Jones, R. "Report Trujillo Paid Off U.S. Aides Probed,"
    Indianapolis Star, January 22, 1963.

Juárez, J. R. "The U.S. Withdrawal from Santo Domingo,"
    Hispanic American Historical Review 42 (1962): 152-92.

Kent, G. "God and Trujillo: The Dominican Republic's
    Dictator," Inter-American 5 (March 1946): 14-16.

Koch, T. "Verlorene Paradiese zwischen Castro und Kennedy:
    Die Dominikanische Republik," Die Zeit (Hamburg),
    April 20, 1962, 4.

Levin, U. "Dominican Republic: The U.S.A. Uses the 'Big
    Stick,'" International Affairs (Moscow), 1962, 94-95.

Logan, R. W. "Dominican Republic: Struggle for Tomorrow,"
    The Nation 210 (December 16, 1961): 488-90.

Maas, P. "Boswell of the Jet Set," Saturday Evening Post
    236 (January 19, 1963): 28-31.

Marchant, R. "El legado de Trujillo," Cuadernos, November
    1961, 71-75.

Mejía, N. W. "El peligro communista," Boletín de la Secre-
    taría de estado de relaciones exteriores y culto no.
    72 (April-June 1955): 22-28.

"Missing Link in Dominica," National Review, December 16,
    1961, 4-6-07.

Ornes, G. E., and J. McCarten. "Trujillo: Little Caesar on Our Own Front Porch," Harper's Magazine 213 (December 1956): 67-72.

Pan American Union, "El caso dominicano," Américas 12, no. 8 (August 1960): 20.

_____. "Crisis y conferencias," Américas 12, no. 9 (September 1960): 2.

_____. "Estudio de supuestas violaciones de derechos en la República Dominicana y Cuba," Américas 14, no. 2 (February 1962): 12.

_____. "Nueva era para la República dominicana," Américas 14, no. 3 (March 1962): 31.

_____. "Ayuda a la República Dominicana," Américas 14, no. 5 (May 1962): 31.

"Premature Joy," New Times (Moscow), November 4, 1961, 4.

Pulley, R. "The United States and the Dominican Republic, 1933-1940: The High Price of Caribbean Stability," Caribbean Studies 5 (October 1965): 22-31.

Romualdi, S. "Trujillo on the Carpet," Inter-American Labor Bulletin 11 (March 1960): 1.

Sinks, A. H. "Trujillo: Caribbean Dictator," American Mercury 5 (October 1940): 164-71.

Slater, J. "The United States, the Organization of American States, and the Dominican Republic, 1961-1963," International Organization 18 (Spring 1964): 268-91.

Szulc, T. "Uneasy Year 29 of the Trujillo Era," New York Times Magazine, August 29, 1959, 9 ff.

Thomson, C. A. "Dictatorship in the Dominican Republic," Foreign Policy Reports 12 (April 15, 1936): 30-40.

Thorning, J. F. "The Dominican Republic: Twenty-Five Years of Peace and Prosperity," World Affairs 118 (Summer 1955): 45-47.

Trujillo, Flor de Oro. "My Life as Trujillo's Daughter," told to Laura Berquist, Look 29 (June 15, 1965): 44 ff.; and (June 29, 1965): 52 ff.

Trujillo, R. L. "Trujillo declara que América debe oponer un frente a la amenza comunista . . . ," Boletín de la Secretaría de estado de relaciones exteriores y culto no. 73 (July-September 1955): 22-27.

_____. "Benefactor niega existo conflicto entre la Iglesia y el Estado Dominicano," Boletín de la Secretaría de estado de relaciones exteriores y culto no. 91 (April-June 1960): 12-14.

U.S. Department of State. "U.S. Severs Relations with Dominican Republic," Bulletin 43, no. 1106 (September 12, 1960): 412.

_____. "OAS Condemns Government of Dominican Republic," Bulletin 43, no. 1106 (September 12, 1960): 355-58.

_____. "Dominican Republic," Bulletin 45, no. 1168 (February 12, 1962): 258-59.

"U.S. Finds Dominicans Difficult," People's World (San Francisco), February 3, 1962, 5.

Villard, O. G. "Men and Issues--Santo Domingo, 1937," The Nation 144 (March 3, 1937): 323-24.

Whitney, T. P. "Comment," New Republic 142 (November 30, 1961): 8.

_____. "In the Wake of Trujillo," New Republic 143 (December 11, 1961): 6-8.

_____. "The U.S. and the Dominicans: What Will Be Done with Trujillo Properties?" New Republic 146 (February 12, 1962): 13-14.

Wiarda, H. J. "The Changing Political Orientation of the Church in the Dominican Republic," Journal of Church and State 7 (1965): 238-54.

_____. "The Politics of Civil-Military Relations in the Dominican Republic," Journal of Inter-American Studies 7 (1965): 465-84.

_____. "The Development of the Labor Movement in the Dominican Republic," <u>Inter-American Economic Affairs</u> 20 (1966): 41-63.

_____. "From Fragmentation to Disintegration: The Social and Political Effects of the Dominican Revolution," <u>América latina</u> 10 (1967): 55-71.

_____. "Dictatorship and Development: The Trujillo Regime and Its Implications," <u>Southwestern Social Science Quarterly</u> 48 (1968): 548-57.

Wright, T. P. "The United States and Latin American Dictatorship: The Case of the Dominican Republic," <u>Journal of International Affairs</u> 14 (1960): 152-57.

Ziegler, J. "Santo Domingo: Feudo de Trujillo," <u>Cuadernos</u> no. 46 (January-February 1961): 98-102.

Books on Rhodesia

Alport, Lord C. J. <u>The Sudden Assignment: Being a Record of Service in Central Africa</u>. London: Hodder & Stoughton, 1965.

Barber, J. P. <u>Rhodesia: The Road to Rebellion</u>. London: Oxford University Press for the Institute of Race Relations, 1967.

Barber, W. J. <u>The Economy of British Central Africa</u>. Stanford: Stanford University Press, 1961.

Bell, R. G. <u>Rhodesia: Outline of a Nonviolent Strategy to Resolve the Crisis</u>. London: Housmans, 1968.

Boutros-Ghali, B. <u>L'Organisation de l'unité africaine</u>. Paris: Colin, 1969.

Bowman, L. W. <u>Rhodesia: White Power in an African State</u>. Cambridge, Mass.: Harvard University Press, 1973.

Brelsford, N. V., ed. <u>Handbook to the Federation of Rhodesia and Nyasaland</u>. London: Cassell, 1960.

Bull, T., ed. <u>Rhodesian Perspective</u>. London: Joseph, 1967.

Clegg, E. M. Race and Politics: Partnership in the Federation of Rhodesia and Nyasaland. London: Oxford University Press, 1960.

Clements, F. Rhodesia: The Course to Collision. London: Pall Mall Press, 1969.

Cunningham, G. Rhodesia: The Last Chance. London: Fabian Society, 1966.

Day, J. International Nationalism: The Extraterritorial Relations of Southern Rhodesian African Nationalists. London: Routledge & Kegan Paul, 1967.

Gann, L. H. Central Africa: The Former British States. Englewood Cliffs, N.J.: Prentice-Hall, 1971.

Gray, R. The Two Nations: Aspects of the Development of Race Relations in the Rhodesias and Nyasaland. London: Oxford University Press, 1960.

Hanna, A. J. The Story of the Rhodesias and Nyasaland. London: Falser & Falser, 1960.

Hensman, H. A History of Rhodesia. New York: Negro University Press, 1970.

Holleman, J. Chief, Council and Commissioner: Some Problems of Government in Rhodesia. Leiden: Afrika-Studiecentrum, 1969.

Kaunda, K. A Humanist in Africa. London: Longmans, 1966.

Keatley, P. The Politics of Partnership. Harmondsworth: Penguin, 1963.

Lardner-Burke, D. Rhodesia: The Story of the Crisis. London: Oldbourne, 1966.

Marshall, C. B. Crisis over Rhodesia: A Skeptical View. Baltimore: Johns Hopkins Press, 1967.

Mason, P. The Birth of a Dilemma: The Conquest and Settlement of Rhodesia. London: Oxford University Press for the Institute of Race Relations, 1962.

Mezerik, A. G. Rhodesia and the United Nations. New York: International Review Service, 1966.

421

Mlambo, E. E. M. <u>Rhodesia: The Struggle for a Birthright</u>. London: C. Hurst, 1972.

Mtshali, B. V. <u>Rhodesia: Background to Conflict</u>. New York: Hawthorn Books, 1967.

Murray, D. <u>The Governmental System in Southern Rhodesia</u>. London: Oxford University Press, 1970.

Nyerere, J. <u>Freedom and Unity: Uhuru na umoja</u>. Dar es Salaam: Oxford University Press, 1966.

Palley, C. <u>The Constitutional History and Law of Southern Rhodesia, 1888-1965</u>. London and Oxford: Clarendon Press, 1966.

Peck, A. <u>Rhodesia Condemns: The Perfidy of Albion</u>. London: Britons Publishing, 1968.

Ransford, O. <u>The Rulers of Rhodesia from Earliest Times to the Referendum</u>. London: Murray, 1968.

Samkange, S. J. T. <u>Origins of Rhodesia</u>. London: Heinemann, 1968.

Shamugaria, N. S. <u>Crisis in Rhodesia</u>. London: Deutsch, 1965.

Sithole, N. <u>African Nationalism</u>. London: Oxford University Press, 1968.

Smith, D. <u>Rhodesia: The Problem</u>. London: Maxwell, 1969.

Thompson, W. S. <u>Ghana's Foreign Policy: 1957-1966</u>. Princeton: Princeton University Press, 1968.

Todd, J. <u>Rhodesia</u>. London: MacGibbon & Kee, 1966.

Tow, L. <u>The Manufacturing Economy of Southern Rhodesia: Problems and Prospects</u>. Washington, D.C.: National Academy of Sciences, 1960.

Tredgold, Sir R. C. <u>The Rhodesia That Was My Life</u>. London: Allen & Unwin, 1968.

United Kingdom. <u>Southern Rhodesia: Documents . . . November 1963-November 1965</u>. Cmnd. 2807. London: Her Majesty's Stationery Office, 1965.

_____. Rhodesia: Documents Relating to Proposals for a Settlement, 1966. Cmnd. 3171. London: Her Majesty's Stationery Office, 1966.

_____. Britain and the United Nations. London: British Information Service, 1969.

_____. Rhodesia: Report on Exchanges with the Regime . . . November, 1968. Cmnd. 4065. London: Her Majesty's Stationery Office, 1969.

_____. Rhodesia: Proposals for a Settlement. London: Her Majesty's Stationery Office, 1971.

Welensky, Sir R. Welensky's 4000 Days. New York: Roy Publishers, 1964.

Wills, A. J. An Introduction to the History of Central Africa. 2nd edition. London: Oxford University Press, 1967.

Young, Kenneth. Rhodesia and Independence: A Study in British Colonial Policy. London: Heineman, 1967.

Articles on Rhodesia

Adams, R. "Rhodesia's Economic Prospects," Banker, July 1972, 939-44.

Africa Confidential: "Rhodesia's Public Opinion Poll," January 19, 1968, 2; "Rhodesia: The Strength of the Pack," May 26, 1967, 11.

Alport, Lord. "The Conservative Party and Rhodesia," Round Table, July 1971, 391-99.

_____. "The Proposed Rhodesian Settlement: A Personal View," The World Today 28 (1972): 1-4.

Austin, D. "Sanctions and Rhodesia," The World Today 22 (1966): 106-13.

Barber, J. P. "Rhodesia: The Constitutional Conflict," Journal of Modern African Studies 4 (1966): 457-70.

Bowman, L. W. "Organization, Power, and Decision Making Within the Rhodesian Front," *Journal of Commonwealth Political Studies* 8 (1969): 145-65.

Chenu, F. "La difficulte naissance de la guérilla rhodésienne," *Temps modernes*, 1970, 890-915.

Clarke, D. G. "Economic and Political Aspects of the Rhodesian Franchise," *Journal of Commonwealth Political Studies* 11 (1973): 67-78.

Colvin, I. "The Pearce Commission and After," *South Africa Society*, 1972. (Pamphlet.)

Commonwealth Secretariat. "Commonwealth Sanctions Committee: Communique," 73/42, May 17, 1973.

Day, J. "The Rhodesian African Nationalists and the Commonwealth African States," *Journal of Commonwealth Political Studies* 8 (1969): 132-44.

Doxey, M. "Africa Against Portugal," *Economist, Foreign Report* 908 (May 6, 1965): 3-5.

_____. "Verwoerd and Smith," *Economist, Foreign Report* 913 (June 17, 1965): 1-3.

_____. "Economic Sanctions: Part Lessons and the Case of Rhodesia," *Behind the Headlines* 27, no. 2 (1968): 1-66.

_____. "Mr. Smith's Guerrillas," *Economist, Foreign Report* 1042 (February 15, 1968): 7-8.

_____. "South African Troops for Rhodesia?" *Economist, Foreign Report* 1048 (March 28, 1968): 7-8.

_____. "The Rhodesian Sanctions Experiment," *Yearbook of World Affairs* 25 (1971): 142-62.

Enke, S. "What Would Sanction Involve?" *Optima*, 1964, 183-89.

Fawcett, J. E. S. "The Commonwealth in the United Nations," *Journal of Commonwealth Political Studies* 1 (1962): 123-35.

Fenwick, C. G. "When Is There a Threat to Peace?--Rhode-
    sia," AJIL 61 (1967): 753-55.

Franck, T. M., ed. "Policy Paper on the Legality of Manda-
    tory Sanctions by the United Nations Against Rhodesia,"
    Policy Paper, Center for International Studies, New
    York University, 1969.

Fredland, R. A. "The OAU After Ten Years: Can It Survive,"
    African Affairs 72 (1973): 309-16.

Gann, L. H. "Rhodesia and the Prophets," African Affairs
    71 (1972): 125-43.

Gutteridge, W. "Rhodesia: The Use of Military Force,"
    The World Today 21 (1965): 499-503.

Halpern, J. "Polarization in Rhodesia: State, Church,
    Peoples," The World Today 27 (January 1971): 1-8.

Hargreaves, J. "Pan-Africanism After Rhodesia," The World
    Today 22 (1966): 57-63.

Harris, C. "The Political and Economic Effects of Sanc-
    tions on Rhodesia," The World Today 23 (1967): 1-4.

Hildrew, P. "Rhodesia's Second UDI," The World Today 25
    (1969): 285-88.

_____. "The Rhodesian Referendum: June 20th, 1969,"
    Parliamentary Affairs 22 (Winter 1969/70): 72-80.

Hodder-Williams, R. "White Attitudes and UDI: A Case
    Study," Journal of Commonwealth Political Studies 8
    (1970): 244-64.

Hoogvelt, A. M. M., and D. Child. "Rhodesia: Economic
    Blockade and Longterm Development Strategy." The
    Hague, Institute of Social Studies, 1973. (Pamphlet.)

Idenburg, P. J. "Britse unitverkoop der Rhodesische,"
    Internationale spectator (Netherlands) 26 (1972):
    953-65.

MacFarlane, L. J. "Justifying Rebellion: Black and White
    Nationalism in Rhodesia," Journal of Commonwealth
    Political Studies 6 (1965): 54-79.

McWilliam, M. D. "Economic Factors in the Rhodesian Crisis,"
    The World Today 20 (1964): 322-27.

Maxey, D. "From Rhodesia to Zimbabwe: African Resistance
    to European Rule Since UDI," Fabian Society (1972).
    (Pamphlet.)

_____. "The Fight for Zimbabwe: The Armed Conflict in
    Southern Rhodesia Since UDI." Brentwood, Essex, 1973.
    (Mimeographed.)

Palmer, R. "European Resistance to African Majority Rule:
    The Settlers' and Residents' Association of Nyasaland,
    1960-1963," African Affairs 72 (1973): 256-72.

Roundtable. "The Chiefs Rally to Mr. Smith," Round Table,
    320 (April 1968): 194-98.

Sutcliffe, R. B. "Crisis on the Copperbelt," The World
    Today 22 (1966): 499-502.

_____. "Rhodesian Trade Since U.D.I.," The World Today
    23 (1967): 418-22.

_____. "The Political Economy of Rhodesian Sanctions,"
    Journal of Commonwealth Political Studies 8 (1969):
    113-25.

_____. "Stagnation and Inequality in Rhodesia, 1946-
    68," Bulletin: Oxford University Institute of Eco-
    nomics and Statistics, February 1971, 35-56.

Symonds, J. "The Rhodesian Crisis," The World Today 21
    (1965): 453-59.

Turner, A. C. "Independent Rhodesia," Current History,
    March 1970, 129-34, 179-81.

Von der Ropp, K. F. "Ein neuer Versuch zur Lösung des
    Rhodesien-Problems," Europa-Archiv 2 (1972): 61-68.

Zacklin, R. "Challenge of Rhodesia: Toward an Interna-
    tional Public Policy," International Conciliation,
    November 1969: 1-72.

Zimmerli, C. H. "Human Rights and the Rule of Law in
    Southern Rhodesia," International and Comparative Law
    Quarterly 20 (1971): 239-300.

C. LLOYD BROWN-JOHN is Associate Professor of Political Science at the University of Windsor, Windsor, Ontario.

Dr. Brown-John has published materials on extradition among Commonwealth states and on international law and federal states. He has also published in the field of public administration. Reviews and articles appear in Public Administration, The Canadian Yearbook of International Law, Etudes Internationales, Canadian Public Administration, The Canadian Journal of Political Science, and Nord-Sud. Dr. Brown-John is also a full-time political analyst and commentator for the Canadian Broadcasting outlet in Windsor, Ontario and was recently appointed to the Canadian Consumer Council, a policy advisory agency for the Canadian federal government.

C. Lloyd Brown-John was the recipient of Province of Ontario Graduate Fellowships from 1963 to 1966. He has recently been the recipient of a Canada Council Research Grant for studies in extradition and political offenses in international law. Prior to joining the University of Windsor, he served with the Canadian Department of External Affairs on legal matters and as founder of a desk for British political affairs.

Dr. Brown-John was graduated with honors in Political Science from the University of British Columbia. He received his M.A. and Ph.D. at the University of Toronto.

OCEAN SPACE RIGHTS: Developing U.S. Policy
            Lawrence Juda

TERRITORIAL SEAS AND INTER-AMERICAN RELATIONS: With Case
Studies of the Peruvian and U.S. Fishing Industries
            Bobbie B. Smetherman and
            Robert M. Smetherman

THE UNITED NATIONS AND RHODESIA: A Study in International
Law
            Ralph Zacklin